Competition

Competition

The Economics of Industrial Change

Paul Auerbach

Basil Blackwell

Copyright © Paul Auerbach 1988

First published 1988

First published in paperback 1989

Reprinted 1990

Basil Blackwell Ltd
108 Cowley Road, Oxford OX4 1JF, UK

Basil Blackwell Inc.
3 Cambridge Center
Cambridge, Massachusetts 02142, USA

British Library Cataloguing in Publication Data
A CIP catalogue record for this book is available from the British Library.

Library of Congress Cataloging in Publication Data
A CIP catalogue record for this book is available from the Library of Congress.
ISBN 0-631-15966-5
ISBN 0-631-17235-1 (pbk.)

Typeset in 10 on 11pt Times
by Joshua Associates Ltd, Oxford
Printed in Great Britain by
T.J. Press (Padstow) Ltd, Padstow, Cornwall.

Preface to the Paperback Edition

The changes from the original hardback issue consist of corrections of misprints, the most egregious of which was the mis-spelling of the name of the great operatic soprano Amelita Galli-Curci. If the Gibbon-like opening phrases of the book on the decline and fall of British industry should no longer seem appropriate to some readers, such a circumstance would only reinforce the contention put forth here of the dangers of a static characterisation of events in an inherently dynamic industrial environment.

Paul Auerbach

Acknowledgements

I would like to thank the host of friends who have helped me in the writing of this book. I dare not list them for fear of leaving somebody out, but they know who they are and bear responsibility for creating the benign and encouraging atmosphere without which work is impossible. A few must be named – those who have suffered through the whole manuscript from beginning to end: Jack Campbell, Meghnad Desai, Richard Saville and Peter Skott. I also extend my gratitude to the Nuffield Foundation, whose grant helped me to complete the project. A special note of thanks to the business and financial journalists whose labours are present throughout this book.

Table of Contents

To my father and mother

1

Introduction

General Considerations

The most dramatic and crucial events of contemporary economic life are directly concerned with changes in the industrial environment. In the UK, laggard industries collapse precipitously, reflecting not only the general economic crisis, but unprecedented competitive pressure. In the US, books flood off the press which attempt to develop a strategy to deal with 'The increasing pressures of international competition on domestic industry . . .'[1] Domestic industries traditionally thought to be secure from the competition even of other advanced economies have first had to confront Japan, and now newly industrialising countries such as Taiwan, Brazil and South Korea as rivals, either as bases of multinational production or, increasingly, as originators of productive enterprise. It is our view that these events are a manifestation of a tendency which has always been present in the capitalist market economy for competitiveness to increase over time. If such a tendency exists, then orthodox economic theory[2] is seriously flawed, since its static framework is not capable of explaining these events except on an *ad hoc* basis.

The competitive process and the structure of industry are central to economic life. The popularity of the writings of John Kenneth Galbraith indicates a public concern with issues in industrial economics which goes far beyond their conventional association in the literature of academic economics with anti-monopolies legislation. An enormous gap exists between our day-to-day observation of the changes taking place around us in the sphere of business activity and the tools available to us from orthodox theory to analyse these changes: the corpus of microeconomic theory which serves as a theoretical foundation for research into the economics of industry has been an obstacle to an understanding of the nature and dynamics of the industrial economy. The critique offered here is thus directed at the static approach to competition dominant in economics, which is exemplified by, but not uniquely identified with, the crucial role played by the concepts of 'market' and 'industry'. The argument of the book may be summarised as follows:

1 The literature of industrial economics has developed as a dutiful application of the research programme implied by standard micro-economic theory. It is necessary, therefore, to explore the logic, predictions and conceptual orientation of the standard theory and its implications for industrial economics.
2 This literature is seen to be inadequate as an explanation for the competitive behaviour of business in capitalist market economies. Most especially, due to its ahistorical and static nature, it is unable to illuminate the central questions concerning the evolution of the competitive process.
3 An alternative approach is proposed for an interpretation of historical and contemporary developments in the evolution of competition. This approach puts central emphasis on changes through time in the consciousness and facility of economic actors and how these changes transform the very environment in which economic actors function. Such an approach proves more satisfactory than that emerging from economic orthodoxy.

Economics is usually claimed as a branch of positive science. Its success must therefore be measured not by the elegance and complexity of the associated theory, but primarily by its usefulness in applied fields such as industrial economics. Rigorous and decisive verification tests are difficult (some believe impossible) to construct in all sciences, and most notori-ously so in the social sciences, including economics. But, if it is too much to ask that the theory act as an engine of prediction, we may at least hope that it 'point us in the right direction' and offer us at least *ex post* a mechanism for understanding that which has been taking place around us.

Many of the well-known logical difficulties with standard theory have serious consequences for applied work, especially for the analysis of business behaviour, such as the problems surrounding the delineation of the market for a commodity. Furthermore, in its role as a generator of predictions, many of the central propositions of standard theory seem to be refuted either by the stylised facts of economic history or by formal empirical studies. The failure of these 'refutations' to have any impact on the body of theory taught to generations of students may cause us to question whether the discipline as currently taught and practised is in fact empirically based. The most decisive weakness of orthodox theory is, however, neither its logic nor its role in verification, but its use as a framework for viewing the direction of movement of the capitalist market economy. The economics of industry is the arena in which we shall consider the status of modern economic theory as a scientific research programme.

Science: Logic and Conceptualisation

The critique may be put forth at an abstract level by repeating Thorstein Veblen's venerable query – 'Why is economics not an evolutionary science?'. The question is even more relevant now than when it was posed: economic orthodoxy has progressively calcified into a narrow body of static theory based on axioms of rational choice and it has no methodology for dealing systematically with the influence of different environments on the underlying parameters affecting human behaviour. One consequence of these developments is that the domain of applicability of economic theory has become methodologically unconstrained, both with regard to historical time and to social context. An astronomer viewing a galaxy millions of light-years away proceeds on the assumption that the theoretical structures of contemporary terrestrial physics may be used to interpret this ancient and distant picture. Are we equally confident that an identical toolkit of rational axioms may be applied to explain the actions of a nineteenth century shopkeeper (or perhaps even a medieval vassal) and those of a financial manager of a modern multinational? The rational axiomatic approach is ahistorical and static, and attempts to fit highly variegated types of behaviour into a preconceived and narrow set of categories. Behaviour derived from exogenously specified axioms is of little use in an evolutionary approach to economics.

But nineteenth century evolutionary theory may not be put forth as a viable model for economics. The analogy is deceptive, because *human* behaviour is not only shaped by its environment, but plays a fundamental role in the latter's very construction. An important application of this principle is to be found in the notions of 'market' and 'industry' as they are used in mainstream theory. These concepts will be seen to be inoperative on the basis of the impossibility of constructing such categories in a meaningful and consistent way – problems well known in the literature of economics, but almost invariably ignored. The core of the quandary, however, is not one of logic but of conceptualisation – the market cannot be used to specify an exogenous area of activity since its very extent *is contingent upon the behaviour of the participants*. As a result, the mutual interaction of environment and behaviour becomes crucial to an analysis of the weaknesses of the mainstream theory in its application to cross-sectional analyses of the competitive behaviour of industries.

Of even greater significance are the implications of the critique with regard to long-term trends in the capitalist market economy. A widespread conclusion from the perspective of the mainstream approach has been that a long-term downward trend in competitiveness has taken place. This conclusion is based on the tendency for business concentration to increase over the twentieth century when markets are measured over a given (usually national) extent. On the contrary, from a dynamic, historical perspective this proposition is the reverse of the truth. Capitalists have progressively become more 'capitalistic' – businessmen and women ever more businesslike, knowledgeable and technically proficient, more flexible in their actions, more rapid and efficacious in response to profitable opportunities and less narrow and localised in their concerns. These changes in *behaviour* (themselves engendered by environmental evolution) have caused the functional sphere of competitive activity (the relevant 'markets') to expand over time. Furthermore, these skills and habits of mind, once considered so rare and mysterious have become and are becoming more widespread and available, both within national economies and worldwide.

Orthodox theory is an inappropriate vehicle for understanding the process of change which is an inherent part of the capitalist market economy. A perspective derived from exogenously specified behaviour in the context of a given environment (e.g. a market) is of little use in describing and explaining an evolution which is itself crucially affected by changes in behaviour. If, in fact, there is a dominant tendency for competitiveness to increase in the capitalist market economy for the reasons outlined here, then the perspective of mainstream theory is misdirected.

Science as Prediction

The concern in this book will be exclusively with the positive aspects of the question of competition. This is not due to any notion that normative issues are of lesser significance. On the contrary, the avoidance of normative issues here is in order to refrain from the common tendency to treat them as an afterthought and to avoid entanglements and confusions with the questions at hand. An additional reason for the exclusion of normative analysis is our strong suspicion that the forms this analysis has invariably taken have had a deleterious effect on the development of economics as a science. One example is the distortion brought about by the continued centrality of the model of perfect competition, whose prominence extends far beyond its presumptive scientific virtues of relative simplicity and seeming decisiveness in prediction. The model's key role in the discipline, despite its grave inadequacies as a positive theory, is at least partially maintained by the popular normative propositions (Paretian optimality, etc.) associated with it. Such considerations are a distraction from the task of the construction of a scientific approach to economics.

A further methodological rule to be followed is scrupulous application of Alec Nove's 'law of equal cheating', which suggests that we can often make reasonable conjectures about the rates of change of economic variables even when the absolute levels of these variables are difficult or impossible to measure in a satisfactory way. Thus we have no idea whether or not the contemporary economy is 'competitive', and not only do we refuse to be embarrassed by manifestations and instances of 'uncompetitiveness', but shall point to nominally contradictory evidence as a means of illustrating the dangers of simplistic 'either–or' approaches to human behaviour. In fact, it is not clear that the question 'Is a sector (or an economy) competitive or not?' is at all meaningful outside the static context. The central empirical proposition of this book relates to the direction of *change* of the conditions of competitiveness within the economy. Even this notion is meant only to suggest an underlying tendency and not to point to an invariable empirical 'law'.

An Outline of the Structure of the Book

We have outlined the key themes that will be present in this book on the role of competition in the capitalist market economy. In the chapters that follow the critique of orthodoxy is integrated with the alternative approach being developed. Chapter 2 reviews the notions of competition which have emerged in economic theory – a static one, epitomised by the Cournot–Edgeworth model of competition in the context of a given environment (i.e. a market) and a dynamic one, emerging out of Adam Smith's 'invisible hand' principle of the tendency of capital to flow into areas of high profitability. We ask why the static theory has remained at the centre of attention, both in terms of the alleged practical strengths of the static theory and the weaknesses embodied in contemporary dynamic approaches. Since Marshallian microeconomic theory contains as a central proposition the notion that market structure determines business behaviour, the critique in chapter 3 reiterates and focuses on two well-established conclusions of the economics literature, namely that there is no consistent method either for delineating a market or for drawing simple lines of causation between market structure and firm behaviour. The methodology at the foundation of mainstream industrial economics is thus severely flawed. In chapter 4 the weaknesses of the orthodox methodology are highlighted through an analysis of the mainstream attempts to establish a statistical relationship between industrial concentration and profitability; alternative tests of the 'invisible hand' theorem are also evaluated.

Chapter 5 considers the nature of firm control. The conclusions that emerge contrast sharply with notions of a past golden age of entrepreneurial behaviour. Business history is here characterised by the steady evolution in management technique and improvement in information that have taken place, as well as the long-term changes in the technical competence and, perhaps, the disposition of managers. The crucial effect on the evolution of the competitive process of these events belies the traditional 'black box' approach to the firm of orthodox theory. In chapter 6 the current literature on the modern corporation is critically reviewed as an attempt to fit the old wine of economic orthodoxy into the new bottles of firm level analysis. Chapter 7 analyses the implicit capital market theory buried within standard microeconomics. The neo-classical predictions are evaluated in light of the actual relationship between industry and the financial markets and there is also a consideration of the limitations of static theory as a structure for understanding the current dramatic transformations in the financial world of the 1980s.

With the evolution of both firm control and the financial environment already considered, in chapter 8 we examine the meaning and significance of the emergence of large integrated, diversified and then multinational enterprises in the twentieth century. In chapter 9 we consider from an historical and sectoral perspective the hypothesis that competition has had a long-term tendency to increase in the capitalist market economy. Chapter 10 synthesises and evaluates the developments in competition described above and indicates the appropriate direction for future research.

The analysis here is largely restricted to the 'Anglo-Saxon' (UK and US) economies, and for this fact we feel some regret. No apologies, however, will be forthcoming for failing to phrase all our guesses, surmises and conjectures about the future state of competition as deductions from 'rigorous' utilitarian axioms of choice. Despite the almost complete identification in recent years of this procedure with the permissible domain of theory, there is not the slightest justification within the methodology of science for the exclusion of structures that attempt to use descriptive detail in the formation of behavioural general-isations. The rise of the axiomatic approach has been coincident with a dramatic increase in technical facility within the economics profession, but is this to be taken as *per se* evidence that our knowledge of the external world has increased? A useful development in the subject would be an end to the self-congratulatory atmosphere and its replacement with a serious and frank assessment of the state of knowledge – and ignorance. Such an assessment would be a prerequisite to the development of a serious, as opposed to pompous approach to these vital questions.

Notes

1. Introduction to Zysman, J. and L. Tyson (eds) *American Industry in International Competition* Cornell University 1983, p. 23.
2. For variety, this approach will be referred to as orthodox, static, standard, mainstream, structuralist, neo-classical or Marshallian theory. The 'Marshallian' theory referred to here is that which has become the heritage of industrial economics, and economics in general. In chapter 2 and subsequent chapters differences between alternative versions of the mainstream approach will be explored, although exegetical discussions will, on the whole, be avoided.

2

The Concept of Competition

Introduction

In scholarly publications and text books in economics the view is well nigh unanimously held that competition is the dominant regulatory force of the capitalist market economy. The case, however, is not self-evident. Business in a capitalist society is conducted within a complex web of legal, institutional and financial constraints, and the motivations of individuals derive not only from self-interest, but from habit, slothfulness, and a passion for excellence and precision – factors not necessarily congruent with traditional notions of 'competitiveness' as an explanation for the events which take place within the capitalist market economy. Such is the power of the competitive tradition in economic theory dating from Adam Smith that attempts to assemble a collection of rival doctrines are bo ind to be faltering and the list itself small: all economic thought, to some extent, finds itself in the grip of the 'invisible hand'.

Our initial purpose is not so much to judge rival approaches but to bring into focus the competitive doctrine itself and to introduce themes which counter the competitive orthodoxy and reappear as leitmotivs throughout the book. The opposition to orthodoxy is grouped under two traditions. One, which we dub the 'New Industrial State' unites three schools of dissent, while the second, the Institutionalists, represents a far more radical rejection of orthodoxy and an even more heterogeneous collection of ideas and individuals than does the New Industrial State.

Neither, however, is the competitive tradition a unified whole. There are two distinct approaches to competition – a classical dynamic view of the competitive process and a neo-classical static view. In the exposition below these approaches will be dealt with in reverse historical order, for reasons to be explained. It will be argued that the confused relationship between the classical and neo-classical approaches is due to the dominant influence of the Marshallian synthesis of these two schools, an influence which has been particularly strong in economics of an applied nature such as industrial economics. This synthesis incorporates a predominantly static approach to competition, while adding sufficient elements from the dynamic approach to make it plausible as a practical model. This attempt at synthesis has been a failure, with deleterious effects on the development of industrial economics.

It is to the rivals of competition that we now turn.

Alternatives to Competition

The New Industrial State

The first alternative tradition may be put under the grand heading of the literature of the 'New Industrial State', since all aspects of this view listed below received their most confident and forthright assertion in Galbraith's famous book of that title.[1] The general historical perspective conceives of a development within industrial economies in which competitive, market-based regulation was replaced in the twentieth century by 'something else'. We consider three main variants – the Monopoly Capitalist, Managerialist and Planning schools. These 'replacements' for an analysis based on competitive regulation are inevitably intertwined, but analytically we find it useful to separate out these doctrines as follows:

First, since little meaning could be attributed to bigness *per se* by orthodox theory, the eruption of giant firms in the twentieth century was widely interpreted as a movement from competitive to monopolistic market structures: doctrines which put exceptional emphasis on the growth of monopoly may be grouped together under a stylised Monopoly Capitalist school. A politically radical version of this approach, Monopoly Capitalism, has been conventionally Marshallian in its approach to competition despite original features.[2] A similar analysis in mainstream economics of trends in competition generated the development of monopolistic competition and associated doctrines. The underlying empirical premise of both the radical and mainstream versions of the Monopoly Capitalist school – that competition has decreased in the twentieth century – will be a central point of contention to be discussed throughout this book.

The second school within this tradition developed an elaborate 'managerialist' literature. While as an historical matter 'managerialism' could only emerge after there had been broad acceptance of the afore-mentioned literature on monopolistic market structures, it was potentially a good deal more subversive than the latter: the behaviour of the firm was taken to be significantly affected by its internal locus of decision making, and not strictly determined by its external environment. In the subsequent development of this literature, most of the potentially heretical effect of this doctrine has been lost, as the school has been integrated with the neo-classical theory of choice and has focused almost exclusively on the conflict between owners' and managers' utilities. The dominant tendency in this literature has been to treat managerial volition as a 'bad thing', but with one exceptional and curious aspect: the managerialist school has contained within it members who have voiced, quite uniquely, a dissent from Adam Smith's famous observation that 'It is not from the bene-volence of the butcher, or the baker, that we expect our dinner, but from their regard to their own self interest.' For some managerialists, there is no need either to invoke state intervention or to postulate the existence of an 'invisible hand' of competition as protection from the exercise of this self-interest, since we may rely upon the benevolence of the modern corporate manager to reconcile any conflict between private power and public interest.[3]

A third school has recently emerged within the New Industrial State tradition which emphasizes a choice internal to the firm between planning and the market. The recent popularity of this approach derives from its connection with the historical studies pioneered by Alfred Chandler, where the challenge to standard doctrine is embodied in the by-passing, in fact the irrelevance, of competition as a central explanatory element in the development of the American industrial structure at the turn of the century. The key motive force for change was instead embodied in the decisions made by firms to replace an anonymous market with the 'visible hand' of management for the production and sale of their commodities. In this framework, events crucial to the emergence of modern industrial society were initiated *within* firms and not imposed by the competitive environment. Indeed, they involved a movement away from market relations in favour of administered planning arrangements. No member of this school, however, would claim it offers a unified, coherent picture of how firms integrate within an economy. Furthermore – and this is especially true of the more formal aspects of the analysis as developed by Oliver Williamson and others – the market is in a broader sense the ubiquitous context in which decisions take place and from which emerge the parameters of calculation for internal decision making: it is unclear the extent to which the model may be detached from the overall market context. In general terms, however, 'planning' in various guises remains one of the main rivals to competition as an explanation for events observed in the industrial sector.

The Institutionalists
An older, more radical alternative to competition as a mode of analysis is that offered by the Institutionalists. The tradition has been highly diffuse, embodying the German Historical School, American Institutionalists at the turn of the century, behaviourists, economic historians and a whole range of dissenting, 'underground' and non-academic opinion including business economists and business journalists. Furthermore, this tradition

has been methodologically inchoate, formulating its opposition to standard doctrine often rather naively in terms of its use of 'inductive' versus 'deductive' methods, thereby accepting from an obverse perspective the orthodox separation of 'theory' and 'fact': the institutionalist rejection of 'theory' made its descent into obscurity inevitable, as dominant opinion in academic economics in the twentieth century has become ever more enamoured of the achievements of physical science, with the resultant pressure for the development of 'laws' of human behaviour. Taking advantage of the disparate nature of the ideas associated with this tradition, an exegetical discussion of these economic doctrines will be side-stepped and what is presented below is a synthetic version of the institutionalist dissent against competitive orthodoxy.

The first aspect of the institutionalist critique is an anti-utilitarian bias – a denial of the sufficiency of self-interest as an explanation for the behaviour of economic actors:

> Man as a social being is a child of civilisation and a product of history. His wants, his intellectual outlook, his relation to material objects and his connection with other human beings have not always been the same. Geography influences them, while the progress of education may entirely transform them.[4]

Orthodox theory in its pure form does not deny the influence of societal factors upon preferences, but assumes that these factors and their effects show stability over time.[5] It implies that the influence of these factors can be analysed in terms of a simple uni-directional effect upon the preferences and initial endowments of the individuals comprising the general equilibrium model. A central focus in this book is on historical evolution, where the mutual interaction of the 'preferences' and 'endowments' of individuals with societal factors is the essence of the process, so that the presumption of such a simple relationship is blatantly inappropriate.

The anti-utilitarian bias of Institutionalism leads to the second element of the critique which is, naturally enough, an emphasis upon institutions – legal, financial and otherwise – as having an independent explanatory power and interpretive integrity that is separable from a purely 'functionalist' interpretation. Institutions, traditions, legal systems, etc. shape the way business is conducted, and outcomes in the market-place cannot be accurately predicted without an appropriate knowledge of their role. In its most extreme form, orthodox economics has incorporated the analysis of a whole host of institutions and legal structures in contemporary life by evaluating them in terms of their effects upon the process of the free exchange of commodities:

> The time pattern of hours that an individual supplies to the market is something that, in a very clear sense, he *chooses* ... there is no question that social convention and institutional structures affect these patterns, but conventions and institutions do not simply come

out of the blue. On the contrary, institutions and customs are designed precisely in order to aid in matching preferences and opportunities satisfactorily.[6]

This 'functionalist' approach perceives institutions as mere conduits through which individuals express their preferences, so that institutions themselves are not fundamental in the shaping of final outcomes. But if, as in the above quotation, institutions affect choices and choices affect institutions, we are in danger of running into an infinite regress. Where should we stop, and where should we begin? If we take the institutions themselves rather than preferences as primary, such a functionalist view could easily be turned around to justify a systematic institutionalism.[7] There is clearly little room in contemporary orthodoxy for traditional approaches to the examination of institutions.

A last and related issue has been the role of descriptive realism in the construction of conceptual generalisations. It is intimately connected with the kind of evidence to be taken as legitimately scientific – do we exclude as *per se* irrelevant ('anecdotal') a business person's description of his or her own behaviour? The most analytically advanced attempt to present a descriptively realistic model of business behaviour has come from the Carnegie School,[8] but in mainstream industrial economics there has long been an implicitly 'institutionalist' critique of formal oligopoly theory on the basis of its lack of descriptive realism: the literature of industrial economics has treated the theory of games rather gingerly compared with, for instance, its extensive discussions of the empirically pervasive phenomenon of price leadership; in F. M. Scherer's famous text[9] the number and size distribution of sellers (the central focus of orthodox explorations) is only one among several factors which might limit oligopolistic co-ordination, while some other categories listed, such as 'industry social structure' (i.e. the existence of social networks which facilitate coalitions in restraint of trade) sit awkwardly within the neoclassical worldview.

Within industrial economics, however, such critiques are usually voiced in Aesopian language. For economic historians, the implicit (and sometimes unconscious) critique of economic orthodoxy has always been far less inhibited. For instance, it has long been contended by many economic historians, in direct contradiction to orthodox theory, that the continued influence of family control over enterprises has stultified the development of firms and their 'rational' operation. Among both economic historians and business journalists there has always been an unstated, underground theory (or theories) of economic behaviour and of competition. Thus, many economic historians and business journalists would treat as unexceptional the following statement: 'Recent rationalisation and consolidation in the [domestic appliance] industry has heightened competition',[10] a declaration which would leave most academic economists gasping for breath.

Are such statements mere economic illiteracy or can they be given a rationale? There is a strong emphasis in this book on the evidence and arguments of economic historians and business journalists, those most unapologetic upholders of an institutionalist tradition. It is certainly not invariably the case that their views and approach are to be preferred to those of orthodox economists. But when disagreements exist between the 'institutionalists' and the proponents of orthodox theory, it would be foolish to assume that it is always the former who are at fault.

Despite the important contributions of institutionalism to competitive analysis and to economics in general, and despite the Janus-like approach of most academic economists who, when addressing a public audience, precipitously adopt an institutionalist methodology (not, we believe, merely for reasons of accessibility), the fortunes of this school have never been lower. One endemic problem has been the inability of its spokespersons to give an articulate view of their methodological position:

> Giving a lecture before a convention of scientists at Geneva, Pareto was interrupted from the floor by a patronising cry from Gustav Schmoller [a leading member of the German Historical School]: 'But are there laws in economics?' Schmoller had no personal acquaintance with Pareto at the time. After the lecture Pareto recognised his heckler on the street and sidled up to him in his shabby clothes and in the guise of a beggar: 'Please, sir, can you direct me to a restaurant where one can eat for nothing?' 'Not where you can eat for nothing, my good man', the German replied, 'but here is one where you can eat for very little!' 'So there are laws in economics!' laughed Pareto as he turned away.[11]

For whatever reasons, and contrary to regular claims of an incipient revival, institutional approaches to economics are still in retreat and even recently have lost ground in areas of former predominance:

> Over the past twenty years a branch of applied microeconomics has been developed and specialized into what is known as modern finance theory. ... Prior to 1958, finance was largely a descriptive field of endeavor. Since then major theoretical thrusts have transformed the field into a positive science. ... Forty years ago the faculty [of business schools] were drawn from the ranks of business and government. Today, finance faculty are predominantly academicians in the traditional sense of the word. ... Their interest and training is in developing theories of economic behavior, then testing them with the tools provided by statistics and econometrics. Anecdotal evidence and individual business experience have been superceded by the analytic approach of modern finance theory.[12]

There are many grounds for viewing these developments with less than unalloyed contentment.

Static Conceptions

Classical and Neo-Classical Competition

In contrast to its presumptive opponents, the competitive tradition has the following characteristics. First, self-interest is the prime motive force in the actions of economic participants, these actions emanating from stable, well-defined preference relations. Secondly, as a result of this conceptualisation of human action, the historical evolution of economic behaviour is explained by 'exogenous' shifts in the environmental constraints faced by participants and not by any changes in their underlying 'utility function'. Thirdly, economic outcomes are analysed while abstracting from institutional considerations. Institutions are either outside the domain of economic theory or they are explained as bargaining outcomes. The evolution of financial institutions is a particular problem for orthodoxy, since the theory does not successfully deal with the problems of time and uncertainty which make finance important. Fourthly, an element so far unmentioned, there is an exceptional emphasis within the tradition on the theory of value.

These characteristics are common to all schools within the competitive tradition, but significant differences exist within the tradition itself. Two distinct approaches to competition are embodied in the orthodox tradition. There is a classical dynamic approach which emphasizes the tendency for rates of return to equalise between different economic activities through the behaviour of profit-seeking individuals and a neo-classical, static notion which analyses interactions in the context of a specified environment, so that a situation is *defined* to be competitive if a predetermined set of structural characteristics (large number of participants, etc.) are found to be present. Recent literature emphasizing this distinction[13] has almost invariably compared the static neo-classical approach to the earlier classical theory in an invidious way. But the absence of a consistently dynamic approach to competition in the literature of economics is partially due to weaknesses which all orthodox approaches – classical and neo-classical share in common.

In this reconstruction of approaches to competition, the pure neo-classical (static) approach will be considered first. This view, emerging from Cournot and Edgeworth suggests that with only minimal assumptions about participants' preferences and technology a determinate outcome may be derived for a market containing 'large numbers', the price (and 'profit') in the market being lower than in an equivalent market containing a single seller. Thus, in figure 2.1 the profit margin for the market will descend to a lower bound of 'normal' profit π^n when there is a large number (or low concentration) of sellers in the market (point A), while it will have a monopoly profit margin π^m when there is only a single seller (point B, where the concentration index is equal to unity).

Observe that despite the purely static, timeless framework in which this model is constructed, what emerges is a powerful presumption of an

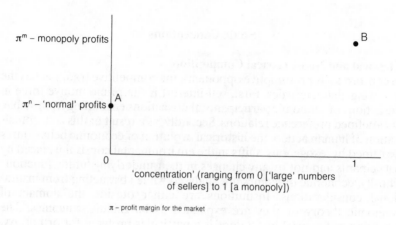

Figure 2.1

unidirectional movement of events: market structure (concentration, etc.) dictates market outcomes (prices and profits) by way of strictly determinate behaviour. The decisiveness of this outcome makes many economists very hesitant about surrendering it despite its problems and lack of 'realism'; much of contemporary economic theory has been concerned with recapturing its determinate quality in more 'acceptable' frameworks.

There are special problems in this analysis which will not detain us, including the existence of equilibrium solutions. More central here is the question of what takes place in market situations 'in between' those of competition and monopoly: unless some sort of monotonic relation is maintained between concentration and profits so that the model is applicable to highly concentrated oligopolies, we are in a difficult situation indeed, since private monopolies in the pure sense of the word are everywhere a rarity.

A commonly proposed solution[14] yields a straight line connection between the two points in figure 2.1. Let

$$\pi_i = pq_i - c_i(q_i)$$

be the profit function for the ith firm, where p is the (uniform) market price, q_i is the firm's output and $c_i(q_i)$ is the firm's total costs. If each firm proceeds to maximise profits, the equilibrium outcome for the market as a whole is as follows:

$$\rho = \gamma \times H/E,$$

where ρ is the market's profit margin, E is the market demand elasticity (defined to be a positive number) and H is the Herfindahl index of concentration. This popular index is simply the sum of the squares of the market shares of every participant in the market. Thus, if we have two market participants, one with two-thirds of the market and the other with one-third, the H index is

$$(2/3)^2 + (1/3)^2 = 0.56.$$

For firms of equal size, the H index approaches zero as the number of firms becomes very large and is equal to one for a monopoly.

The crucial parameter is γ, the index of conjectural variation. For the representative (i^{th}) firm, it is equal to dQ/dq_i, where q_i is the firm's own output and Q is the output of the whole market. If firm i conjectures that γ is equal to unity, it believes that changes in its own output dq_i will not be matched by any additional changes in other firms' output, so that $dq_i = dQ$. The assumption that firms will behave in this way is the famous Cournot postulate, but clearly other conjectures are possible and even likely, especially as we approach the 'oligopolistic' (high H) section of figure 2.1. Indeed it has been suggested that the whole of the oligopoly literature (in the absence of entry) has consisted of arguments about the parameter γ.[15]

To derive the straight line solution, the Cournot conjecture that $\gamma = 1$ has been used. Although this behavioural assumption is generally considered 'naive', it was thought to yield the powerful result that market profitability is continuously and strictly determined by the degree of market concentration H and the inverse of the market demand elasticity. In fact, this result does not hold[16]. In general, given the behavioural postulate of profit maximisation for each firm, the cost functions of the firm and the behavioural parameter γ, the equilibrium market share of each firm and therefore the H index of concentration will be determinate: it is impossible to vary the level of H for a given cost function $c_i(q_i)$ and a given conjectural variation parameter γ, because the level of H will already be uniquely determined by these parameters. *There is no sense here in which H can be seen as a structural determinant of behaviour* since it is merely an amalgamation of firms' market shares – it is as much a *result* as a *determinant* of market behaviour.

This minor episode in the history of economic thought – the failure of the Cournot solution to generate a positive monotonic relationship between market concentration and profitability – illuminates some fundamental tendencies in economic theory. First, the intention of the formulation of the model was to use the H index as an independent, structural determinant of market behaviour. Secondly, the form of the behavioural response was passive, mechanistic and utterly predictable. This model, of the form

(market) structure → (business) behaviour

has been, and remains, the goal of most academic theorising in industrial economics. The attraction of such models is clear, but the goal is elusive.

Once participants' behaviour is brought to the centre of the stage, it is not evident that simple lines of causation can be drawn. As an economic historian has written about the fine writing paper manufacturers in the US at the turn of the century, 'it was the firms' predisposition to restrict output and support prices that had made collusion so successful in the past, not the reverse'.[17] Even in purely static market models, someone must initiate action[18] (whence Walras's *deus ex machina*, the auctioneer): total avoidance of questions concerning the behaviour of participants is impossible.

Despite these caveats, the models associated with the static approach to competition are very powerful, with a level of analytical precision and coherence which is rare in the social sciences. In the end, few would dispute the logic of the notion that *ceteris paribus* increases in concentration will decrease competition in most market situations: the real questions concern the practical applicability of the model and the appropriateness of the *ceteris paribus* assumption.

The discussion here of the earlier, classical tradition will be very much a stylisation of the logic and tendencies embodied within it, since the central concern of Smith, Ricardo, and other classical writers with growth and distribution precluded detailed consideration of those 'allocative' questions usually associated with the competitive process. The classical perspective on competition emphasized a tendency for 'profits' to equalise between economic activities. In contrast with models of the Cournot–Edgeworth type, exceptional care must be taken here in measuring profits or profitability. In the classical context, where the passage of time is unambiguously present, we must consider the relative merits of different measures of the rate of return on invested capital, as investors make judgements on perceived future profits (a flow) versus a present commitment of capital (a stock). On the other hand, the classical tendency towards profit equalisation between economic activities may be interpreted as taking place across industries, firms, and even projects. The classical approach thus appears less demanding than the static neo-classical framework in the need for precise delineation of the relevant domain of competitive activity: since the neo-classical model *identifies* the level of competition with some measure of concentration *in a particular market*, an exact and consistent measure of its boundaries is a necessity. The dominant Marshallian synthesis embodies the difficulties of both traditions – it inherits the time-related problems which the static paradigm ignores, but on the other hand it must confront the demands for precision inherent in the static framework for the delineation of markets or commodities.

Consider some other characteristics of the classical approach. First, the tendency for rates of return to equalise as economic actors 'compete' puts no special emphasis on price competition. Its very openness and generality in this respect is simultaneously a great strength and weakness. The freedom in dynamic, classical models to discuss entry, investment, and innovation as modes of competition is very attractive, but the resultant structures lack the simplicity and decisiveness of static models of price competition. Secondly, the obvious counterpart in the classical tradition to the static model's use of market concentration as a measure of competitiveness *would have been* an index of the rate of convergence of profitability. But such a discussion is not to be found in the developed classical literature, since the universal obsession with the theory of value dictated the assumption that equalisation of profits had taken place.[19]

The inheritance by the Marshallian tradition of the emphasis on price competition from the static Cournot tradition and on the fact rather than the process of equalisation from the classical school have been further obstacles to its ability to analyse the process of competition. The failure of the classical tradition to develop fully an analysis of the process of competition is related to its embracing of utilitarian psychology: a system which assumes that equalisation 'perfectly' takes place is felicitously associated with the 'perfectly' rational entrepreneur, so that questions related to behaviour and to the process of equalisation (or limitations to its consummation) may be subsumed and ignored. The classical system failed to develop a theory of the evolution of competition which was linked to changes in behaviour, despite the potentialities inherent in its structure. Since an even more systematic utilitarianism was embodied in the neo-classical approach, the ghost of Jeremy Bentham (whether in Paretian guise or not) inevitably haunts the Marshallian synthesis.

The Marshallian Synthesis

The presentation here has to some extent reversed historical chronology, but it is not totally fanciful: the Marshallian synthesis, which has emerged as the source of orthodoxy in the Anglo-Saxon world for much of the twentieth century, has been dominated by considerations emanating from the pure static approach, with the classical, dynamic elements given very definitely a second place. As late as the 1940s, a seminal discussion of the problem of oligopoly was solely concerned with actions between participants already existent in the market.[20] The now extensive literature on entry did not even begin to emerge until the mid 1950s.

The synthesis consists of three elements, the first being that which has so exercised theorists in the present century, namely, the substitution of partial for general equilibrium. Two other aspects are crucial – the introduction into the static framework of questions explicitly related to the passage of time and a less tangible but related aspect, the presumption that this model is suited in a fairly literal way to deal with 'practical' real world issues. The latter conviction is probably the most important aspect of the heritage from Alfred Marshall himself.

Time is introduced into the Marshallian synthesis through the construct of a duality between a short run with fixed capital, in which neo-classical static considerations are dominant, most especially the number (or concentration) of participants within a given market and the modes of rivalry undertaken by them, and a classical long run in which the flow of new capital in and out of the market (or in this case the industry) is possible. Theorists have then been left with a somewhat overdetermined scheme for deciding when a situation was 'competitive': one solution which achieved a limited popularity was to declare the competitive situation in a market as 'pure' when the large numbers and associated criteria were met, while the designation 'perfect' demanded the further condition of free entry.[21]

In recent years there has been a shift away from the pure neo-classical characteristic of concentration as the key indication of competitiveness. There is now a greater emphasis on the sufficiency, at least in an approximate sense, of free entry, even in relatively 'monopolised' situations.[22] Even more troublesome for the static tradition are contexts in which the venerable 'numbers' criterion is not even a necessary condition for a 'monopoly', such as the provision of medical doctors' services in the US, widely touted by economists as an example of the use of monopoly power. In this case, 'special' considerations such as a high degree of consumer ignorance seem to make limitations on entry a sufficient condition for substantial market power even in the absence of any obvious market concentration.

The burden of practical relevance is further increased by the demands of industrial economics on the Marshallian synthesis. From the static perspective, industrial economics makes demands on the short run aspect of the Marshallian model for a descriptively realistic view of the world – for the inclusion of factors such as industry social structure and non-price forms of competition. The tension between logic and practicality manifested itself in the upheavals which took place in Marshallian theory after the First World War. But the resultant development of the theories of monopolistic competition and imperfect competition did not receive its impetus because of strong disquiet over the empirical irrelevance of diminishing returns (marginal cost curves in this literature continued to be drawn in an upward sloping direction). Nor did the doctrines surface because they possessed partial equilibrium solutions to the theoretical conundrums of perfect competition. What then was the cause of these upheavals?

In essence, these revolts from within the palace were engendered by a strong reaction to the dramatic changes which seemed to be taking place in the industrial structure – the growth of giant 'monopolies', of advertising and of product differentiation: the Marshallian tradition, with its emphasis on practicality, seemed to be losing its way.

Subsequently, however, all attackers, both from within and without, have been repelled, preserving the traditional approach to monopoly and competition in a way that would have been recognisable to Alfred Marshall himself.

The Victory of Perfect Competition
Economics has periodically been greeted with claims of the incipient overthrow of orthodoxy. In the 1940s, Hayek's optimistic prediction with reference to the work of J. M. Clark and Fritz Machlup that 'There are

signs of increasing awareness among economists that what they have been discussing in recent years under the name "competition" is not the same thing as what is thus called in ordinary language'[23] has remained un-fulfilled. Indeed Machlup's subsequent book[24] was firmly in the main-stream tradition. An examination of the most popular present-day textbooks on microeconomics evidences less of Hayek's dynamic approach to competition than ever before, and the more advanced the level of analysis of the text, the more static the approach.[25]

Even more striking is the retreat to the monopoly–competition dichotomy used by Marshall himself, with the practical abandonment of 'intermediate cases'. The dominance of 'monopoly' over models of small group oligopoly in empirical work is due to the 'indecisiveness' of the latter in its predictions: the economic writings devoted to measuring the burden to society of high industrial concentration do not mention oligopoly at all, but are quite unselfconsciously known as the 'welfare losses due to monopoly' literature.[26] Equally disconcerting for those who believe in the possibility of progressive refinement of existing economic theory has been the abandonment of attempts to develop alternatives to the model of perfect competition, an activity which so occupied the economics profession in the first half of the twentieth century.

The present role of monopolistic competition as the plaything of High Theorists is particularly ironic, given the prominent place it had in inspiring and structuring early work in industrial economics.[27] It is unfortunate that the substantive debate has petered out, since the original issues which engendered the growth of this literature remain unresolved. There seems to have been an implicit acceptance within much of mainstream economics of the curious Chicago proposition that for practical purposes one can do 'well enough' at prediction with a judicious mixture of the models of monopoly and perfect competition, these latter having defeated their presumptive challengers – 'small group' oligopoly theory in the case of monopoly and 'large group' monopolistic competi-tion versus perfect competition in the context of unconcentrated markets. The continued refinement of the pure theory (or theories) of oligopoly and the occasional application of specific models in empirical contexts[28] has proceeded apace. But in mainstream economics, perfect competition has continued to be the predominant model in economic situations which are 'competitive', with monopoly rather than one of the maze of oligopolistic alternatives as the central focus in 'non-competitive' situations.

What seems to have been forgotten in the mainstream preservation of the monopoly–competition dichotomy is that in several important instances, researchers have found that the predictions of the latter model seem to have been falsified in the real world. Perfect competition fails to predict behaviour accurately in many 'large group' situations where it would be expected to serve and which, in a heuristic sense at least, monopolistic competition deals with more successfully: advertising, product differentiation and price discrimination are all phenomena which are commonly observed in unconcentrated markets – impossible in a world of perfect competition, but seemingly consistent with models of monopolistic competition. It is clear we would need some such construct to explain Scherer's example of price discrimination in barber shops, where adult prices are higher than childrens' due to home competition 'despite the higher input in shearing a wiggling object'![29] A list of failures of prediction by the perfectly competitive model would be long indeed. *Ad hoc* manipulation may always be attempted, but becomes progressively less convincing.

But the challenge from monopolistic competition failed. A leading objection to the use of the model of monopolistic competition is that it does not yield unambiguous predictions without much stronger and more restrictive assumptions than would be necessary in the perfectly competitive model.[30] Furthermore, in general equilibrium formulations the monopolistically competitive firm does not really take the place of the perfectly competitive firm as 'typical', since the former must exist in what is essentially a sea of perfect competition and only a limited part of the classic Chamberlinian results can be formulated in this context.[31] Another reason for the long-term unpopularity of the model is the suspicion of economists that even the large numbers zero profit equilibrium may not be totally consistent with their pursuit of the Holy Grail of Paretian optimality.

An even more curious criticism, centred around the University of Chicago, is that since there is an assumption (or possibility) of differentiated products under monopolistic competition, that is to say, products which cannot necessarily be labelled and segregated one from the other in a mechanical way as in perfect competition, one encounters grave difficulties in the setting of market boundaries. This is often couched as part of a defence of perfect competition, *as if a meaningful problem in the real world can be made to disappear by assuming it away in the appropriate model*. Indeed, it is one of the lasting contributions of the literature of monopolistic competition to point to the need for clarification of this substantive, unavoidable question.

There has been one more significant 'alternative' to perfect competition – 'workable competition' – which, though rarely discussed in the context of formal theory has had a pervasive influence on the literature of industrial economics. This concept, which traces its origins to an article by J. M. Clark[32] was an attempt to go 'beyond' perfect competition, whose assumptions were thought to be overly rigorous, both in the sense that the formal criteria were too exacting in real life circumstances (e.g. perfect knowledge) and that there were many instances known to practical investigators where, when all relevant factors were considered, no action of public policy was likely to improve performance even in a highly concentrated industry.[33]

An examination of those workable competition criteria which depart from mainstream analysis reveal them to be of two kinds: first, they include structural variables which are not subject to easy quantitative treatment (e.g. the technological opportunities open to an industry) and secondly, there are a set of behavioural characteristics (e.g. the tendency of the firms in an industry to exploit these technological opportunities). It is difficult to subscribe to the commonly held view that it was simply the vagueness of the workable competition criteria which limited the model's popularity within industrial economics, since the precision of any formal theory will have to be modified in practical applications: the mainstream monopoly–competition dichotomy loses much of its precision in the analysis of substantive issues. The real reason for the theory's loss of popularity within industrial economics was, as Joe Bain suggested, that

> Whatever the degree of association within oligopolies between competitive behaviour and results, it seems quite likely that such behavior may be in turn either influenced or determined by certain characteristics of the underlying market structure. If so, a demonstrated association between market structure and results would establish the more fundamental determinants of the workability of competition.[34]

In other words, a correct specification of structural characteristics should be sufficient to describe an industry, without any need to define behavioural characteristics as anything other than dependent variables within the model. If it were conceded that these behavioural characteristics (e.g. how firms respond to technological opportunities) were necessary to adjudge the competitiveness of an industry, it would be an implicit concession of the failure of the Marshallian paradigm.

As workable competition never presented a consistent theoretical alternative to the Marshallian approach, its failure was inevitable. On the other hand, the persistent sympathy which it receives from practical researchers is symptomatic of the weaknesses implicitly felt to exist within the Marshallian paradigm and of the impossibility of modelling competition in purely structural terms. Thus, in the orthodox view[35] it is the superior precision of the market structure approach to competition compared with its classical alternatives which accounts for its predominance. This approach is 'precise' in the sense that

1 Competition is conceived in a manner that makes it amenable to objective measurement, with a focus on the inverse of some index of the concentration of firms within a market.
2 Decisive predictions can be derived of an inverse relation between profitability within the market and this measure of competition.
3 It is possible to construct statistical tests with this measure of competition as the key independent variable which (successfully) explain the level of profitability within an industry.

The literature of industrial economics thus manifests in practical terms many of the tensions of earlier theoretical controversies. It frequently juxtaposes a richly descriptive 'workable competition' approach in case studies that uses both behavioural concepts and non-quantifiable structural variables with a statistical methodology based on orthodox Marshallian theory. The latter methodology substantively accepts one or another measure of concentration as an accurate summary of the industry's ability to behave collusively, and accepts, as a matter of faith and with only limited modification, the categories offered up by the Census of Industry as surrogates for market measurement.

In summary, the ultimate justification for the dominance of orthodox approaches to competition is that the models contain a high level of conceptual precision. It will be argued that the claim to conceptual precision in orthodox models is in fact a weak one, especially once we enter the domain of practical implementation. In the absence of a coherent method for delineating markets, little remains of the orthodox approach to competition. A dynamic, classical view of the competition can not only avoid many of these difficulties, but also offers the possibility of a much richer, more 'realistic' view of the competitive process.

Dynamic Conceptions: the Challenge from Hayek

The most prominent contemporary advocate of a dynamic approach to competition and the most persuasive critic of the orthodox approach is Fredrich Hayek. Hayek's attacks on the mainstream approach to competition linger in the guilty conscience of economists: 'the theory of perfect competition . . . has little claim to be called "competition" at all. . . . If the state of affairs assumed by the theory . . . ever existed, it would not only deprive of their scope all the activities which the very verb "to compete" describes but would make them virtually impossible.'[36]

Thus, the emphasis upon perfect competition as a static equilibrium paradoxically excludes all manifestations of agents actively *competing*: 'Advertising, undercutting, and improving ("differentiating") the goods and services produced are all excluded by definition – "perfect competition" means indeed the absence of all competitive activities.' For both lawyers and industrial economists involved in anti-trust cases, it may be some solace to read from such an eminent source that the perpetual 'confusion' about whether a homogeneous price in a market is a *per se* indication of the existence of a competitive equilibrium or of a successful price-fixing agreement is not their own, but existent in the theory itself. The same is true of questions about whether non-price competition represents 'real' competition: 'the talk about the defects of competition when we are in fact talking about the necessary difference[s] between commodities and services conceals a very real confusion and leads on occasion to absurd conclusions'.

The foundation of Hayek's approach to competition as a dynamic, behavioural activity is an analysis of how knowledge is acquired and communicated in an economic system. For him, the neo-classical assumption of perfect knowledge has a paralysing effect on the investigation of the very behaviour one would want to explore: '[producers] are assumed to know the lowest cost at which the commodity can be produced. Yet this knowledge which is assumed to be given to begin with is one of the main points where it is only through the process of competition that the facts will be discovered'. The worst characteristic of monopoly is not the potential escalation of profit margins, but its tendency to generate costs which are higher than they otherwise would be, a point anticipating the development of the concept of X-inefficiency (see chapter 3), though from a perspective which is a good deal more heretical than the latter: even under 'competition' the existence of minimum costs cannot be presumed, but requires 'constant struggle, absorbing a greater part of the energy of the manager'.[37] Such a view of costs is a commonplace among individuals engaged in the solution of managerial problems. As Henry Ford reminds us:

> although one may carefully calculate what a cost is, and of course all our costs are carefully calculated, no one knows what a cost ought to be. One of the ways of discovering what a cost ought to be is to name a price so low as to force everybody in the place to the highest point of efficiency. The lowest price makes everybody dig for profits.[38]

Similiar sentiments may be found from a very different source:

> Unprofitable production is a signal not for the raising of prices, but above all for the search for more economical solutions to the mobilisation of resources and the lowering of the costs of production.[39]

It would seem that the orthodox economic theorist is quite alone in conceptualising costs as objective, exogenous, binding constraints imposed upon management and the enterprise by the exigencies of the production function. In his approach to this and other aspects of the competitive process Hayek's isolation in the academic world may be contrasted with how unexceptional his pronouncements seem to practitioners engaged in solving substantive, real world problems.

A central concern in the Hayekian approach is the acquisition and use of knowledge in economic decision making:

> It has become customary among economists to stress only the need of knowledge of prices, apparently because – as a consequence of the confusions between objective and subjective data – the complete knowledge of objective facts was taken for granted ... price expectations and even the knowledge of current prices are only a very small section of the problem of knowledge as I see it. The wider aspect of the problem with which I am concerned is the knowledge of the basic fact of how different commodities can be obtained and used and under what conditions they are actually obtained and used.[40]

In other words 'knowledge' is not just a mastery of the (technical) states of the art which are taken as given in static analysis. It also embraces a host of ways of doing business in those situations where the orthodox assumption of a technical 'set of blueprints' for production in every contingent circumstance is inconceivable. Furthermore, for Hayek it is impossible to believe that this kind of information is universally and costlessly available, especially to those not on the scene of a specific situation. The entrepreneur does not proceed to maximise an objective function subject to a set of exogenously specified and universally known constraints, dictated by the state of technical knowledge and by the preference functions existent in the market. On the contrary, through a process of interaction with the environment, the entrepreneur explores and develops *new* methods of production (even in the absence of fundamental technological innovation) and offers *new* products in response to that unique and concrete situation.

It is clear that Hayek's 'theory of the firm' is intimately connected with a *process* of discovery – with behaviour. The firm is not simply subject to the constraints of an exogenously specified production function: it is the very task of the entrepreneur to move and manipulate those constraints. In a precisely parallel way, it is impossible to specify an exogenous market which exists as a structural constraint upon competitive activity, since it is the very nature of entrepreneurial activity to break down and make irrelevant any such encumbrances, to create new markets and stretch old ones as part of their creative activity and process of discovery: 'The conception of the economic system as divisible into distinct markets for separate commodities is after all largely the product of the imagination of the economist and certainly is not the rule in the field of manufacture and of personal services, to which the discussion about competition so largely refers.'[41]

Hayek's critique of standard approaches to competition is so eloquent and fundamental that some care must be taken to distinguish it from the position taken in this book. Furthermore, the success of orthodoxy at repelling this and similar Austrian attacks must be explained. Ironically, what would seem to be an even more radical assault upon standard competitive theory by an Austrian (in a literal and only marginally in a figurative sense), Joseph Schumpeter, has received a good deal more attention in the literature than Hayek's. Unlike Hayek's analysis, in which entrepreneurial price calculations are seen in a new light and in which an environment of 'rational' market-based prices is a necessary prerequisite for meaningful decisions to be made at the microeconomic level, Schumpeter's 'gales of creative destruction' make irrelevant or trivial these price calculations. His pronouncements on these questions have been widely discussed, but relegated in the literature of economics to a specific sub-topic in the theory of competition, namely technological change, and there they have stayed. The relevance of his ideas to the theory of the competitive process in a broader sense has been largely ignored, but they will be considered in the context of technological diffusion in chapter 9.

Hayek, an Austrian in the figurative as well as literal sense embraces that school's central contribution to the development of marginal utility: his critique of the use of 'equilibrium' analysis stops at 'the analysis of the action of a single person'.[42] Such a pronouncement is not surprising, given his desire to demonstrate the efficacy of free market institutions under all conditions. Furthermore, he uses a methodology found in Ludwig von Mises's *Human Action*,[43] where (human) behaviour can be described, not from observation but from the 'necessity' which emerges from its inherent ('rational') nature. That this is at the basis of Hayek's approach, despite protestations to a Popperian falsification methodology is clear:

> Assume that somewhere in the world a new opportunity for the use of some raw material say, tin has arisen. . . . All that the users of tin need to know is that some of the tin they used to consume is now more profitably employed elsewhere and that, in consequence, they must economise on tin. . . . The whole acts as one market, not because any of its members survey the whole field, but because their limited fields of vision sufficiently overlap so that through many intermediaries the relevant information is communicated to all.[44]

This (optimal) result seems to come about as an inherent consequence of the existence of market relations, without any necessity to specify historical circumstances or conditions of trade. Apparently, it will be necessarily true in all times and places, for all conditions of exchange, that the information communicated by prices to individual traders will be collectively of a greater magnitude and more useful than that to any central source, and that whatever the customs, traditions, habits, superstition or ignorance within this market these prices will always guide the optimal use of these resources by these individual traders. Neo-classical economics often comes to similar conclusions, but when properly presented, it offers a scrupulous listing of the necessary pre-conditions for such a result.

Hayek's somewhat tautological approach to normative questions is not to be confused with his epistemological position, which insists on a separation between the subjective 'data' which are available to individuals on the one hand, and the objective 'facts' on the other. Confusion has often resulted from the two very different conceptions of subjectivity found in Hayek's writings. The first conception is that competition is a dynamic, behavioural process rooted in, among other things, the subjective perceptions by the participants of an objective reality. The second is that an understanding of the competitive process may be gained by a subjective, introspective analysis of 'rational' action. The first of these conceptions suggests that since analysis of competition is intimately concerned with peoples' subjective perceptions, empirical verification may be very difficult indeed, but it is not in principle excluded. The second conception seems to derive the competitive process logically from its inherent *necessity* in the context of rational action (and the absence of government interference), something which may be subjectively perceived a priori by the economist.

As Hayek and his followers have embraced the second as well as the first of these approaches, free market situations always appear optimal and little can be said about the process of economic change. They are often forced to retreat to Marshallian structuralist categories in order, for instance, to demonstrate empirically that competition in the economy is increasing,[45] since they are bereft of a methodology for the verification of their own very different perspective on competition. While the difficulties of empirical verification have proved a major obstacle to the acceptance of the Hayekian concept of competition, it is only with the second conception of subjectivity that Hayek himself excludes this possibility.

Hayek's categories are deeply rooted in the static utilitarian calculus of choice inherited from the earlier Austrian School of Menger and others, and they rest uneasily with his dynamic behavioural notions of the competitive process. For the theorist it is easy to argue that Hayek is trying to have the best of all possible worlds – a convincing, realistic picture of the competitive process, but with normative conclusions as decisive as those emerging from the most carefully constructed (and constrained) static neo-classical formulations. As the perspective on the competitive process presented here has aspects akin to those of Hayek, we shall wish to demonstrate that a behavioural, dynamic approach to competition can be constructed using the traditional methodology of science, one which concedes in principle the possibility of empirical refutation.

Perhaps all notions of competitiveness which are viable for empirical and (especially) statistical work will confront many of these difficulties and inevitably vitiate some of the grandeur of the constructions of Hayek and Schumpeter. To some extent, in any dynamic approach, the distinction between a modelling of *ex ante* decision making and *ex post* observations is an inherent problem: we cannot rely on static, timeless equilibrium to solve this problem for us. Hayek emphasizes that 'it is important to remember that ... all facts given to the person in question [are] the things as they are known to (or believed by) him to exist, and not, strictly speaking, objective facts'.[46] Not surprisingly, the reaction of those few orthodox theorists who have addressed themselves to the issues raised by Hayek has been sharp indeed: 'no competent theorist regards static–equilibrium theory as the last word of economic analysis ... Hayek's discussion is less a "refutation" ... than ... an obscurantist effort to undermine all of the standard techniques of economic analysis'.[47]

There is an important element of validity in this critique, since Hayek's methodology often seems to deny, even in principle, any standard for independent verification of the relationship between the subjective perception of reality and the 'thing in itself'. Furthermore, there is a strong presumption, with more than a little ideological flavour, that if events take place under the appropriate conditions (i.e. those of a free market), *it must be* that all information available will have been processed 'as well as possible'.

Unfortunately for the upholders of mainstream theory, Hayek's methodological position is essentially correct. Once we depart from pure static equilibrium models, the propositions of economic theory, as Hayek suggests, refer to things which are defined in terms of human attitudes towards them. The misunderstanding of this point is a source of much confusion: 'I am not certain that [mainstream economists – dubbed by Hayek as 'behaviourists'] are quite aware of how much of the traditional approach they would have to abandon if they wanted to be consistent or that they would want to adhere to it consistently if they were aware of this.'[48]

Thus, the orthodox notion of opportunity cost, a subjective concept, has no correspondence to the statistical cost curves used in applied work.[49] If such difficulties exist in the Marshallian theory, which prides itself on empirical applicability, it may prove impossible to formulate statistical tests using a truly dynamic approach. But would such a failure be considered fatal and would rejection of the dynamic approach be justified in the pursuit of 'objective' results? These questions relate to the issue of what kind of empirical information is relevant for the confirmation of a theory.

Orthodox theory in the past has been presented as appropriate for statistical and economy-wide testing and thus well in line with the popular desire to establish broad-based scientific generalisations, alongside which the individual case study gives the impression of lacking purpose and direction. Unfortunately for the dynamic approach, it is the latter which is most conducive to it. Since the primary focus of the dynamic approach is upon behaviour, the distinction between *ex ante* intentions and perceptions and *ex post* outcomes is critical, but difficult to disinter from statistical data, as are the subtle interactions between structure and behaviour. Furthermore, there is invariably a host of side information (i.e. information about behaviour) available in a case study which becomes invisible in a statistical test. In chapter 4, the dynamic approach is 'watered down' and analysed in the context of statistical tests. The motivation for this procedure is that the ability to formulate such tests in principle is an indication of some minimum level of coherence in the dynamic approach which would be difficult to demonstrate in any other manner, even if there inevitably remain serious limitations to statistical tests of dynamic processes.

In the next chapter it is argued that the use of 'precise' market measurement which is central to Marshallian theory is not in fact a viable procedure. Economists often tell the story of the inebriated gentleman who staggered around the lamp-post looking for his keys despite the fact that he lost them at the other end of the street 'because the light is better' under the lamp-post. The problem is not merely that the use of these market and industry measures leads to some academic embarrassments and conundrums, but that they are unusable for comparative purposes and they give a fundamentally inaccurate picture of the development of the competitive process over historical time. We may then be forced to desert the brilliantly illuminated static approach to competition in favour of a more dimly lit dynamic alternative.

Notes

1. Galbraith, J. K. *The New Industrial State* Signet Books 1967.
2. Auerbach, P. and P. Skott, 'Concentration, Competition and Distribution – A Critique of Theories of Monopoly Capital' *International Review of Applied Economics* 2(1) January 1988: 42–61. An extremely influential example of the monopoly capital school is Baran, P. and P. Sweezy *Monopoly Capital* Penguin 1966 and a prominent recent example is Cowling, K. *Monopoly Capitalism* Macmillan 1982; a brief discussion on this topic ensues in ch. 10.
3. See for example Berle, A. *The American Economic Republic* Harcourt Brace & World 1965.
4. Bruno Hildebrand of the German Historical School, quoted in Gide, C. and C. Rist *A History of Economic Doctrines* (English translation) Harrap 1915, pp. 400–1.
5. See for instance Hahn, F. 'On the Notion of Equilibrium'. Inaugural lecture Cambridge University 1973.
6. Lucas, R. E. *Studies in Business Cycle Theory* Basil Blackwell 1981, p. 4.
7. This point is made by Skott, P. 'On General Equilibrium Theory, Rationality and the Costs of Spurious Generality' *British Review of Economic Issues* 8(18) (Spring 1986): 29–50.
8. Major writings from this school include March, J. and H. Simon *Organizations* John Wiley 1958, Cyert, R. and J. March *A Behavioral Theory of the Firm* Prentice-Hall 1963 and Simon, H. *Administrative Behavior* Free Press 1965. The most prominent representation of this tradition in recent years is Nelson, R. R. and S. Winter *An Evolutionary Theory of Economic Change* Harvard University 1982.
9. Scherer F. M. *Industrial Market Structure and Economic Performance* Rand McNally second edn 1980, ch. 7.
10. 'Keeping America Cool' *Financial Times* 26 September 1985.
11. Biographical note by A. Livingston to Pareto in Pareto, V. *The Mind and Society* Jonathan Cape 1935, p. xviii. In fact, Schmoller's methodological position was a good deal more subtle than is indicated by this anecdote – see Gide and Rist (note 4), p. 385.
12. Copeland, T. and J. F. Weston *Financial Theory and Corporate Policy* second edn Addison Wesley 1983, p. viii.
13. McNulty, P. 'A Note on the History of Perfect Competition' *Journal of Political Economy* 75 part 1(4) (August 1967): 395–99, his 'Economic Theory and the Meaning of Competition' *Quarterly Journal of Economics* 82(4) (November 1968): 639–56 and Gram, H. and V. Walsh *Classical and Neo-Classical Theories of General Equilibrium* Oxford University 1979.
14. See Waterson, M. *Economic Theory of the Industry* Cambridge University 1984, ch. 2 and Schmalensee, R. 'The New Industrial Organization and the Economic Analysis of Modern Markets' in Hildenbrand, W. (ed.) *Advances in Economic Theory* Cambridge University 1980, ch. 10.
15. See Cowling (note 2), p. 35.
16. See Clarke, R. and S. Davies 'Market Structure and Price-Cost Margins'

Economica 49 (August 1982): 277–87; for a different development of the same point see Auerbach, P. and P. Skott 'A Critique of Theories of Monopoly Capital' *University College London Discussion Paper* No. 85–19 1985.

17. Lamoreaux, N. *The Great Merger Movement in American Business 1895–1904* Cambridge University 1985, pp. 26–7.
18. Arrow, K. 'Towards a Theory of Price Adjustment' in Abramovitz, M. (ed.) *The Allocation of Economic Resources* Stanford University 1959, pp. 41–51.
19. For Marx 'the general rate of profit is never anything more than a tendency to equalise specific rates of profit' (Marx, K. *Capital* vol. 3 International Publishers edn of 1977, p. 366), but the formal model presented in vol. 2 of *Capital* makes him liable for the comments made here.
20. Fellner, W. *Competition Among the Few* Augustus M. Kelley 1965; originally published in 1949.
21. Machlup, F. *The Political Economy of Monopoly* Johns Hopkins University 1952, ch. 1.
22. Fama, E. and A. Laffer 'The Number of Firms and Competition' *American Economic Review* 62(4) (September 1972): 670–4, and Baumol, W., J. Panzar and R. Willig *Contestable Markets and the Theory of Industry Structure* Harcourt Brace Jovanovich 1982.
23. Hayek, F. 'The Meaning of Competition' as reprinted in a collection of articles by Hayek *Individualism and Economic Order* University of Chicago 1948, pp. 92–106.
24. Machlup (note 21).
25. A typical example of an advanced microeconomics text is Gravelle, H. and R. Rees *Microeconomics* Longman 1981.
26. See Harberger, A. 'Monopoly and Resource Allocation' and Bergson, A. 'On Monopoly Welfare Losses' in *American Economic Review* 44 (May 1954): 77–84 and 63 (December 1973): 853–70 respectively.
27. See Bain, J. 'Chamberlin's Impact on Microeconomic Theory' reprinted in Bain, J. *Essays on Price Theory and Industrial Organization* Little, Brown and Co. 1972, ch. 14; a bibliography of contemporary theoretical work on monopolistic competition may be found in Hart, O. 'Imperfect Competition in General Equilibrium: An Overview of Recent Work' in Arrow, K. and S. Honkapohja (eds) *Frontiers of Economics* Basil Blackwell 1985, pp. 100–49.
28. A recent example being Domovitz, I., R. Hubbard and B. Petersen 'Oligopoly Supergames: Some Empirical Evidence on Prices and Margins' *Journal of Industrial Economics* 25(4) (June 1987): 379–98.
29. Scherer (note 9), p. 318.
30. Archibald, G. 'Chamberlin versus Chicago' *Review of Economic Studies* 29 (October 1961): 2–28.
31. Negishi, T. 'Monopolistic Competition and General Equilibrium' *Review of Economic Studies* 27(3) (June 1961): 196–201 and Arrow, K. 'The Firm in General Equilibrium Theory' in Marris, R. and A. Wood (eds) *The Corporate Economy* Macmillan 1971, pp. 68–110.
32. Clark, J. M. 'Toward a Concept of Workable Competition' *American Economic Review* 30 (June 1940): 241–56.
33. Markham, J. 'An Alternative Approach to the Concept of Workable Competition' *American Economic Review* 40(3) (June 1950): 349–61.
34. Bain, J. 'Workable Competition in Oligopoly: Theoretical Considerations and Some Empirical Evidence' *American Economic Review* 40(2) (May 1950): 35–47.

35. Stigler, G. 'Monopolistic Competition in Retrospect' in *Five Lectures on Economic Principles* London School of Economics 1949.
36. Hayek (note 23).
37. Hayek, F. 'The Use of Knowledge in Society' in *Individualism* (note 23), pp. 27–91.
38. Henry Ford *My Life and Work* (with Samuel Crowther) quoted in Chandler, A. *Ford, General Motors and the Automobile Industry* Harcourt Brace and World 1964, p. 99.
39. Petakov, N. 'Tsena – Richag Upravleniya' ['Pricing – The Lever of Management'] *Ekonomicheskaya Gazeta* (USSR) 16 April 1986, p. 10.
40. Hayek, F. 'Economics and Knowledge' in *Individualism* (note 23), pp. 33–56.
41. Hayek (note 23).
42. Hayek (note 40).
43. von Mises, L. *Human Action* Contemporary Books third edn 1966. Originally published in 1949.
44. Hayek (note 37).
45. See Reekie, W. *Industry, Prices and Markets* Phillip Alan 1979, ch. 2.
46. Hayek (note 40).
47. Bishop, R. 'The Theory of Monopolistic Competition after Thirty Years: the Impact on General Theory' *American Economic Review* 59(3) (May 1964): 33–45.
48. Hayek (note 40).
49. See the discussion in Buchanan, J. *Cost and Choice* Markham 1969.

3

Markets and Industries

Introduction

The 'market' is central to the orthodox concept of competition in both its pure static and Marshallian varieties. In this chapter, three major conclusions arise:

1 *Objective and consistent criteria to delineate markets for the purpose of cross-sectional comparisons do not exist*. This is a critical weakness in the orthodox theory of competition. The central methodology emerging from orthodox theory for comparing two competitive situations (i.e. two 'industries') is to compute an index of market concentration (for instance a Herfindahl index) for each of them and to declare the industry with the higher index to be less competitive. But if objective and consistent criteria for market delineation do not exist even in principle, the resulting indices have little meaning. It makes a mockery of the orthodox claim to an exceptional precision compared with alternative doctrines. It is as if the relative population densities of cities were to be calculated in the absence of any basis, even in principle for delineating the boundaries of 'a city'.

2 *Measures of market concentration cannot be used to trace the historical evolution of the competitive process through time series comparisons*. In the absence of a methodology for delineating market boundaries and explaining changes in these boundaries over time, historical movements in market concentration cannot be used to measure changes in the competitive environment.

3 *In the context of orthodox theory, market delineation must be specified independently of the behaviour of participants in that market. Because of*

*the necessary interaction between structure and behaviour in the generation
of market boundaries such a task is in fact impossible*. At a theoretical
level, it is this failure which generates most of the problems specified
above. In practical work, it explains why case study research invariably
takes into consideration the behaviour of participants in drawing industry
boundaries if these boundaries are not to be totally arbitrary. The
necessity for such a procedure raises serious questions about the claims to
practical utility of the Marshallian research programme.

In addition to these problems which exist in principle, there are a series
of secondary considerations concerning the practical applicability of
existing data to empirical questions. These other difficulties prove to be
extremely daunting. Since, however, these empirical procedures are not
supported by an intellectually coherent theory, there is no reason to think
that if these practical obstacles were overcome the results would be
worthwhile. Little that is useful emerges from the orthodox approach to
market delineation.

Cross-sectional Comparisons of Market Structure

Pure Static and Marshallian Approaches

The pure static theory cannot dispense with an explicit delineation of the
domain of the market[1] in which transactions take place. For Edgeworth,
one of the founders of the tradition, it was an issue of major importance:

> Edgeworth certainly perceived ... the enormous problems of
> competitive grouping. The variability in the composition of the
> competitive 'units' is as much a source of theoretical indeterminacy
> as is the limitation in the numbers of these units, however they may
> be defined. So horrified was Edgeworth by the thought of a
> wholesale collapse of economic theory and of the scientific enter-
> prise, that he attempted to dispose of this profound difficulty by
> resorting to some rather obscure technical jargon. In so-called
> 'perfect competition', the indestructible competitive unit was taken
> to be the 'catalectic molecule', the bare, and irreducible individual
> human being.[2]

Modern general equilibrium theory has 'solved' Edgeworth's problem.
In this model, goods are simply labelled qualitatively, as well as in time and
in space. Since the good is defined in space, the delineation of the market is
identical with the delineation of the product, which is why these problems
are often conflated in the literature. But no guidance is given for a host of
problems in the fitting of the model to reality:

1 Over what time dimension do we measure the relevant parameters? For
   instance, if we want to calculate elasticities of demand as part of our

procedure for market delineation, should we use long or short run elasticities?

2 Is our delineation on the basis of markets (the 'short run') or in terms of industries (the 'long run')? The existence of more than one method of delineation implies not only alternative and possibly conflicting systems of classification of products based, on the one hand, on substitution in consumption (elasticity of demand) and in production (elasticity of supply), but as well a geographical conflict between where goods are consumed and where they are produced.

3 How do we deal with changes over time, such as movements in technology which challenge the validity of our initial categories?

4 *Most significantly*, how can we maintain our market delineation in a consistent, independent way over time when these markets are inevitably shaped by, and changing with the behaviour of participants?

In pure static theory, all of the above problems are solved by assuming them away: conceptual difficulties in market delineation do not exist. If one of the purposes of theory is to focus on the important issues, *the clear implication from general equilibrium theory is that the problem of market delineation is one of relatively trivial consequence*.

The Marshallian theory, with its greater pretence to practical realism, has not been able to avoid the issue of market delineation so easily. What in fact would be the prerequisites for a successful market measure in the Marshallian context? The following characteristics are crucial for an *ex ante* specification of market extent:

1 *Qualitative delineation*. It must be possible to separate these markets *qualitatively* one from the other, with unambiguous lines of demarcation.

2 *Consistent delineation*. The criterion/criteria for delineation must be *consistent* between markets and over 'time', the latter concept referring both to
(a) Marshallian 'time', in which we distinguish between the short and long run and
(b) historical time. Here, if the measure is not to be constant over different periods, we must demonstrate that a systematically and uniformly applicable methodology for showing changes in the boundaries of the market is available.

3 *Independent specification*. The market must be specified in a manner which makes its delineation independent of the behaviour of the participants in that market, if the statement 'market structure affects conduct' is to be meaningful in the powerful form in which it is put forth in standard theory.

In applied work, it has always been implicitly recognised that the above criteria are incapable of realisation. Most specifically the delineation of industry boundaries for anti-trust purposes has always taken place using an interaction of structural and behavioural variables, but often rather apologetically. It is generally implied that a 'correct' Marshallian solution would be used *if only enough information were available*.

From these theoretical traditions – the pure static and the Marshallian – have emerged two classes of solutions in industrial economics to deal with the problem of market delineation. The first, inspired perhaps by the static theory's light-hearted perspective on the issue, offers off-hand practical solutions as if they were sufficient to deal with the difficulties confronted. The second, emanating from the Marshallian tradition attempts a principled solution, the cross-elasticity of demand. Neither of these approaches is a successful method of market delineation.

'Solutions' to the Problem of Market Delineation

In economic theory *the market must be considered (like the cost curve) as an* ex ante *concept*. When market analysis is used to explain and predict economic outcomes, the purpose is to examine how the market constrains and affects the behaviour of participants within its domain. Let us, for instance, assume that there were only two shops selling food in each of two neighbourhoods of London. If the first neighbourhood were in Brixton, we might well believe that its indigent inhabitants were limited to these two shops by *objective conditions* (distance, cost of transport, etc.) and that a duopoly analysis of this market is appropriate. On the other hand, the affluent, car-mobile residents of Surbiton are in a far different position. We would be reluctant to use a duopoly analysis even if almost every household purchased its food in the two shops in this neighborhood. If with small price differentials purchasers were in a position to break their habit of neighbourhood shopping and use an alternative venue, it would seem pointless to delineate the neighbourhood as the relevant unit of analysis for explaining and predicting the behaviour, prices and profits of the two local shops.

In other words, it would be impossible to delineate the market until we had separated necessity from convenience[3] for the shoppers in this case and more generally had specified the market's domain *independently of the actual behaviour of its participants*. Even in our example we have made an implicit assumption about price rationality on the part of buyers – we have presumed that if objective conditions permit them to pursue cheaper alternatives they will do so, and they will not persist in their present behaviour out of custom, laziness or consumer loyalty.

Of the several attempts to deal with the problem of market delineation perhaps the most venerable is that attributed to Cournot and to Marshall, whereby the domain of the market is set where the price (inclusive of transport costs) of the commodity is uniform. There is an important sense in which this is a useful tool of analysis. For instance, an indication of the internationalisation of world grain production and of the elimination of insulated submarkets (especially in the Third World) since the end of the Second World War has been the development of universally applicable international grain prices.

For all its attractiveness, this notion cannot be the foundation of a market measure, as it precludes by definition the possibility of testing the usefulness and applicability of the perfectly competitive model's prediction that deconcentrated markets will tend to price uniformity.[4] It makes nonsense of any attempt to explore, for instance, why two brands of aspirin, side-by-side on the counter shelf, sell for different prices, since we would have to declare them to be in different markets in order to be consistent. The definition would thus exclude many central issues in market analysis concerning the possibility of price discrimination, countervailing power, consumer ignorance or other forms of market failure. The long list of assumptions about the *behaviour* of both producers and consumers which would be needed to generate this practical solution to the problem of market extent makes it inappropriate as a structural measure.

The other attempt at a straightforward solution to the problem is to specify the domain of the market so that it includes all those firms which are conscious of each others' behaviour.[5] Such a definition would at best be limited to situations of apparently high concentration: it would exclude perfectly competitive situations and all others in which firms are not conscious of the behaviour of others, or in which they do not respond reactively to changes in the behaviour of other individual firms. To remove this objection, we might choose to broaden the definition to include not only those firms possessing a common sense of rivalry, but all those which observe and respond to a common set of parameters (e.g. market prices).

Variations on this definition are commonly used in research of a case study kind. Clearly, such an approach has little connection with the demands of economic orthodoxy, where the exogenous market structure must be determined independently of the behaviour of participants. The necessity for taking participants' behaviour into consideration in this definition results in two substantive problems. First, in an economy consisting of firms which are increasingly diversified, it is likely that the strategic perceptions which firms have about a particular market will become progressively more asymmetric: a small beer-maker's perception of price and quality changes by other firms in the beer market is likely to be very different from that of a beer subdivision of a multinational firm which sells products which are both substitutes and complements for beer.[6]

Secondly, this definition, since it is based on the subjective perceptions of participants, would seem to exclude behaviour on the part of firms which is other than knowledgeable and rational. In the case of our food stores in London, the two sellers in Brixton might correctly perceive that they have no substantive rivals, in which case the prices and profits emerging from a duopoly analysis of this market might yield an accurate prediction. The two sellers in Surbiton, however, might delude themselves into thinking that, for them as well, joint profit maximising behaviour was a rational strategy, even though an objective delineation of the market's domain would imply that this was a misperception of the functional domain of competition. These two sellers might not be conscious of anyone else's behaviour, but they may indeed be in competition with food stores in other neighbourhoods. Such delusions and mistakes on the part of firms are a significant fact of economic life, most especially when we consider the qualitative and geographical differentiation of products, where miscalculations and uncertainty about the identity of one's rivals are common events. A striking example of this phenomenon in recent years was the failure of the British motorcycle industry to take any cognizance of Japanese imports, even after significant market penetration had taken place.[7] As far as the British manufacturers were concerned, Japanese motorcycles were not in the same market.

Thus, while both these practical solutions to the problem of market delineation are useful in applied work, neither can serve as a principled solution for the purposes of orthodox analysis.

The cross-elasticity of demand is the central device suggested for the delineation of the market in almost every textbook where the issue is raised.[8] It has retained its status as a principled solution to the problem despite the fact that it has rarely been used in practice, on the grounds that the obstacles to its use could be overcome if sufficient information were available. This is indeed a curious state of affairs, since the arguments presented below suggesting the unviability of the elasticity of demand are extremely well known. The usual presumption has been that this measure of the substitutability between two products could be used to group them in a common category if the cross-elasticity exceeded some pre-determined positive value.

The essential problems with the use of cross-elasticities to delineate market boundaries are that the level of 'cut-off' is completely arbitrary from the point of view of economic theory and that these elasticities cannot be applied in a consistent and meaningful way. Since all demand elasticities are contingent on the level of aggregation, they cannot be used to determine the initial level of aggregation in a consistent way. In deciding whether sausage is meat or bread, we may choose to examine the cross-elasticity of 'sausage' and 'beef' compared with that of 'sausage' and 'brown bread'. But this is an arbitrary procedure. Why should we decide to use sausage as a basic category, instead of more sharply defined ones such as German Bratwurst, English bangers, Italian salami, etc., or even more narrow ones contingent on the packaging, quality, etc. of these products?

Now, in the real world, these problems will be decided for us by the levels of initial aggregation set by the Standard Industrial Classification system, which, being largely decided on supply considerations, are irrelevant to the needs of a consistently demand-based criterion. We could base our cut-off on the 'intrinsic' difference between, say, sausage and bread (or could we?), but such a procedure would defeat the whole purpose of having an objective measure and would not be very helpful in the context of using this tool to decide the geographical delineation of the market, where the same problems are confronted. Cross-elasticity cannot be used in a consistent, systematic way to deal with the level of commodity aggregation, since its own value will be contingent on the prior level of aggregation.

Furthermore, these issues are invariably discussed in a purely static context. Once we enter the dimension of time, it is impossible to ignore the Marshallian distinction between the short and long run, since market delineations based on substitution in demand may be very different from industry (long run) delineations based on substitution in supply. Nicholas Kaldor's observations on this question are apposite:

> [Mrs. Robinson's concept of an industry] implies the assumption that the products of different firms consist of a 'chain of substitutes' surrounded on each side of a 'marked gap' within which the demand for each firm's product is *similarly sensitive* with respect to the price of any of the others. The 'boundary' is thus defined as the limit beyond which this sensitiveness ceases or at any rate becomes a different order of magnitude. No doubt for each particular producer there exists such a boundary. But there is no reason to assume (except in very special cases, involving a peculiar grouping of consumers) that this boundary is the same for any group of producers; or that the sensitiveness of demand for the products of any *particular* producer is of the same order magnitude with respect to the prices of any group of his rivals. Some producers will be 'nearer' to him, others 'further off'. *If the demand for cigarettes in a particular village shop is more affected by the price of beer in the opposite public-house than by the price of cigarettes in the shop at the nearest town, which of the two would Mrs. Robinson lump together into 'one industry': the seller of cigarettes plus the seller of beer in the village, or the seller of cigarettes in the village plus the seller of cigarettes in the town?*[9] (italics added)

It is worth noting why Kaldor's question is a paradox at all. While the discussion of this question proceeds purely in terms of elasticity of demand, it is implicit that there would be something a bit absurd about aggregating cigarettes and beer, to the exclusion of cigarettes more geographically separated, since these 'market' categories based on elasticity of demand will have to serve as 'industry' delineations (Mrs. Robinson's seller-oriented concept) as well. This aspect of the problem sometimes results in the rather casual comment that delineation should be based upon elasticities of demand and (?) supply,[10] though the integration is never clearly specified. The market–industry distinction creates a conflict between a demand-oriented butter and margarine delineation and the supply-oriented delineation between butter and cheese. This problem creates great confusion in statistical tests of the Marshallian model of competition. Moreover, the geographical domain of production may differ from the geographical domain of consumption. An obvious example (to be discussed below) arises in the context of international trade.

In summary, if cross-elasticity of demand were not so impractical as a market measure, it would fail on grounds of principle. If it did not fail on such grounds, it would still be inadequate for any practical application.

Empirical issues
Industry analysis in economics is so ubiquitous that defences of its use are hard to come by:

> Flippant examples purportedly destructive of the industry concept in a product differentiated economy (such as the alleged close substitution of nightclub admissions, pleasure cruises and cold showers) are not persuasive; for each of these there can be twenty queries such as those concerning the evident degree of substitutability between cigarettes and kitchen sinks, automobiles and roller skates, or concrete and gunpowder. A serious endeavor to couple our powers of observation with our knowledge of the concept of cross-elasticity of demand might have shut off a great deal of pseudomethodological quibbling over the acceptability and validity of the industry concept in a price theory that deals with a product-differentiated economy.[11]

It is easy to be sympathetic with practical economists such as Bain who have to 'get on with the job', whatever the objections of theorists. For Bain, in the absence of a usable alternative the industry will retain its central role because of the need felt to order firms (or the activities of firms) in some other way than as an arbitrary agglomeration.

The pervasiveness of industry analysis has not lessened. On the contrary, its domain of applicability in statistical tests has spread far beyond the traditional concern with profitability to a whole host of other issues.[12] Thus, for a wide set of topics in which the level of industry competitiveness is thought to be an appropriate independent variable, the following 'boiling down' procedure often takes place: first, there is a discussion of the competitive process in which it is sometimes pointed out that the latter involves, in reality, a complex interaction of structural and behavioural variables. Secondly, an approximation to the level of competition is made using a purely structural approach. Thirdly, the market concentration ratio is offered as a surrogate for all these structural factors. Finally, the actual measure used as an appropriate first approximation to market concentration is the national concentration ratio uncorrected either for the existence of local submarkets or for international considerations, even in the case of open economies like Great Britain or Belgium.[13] If it were to be judged purely on the basis of popularity, then industry analysis is alive and well: it must be questioned whether such a 'try it and see' approach has much validity.

The statistical data used to designate the industry may now be explored. The major reservation we have with the ubiquitous use of these data in an unquestioning manner is that there are quite enough difficulties involved with the implementation and interpretation of firm data *even without* the further set of arbitrary assumptions, conjectures and surmises necessary for the construction of industry statistics. The system of industrial classification is international, with the problems and philosophy of implementation especially close between the US and the UK,[14] though differences make straightforward national comparisons difficult.

If we look at the UK classification system, note that it 'has been prepared to conform with the organization and structure of industry and trade as it exists within the United Kingdom. All relevant factors such as the commodity produced or service given, the raw materials used and the nature of the process or the work done, has been taken into consideration'.[15] Clearly, what we have here is some sort of industry or supply side delineation. The economist confronting these rather loose criteria for the first time may demand to know why they cannot be made more 'rigorous'. The main reason is that the industrial census is made to serve multiple purposes and a certain vagueness is, therefore, inevitable. A common grouping on the basis of supply characteristics might take a different form if its purpose were to register industrial competitiveness than if it were used to measure the use of raw materials or trends in the evolution of the labour market between manual and non-manual work. In reality, it is made to serve all these needs simultaneously.

If we look at the 1968 Standard Industrial categories, we see that they break down into 27 broad based Orders, such as:

Order III – Food, Drink and Tobacco
Order VI – Metal Manufacture

Within these Orders may be found 181 Minimum List Headings. Within Order III – Food, Drink and Tobacco, we find as a partial listing

217 Cocoa, Chocolate and Sugar Confectionery
218 Fruit and Vegetable Products
219 Animal and Poultry Foods
221 Vegetable and Animal Oils and Fats

These Minimum List Headings are sometimes further broken up into product listings. It has been implied upon occasion that the Minimum List Headings can be used to represent industry or supply characteristics, while the product designations closely approximate market or demand delineations. A brief glance at the SIC catalogue makes it clear that this is not so, and that the main purpose of the product listings is to disaggregate further the supply-based Minimum List Headings. Under MLH 217, for instance, there are two further divisions:

1. *Cocoa and chocolate*
   Manufacturing cocoa powder, drinking chocolate and chocolate confectionery of all kinds. Cocoa butter is included.

2. *Sugar confectionery*
   Manufacturing boiled sweets, toffee, caramels, marzipan, liquorice, chewing gum and all other types of sweets.

Neither of these groupings, especially the first one containing both beverages and confectionery is likely to be thought to describe 'market' in a meaningful way.

Under the EEC system introduced into the UK in 1980 there are 10 Divisions (ranging from 0–9), 60 Classes (2 digit), 222 Groups (3 digit) and 334 Activity Headings (4 digit). Thus, in Division 4 ('Other Manufacturing Industries'), there is Class 41/42 ('Food, Drink and Tobacco Manufacturing Industries') which contains Group 421 ('Ice Cream, Cocoa, Chocolate and Sugar Confectionery'), within which may be found Activity 4214 ('Cocoa, Chocolate and Sugar Confectionery'). This Activity is then broken down (as was MLH 217 above) into 'Cocoa and Chocolate' and 'Sugar Confectionery'.

Two elements of caution should be added. First, in the case of other sectors, there does not exist such an easy correspondence between the old MLH and the new Activity categories, so that time series comparisons now confront a new series of practical difficulties over and above the conceptual problems which have always existed in such comparisons. Secondly, the present guide to the Standard Industrial Classification system warns that breakdowns below the level of the activity are 'descriptive and intended primarily for ease of exposition. Their use for statistical purposes will be limited'. These limitations reinforce the fact that available data are oriented to supply-based de-lineations: *market* extent and therefore market concentration, a demand-based concept, is non-operational for practical as well as conceptual reasons.

In a world made simple for the census (and for Marshallian theory) each firm would have its activities allocated to a specific classification. As firm activity becomes progressively more diversified, the need for allocation of these activities becomes more pressing, though the problem may be somewhat eased by long-term improvements in the quality of firm accounting data. The census takes its unit of classification to be the 'establishment', which is:

> the smallest unit which can provide the information normally required for an economic census, for example employment, expenses, turnover, capital formation. ... Frequently distant activities characteristic of different industries are carried out at one address, e.g. cotton weaving and the making up of household textiles, but normally these are not classified separately and *the whole of the establishment is classified according to the main activity*. If, however, the required range of data can be provided for each activity, each is taken to constitute a separate establishment.[16] (italics added)

The allocation of all of an establishment's activity to one product category could lead to an overestimate of the importance of principal activities or a misrepresentation of the distribution of the production of certain products where a large percentage of output is produced by firms as ancillary activities. In the case of the 1963 UK Census, the average industry homogeneity for all manufacturing establishments was 90 per cent,[17] which would seem to indicate that the problem was of a trivial order of magnitude. However, the 1947 US Census, which reported the same average level of industry homogeneity, found it necessary to incorporate a 'resistance factor' so that 'abrupt and unrealistic' small changes in the balance of an establishment's activities would not result in industry code changes.[18] Thus in the past this problem has seemed somewhat worrisome to those close to the source of data collection.

The rubric from the census to enterprises does not indicate what measure they should use to designate 'principal activity', such as sales, value added, total assets, net assets, or labour employed (each of which would imply a different theory of business behaviour). Whenever it is possible to do so, ancillary activities such as transport, wholesale and retail distribution are listed as separate establishments (the necessary detail is likely to be forthcoming only from the larger firms). Failing that, ancillary activities are allocated to existing establishments. In the 1963 and 1968 census, products with sales of less than £10 million were excluded and the outputs of certain establishments have been aggregated in a more or less arbitrary way when the products seemed to be reasonably 'homogeneous'.[19]

At least the census categories are fairly consistently based on supply characteristics. This makes them more useful than the muddle which would result if the advice of some economists were followed and greater aspects of demand were incorporated.[20] As it is, census categories may be useful and indeed indispensable for certain practical applications, but they are not suitable for making measurements of the competitiveness of the economy.

Time Series Comparisons of Market Structure

Movements in Market Concentration Over Time
Market concentration is thus problematic when it is used in cross-sectional analyses to compare levels of competitiveness within sections of the economy. Another important use of this concept is as a measure of trends in competitiveness. In a time series context, if the average level of market concentration in various sectors (suitably aggregated) has risen, it has often been deduced that competitiveness in the economy has been reduced.

There are two issues here – first, the general problems connected with time series measurements of market concentration and secondly the modifications which must take place due to the existence of international trade. In addition, there remain fundamental questions concerning the inherent meaning of market concentration as a measure of competitiveness from a dynamic perspective.

The major studies on trends in national concentration (i.e. without modifications for international trade) show a small, but clear rise in overall market concentration for the US in the post-war world, while for the UK, a powerful upward trend can be traced from the mid 1930s to the late 1960s.[21] Examining the UK studies, it is suggestive of the kinds of problems encountered that a continuous series back to the early part of the century cannot be constructed even approximately. One must be content to demonstrate rises in concentration within subseries, such as 1935 to 1951 and 1951 to 1958, since changes in industrial census classifications make longer periods incommensurate. Even within these subseries, only a fraction of industries are available for comparison.

Thus, because of changes in industry definitions and product designations, the introduction of new categories and the elimination of obsolescent ones, only a proportion of these industries are available for any comparison over an extended time span.[22] While some of the alterations in census categories take place for reasons which are incidental for our purposes, the fact that only a fraction of these categories is continuously available over a long period of time is indicative of the contradictions encountered in trying to fit technological transformations and the creation of new products – the very stuff of competitiveness – into a rigid corset of predetermined categories. At least some of the changes in definitions and categories are responses to the evolution of the competitive process and, most especially, technological innovation, so that they take place in a non-random fashion, leaving the remaining categories unsuitable as a sample to illustrate or measure changes in competition over time.[23]

Another serious difficulty with the use of concentration data to analyse time trends in the level of competition is that such a procedure *implicitly assumes that the relevant markets – the domains of competitiveness – have remained constant over decades*. Concern, albeit limited, has been evidenced about this problem in the context of international trade. This phenomenon, however, has continued to be of major significance at the intranational level. As Leslie Hannah suggests:

> What the twentieth century has seen (but what national concentration figures fail to reveal) is a transformation of many local oligopolies into regional, national or international oligopolies. Competition may not, then, have been reduced if the average size of markets has been increasing over time. Given the trend reduction in transport costs (partly a result of road-rail competition and, more recently, of the introduction of containers) it does appear that effective market areas both at home and abroad have indeed been greatly expanded. Moreover, with urbanization and the spread of universal education and a national press and television, demand in these enlarged markets has become increasingly standardized. Thus

while many of the consumer goods industries in the late nineteenth century served mainly local markets with local tastes, the more concentrated industries of today (for example, the producers of domestic electrical goods) serve a mainly national and standardized market. In these circumstances it is, of course, possible that a modern firm, even though it has a larger share of the national market in a given product, will face more competition than its predecessors in the last century who enjoyed protected local markets.[24]

Thus, time series studies which document trends in market concentration can be faulted not only for making the unreasonable presumption that market extent has remained constant throughout the century, but for not even making this powerful assumption explicit in the analysis. While such a procedure is questionable even in the context of static theory, the casual approach to market extent is typical of the literature derived from economic orthodoxy. The elucidation of changes in the domains of competitiveness and the documentation of the extent of these changes must be a central aspect of any analysis of the evolution of competition. But such an analysis is more problematic than it first appears, as may be seen when the international domain of the market is considered.

International Considerations
An obvious modification of the above data would be to take into consideration the effects of international trade. In the studies previously cited, even crude corrections for market delineation (subtracting production which is exported and adding imports) are often not performed, even in the case of open economies like the UK. The arguments made (besides those that relate to data limitations) are that:

1 Some imports are not competitive, since they are merely inputs into domestic production. (This may not be clear from the SIC categories.)
2 Some imports are controlled by domestic producers and multinationals.
3 The *threat* of imports may be as important as the imports themselves.

These arguments are often used to suggest that the whole question can be ignored.[25] However, when import corrections are made, the conventional conclusions suggesting a rising level of market concentration for the 1960s and 1970s in Britain seem to be reversed. This result holds even when (incorporating objection 2) it is assumed that as much as one quarter of these imports are controlled by domestic companies. For the US, import competition is one of the key factors identified by William Shepherd as having changed the conditions of competition in the period 1939–80, conditions which are largely identified with levels of market concentration: 'Theorists assuming the economy to be competitive have been one-half wrong until the 1960s: now they are only one-fourth in error'.[26]

Even with these corrections, such a procedure is not even approximately valid, since the market as an *ex ante* concept must dictate a sphere of *potential* competition. It is no more legitimate to decide on the level of international incursion into a domestic market by examining the level of imports than it would be to plot a demand curve for a product by looking at sales figures. Thus, domestic appliance manufacturers in the US are said to be responding to the threat of foreign competition by lowering costs and improving their quality[27] – by becoming more competitive. If such a strategy is successful then no actual imports may be recorded. However, if US firms remain uncompetitive, then import penetration may rise as foreign competitors move in. A lack of competitiveness could then show up as a decline in profitability or as increased import penetration.

But even if we should observe that imports are controlled by domestic producers, this does not mean that nothing has changed in the competitive environment. In the US, television manufacturers in the late 1960s responded to the threat of Japanese competition by shifting their production off-shore to foreign subsidiaries and affiliates of US-owned firms.[28] This shift in behaviour was a competitive response to an increasingly competitive environment but by itself it did not cause any change in market concentration statistics.

On rare occasions, there have been attempts to build up theoretically appropriate *ex ante* delineations of markets. In a study by Leonard Weiss,[29] geographical submarkets are defined not *ex post* where sales are seen to take place, but in terms of an *ex ante* delineation based on an index of transport costs. But this study is an exception, and this issue like others in market delineation is largely ignored in both the theoretical and applied literature.

It is perhaps forgivable that applied economists have not worked too extensively in this area. For those involved in practical research, the delineation of the market and the specification of its associated structural variables are only a small part of the problems involved in determining the nature of the competitive environment, which is inevitably a function of how participants *behave*. The structural perspective, however, is still of overwhelming dominance in the catechism of economics, dictating correct procedures in case study work and forming the basis of the statistical methodology of industrial economics. It is to a consideration of this perspective which we now turn.

The Market: Interaction of Structure and Behaviour

The Phillips Critique

In Bain's pioneering study,[30] the largest barrier to entry identified in consumer goods industries had been product differentiation due to advertising. This raised for Almarin Phillips the disturbing possibility that, for the oligopolistic sector of the economy, there might well be a reversal in the presumptive lines of causation of the structuralist model where, for instance, technological factors generate high minimum efficient scale in an industry, which acts as a barrier to entry and results in high concentration. Phillips suggested that an oligopolistic industry may adopt *a strategy* designed to exclude entry through collective agreements, the creation of product differentiation barriers to entry and a host of other practices. In Phillips's words – 'Structure, Conduct and Performance – and Performance, Conduct and Structure?'[31]. Other writers have suggested that such structural variables as the level of excess capacity in an industry may be used as part of a strategy of oligopolistic manipulation against potential rivals.[32]

Bain had been able to maintain a purely structuralist conception of barriers to entry partially because his estimates of the level of entry barriers were based on his own subjective determination. When explicit statistical estimates have been attempted, the fact that these 'structural' barriers are contingent on participants' behaviour becomes difficult to ignore. It might be barely possible to accept in structuralist terms of reference that high barriers to entry into the sulphur industry might be due to control of the raw material by dominant firms, or into the ethical drugs industry due to patent protection, but can one consider the product differentiation barrier in the chewing gum industry[33] to be a structural, exogenously determined parameter? Similarly, one may choose to consider an estimate of the capital requirements and the 'risk' of an industry as first approximations to structural barrier to entry parameters, but what is one to do in a purely structural context with such variables as the intensity of research and development and of advertising?[34] Such variables clearly embody behavioural considerations. The Phillips critique – that in fact behaviour can determine structure – is applicable, however, to all structural categories in the context of problems well established in the economic literature.

The problem of the endogeneity of structural variables manifests itself even in such 'deep' structural variables as the firm's level of costs and the form of its production function. In recent years, this issue has surfaced in the controversy over X-inefficiency.[35] The latter notion suggests the fairly commonsense possibility that firms with substantial market power might not realize their gains in the form of monopoly profits, but

1 through a redistribution of the firm's profits from the owners of the firm to its professional managers, either in the form of higher remuneration or more luxurious working conditions, both of which would show up as costs on the firm's books,

and/or

2 through a behavioural effect on the firm's operations, whereby the absence of competition manifests itself in gratuitously higher costs and lack of innovation. This was long ago presaged by John Hicks's often quoted 'The best of all monopoly profits is a quiet life'.[36]

The dynamic effects of X-inefficiency may be even more consequential, and indeed have always been part of the traditional lore of practical economics (in, for instance, the recounting of the decline and fall of US Steel from the heights of industry dominance), but until the explicit development of the analytical framework of X-inefficiency such discussion was always treated as anecdotal, since it could not be coherently framed within a Marshallian context.

This and other managerial theories open up a Pandora's box: industrial activity becomes indeterminate unless the internal workings of the firm are understood. Not only does it raise the possibility that such traditional predictions as the level of monopoly profits may not be available in a determinate form, but perhaps even basic structural parameters such as average costs, minimum efficient scale, etc. may be contingent upon firm behaviour.

The Phillips critique emphasizes that when firms have substantial market power, it is impossible to describe economic outcomes in structural terms, i.e. with those minimal assumptions about behaviour hitherto thought sufficient: oligopolistic strategy and behaviour shape the very environment in which firms exist. The contention we are making here, however, is more general – one that cannot be confined to oligopolistic markets: *the behaviour of participants in a market can never be determined exclusively by a set of market parameters which are exogenous to this behaviour*.

'Uncertainty, Evolution and Economic Theory'

The critique presented here of the structuralist approach under all conditions, whether oligopolistic or not is best explained with reference to the well-known article by Armen Alchian.[37] Therein is established in its most extreme form the basis of the structure–performance paradigm. Alchian argues that concerns about the internal workings of a firm, about whether they actively or consciously pursue the goal of profit maximisation, are irrelevant. In a competitive environment the survivors will be those who successfully adapt. In this conception – essentially a Social Darwinist one – reservations about the standard theory which stem from the impossibility of profit maximisation in a world of uncertainty, or about the unrealistic nature of the assumptions in an empirical sense are irrelevant. The pressure to survive will in the long-term dictate the behaviour of firms, since only those following a correct course will continue to exist. We can thus describe and predict behaviour without reference to the desires and propensities of the individual entrepreneur.

Alchian's conception is illustrated below in a purely static model, which somewhat distorts its probabilistic character but embodies the essential message. In long-term equilibrium, the firm (figure 3.1a) in the perfectly competitive market (figure 3.1b) can only survive by producing at what is in fact the profit maximising output q_c, and selling it at the market price. Any factor which prevented the firm from selling at this price, such as

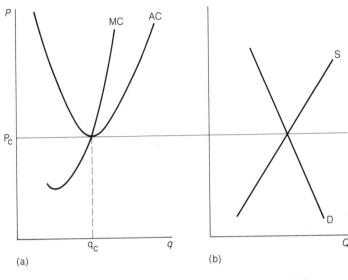

Figure 3.1a   Figure 3.1b

inefficiency or benevolence (in a probabilistic model it may be due to randomly distributed bad luck), would cause it to disappear.

The key difficulty with this formulation may be seen by imagining a county in England in the late Middle Ages populated by villages each of which possesses its own (solitary) shoemaker. Let us assume that transport costs are inconsequential, so that the market as objectively measured covers more or less the whole county. What if, as a result of habit, tradition and ignorance on the part of all concerned, shoes are only purchased and sold within each village, with the resultant price, set by custom and tradition substantially above 'minimum long run average cost' (whatever that may mean in this context)?

It is clear here that that objective specification of a (deconcentrated) market environment is not a sufficient condition to predict either the functional delineation of the market or the price(s) resulting in such a market. The market environment specified by Alchian implicitly includes not only the physical possibilities for exchange (as dictated by transport costs, etc.) but a repertoire of abilities, attitudes and propensities on the part of the participants in the market ('entrepreneurs' and consumers) which would make the environment in which business takes place competitive. As F.M. Scherer succinctly puts it, 'if no firms in the industry happen to conform to the optimal pattern, the selection process can bog down altogether for there will be no "fit" to expand, multiply and drive out the less fit'.[38] Thus, until we have a precise idea of the pattern of behaviour to which firms *do* adhere, it will be impossible to delineate in a meaningful way the boundaries of the very industry to which these firms belong.

It may be suggested that we have misrepresented or misunderstood the Alchian argument, and that its very purpose is to illustrate that only 'minimalist' assumptions about business behaviour are necessary to generate a competitive environment – that they involve only the lowest level of self-seeking and desire to survive:

> suppose that, in attempting to predict the effects of higher real wage rates, it is discovered that every businessman says he does not adjust his labor force. Nevertheless, firms with a lower labor–capital ratio will have lower cost positions and, to that extent, a higher probability of survival. The force of competitive survival, by eliminating higher-cost firms, reveals a population of remaining firms with a new average labor–capital ratio.[39]

In other words, a natural selection process combined with only minimal (implicit) assumptions about firms' self-seeking behaviour (those necessary to create the 'force of competitive survival') are enough to generate a competitive *outcome*. Alchian's article converged nicely with Milton Friedman's contemporaneous attack on the role of assumptions as opposed to predictions in economic theory.[40]

But Alchian's approach focuses exclusively upon *outcomes* as opposed to processes and it has therefore a rigid, all or nothing quality. Let us, for the sake of argument, assume that a minimal amount of self-seeking on the part of our shoemakers would *eventually* result in a competitive outcome by virtue of the Darwinian iterative process outlined by Alchian. *But what is the time period necessary to bring about this outcome?* Is it one year or a hundred? How quickly will this process have to reach its conclusion for us to declare that the environment in which it takes place is competitive? Alchian's analysis of competition is in static terms, and the focus on final outcomes ignores the dimension of time, which is central in the context of competition as a dynamic process of equalisation.

The claim in Alchian's analysis is that given the most minimal assumptions about the behaviour of individual firms, we can use an exogenously specified market structure to predict (final) outcomes. On the contrary, we argue that whatever the long run static outcome, the behaviour and attitude of firms will crucially affect the process of competition and the functional specification of the market as surely as a change in the objective variables affecting market structure. A change towards 'rational' self-seeking profit maximising behaviour on the part of our shoemakers, an increase in the efficacy of their business practices and a widening of their horizons in a geographical sense away from the traditional village will affect the actual extent of the market and the speed with which profits tend to equalise between firms as surely as a reduction in transport costs. (Indeed, a reduction in the latter, far from being purely exogenous may well be triggered by a change in attitudes, just as this 'psychological' change may be set off by improving technological possibilities.)

If we view competition as a dynamic process and desire to study its evolution over time, it will be impossible for us to ignore the changes in entrepreneurial behaviour that have taken place. This consideration is a central motivation for our critique of the structuralist approach. If an alternative, dynamic view of competition had reached the same conclusions about the evolution of the competitive process as the static approach, there would be little motivation for pursuing our critique, even if the former were more 'correct' in a strictly theoretical sense. We believe, however, that the static approach yields a fundamentally incorrect perspective on the historical evolution of the competitive process, much of which is due to its inability to deal successfully with the 'managerial revolution' to be discussed in chapter 5.

The Market in a Practical Context: the Case Study Perspective

The inevitable interaction between structure and behaviour also manifests itself in empirical research. While the statistical work of industrial economists attempts to operationalise the structuralist paradigm using 'exogenous' structural variables (e.g. market concentration) to explain, for instance, levels of industry profitability, the great bulk of the work of economists in industry studies is of a case study variety. Whatever the nominal obeisance of economists to the 'objective' results offered up by structural statistical tests, the methodology which ends up being used in these case studies is by necessity quite different.

Case studies can embody a good deal more empirical detail than a statistical study, are able to explore the historical development of a sector and can attempt to deal with such difficult-to-measure variables as responsiveness to technological change and the role of the political environment. These elements of superiority are well known: the usual response is that these advantages are at the cost of a loss of generality and of the supposed consistency of approach between sectors accruing from the statistical methodology. Much of this consistency is spurious, as we have seen in the context of market delineation.

The most fundamental advantage of the case study approach, however, strikes at a key weakness in the orthodox methodology. The case study does not find it necessary to make those artificial distinctions and uni-causal links between industrial structure and firm behaviour which are present in orthodox approaches and in their associated statistical tests. In much practical analysis of the competitive environment, a key task will be the determination of the functional sphere of competitive activity: orthodox analysis and its associated statistical tests offer up the concept of the industry with its exogenous specification of the environment, while with the case study methodology there is no pretence that structure can be specified exogenously from behaviour.

When looking at substantive cases of market analysis, two facts strongly emerge. First, economists have not even come close to formulating a methodology for the delineation of markets in a straightforward and consistent way which can be used in practical applications. Secondly, the discussions and debates which have ensued make it clear that economists rarely pretend to put forth and defend a specification of the domain of competitive activity which is independent of behaviour.

In response to the first issue, it has been argued that orthodox market analysis can be valid because *some* markets are well-defined.[41] This is undoubtedly true. The ready-to-eat breakfast cereal industry is highly concentrated in both the UK and the US on a national basis.[42] The high concentration ratios undoubtedly reflect substantial market power; caveats about substitutability from porridge, croissants and bacon and eggs would be rightly regarded as irrelevant. Even in this case, however, the second issue emerges: it is impossible to explain the structure of this industry independently of the behaviour of the key participants in the oligopoly who have been so successful at excluding entry into this sector.[43]

Far more typically, however, the industry boundary is manifestly unclear, and one cannot even begin to delineate it without a clear understanding of how actors behave. A thoroughly explored example of these problems is the thirteen year anti-trust case against IBM, which was finally dropped by the US Justice Department in 1982.[44] A key element of contention between the litigants was over the attempt to define the relevant domain of competitive activity – the functional market. When attempting to define the market for mainframe computers, several classic problems were confronted. (Needless to say, none of the participants even pretended that the issue could simply be resolved with the use of a concentration statistic from the Standard Industrial Classification of the census.)

The problems of delineation are enormous. On the demand side, should the market be treated broadly, in terms of the total of electronic data processing equipment? In this case, IBM's share appeared relatively smaller than with a narrower definition, and there appeared to be a long-term tendency for its share to decline. If, on the contrary, there is a focus on the largest mainframes, IBM's share was significantly larger and was increasing over time. On the supply side, should consideration be given merely to those manufacturers who can match IBM in full integration of all aspects of mainframe production? Alternatively, should one consider as competitors (i.e. in the same industry), for instance, those firms who are able to assemble full mainframes and sell them to the public, even though these firms purchase some or all aspects of the mainframe from other producers?

More significant for our purposes is the role of behaviour in determining structure. Are plug-compatible manufacturers (PCMs – manufacturers whose equipment is made to be compatible with that of IBM) to be considered as competitors with IBM in judging the latter's market power? This would clearly be contingent on the actions taken by IBM. If, for instance, IBM 'bundles' its sales – if it either offers substantial discounts on the purchase of the whole computer compared with the price of the parts (e.g. the central processing unit) separately, or it refuses to sell anything but whole mainframes (these are both forms of price discrimination) – it becomes much more difficult for PCMs to function as competitors with IBM. IBM's *behaviour* then determines the functional *structure* of the market in terms of the relevant measure of the market and the corresponding level of market concentration. IBM's actions may well be contingent on the past or present legal environment created by the antitrust authorities. Much of the dispute between economists in the IBM case was over considerations of this kind, and they resulted in dramatically contrasting pictures of the nature of the mainframe computer market.

Developments in the 1980s have been complicating issues even further, and progressively the boundaries between mainframes and desktop computers, and even with telecommunications equipment, are becoming unclear (see chapter 9). Even in industries less volatile than electronics, the basic problem of the interaction of structure and behaviour emerges. The fact that well-defined boundaries can occasionally be drawn around sectors is not very comforting. In the overwhelming number of situations in an economy, it is the very nature of the competitive process to cause these boundaries to be fluid, as they are affected by the activities of participants.

These considerations – the interaction between structure and behaviour, and the difficulties of drawing well-defined industry boundaries – are confronted by all economists in case study work. They are often forgotten, or seen to disappear when 'objective' statistical tests are performed on the relation between structure and behaviour. But a definitive solution to the problem of market delineation is not to be found, because a market is not a 'thing' but a behavioural relation.

Notes

1. In much of the theoretical literature on the delineation of these 'competitive groupings', the problem is defined not in terms of market delineation but of commodity delineation. The terminology of market delineation proves more useful and more general. It deals not only with the well-known questions surrounding the qualitative delineation of commodities (are bitter and lager in the same market, i.e. are they the same commodity?) but underlines as well the existence of problems such as the geographical extent of the market (is the market for beer local, national, or international?). Furthermore, this terminology points up the specifically Marshallian confusions concerning the relationship between the 'market' and the 'industry' (can we simultaneously define a market for beer which is coincident with the beer industry?).
2. Dennis, K. '"Competition" in the History of Economic Thought' Oxford University Doctoral thesis 1975, pp. 230–1.
3. Steiner, P. 'Markets and Industries' in the *International Encyclopaedia of the Social Sciences* vol. 3 Macmillan (US) 1968.
4. Ibid.
5. Ibid., Robinson, E. A. G. *The Structure of Competitive Industry* Cambridge Economic Handbooks 1931, p. 12 and Mason, E. 'Price and Production Policies of Large Scale Enterprise' *American Economic Review* 29(1) part 2

supplement (March 1939): 61–74: '[a seller's market] includes all buyers and sellers, of whatever produce whose action he considers to influence his volume of sales'.

6. See the references in ch. 4 (note 17) on this question.
7. See Boston Consulting Group, Ltd. *Strategy Alternatives for the British Motorcycle Industry* HMSO 1975.
8. Extensive bibliographies of this debate may be found in Bain, J. *Essays on Price Theory and Industrial Organization* Little, Brown and Co. 1972, pp. 191–3, and Ferguson, C. *A Macroeconomic Theory of Workable Competition* Duke University 1964, p. 32. An extended treatment of the questions in this chapter will be found in Auerbach, P. 'Market Structure and Firm Behaviour: An Empty Box?' *Thames Papers in Political Economy* (Autumn 1985).
9. Kaldor, N. 'Mrs. Robinson's "Economics of Imperfect Competiton"' *Economica* new series 3 (August 1934): 335–41, footnote omitted.
10. 'In economic theory, an industry is a collection of firms making products which are highly substitutable; formally they have high cross-elasticities of demand *or* supply': Hart, P. E. and R. Clarke, *Concentration in British Industry 1935–1975* National Institute of Economic and Social Research 1980, p. 2 (italics added) and 'the Census of Production industry used here . . . is not in practice always closely related to the economists' definition of an industry as a group of products with high cross price-elasticities of demand *and* supply', ibid. p. 11 (italics added).
11. Bain (note 8), p. 192.
12. Examples are Hart and Clarke (note 10), ch. 6 and Philips, L. *Effects of Industrial Concentration* North-Holland 1971.
13. See Philips (note 12).
14. Central Statistical Office *Standard Industrial Classification* HMSO 1968. This publication offered the most detailed, albeit brief description of the rationale of the classification system. For 1980, 'an attempt was made to align the United Kingdom classification as closely as practicable with the NACE, the classification in use by the Statistical Office of the European Community' (*Report on the Census of Production* Business Monitor 1980 HMSO Business Statistics Office PA-1002). The emphasis here on the international standard industrial classification of the United Nations which forms the basis of the US and pre-1980 UK system is in order to link it to existing empirical work in these countries.
15. *Standard Industrial Classification* (note 14).
16. Ibid.
17. Sawyer, M. 'Concentration in British Manufacturing Industry' *Oxford Economic Papers* 23(3) (November 1971): 352–75.
18. Conklin, M. and H. Goldstein 'Census Principles of Industry and Product Classification, Manufacturing Industries' in National Bureau of Economic Research (introduction by G. Stigler) *Business Concentration and Price Policy* Princeton University 1955, pp. 15–55.
19. Hart and Clarke (note 10), pp. 131–2.
20. As in Suits's commentary on Conklin and Goldstein (note 18), pp. 48–55.
21. For the US, see Mueller, W. and L. Hamm 'Trends in Industrial Market Concentration, 1947 to 1970' *Review of Economics and Statistics* 56(4) (November 1974): 511–20; for the UK, see Hart and Clarke (note 10), chs 1 to 3, Aaronovitch, S. and M. Sawyer *Big Business* Macmillan 1975, chs 3 to 7

and the summary of studies in Clarke, R. *Industrial Economics* Basil Blackwell 1985, ch. 2.

22. Hart and Clarke (note 10), ch. 2.
23. Hart, P. E., M. A. Utton and G. Walshe *Mergers and Concentration in British Industry* Cambridge University 1973, p. 24.
24. Hannah, L. *The Rise of the Corporate Economy* Methuen 1976, pp. 186–91.
25. Hart and Clarke (note 10), pp. 105–6 and Cowling, K. *Monopoly Capitalism* Macmillan 1981, ch. 6.
26. For the UK, see Utton, M. and E. Morgan *Concentration and Foreign Trade* Cambridge University 1983, ch. 2. Unadjusted five firm concentration for 121 products was 56.5 in 1958, 64.8 in 1968 and 64.5 in 1977; when adjusted for imports it was 58.8 in 1968 and 54.8 in 1977 (table 2.3, pp. 14–15); Shepherd's article seems to embody the doubts arising among mainstream industrial economists about the use of concentration statistics: Shepherd, W. 'Causes of Increased Competition in the US Economy, 1939–1980' *Review of Economics and Statistics* 64(4) (November, 1982): 613–26.
27. 'Appliance Repairmen Are Getting Lonelier' *Business Week* 8 June 1987.
28. Millstein, J. 'Decline in an Expanding Industry: Japanese Competition in Colour Television' in Zysman, J. and L. Tyson (eds) *American Industry in International Competition* Cornell University 1983, pp. 106–41.
29. Weiss, L. 'The Geographical Size of Markets in Manufacturing' *Review of Economics and Statistics* 54(3) (August 1972): 245–57. In antitrust cases in the US, Federal courts have accepted evidence on transport costs in determining market extent in the beer industry: see Elzinga, K. 'The Beer Industry' in Adams, W. (ed.) *The Structure of American Industry* Macmillan (US) sixth edn 1982, pp. 218–48. Concentration ratios produced by the Department of Commerce embody a series of modifications from the census data, including corrections for regional submarkets.
30. Bain, J. *Barriers to New Competition* Harvard University 1956.
31. Phillips A. 'Structure, Conduct and Performance – and Performance, Conduct and Structure?' in Markham, J. and G. Papanek (eds) *Essays in Industrial Organization and Economic Development in Honor of E. S. Mason* Houghton-Mifflin 1970, pp. 26–37.
32. See Williamson, O. 'Selling Expense as a Barrier to Entry' *Quarterly Journal of Economics* 77(1) (February 1963): 112–28 and Spence, A. M. 'Entry, Capacity, Investment and Oligopolistic Pricing' *Bell Journal of Economics* 8(2) (Autumn 1977): 534–44.
33. These examples are from appendix A of Mann, H. M. 'Seller Concentration, Barriers to Entry and Rates of Return in Thirty Industries, 1950–1960' *Review of Economics and Statistics* 48(3)(August 1966): 296–307.
34. See Orr, D. 'An Index of Entry Barriers and its Application to the Market Structure Performance Relationship' *Journal of Industrial Economics* 23(1) (September 1974): 39–50. Orr also includes market concentration as a barrier to entry.
35. The most complete exposition is to be found in Leibenstein, H. *Beyond Economic Man* Harvard University 1976.
36. Hicks, J. 'Annual Survey of Economic Theory: The Theory of Monopoly' *Econometrica* 3(1) (January 1935): 1–20.
37. Alchian, A. 'Uncertainty, Evolution and Economic Theory' *Journal of Political Economy* 58 (June 1950): 211–21.

38. Scherer, F. M. *Industrial Market Structure and Economic Performance* Rand McNally second edn 1980, p. 38.
39. Alchian (note 37).
40. Friedman, M. 'The Methodology of Positive Economics' *Essays in Positive Economics* University of Chicago 1953, pp. 3–43.
41. Waterson, M. *Economic Theory of the Industry* Cambridge University 1984, p. 3.
42. For the UK, see the Monopolies Commission *Report on the Supply of Ready Cooked Breakfast Cereals* HMSO February 1973 and for the US, Scherer, F. M. 'The Breakfast Cereal Industry' in Adams (note 29), pp. 191–217.
43. Ibid. and Schmalensee, R. 'Entry Deterrence in the Ready-to-Eat Cereal Industry' *Bell Journal of Economics* 9(2) (Autumn 1978): 305–27.
44. Sources for this discussion include Fisher, F., J. McGowan and I. Greenwood *Folded, Spindled and Mutilated-Economic Analysis and US vs. IBM* MIT 1983. Fisher worked with the defence in this case while McAdams, A. 'The Computer Industry' in Adams (note 29), pp. 249–97 represents part of the case put forward by the prosecution.

4

The Testing of the 'Invisible Hand' Theorem

The Conceptual Framework

Static Versus Dynamic Approaches

The static, structuralist view of the competitive process is contrasted here with a dynamic approach. The two sharply contrasting paradigms are illustrated in figures 4.1 and 4.2. These two paradigms form the logical basis for the empirical tests to be examined in this chapter. Figure 4.1 represents the structuralist view of the competitive process. Here industries are specified as independent variables, both in the sense that the forces generating industrial structures derive from outside the model and that the industries are 'independent' of one another, so that separate delineation is meaningful. The economy consists of industries 1 to 5 which contain firms A to P. For instance, industry 2 contains firms 2D and 2E. An exceptional case is firm C, which operates in industry 1 but also has entered industry 4. Thus, firms such as (1/4)C may diversify, but the picture is primarily of firms labelled according to the industry to which they 'belong'.

Firm behaviour takes place within the structural constraints of an industry, and these constraints are often lumped together in an un-differentiated way in standard exposition. The problems with this approach become particularly obvious in statistical tests where they are used as exogenous variables, a role for which none of them qualify. These structural constraints may be broken down into three categories, in descending levels of exogeneity:

1 The first category reflects deep structural constraints – the underlying, often technological parameters in the industry, such as the durability of

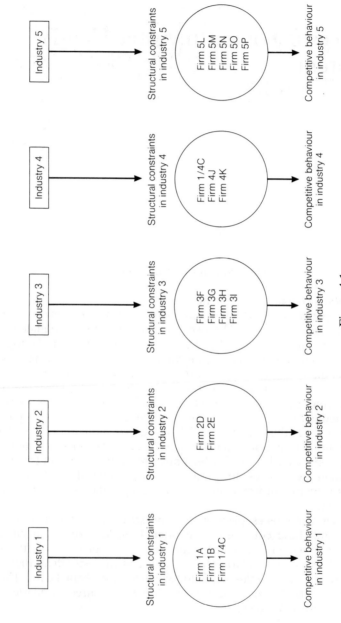

Figure 4.1

the product or the minimum size of plant necessary for engineering efficiency.

2   A second category embodies the facts of the market as they are, of which the most important is the level of concentration among existing participants. Concentration indices are invariably treated as structural constraints upon behaviour, even when these indices are mere amalgamations of firms' market shares (e.g. the H index), which are as much determined by as determining behaviour.

3   A typical list of structural variables in the third category will often include what are clearly behavioural considerations such as the level of advertising pursued by firms in an industry. These variables are meant to be proxies for the structural constraints imposed upon existing firms and potential entrants by, for instance, the technological environment, but to measure such constraints with their behavioural manifestations is to create serious problems of circularity.

The Hayekian notion is that even deep structural constraints of the first category are not simply given by an exogenously defined technology, but may be transformed by entrepreneurial discovery in the act of competing. As a recent book on manufacturing planning has noted 'Many people think of lead time as a constant. . . . In fact it is not a value to be measured as [much] as a parameter to be managed. ... Studies have shown that for many plants, setup and run time only constitute 10 to 20 per cent of the total lead time. The rest is slack that can be substantially cut'.[1] Behaviour affects even the deep structural constraints in an industry and thus there is no exclusive line of causation from structure to behaviour. This line of causation is even weaker for the second and third categories. Amalgamation of these categories in standard expositions is a further cause of incoherence, but it emerges from an attempt to do that which is in fact impossible – to delineate neatly the concepts of structure and behaviour and then arrange them in terms of cause and effect.

This static model may be contrasted with an alternative dynamic view of the competitive process as illustrated in figure 4.2, where it is assumed, for simplicity of exposition, that no new firms are created in the economy. In this case, it is the firm which is the moving force, and whose delineation from other entities is clearly specified. There are distinct capital market layers, ranked from I (highest) to VI (lowest), level I representing, for instance, the domain of giant multinational firms. The meaning and significance of these layers will be explored in depth in chapter 7.

The process of competition is illustrated in detail for level I. Firms 1 to 8 pursue projects by operating in spheres of activity A to N, so that for instance firms 1, 4 and 8 operate projects in sphere A; firms 4 and 8 are diversified and pursue projects in distant spheres of activity, while firm 3 is highly specialised. The greater the speed, freedom and efficacy with which firms pursue projects in different spheres, the more competitive the economy.

The firm in this model is not simply the passive respondent to the

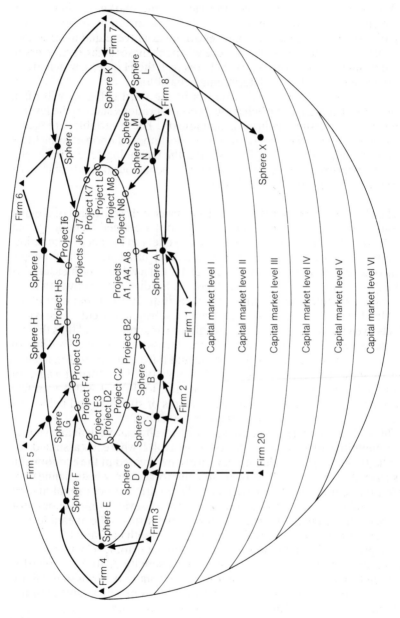

Figure 4.2

constraints imposed on it from the outside. To a great extent, it creates its own environment – the number of spheres in which it chooses to operate, etc.: from this perspective, a significant constraint upon a firm is imposed by the limitations of its own management. The distance between spheres may at first seem to be determined by the same objective technological constraints as in the static approach, but even these constraints are ultimately definable in terms of managerial limitations.

The second major constraint upon the firm is that imposed by the capital market layers. In figure 4.2, firm 7, a multinational producer of cars, may choose to pursue a project in capital market level III, sphere X (e.g. the production of computer software). This act is represented by a solid arrow, since few difficulties exist for raising capital for projects in lower spheres. Only with great difficulty, however, could a firm from capital market layer III (firm 20) pursue a project in layer I, and such an act is represented by an arrow with a dotted line.

A numerical parameter in a dynamic context which would be analogous to the static procedure's use of the weighted average concentration ratio as a measure of competitiveness for an economy would be

$$\beta, \text{where } 0 < \beta < 1$$

from the equation

$$\pi_{i,t} = \pi_{i,t-1} - \beta(\pi_{i,t-1} - \pi_{t-1}^n), \text{over all firms } i = 1 \ldots k \text{ in the economy. (4.1)}$$

In equation (4.1), firm profitability which is greater than 'normal profitability' π^n in the period $t - 1$ should be reduced in period t due to the competitive actions of other firms. The larger the value of β, the more competitive the environment. The magnitude of β depends not only the behaviour of firms at a given capital market level, but upon the distance between these levels: the more fluid the market for finance – the more the capital market layers are squeezed – the greater the likelihood that a firm from a lower level might move up and pursue a project at a higher level in competition with existing firms.

The spheres of activity may look suspiciously to some readers as if they were surrogates for industries, but there are significant differences between these concepts: these spheres, unlike industries, are attached to one another as an indication that discontinuous delineation will not be possible. The failure to delineate these spheres precisely is not critical, for unlike industries they do not dictate or structure firm behaviour. In fact, individual firms' perceptions of the delineation of these spheres is likely to differ depending on their firm-specific advantages and strategies. At least in principle, competition between firms may be conceptualised without reference to these spheres of activity, as firms choose between alternative projects.

The concept of the sphere of activity, however, is a convenient way of clarifying the meaning of 'competitive entry', since if every project of a firm is identified with only one sphere of activity, it is unambiguous to suggest that firm 6 has started to compete with firm 5 if it should initiate a project in sphere G (see figure 4.2). Furthermore, such a concept is helpful in conceptualising the question of diversification, which is in some sense a more natural process in figure 4.2 than it is in figure 4.1, where a firm is pictured as being 'born' into an industry.

One way of viewing the alternative emphases existing in the two approaches to competition is to consider the question of product differentiation, which in figure 4.1 would be one of the structural constraints dermining the nature of behaviour within an industry, while in figure 4.2, as in most literature on marketing strategy, it functions primarily as a decision variable on the part of individual firms. As a further contrast, in figure 4.1 the focus of competition is upon activity within an industry and most specifically upon pricing policy. Other decisions, such as whether to enter a new industry or to undertake new investment, are segregated and treated as conceptually different issues. In figure 4.2 the different aspects of competitive strategy cannot be broken up in this way.

Once activities such as new investment and entry are considered as central to the competitive process, explicit attention must be given to the role of the capital market. In figure 4.1, a great deal can be said about the competitive process even in a world of perfect capital markets, since firm behaviour is constrained within industries. In figure 4.2, by contrast, the constraints upon the activities of firms include those limitations emanating from the capital market. These limitations will affect the ability of firms to raise finance for these new projects both within a given capital market layer and at larger scales of operation (higher capital market levels).

Figures 4.1 and 4.2 represent economies in which no new firms are created. Clearly this is a much more debilitating assumption in the context of figure 4.2, since a dynamic approach with its emphasis on entry and new investment will be critically affected by overall levels of economic activity, which may promote the propagation of new firms and the destruction of existing ones: the structuralist approach more easily ignores these considerations.

These two models tend to shape our views of events in alternative ways. From the perspective of the structuralist approach with its emphasis on pricing policy, recessions in overall economic activity are often associated with increases in competition, as when price wars break out in highly capitalised industries such as steel and ship-building. It is boom periods, on the contrary, which may seem most conducive to competition in the dynamic context of figure 4.2, with the entry into spheres of activity by existing or newly created firms. Both perspectives thus offer alternative views on the question of macroeconomic activity and the competitive process even before we have made a single measurement.

A Definition and its Difficulties
A dynamic definition of competition or competitive behaviour suggested by equation (1) is the class of activities pursued by firms and other

economic entities (banks, etc.) which (other things equal) tends to put downward pressure on the profitability of rivals. Note that there is no explicit delineation into pricing, investment or other activities, and the definition encompasses a broad range of business situations, including competition from firms not obviously in the same industries.

The suspicious reader may scent a whiff of tautology in the use of the word 'rival', but its purpose is to exclude the possibility, for instance, that assiduous activity on the part of an electronics component manufacturer might *raise* profits for a producer of television sets to whom he or she sells, even if profits are cut to other component manufacturers. In order to avoid anomalies brought about by the sales of inputs and of complementary goods, we use the word 'rival', which describes the relationship between firms operating projects within the same sphere of activity. In empirical work, the measurement and delineation of these spheres must be by-passed for the reasons we have made clear in chapter 3: the inherent nature of the competitive process dictates that such delineation is impossible. These spheres function as intermediate (and largely unobservable) variables, and in theoretical terms they are not structural determinants of behaviour. This concept does not solve the problem of market and industry delineation. On the contrary, these difficulties are so severe that the most fruitful way of dealing with them is to relegate the concept of the industry from the centre of the analysis to a more secondary role.

Of a more serious nature, especially from an empirical point of view, is the necessity for the ubiquitous clause 'other things equal'. In principle, it would appear that more assiduous, more competitive behaviour on the part of a manufacturer of, say, video recorders would put downward pressure on the profitability of rivals. Such a presumption is indubitable when the 'other things equal' clause is intact. In the real world, it is conceivable that a lively, innovative, competing group of rivals, perhaps responding to the initial impetus of greater competitiveness from one of them will make higher rates of return than if they had remained sluggish and uncompetitive. Hayekian competitiveness and Schumpeterian inventiveness may result in a positive relationship between competitiveness and profitability, even if the *ceteris paribus* relationship between the profitability of rivals and an increase in competitiveness from one of these firms is negative. Furthermore, profitability may cease to possess its presumed relationship to competition in a world which is pervaded by X-inefficiency, since an increase in competitiveness might awaken otherwise sleeping firms, causing their observed profitability to rise. A last difficulty is that the Schumpeterian hypothesis cannot be well contained within the confines of figure 4.2, simply because that hypothesis is largely concerned with the creation of new spheres of activity.

A related problem is embodied in the limitations imposed by the global π^n of equation (4.1), the universal level of normal profits to which all firms descend. Historically, outbreaks of intense competition have often taken place within a localised domain – one localised by sphere of activity and/or geography. Such eddies of competition erupted early in the industrial revolution – within, for instance, the Sheffield cutlery industry. If competition in an economy (defined nationally or internationally) may be characterised by outbursts of local competition, where 'local' refers either to the geographical area (Sheffield, Silicon Valley) or the product (cutlery, electronics), then the invisible hand tradition dating from Adam Smith, which implies a generalised pressure on profitability towards a universalised norm π^n may be inappropriate. There may be no generalised pressure towards a universal norm of profitability, but if the pressures on profitability have increased within these localised centres of competition – each with its own 'normal' level, we may well choose to regard the resultant economy as more competitive than formerly. Such a possibility further complicates the conceptualisation of the competitive process.

We proceed next to consider the empirical literature which has attempted to put into effect the static paradigm.

Static Formulations

The Concentration–Profits Relationship

The statistical tests emerging from the structure–behaviour paradigm more than anything else have made the Marshallian approaches to industrial economics co-terminous with acceptable academic approaches. Previously, orthodoxy was weakened in the practical domain by the fact that the established methodology of empirical research – the analysis of case studies – seemed a good deal more congruent with workable competition than with orthodox analysis. With the coming of statistical tests based on Marshallian theory, case studies were seen to be *ad hoc*, anecdotal and lacking in general applicability – in short, they were not in the mainstream of contemporary science. If problems, anomalies and contradictory results emerged from these statistical tests, they would soon be corrected with the use of more sophisticated techniques. So infatuated has been the economics profession with this application of statistical methodology that the outpouring of studies has been torrential.[2]

Two rather contradictory results have been witnessed in recent years. On the one hand, the methodology of these statistical tests and the key variables contained within them such as industry concentration have been used to explain phenomena far beyond the domain of the original concentration–profits studies (e.g. the extent of racial discrimination by employers) and, on the other, the very basis of the original studies has come under severe attack.[3] However, many of the failures pointed out by critics are due not to inadequacies in the methods used by researchers, but are inherent in the Marshallian conception and bring into question whether the extension of this statistical methodology into new areas is advisable. It is upon these fundamental inadequacies that we shall be focusing.

Bain's pioneering statistical study of 1951[4] investigated whether profits (weighted averages of industry rates of return on equity over a five year period) could be explained by the degree of industry monopolisation (the eight-firm concentration ratio). While, in the words of commentators on these studies, Bain's results were 'successful', i.e. he found that such a relationship existed, for Bain and others the results were unsatisfactory. What was in fact being tested was a form of the pure, static transactions theorem in which profit margins would be linked to the number of participants in the market. This latter hypothesis has subsequently been tested (for 'monopsonists') in the appropriate setting – in auctions – to determine whether the number of bidders has a decisive effect on the ratio of the actual transaction price to the sellers' reserve price.[5] Bain's intention, however, was to capture not only this pure neo-classical half of the Marshallian synthesis, but the classical half as well (as witnessed by the use of rates of return on equity as a profits variable), which accounts for his subsequent contribution in the development of estimates for industry barriers to entry. In general terms, a great many of the studies which have followed have taken the following form:

$$\pi = f(\mathrm{CR}, \mathrm{BE}, x_1 \ldots x_n, \varepsilon) \qquad (4.2)$$

where π = a measure of industry profitability
         CR = an index of industry monopolisation
         BE = alternative measures of industry barriers to entry
   $x_1 \ldots x_n$ = other variables necessary to complete the particular researcher's specification
         ε = error term

As a rule, these tests are carried out as cross-section analyses of these variables averaged over several years, but the search is clearly for economy-wide parametric estimates which would indicate what kind of alterations in performance would take place within industries when 'exogenous' movements in the structural variables take place. Indicative of the intentions of researchers, and of the literalness with which they have taken their parametric estimates has been the attempt to find a 'critical' concentration ratio, an economy-wide value which if exceeded causes an industry's profitability to increase decisively because of successful collusion.[6] Studies of this class have not strayed very far from a basic Marshallian competition–monopoly dichotomy and only to a limited extent have been able to incorporate developments in contemporary orthodoxy, to wit

1 General equilibrium. Each industry exists in a 'sea' of perfect competition for the purchase of inputs (including labour), so that problems of bilateral monopoly and countervailing power are excluded, as are (other) reflexive effects of monopolisation in one industry (e.g. X-inefficiency) upon others.
2 Oligopoly theory. A Cournot-like presumption (in the sense described

in chapter 2) is present so that there is a monotonic (usually linear) relationship between industry concentration and profits.

3 Barriers to entry. A similar Cournot-type assumption is made about barriers to entry, by which higher barriers are associated with higher industry profitability in a strict way, despite the complex theoretical literature which has now emerged on the topic of entry barriers.

4 Deviations from profit maximising behaviour. The statistical tests implicitly exclude hypotheses concerning deviations from profit maximisation by monopolists, either due to managerial effects or X-inefficiency. Tests of monopoly power may still yield the 'correct' sign on the coefficient between profitability and concentration, but will not properly measure the impact of non-profit maximising behaviour in different industries.

The tests often exclude considerations which would be recognised as reasonable even in the most traditional theory: the analysis makes the implicit assumption of the presence of cost conditions which are the same for firms at all scales of output within the industry, so that it is impossible to disinter profits from rents accrued due to low average costs at high levels of output; it by-passes questions concerning size and/or monopoly power and technological dynamism; it often excludes the market elasticity of demand as an explanatory variable and invariably avoids the possibility of price discrimination. Many of these simplifications and compromises are dictated by the exigencies of statistical testing and in various contemporary studies refinements have been introduced to deal with some of them, for instance countervailing power problems are dealt with by incorporating buyer concentration ratios.

However, our major interest here is not to focus on the difficulties listed above, but upon those which emanate directly from the logic of the Marshallian theory underpinning these tests. These problems have received prominent airing in the literature, but the inevitable conclusions have not been drawn because of an unwillingness to trace the difficulties back to the very logic of Marshallian analysis and due to a hesitancy about surrendering this methodology in the absence of an alternative set of statistical tests of the invisible hand. The problems with tests of the form of equation (4.2) on which we should like to concentrate are as follows:

1 *The causation system embodied in them.* High correlations between variables are insufficient as an explanation without a well-defined line of causation from the independent to dependent variables. If a relation between industry profitability and concentration can be accounted for by the effects of a third variable (e.g. scale economies), or, if as a result of an admixture between behavioural and structural variables (e.g. advertising and concentration)[7] there is a complex series of interactions between these independent variables, successful statistical results may be brought into question. Thus, in Phillips's critique described in chapter 3 high concentration in an industry may result in the generation of

advertising as a product differentiation barrier to entry, which may subsequently affect the level of and trends in concentration in that industry. On the other hand, even in the logic of the theory an industry which is (technologically) predisposed to entry barriers (with, for instance, high minimum efficient scale relative to the market) is more likely, other things equal, to be highly concentrated.

These fundamental problems are embodied in the logic of Marshallian theory. As we have seen in chapter 2, even in principle it is impossible to consider the sales concentration ratio as an independent variable affecting industry profits; the quantification of entry barriers invariably embraces everything from attempts to measure the deep structure of the industry (e.g. its level of minimum efficient scale) to behavioural variables like advertising, which are as much the effect as the cause of industry concentration. There is little mystery, then, about the eclectic and improvised nature[8] of these empirical studies. The theory, by postulating a line of causation from structure to behaviour, when all to be seen in the real world are myriad interactions between structural and behavioural variables, has posed insoluble problems for researchers trying to apply an inapplicable theory.

2   *The static, 'snapshot' nature of the tests*. Borrowing from the comparative static methodology of Marshallian theory, the presumption is that a cross-section of industries at one moment will capture what is in fact a time-related process. The level of market concentration, for instance, should have its effect upon industry profitability in the present, but, depending on the theory of entry assumed, the imposition of barriers to entry in an industry may only affect (ordinary measurements of book) profitability over several years. In specific industries, high concentration may historically have preceded the imposition of barriers to entry and then caused their construction, while in other industries, high barriers to entry may have permitted the growth of concentration. The snapshot of the statistical test disguises the differences both in the timing and in the causation system embodied in the two sequences of events.

In general the framework has difficulties dealing with the possibility that the industry is in other than static equilibrium, since it is testing for the existence of equilibrium rather than a tendency towards equalisation. It usually deals clumsily, for instance, with the effect of growth in industry demand upon profitability by incorporating industry sales as an independent variable, a measure which is econometrically underidentified: growth in sales is not the same thing as growth in demand, sales reflecting not only demand but supply conditions, which means that both costs and the effects of past profitability on present levels of costs and capacity will influence current sales. Furthermore, to the extent that there are stochastic factors affecting the firm (e.g. the discovery of an oilfield) which are independent of those on the industry as a whole, it is possible to generate a relationship between market share (and therefore concentration) and book-value profitability which is purely fortuitous.[9] Of greater significance is that such a relationship may also emerge from a firm whose success is due to systematic factors (i.e. efficiency) and this realisation, as we shall see below, has proved extremely bothersome to mainstream industrial economists.

3   *The mixing of classical and neo-classical concepts*. The standard statistical tests use both concentration and barriers to entry as explanations for industry profitability, and yet persistent confusion exists on the relation between them as necessary and sufficient conditions for the generation of monopoly. Furthermore, the two halves of the Marshallian theory are difficult to test simultaneously in other ways. For example, the concept of the market for biscuits which is relevant in a pure neo-classical conception (i.e. applicable for a concentration measure) is very possibly more narrowly defined than the classical domain of the industry for the same commodity, which is needed for the construction of a measure of entry barriers; the tobacco industry might be overly broad for delineating functional market concentration, even if it contains the relevant domain for the measurement of entry barriers.[10] No reasonable solutions are possible to the problem of incorporating these different conceptualisations of the competitive process into a single statistical test.

4   *The use of the industry concept*. There are difficulties, both practical and conceptual, in attempting to use a measure of industry profitability in a statistical test. The construction of the latter measure from weighted averages of firm profitability can result in an observed relationship with market concentration which is purely a statistical artefact, telling us nothing about the cause and effect relationship between monopolisation and industry profitability. For instance, let us suppose we have two industries, A and B, with industry A's four largest firms having 60 per cent of the market and an average profit rate of 25 per cent, and with the rest of the firms in the industry having an average profit rate of 10 per cent. For industry B, the four largest firms have 40 per cent of the market and an average profit rate of 25 per cent, with the remaining firms in the industry also having an average profit rate of 10 per cent. Industry A will register higher concentration and higher average profits simply because of the greater weight given to the largest firms.[11] In other words, the concept of the industry, which necessitates the use of industry averages of profitability, leads to substantial problems of statistical identification.

An additional set of problems exists for the concept of the industry besides those discussed in 1 above: not only must the industry be an exogenous constraint on firm behaviour, but its parameters must affect all firms symmetrically. There are two implicit presumptions here. First, in order to construct an index of market concentration, the sales (or value added) of multiplant firms have to be allocated to different industries. The index of concentration is then constructed as if, for instance, a firm existing wholly in one industry with a 15 per cent market share is equivalent in its market power to a large conglomerate whose subsidiary has the same share in that industry. The resultant concentration–profits test thus contains the (implicit) joint hypothesis that there exists a perfect capital market or some comparable construct to ensure that the absolute size of the firm does not affect its influence in specific markets. Thus, it seems difficult to separate the concentration–profits hypothesis from one concerning the existence of a perfect capital market. Secondly, the environment which firms face in a particular sphere of activity must be uniform enough *vis-à-vis* different firms' strategies so that it is meaningful to group their activities together. Recent literature discussed below has brought into question whether even this minimally necessary though far from sufficient condition can be fulfilled in a range of substantive competitive situations.

Alternative Formulations
The last few years have witnessed an 'empirical renaissance in industrial economics'[12] in order to deal with various aspects of the problems discussed above. We review here the most notable lines of approach. Certain developments have been connected with the use of the PIMS data set, which in the US allocates a firm's activities to 261 manufacturing and 14 non-manufacturing categories defined by the Federal Trade Commission, and includes, among other things, firms' price–cost margins as allocated to these different activities as well as their market share.[13]

This data set has proved popular for two reasons. First, firm-level allocation of profits to different activities should be less flawed than the artificial constructs put together by researchers in traditional concentration–profits studies. Secondly, and more importantly, the concept of market share has come to symbolise an alternative line of explanation to that found in the concentration–profits literature and to the welfare implications embodied in it. Thus, in the 'new industrial economics' it is suggested that the 'snapshot' showing a relation between industry profits and concentration in, for instance, the mainframe computer industry is a reflection of IBM's greater efficiency (perhaps itelf due to scale economies) compared with other firms, which results in both its large market share (with high industry concentration) and its high profitability.[14] The PIMS data set has been used to differentiate this firm-specific basis of profitability (which is taken to represent the efficiency explanation) from the industry-wide, or monopolistic causes of profitability. If the firm-specific efficiency explanation is indeed the appropriate causal nexus, it has been suggested that the traditional welfare implications of concentration–profits studies should be put aside. The emergence of the PIMS data has also coincided with the use of market share as a magical explanation for firms' success on the part of marketing consultants. With the inevitable emergence of the realisation that high correlation between variables does not necessarily imply cause and effect, this particular fashion now seems on the decline.

Recent statistical tests have tried to incorporate both the firm's market share (identified with an 'efficiency' explanation) and market concentration (identified with a 'monopoly' explanation) in statistical tests of industry profitability, these being an attempt to see which of these variables is better at explanation. However, there is no justification in statistical methodology for these races between variables, most especially when, like market concentration and large firm market share, they are so intimately related. The real significance of the market share – concentration controversy is that it illustrates the inadequacy of timeless static tests for discriminating between alternative explanations of the path of industrial evolution, and it is a manifestation in the practical domain of the well-known theoretical problems which exist in attempting to distinguish between income and rent, problems which are at the core of this controversy.

An article by Nickell and Metcalf, 'Monopolistic Industries and Monopoly Profits or, are Kellogg's Cornflakes Overpriced?',[15] attempts to avoid the problems created by the use of industry-wide profits or price–cost margins in concentration-profits studies. They use a measure of the difference between the proprietary brand price (e.g. Kellogg's Cornflakes) and own-brand price (e.g. cornflakes under the label of the retailer) as a surrogate for the monopoly markup. This markup is then explained in the usual way by market concentration, advertising expenditure per unit sales, elasticity of demand (a negative relationship expected here), growth of sales, minimum efficient scale and other barriers to entry.

But how can this test be taken to be a measure of the effects of monopoly power? Consumers in the cases used for the tests are, to quote a famous phrase *free to choose* between proprietary and own brands. Therefore the higher markup on some goods must reflect the influence of a third variable, such as quality differences perceived by consumers or consumer ignorance. There are two possibilities. First, the different brands may be identical, in which case the price differential reflects ignorance and/or the non-autonomy of consumer preferences (e.g. the influence of advertising). The latter interpretation might be quite interesting in its own terms, but would have little to do with the neo-classical theory of monopoly power under test here. Alternatively, quality differences may exist, in which case the test is quite pointless. Some element of these effects may be captured by the advertising variable, but commodities may have differing levels of potential differentiation (e.g. the public may be more susceptible to being convinced that there are real differences between different brands of hair shampoos than between different brands of aspirins) which are not easily captured by *ex post* measures of variables like advertising.

The fundamental problem is the use of a snapshot observation to capture a dynamic, evolving process. It cannot distinguish between a price gap which results from a retailer's countervailing power competitive response and one which is simply due to monopoly price discrimination on the part of the manufacturer. In the countervailing power case, the emergence of a price gap may be a manifestation of the intensification of competition where none was present before. Even if both commodities originate from the manufacturer, this is not *per se* evidence of price discrimination since the production of the own brand product may represent a concession to retailer pressure. If it results from an attempt to ward off incipient competition and therefore qualifies as price discrimination, the emergence of the own brand commodity may be a manifestation of a monopolist's response to an increasingly competitive environment. The static picture of competition presented by this and similar studies is thus inadequate for analysing the process of competition and its evolution.

The last few years have witnessed attempts to salvage elements of a structuralist approach to competition. Perhaps the most imaginative of these has been from Michael Porter, who has incorporated ideas from the literature of management strategy embodied in his book *Competitive Strategy* into tests of profitability.[16] He has elaborated the concept of 'strategic groups', which are clusters of firms within industries following similiar strategies. The profitability of the industry as a whole depends on modified versions of the traditional factors – the number and size distribution of the groups as well as other variables which relate to interdependence between these groups, but the performance of individual firms is determined at the level of the group. The height of mobility barriers protecting a particular strategic group determines its potential profitability.

How are are these strategic groups constructed? '[The] differences in firms' strategies that define strategic groups imply differences in marketing methods, technologies and scales of activity that can make the standard sources of entry barriers – economies of scale, product differentiation, heavy requirements for capital, cost advantages and proprietary knowledge – vary by strategic group', and these differences explain why some firms earn higher profits than others. Furthermore,

> different strategic groups may enjoy greater bargaining power vis-à-vis suppliers and customers than others due to differences in scale, threat of vertical integration or product differentiation following from their differing strategies. Differences in product differentiation, quality control and other characteristics resulting from strategy differences can also lead to differences among strategic groups in the overall elasticity of demand due to substitute products produced by other industries.

Thus, firms are linked together in groups by an amalgam of volitional, behavioural factors (as implied by the name 'strategic group'), structural technological factors close to those of orthodox industry theory (though Porter denies that these groups are merely 'properly defined industries', strategic groups merely reflecting 'different approaches to operating in the same competitive arena') and, by implication, capital market limitations on smaller entities.

These groupings, which combine structural and behavioural variables – a partial salvaging of orthodoxy – had to be abandoned in statistical tests, and one of the reasons we find particularly instructive: 'becoming sufficiently well informed about a large sample of industries to identify their configurations of strategic groups is a formidable task, because almost an industry study of each industry would be required'. In fact, each industry was split into two groups, leaders and followers, with the leaders being those firms accounting for 30 per cent of the sales revenue in the industry. Having created this rather arbitrary distinction between groups, in which the behavioural considerations which had been part of their *raison d'être* have been eliminated, the variables used to explain differences in profitability between the groups are all traditional structural ones geared to the size differences between the firms:

> Different elements of industry structure will provide mobility barriers or affect the pattern of rivalry for different strategic groups. Heavy scale economies in production, distribution or service, for example, would act as mobility barriers for broad-line, integrated firms in the leader group but not for followers. Thus a central prediction of the theory is that different structural models will be appropriate to explaining average firm profitability in the leader and follower groups, given the likely differences in strategy between firms in the two groups.

Porter's results confirm some of his suppositions, with a very low (0.14) correlation between leader and follower firm profitability within the same industry. But, as can be seen in the above paragraph, in the division between groups used here all of the advantages should have been on the side of the leader group (since the size factors mentioned merely give options to the leaders which are not available to the followers) and yet the latter's level of profitability only averaged slightly higher than that of the followers overall (11.68 per cent compared with 10.84 per cent), and there were several cases where the follower group had greater profitability within an industry.

Ultimately, Porter's idea that there exist strata within the industry partially shaped by behavioural considerations which have more effect on the firm's profitability than the industry itself is subversive of orthodox theory. Whether a proper statistical test of the hypothesis could be performed, with the behavioural considerations dealt with in a non-arbitrary manner, is an open question. While it may prove useful for certain limited empirical purposes to cluster firms into groups, such groupings are in conflict with the very nature of competition as a dynamic process. If these groups existed in the past, they are ever less likely to do so in the future, with the growing aggressiveness of firms and an environment growing increasingly competitive. Furthermore, the symmetry of attitudes between firms necessary for the formation of these groups is far less likely than in former times with the substantial increases in diversification which have taken place (this was another reason for Porter's data problems). Our own belief is that Porter's move away from the concept of the industry has not been radical enough and that ultimately it is the firm which is the irreducible unit upon which analysis of business behaviour must be based.[17] It is to this question which we now turn.

The Special Problems of Dynamic Analysis

The Firm as a Unit of Analysis

It will be argued in subsequent chapters that the firm rather than the industry is the unit around which the competitive process should be conceptualised. In this section we offer a more limited proposition – the firm should serve as an alternative candidate to the industry as the unit of analysis for statistical tests of the invisible hand theorem. Given the difficulties suggested above with inter-industry tests, it would be preferable to test the proposition that excess returns are eliminated between firms, rather than between industries. However, any contest between the firm and the industry may seem pointless, as the two concepts are incommensurable. The industry has multidimensional uses in economics. It is

1 a method of ordering firms in an economy
2 an exogenous constraint on firm behaviour
3 a unit of analysis for theoretical and statistical work.

Only with the last of these purposes is it possible to compare the uses of the firm and the industry in economics. The use of the firm as a unit of analysis emerges from a belief that existing legal and institutional structures make such a delineation possible, in contrast to the concept of the industry which, far from being a 'thing' at all with well-defined boundaries, is in fact a behavioural relation whose limits are constantly changing. But conceptual problems exist for firm delineation as well: 'If an apple orchard owner contracts with a beekeeper to pollinate his fruits, is the result one firm or two firms? The question has no clear answer. The contract involved may be a hire–rental contract, a wage contract, a contract sharing the apple yield, or in principle, some combination of these and still other arrangements.'[18] There is no general solution to these kinds of conundrums, but in most practical contexts there is a possibility of drawing on a qualitatitive, legal definition of the firm for the delineation of its boundaries. The definitive nature of the identity of the firm in ownership terms is most clearly attested to by partnerships, private and family firms which make up the vast majority of enterprises.

However, in dealing with large incorporated enterprises we face difficult empirical questions. The accounting distinctions which exist between different kinds of company holdings seem arbitrary from an economic point of view. In the UK accounting regulations there is a distinction between a company holding of a marketable security and a trading investment, with the latter supposedly held for long term commercial reasons. A company which has a trading investment of normally 20 per cent or more of the voting rights of a firm can account for it as an associated company [SSAP 1]. The parent's share of the latter firm's profit and loss account is incorporated with the dominant firm, though its assets (except for the purchase price of its shares) do not appear on the parent company's balance sheet. To be a fully fledged subsidiary, consolidated in the parent firm's balance sheet, the parent company's holding must be over 50 per cent of the voting rights of the firm. In this case the whole of the subsidiary's assets and liabilities appear on the parent's balance sheet, with the non-owned fraction shown as a minority interest [SSAP 14]. These ambiguous boundaries of the firm are indeed subject to manipulation:

> Retailing giant Burton Group has raised £100 million off balance sheet finance with the creation of a 50% property holding associate. The careful equity structure means that no capital gains should arise even though the new company is outside the group for trading loss purposes. The equity structure gives Burton just under half the votes but more than 75% of the share capital. This means that assets can be passed between the two companies without a charge. But trading losses will not be transferable because Burton does not have formal control.[19]

Thus it is possible to imagine legal and institutional situations which in fact make the firm analytically unviable as a separate entity, either because of the ambiguity of its extent (perhaps industrial conglomerations in Japan manifest this problem)[20] or because share ownership is so hemmed in with restrictions (as in Europe in earlier centuries) that the identity of the firm is extremely ambiguous. Contemporary movements by firms into joint ventures are creating similiar ambiguities.

Any convincing demonstration of the utility of the firm as a unit of analysis will have to show that such phenomena can be dealt with in a convincing way. If firm analysis of the invisible hand theorem is shown to be a viable alternative to statistical tests based on the industry, it would be an important part of the critique of industry studies, and some attempts at firm level analysis will be examined below. First, however, we have to consider how the firm's income is to be measured, and how the firm is to be valued.

Income, Profits and Rent

Crucial to any test of the invisible hand is a consideration of the measurement of firm income and firm valuation. In the studies discussed above, the measurement of firm income is often treated in an extremely cavalier manner,[21] it sometimes not even being clear whether the dependent variable under test is a rate of return on sales or, as usually would be more appropriate, a rate of return on capital. The indolence of researchers emerges from the *implication* of the static theory that these questions are of little consequence: 'In statics [or] ... in the economics of the stationary state ... the difficulty about income does not arise. A person's income can be taken without qualification as equal to his receipts (earnings of labour, or rent from property). Sleeping dogs can be left to lie.'[22]

In the dynamic approach to the invisible hand being considered here, as in the real world, such luxuries do not obtain. Here, a flow of returns in the present and in an uncertain future must be compared with an existing stock of capital in order to measure the effect of these returns on the value of the firm. Rapid technological change and the periods of high inflation witnessed in recent decades have made it increasingly evident that traditional book value calculations of firm income are adequate neither for the purposes of empirical research by economists, nor for a correct evaluation of firm performance. The procedure followed here will be to outline the prerequisites of a 'correct' measure of firm income for the purposes of the invisible hand. This line of approach may seem odd to those researchers who, for instance, use historic cost accounting data because they work just as well as the figures corrected for inflation, but we reject the 'try it and see' methodology which chooses measures on the basis of their 'success' in the statistical test conducted by the investigator.

We proceed to search for that variable involved in the process of equalisation which would correspond to a *normatively correct* decision rule on the part of economic actors. An alternative, behaviourally derived construct (e.g. the use of historic cost profits) might more closely correspond to the variable which is in fact used by business people when we observe them directly and might yield results which are interesting and no less robust empirically. But here we are less interested in descriptive realism than in considering the appropriate variable – that which embodies the most rational criteria for an empirical test of the invisible hand hypothesis embodied in the competitive tradition.

The variable for which we are searching will be expected to play a dual role – it will act as a *signal* for competitive equalisation, and it is the variable *which will be equalised*.[23] Any test of whether this variable equalises is a joint hypothesis with the notion that it is also the appropriate signal for equalisation. We shall be dealing with these issues jointly, but for clarification it will be worthwhile to consider each of these issues in turn:

1　*The variable which is a signal for equalisation.* The search for an appropriate measure must embody the fact that 'the quality of the profit figure as an indicator depends upon someone's opinion with respect to the future. ... Different people will hold different opinions, with differing degrees of confidence; and they may arrive at conclusions at different points of time'.[24] Because individuals' conjectures may differ in a world of less than perfect information, the role of profits may not always be what we expect it to be: 'while the standard view is that excess industry profits induce entry, [our] theory suggests that high profits, ceteris paribus, may well signal the presence of very successful and difficult to imitate competitors and thereby impede rational entry attempts'.[25] If, however, we stay within the dominant tradition of the invisible hand and assume that high profits are a positive incentive to compete in a sector, the following considerations would seem to be relevant to the measurement of profitability:

a Alternative measures (book profits, cash flow, etc.). Which of these is used by prospective competitors as their best proxy for their own likelihood of success in that sphere of activity, and by existing participants as a green light for further expansion? While new rivals may base their decisions on their independent perceptions of their future revenues and costs, it is hard to conceive that the accounts of existing firms do not serve as a basis for calculation in many circumstances.
b Alternative specifications of these measures. Do prospective rivals see through differences between firms in their depreciation write-off techniques and other accounting practices?
c Alternative time dimensions. Is the appropriate signalling mechanism current profits, or, perhaps, average profits over recent years?

2   *The variable which is to be equalised.* A not quite identical set of problems exists here.

a Measurement problems. How will the presence of competition manifest itself on the company's books? We shall have to discuss, for instance, the relationship between income and rent. The issue of entrepreneurial withdrawals seems incapable of any satisfactory resolution: the hopelessness of ever resolving the question of what the entrepreneur *would* have been paid if he/she had hired himself/herself on the free market leads us to question the validity and usefulness of comparisons of profit rates between large firms and those small enough for these withdrawals to be of significance.[26]
b The domain of equalisation. There may be circumstances under which equalisation is taking place at the level of the project or sphere of activity, but is not observable at the level of the firm. Since an important part of our critique of orthodoxy is that the former sphere is unobservable, we shall not be putting undue emphasis on these arguments!

A further issue in the measurement of firm income is the problem of the distinction between firm income (profit) and rent, a question so fundamental that it has been linked to the way we conceptualise the firm itself.[27] In the statistical tests discussed above the problem is particularly acute, since the attempts to explain excess profitability by concentration have to be based on the notion that these profits contained no element (or for every firm/industry, an equal–proportionate) element of rent, since *rents themselves are not explicable by the level of concentration*. (If company profits contain a substantial element of rent, they are also a poor *signal* for equalisation, but we shall put this problem aside.) If income and rent are inextricably mingled in company accounts, then the Marshallian theorem is untestable for yet another reason, that is, the variable to be equalised – pure return without rent – is unobtainable, and the controversies we have discussed above concerning monopoly versus efficiency explanations of this aggregate containing both profit and rent are inevitable and insoluble.

As an example, in examining IBM's accounts prior to a concentration–profits test we would have to assure ourselves that we have removed all remuneration due to patents and special skills and processes, all of which would have to be assigned a market value. We would then have to subtract any cost advantages due to economies of scale by comparing IBM's average costs with those which would have been present in a typical firm which was small enough to have existed in sufficient numbers to make the market perfectly competitive. Such a happenstance seems as if it would be quite unlikely, since the industry manifestly evidences significant economies of scale! Lastly, we would have to distinguish these 'intrinsic' economies of scale from any economies in, say, marketing and selling stemming from IBM's initial monopolistic advantage. There is clearly enough here to tax a medieval schoolman.

If one is testing the general proposition of invisible hand equalisation, but not in the concentration–profits context, an alternative to the impossible task outlined above is to view the mass of profits as 'the ability of a firm to generate revenues in excess of expenses'[28] and abandon all attempts to separate income from rent. If, for instance, we suggest that the present day economy is more competitive than that in the seventeenth century, it is not necessarily because we claim that the earlier period evidenced more monopolies in a strict Marshallian sense, but that immobility, ignorance and lack of replicability of physical artefacts meant that rents were widespread in skills and resources. Indeed, as we have seen, the income–rent distinction is undefined outside of an environment dominated by competitive markets. While this issue remains a troublesome one, it is sufficient for tests of general failures in the equalisation process to use the income–rent aggregate as a measure, while such an option is unavailable in the Marshallian context, with its explicit claim to a monopoly power explanation for the profit component of this aggregate.

Standard Accounting Approaches

We have already noted some of the difficulties of trying to create an industry aggregate measure of profitability. Clearly, the 'primary industry' method of allocating every firm to a specific industry has become more and more difficult with increasing levels of diversification. On the other hand, attempts to create price–cost margins for the firm's activities, which are then allocated by researchers to each particular industry in which the firm operates leave many issues unclear under the best of circumstances, including the allocation of centrally derived expenditures such as administration, advertising and research and development and the problems resulting from inter-divisional transfer prices used by firms.[29] Even more disquieting is the rather lighthearted approach in most empirical studies to the question of subtracting a charge for capital in order to transform the profit margin measure into a rate of return equivalent: as we shall see, considerations of asset measurement cannot be dealt with lightly, even for the firm as a whole, and the idea of having the additional burden of allocating capital and calculating rates of return for the firm's separate activities is indeed hair-raising, since it is usually considered quite a difficult task even for the firm's internal accountants! The calculation of profitability or its equivalent will prove quite difficult enough even at the level of the firm without adding an additional set of complications caused by splitting up the firm's activities into industrial activities.

What we usually refer to as profit is the result of a smoothing operation performed by accountants on cash flow to eliminate unrepresentative events in any one year, such as expenditure on a capital good (which is depreciated in the accounts over time), or the effect of what are called extraordinary items (e.g. sale of a capital asset). These attempts to give an accurate snapshot of firm performance in any one year should be distinguished from conscious self-interested attempts to smooth the path of firm income over time, but scope for irregularities of this kind is given by the initial departure from the most primitive statistic, which is the firm's cash flow. Even this statistic, however, is linked to the (arbitrary) length of accounting periods.

Can accounting practices be reconciled with a 'correct' measure of return? Some critics of standard accounting practice in recent years have pointed to the fact that the standard rate of return statistic, far from being representative of a project or firm's performance in a given year, may deviate substantially from that project or firm's internal rate of return, so that 'the accounting rate of return [is] a hodge-podge devoid of information about economic rate of return'.[30] However, this conclusion is too extreme, since as a smoothing operation on cash flow, the internal rate of return can always be shown to be equal to a weighted average of accounting rates of return plus a correction for resultant errors in asset valuation.[31] Unfortunately, this is no great consolation for standard practice, since this scheme will work equally well for any accounting modifications performed on the cash flow statistic, no matter how arbitrary.[32]

Once we have deviated from the cash flow statistic, the number of practical problems involved in constructing a profit statistic that is representative for a given year are substantial. It is necessary to consider how to treat changes in the value of firm-specific company assets (over and above any adjustment made for general inflation), especially those involving assets which are rarely traded such as land,[33] the treatment of advertising and research and development either as a current expense or as a depreciating investment[34] and the significant differences in the regimes of depreciation adopted by firms.

In partial mitigation of these problems, we may note that cross-sectional studies ordinarily use averages of profitability over several years and that there is some evidence that financial markets are capable of 'seeing through' changes in accounting conventions.[35] Clearly, however, we who are interested in the time path of earnings can avoid some of these problems by returning to the primitive cash flow statistic, unmodified by attempts to make it suitable for a single year, and leave these conundrums to the adherents of static theory.[36]

Firm Valuation

What is the relationship between firm income and value? A good place to begin is with an identity which relates the two:[37]

$$Y_t = D_t + (A_t - A_{t-1}) \qquad (4.3)$$

where Y_t = income in period $t - 1 \rightarrow t$
D_t = net distributions to shareholders in period $t - 1 \rightarrow t$
A_t = asset value at time t.

Note that in this definition we may observe a correspondence between income measurement and asset valuation and the conception of income as a surplus after capital maintenance. What becomes clear from this definition is that due to the intimate relation between income and asset valuation, a false kind of equalisation of rates of return is bound to take place unless the size of firm is measured in a way which is uncontingent on its net return.

Before we can even begin to consider the issue of firm valuation, it becomes evident that the problems discussed above concerning the boundaries of the firm impinge themselves in the necessary prior judgement of what components should be considered as part of the firm's assets. These assets may be limited to the current value of plant, equipment and inventories and may be extended to include net non-interest bearing assets, but 'there is no reason in principle to stop with this latter definition of capital employed. More broadly conceived the capital stock could also include human capital, property rights (particularly patents and copyrights) the results of research and development (R&D) and advertising, and special earnings opportunities open to the firm'.[38]

We are interested in value for two reasons: first, if we are concerned with cash-flow or income comparisons between firms and over time, these measures must be scaled for size in a manner which is consistent both between firms and over time so that we can create a viable measure of return on investment. Secondly, there are reasons why we may wish to depart altogether from the return on investment approach: as a variable to be equalised, it may be inadequate because it does not exhaustively embody all the qualities that investors should consider in choosing an income earning asset – most especially it does not measure the risk attached to that asset. Alternatively, the rate of return in one year or in any finite time span may not be considered a good signal – a total embodiment of all available information about future returns.[39]

Currently the most popular approach to these questions is through consideration of Tobin's q, which is the (financial) market value of a firm's reproducible real capital assets divided by the replacement cost of those assets. The concept of q clearly emerges from the literature on project evaluation, but in practice it will usually be impossible to identify separately the component projects in a firm because of the interrelationships and dependencies, the joint costs and benefits between projects, so that no aggregates smaller than the firm are viable.

The use of q as a signal for investment and equalisation rests on the presumption that average q is a good proxy for marginal q.[40] This implies first that the rent component in the former is rather small and secondly that in a world in which equalisation does indeed take place, firms make a Cournot-type assumption about the investment behaviour of other firms: the others, it is assumed, will not be tempted to enter a sector just when they are.

Of more significance is the theory's identification of the maximisation of the market value of the firm's assets with the maximisation of firm wealth. Gyrations in the financial market values of firms compared with their long-term valuation have caused some analysts to question the empirical relevance of the doctrine of financial market efficiency (see chapter 7), so that the matter is not to be thought of as a mere tautology. Furthermore, there is a substantial literature emanating from various sources which contends that investors in financial markets interfere with managers' desires to maximise firm wealth due (implicitly) to investors' lack of detailed information about firms' internal operations and future prospects and to the overly high rate of discount that they apply in their valuation.

In addition, 'since the q theory, allowing the divergence between the value of capital evaluated in the financial market and the price of capital goods, is a theory which explains how investment (change in capital stock) is motivated by this apparent short-run disequilibrium',[41] it may be in conflict with those theories of finance which establish the sovereignty of financial market valuation in the first place, since these theories presume a general equilibrium between asset and financial markets. In other words, the q hypothesis is not only coextensive with theories of firm wealth maximisation, but implies as well some notion of financial market equilibrium with which it rests uneasily.

In the calculation of q[42] for firms, the numerator – the market value of the firm's financial assets – is straightforward conceptually.[43] But to what do qs converge? We cannot answer this question until we consider the suggested alternative forms of evaluation of firm assets – our denominator – which are as follows:

1 historic cost;
2 economic value;
3 net realisable value;
4 deprival value;
5 replacement cost;

There is one possible justification for the use of historic accounts above and beyond the pragmatic ones given above, which is that it eases what is otherwise a major difficulty, that of measuring our denominator in a way which is independent of our numerator. In each of the measures 2–4, this is a serious problem indeed, since each measures the value of the firm's assets (economic value: the net present value of the firm's assets; net realisable value: their value if sold off; deprival value: 'the adverse value of the entire loss that the owner might expect to suffer if he were deprived of the property'[44]) will be linked in a causative chain with the numerator – the (financial) market value of the firm. While this is not meant as an argument in favour of historic cost measuring, it does point out difficulties which must be reluctantly admitted – reluctantly, especially, since a 'q' ratio formed with measure 3 in the denominator would be an interesting place to begin an exploration of firm bankruptcy.

We are left then with the need for a calculation of replacement costs of assets under the assumption that assets are replicable in a way which is uncontingent on the level of demand for those assets (which would obviously be linked to the numerator), in other words, that we live in a linear homogeneous world. Only under these particular circumstances, furthermore, is there any special merit in the intuitive presupposition that qs should normalise to a value of unity. If there are high short run costs to the adjustment of the capital stock,[45] it is not clear that replacement costs can be measured in a way which is not contingent on firm profitability, since, for instance, periods of high profitability will build up the demand for, and the replacement cost of capital goods.

There are further conceptual issues concerned with replacement cost in the context of technological change. Replacement cost is the outlay needed to purchase the current productive capacity of the firm at minimum cost and with the most modern technologies available. 'This concept is more complex and more difficult to measure than is reproduction cost, which measures only the inflation-adjusted cost of plant if reproduced in kind. To determine replacement cost we must also adjust for varying levels of technological advance across plant categories and product types, and for varying rates of "real" (versus book) depreciation'[46] – a challenging task indeed.

We thus have available two viable measures for testing the invisible hand theorem – a cash flow measure divided by the replacement cost of assets, and q. If the problems of proper measurement seem daunting in this context, they merely clarify how many important issues were 'pushed under the carpet' in the static analysis. But the problems themselves were always there.

Time Series Approaches

Higgledy Piggledy Growth and Other Tests
There were three major problems with the concentration–profits studies discussed earlier under the heading 'Static Formulations'. First, as static, cross-sectional tests they are unable to embody the logic of the dynamic

process postulated by invisible hand equalisation. The statistical results emerging from such studies embody an intolerable confusion in the cause–effect and sequential relationship between variables. Secondly, severe difficulties emerge from the use of the industry, as opposed to the firm as a unit of analysis. Thirdly, as a matter of record, most of these studies have been quite casual about the measurement of income and value, a casualness emerging out of the perspective of static theory. Of these problems, the first is the most significant. The studies to be discussed in this section – time series tests of earnings – form a far more convincing framework for the consideration of the invisible hand hypothesis than the static tests, even when these time series studies were intended for other purposes. They form as well the closest existent approximations to the dynamic model of equalisation outlined in the first part of this chapter.

The time series tests to be discussed here fall into two categories – those using firm and those using industry data. The firm studies were initiated with the famous study of I. M. D. Little,[47] whose intention was to examine whether companies which had high growth in earnings per share in one period tend to persist with high growth in a later period – in other words, are there such things as 'growth stocks'? Little's negative answer to this question has been confirmed many times by subsequent researchers – earnings per share move in a random walk, 'higgledy piggledy' fashion:

$$E(Y_t) = Y_{t-1} + \delta \qquad (4.4)$$

Thus, as in equation (4.4) the best estimates of earnings in the present period have been found to be earnings in the last period plus a drift factor (δ). While such studies were not intended as tests of invisible hand equalisation, similar results have been found on returns measured by net income/assets and net income/equity. Such results appear to contradict a tendency to equalisation, since abnormally high returns should move, not in a higgledy-piggledy fashion, but systematically in the direction of a universal norm for all firms.

However, some of the investigations using net income/assets and net income/equity as measures of Y have found a tendency for reversion to mean levels within the period studied,[48] a movement which could be signalling the effects of competitive equalisation. Even this process of reversion towards a firm's own mean level of profitability, should it exist, is still far from a convergence to a normal rate of return governing, at the very least all firms in the economy. The conceptualisation and the measure of this normal rate remains a central difficulty with all attempts to measure the process of equalisation. Of available methodologies, the higgledy-piggledy approach, being both dynamic and firm based may, if appropriately adapted, prove in the future to be the most likely candidate for a correctly specified test of the invisible hand theorem.

The higgledy-piggledy literature does not precisely confront the question of competitive equalisation, but the results must be viewed as somewhat disquieting for that hypothesis. The only direct address to the issue of the invisible hand in a time series, firm-based context is that by D. C. Mueller,[49] where he adopts statistical techniques which had been developed to study the mobility of individuals between higher and lower social groupings and employs them to study the mobility of 472 US firms between higher and lower bands of profitability from 1949 to 1968. The methodology proceeds by ranking firms according to their profitability in successive time periods. The equalisation hypothesis is taken to imply that a firm's profitability rank after a sufficient number of time periods will be unassociated with its opening rank. The firms were allocated each year into one of eight ranked bands of profitability, which allowed Mueller to define P_{ijt} as the proportion of firms which, being initially in group i, had by time period t moved to group j. The hypothesis that non-normal profits are transient was then tested via the regression equation:

$$P_{ijt} = \alpha_{ij} + \beta_{ij}/t + \varepsilon_{ijt} \tag{4.5}$$

and implied that

$$\alpha_{ij} = 0.125, \tag{4.5a}$$

so that after the passage of sufficient time a company has an equal chance of being in any profit band.

$$\beta_{ii} > 0, \tag{4.5b}$$

so that the probability (P_{iit}) that a company remains in its initial band is relatively high in the first instance but approaches the limiting value of 0.125.

$$\beta_{ij} < 0 \text{ for } i \neq j, \tag{4.5c}$$

so that the probability of movement between bands is initially low but approaches the limiting value 0.125 as time progresses.

Mueller's results indicate substantial non-equalisation. While the estimated βs were small in absolute value (which would indicate rapid convergence), 43 of the 64 estimated values of α_{ij} are significantly different from 0.125. The probability, for instance, of a firm starting in the highest group and staying there is 0.34 and its probability of moving to the second category is equal to 0.17, but the probability of it descending to the lowest two profit groups are 0.07 and 0.08 respectively.

This study and its results are of great interest, but two criticisms come to mind. First, the social mobility model does not precisely correspond to that of the invisible hand. The latter theory suggests that the invisible hand of competition should drag down a firm's exceptionally high profitability, and the higher the profitability the more rapidly it should be dragged down: the social mobility presumption is that there is no relationship between starting category and final category of profitability.

Secondly, the use of relative profitability categories in each year (with the implicit presumption that the median level represents normal profitability) necessitates that the study is restricted to those which continue to exist throughout the whole (20 year) sample period. Such a procedure contains a strong element of pre-selection bias. This problem is present in most studies of this kind.[50] An independent measure of normal profits, perhaps one linked to a theory of bankruptcy, might permit non-survivors to be included in a sample, but such notions of normal profits have as yet not been developed.

Relatively few attempts have been made to make time series tests of the invisible hand on an industry basis. Two studies are exceptional because they embody careful attempts to measure and use q for this purpose. The study by Lindenberg and Ross[51] calculated q ratios for a sample of firms in the US for the period 1960 to 1977. The invisible hand proposition is not confronted explicitly, but when these firms are grouped into industry categories it is evident that while differences exist – and persist between sectors, exceptionally large values of industry q tend to disappear in the latter part of the period. At the firm level this tendency is corroborated – q levels over time for each firm are not given, but exceptionally high levels (i.e. above 3.5) are far rarer in 1977 (when macroeconomic movements are controlled for) than in 1960.[52] The care which was taken to measure q in this study lends some credence to the notion that what we may be observing here is not merely an artifact of changing accounting conventions but perhaps some genuine acceleration in the process of equalisation.

The second study by von Furstenberg, Malkiel and Watson[53] explicitly confronts the question of equalisation. From a sample of US industries for 1956–76 constructed from the Compustat tape they estimated the equation:

$$d \log q_i = a_{3i} + a_{4i} (d \log q) + a_{5i} \left(\frac{q_i}{q} \right)_{-1} \qquad (4.6)$$

where $d \log q_i$ are changes in the q of each industry i, $d \log q$ are percentage changes in the annual q for the non-financial corporate sector as a whole. The coefficient a_{4i} shows the degree to which the industry q_i changes with the overall market q in percentage terms (analogous to the β coefficent of portfolio analysis to be described in chapter 7) and the coefficient a_{5i} gives us our test of the invisible hand – its sign should be negative. The results of the tests yielded values for a_{5i} which were on the whole negative but not statistically significant. While the invisible hand theorem is thus rejected, there was strong evidence in this study that q does act as a signal for new investment, so that at least part of the equalisation story is substantiated.

The conclusion from these time series studies which, with whatever problems they contain, are far more convincing than the cross-section tests is unanimous – there is no decisive tendency in the direction of invisible hand equalisation.

Problems and Limitations

How are we to interpret the results of existing studies on the invisible hand? As any study will inevitably deal with a small subsample of all firms (most likely firms in the quoted sector), the presence of an equalisation process within the sample would not confirm the existence of a global equalisation process: its absence, however, might imply *a fortiori* that it will not be found in the economy as a whole. The absence of even this semi-global equalisation does not deny the possibility of substantial pockets of competition within the economy, but a methodology for the precise delineation of these domains does not exist, whether by type of commodity (e.g. consumer versus industrial goods), size class of firm, or otherwise. With the exception of the problem of sample limitation, the only other reason why statistical evidence of equalisation might remain unconvincing in a correctly specified time series test is that declining profitability may reflect for a particular firm not competition, but market saturation: it is unlikely that such a phenomenon could be an important factor for a large sector of the economy at any one time.

There are several reasons, on the contrary, why equalisation may be present as an underlying tendency even if it does not show up in statistical results. First, managers may desire to 'smooth' the cash flow of firms (and therefore delay or inhibit any observed equalisation) for several reasons:

1   Thinking of cash explicitly from a *liquidity* perspective, managers may automatically cut back on expenditure when revenues decline for reasons of risk aversion (fears of cash shortfall). Alternatively, if managers use cash in a mechanical way as their source of investment expenditure, net cash inflows at least for a time may be unaffected by any downturn in revenue resulting from competition, as managers constrain or more likely delay even vital investment expenditure. Managerial considerations focusing on liquidity would imply that the firm is faced with something other than a perfect capital market.

2   If, however, managers view cash flow from a *profit* perspective, they conceivably might attempt to maintain a steady trend in cash flow growth (as they do with dividends), even to the extent of abstaining from profitable projects, in order to avoid arousing unsustainable investor expectations: this, however, seems a bit far-fetched. What seems more likely is that managers may engage in accounting manipulations to smooth observed cash flow, or they might intentionally take on a bundle of projects in which long payback projects are balanced by ones yielding shorter term returns.

There are other possibilities concerning equalisation which bring into question standard assumptions of economic theory. Firm level equalisation presumes that a wealth maximising firm will make, at the margin, the same rate of return on all projects, so that project level equalisation will reflect itself at the level of the firm. It is possible, however, that the real world is not, in this case, well-described by the differential calculus and that large discontinuities between the rates of return on different projects undertaken by a firm may swamp the marginal effects of competitive equalisation within projects.

Furthermore, we may, like Kaldor, wish to emphasize the importance of non-convexities or 'learning by doing' in the firm's production function, so that initial success in a project implies the possibility of economies of scale and differential rents in related projects, all leading to a 'virtuous circle'. One could conceive, furthermore, of a financial virtuous circle, in which initial success acts as a signal to financial markets which either lowers the cost or increases the accessibility of finance, making possible the pursuit of profitable opportunities otherwise unavailable to the firm. A last critique subversive of the non-equalisation results using the q measure would be that the financial market values in the numerator of q communicate no objective information other than the (possibly deluded) beliefs of financial markets. This, as they say, is a whole other kettle of fish, into which we shall be dipping in chapter 7.

Thus, while studies of the invisible hand point to substantial non equalisation, the literature is still small and of recent vintage. Furthermore, there are reasons why non equalisation may be observed in statistical tests when in the true state of the world equalisation in fact occurs.

Even if, however, these time series studies do indeed demonstrate the existence of non equalisation, they are still retrogressive compared with the concentration–profits studies in developing a methodology to account for the *causes* of this non equalisation. It seems highly inappropriate merely to add on constructs from the static paradigm (e.g. concentration) in an attempt to explain the non equalisation found in a dynamic framework.[54] But the time series literature represents a great advance on the earlier static tests and demonstrates that dynamic approaches to competition are in principle testable statistically.

Or are they?

Competition is far from being a mechanical process in which excess returns tend to be eliminated between firms and between sectors. At best, an observed equalisation would register the outward manifestations of the workings of a multi-faceted behavioural system. It may in fact be possible to use other statistical procedures such as the level of firm turnover to supplement the equalisation tests in observing the competitiveness of an environment, though measures of firm turnover have as yet proved problematic.[55]

There are more profound implications to a full consideration of competition as a dynamic process than the need to supplement the equalisation tests. We have suggested that observation of equalisation at the level of the firm is more appropriate than at the level of the industry. But unfortunately there is an important flaw in using the firm as the unit to be equalised (though it still remains superior to its industry alternative): the firm, or at least its masters, are not inanimate – if they find themselves being subject to equalisation they are likely to *do something* about it. In a world of diversification and fluid movement between sectors, it becomes increasingly difficult to identify the trajectory of a firm's profits with a specific line of business, so that the effect of equalisation in a particular sector becomes hard to disinter from its countervailing strategies in other sectors. To some extent, both industry and firm based tests of the invisible hand face the same problem: the industry is invalid as a unit of analysis because it is not a *thing* but a behavioural relation between volitional, conscious economic actors. Similarly, it is difficult to presume that observations at the level of the firm merely reflect the effects of the competitive environment and not as well the responses of actors to this environment. It will remain an open question here whether the process of competition can ever be usefully encapsulated or explained in a statistical test.

The firm as the crucial unit through which economic actors make decisions and transform their environment is the subject of the next chapter, but our orientation will shift. In, for instance, our consideration of the role of the historic development of company accounts and of measures of firm profitability there will be an emphasis on movements in the direction of 'defining and improving the quality of the various pieces of information that [the accounts] contain, on which useful analysis can be based, [rather than those] attempting to establish a formula for the calculation of "true" profit'.[56] Thus there will be relatively little discussion of the 'true' or 'optimal' measures which have been at least implicitly a part of the traditional approach to the invisible hand. The emphasis will be rather on the problems which have been confronted historically in improving the quality of the information available to decision-makers, developments which have been of major significance in the evolution of the competitive process. It is to these and related historical developments which we now turn.

Notes

1. Vollmann, T., W. Berry and D. Whybark *Manufacturing Planning and Control Systems* Richard D. Irwin 1984, p. 159.
2. Surveys include Weiss, L. 'Quantitative Studies of Industrial Organization' in ch. 9 of Intrilligator, M. (ed.) *Frontiers of Quantitative Economics* North-Holland 1971 and Scherer, F. M. *Industrial Market Structure and Economic Performance* Rand McNally second edn 1980, ch. 9, and of Clarke, R. *Industrial Economics* Basil Blackwell 1985, ch. 5. A survey of especial interest is Semmler, W. 'Competition, Monopoly and Differentials of Profit Rates: Theoretical Considerations and Empirical Evidence' *Review of Radical Political Economics* 13(4) 1982: 39–52. Recent UK studies include Hart, P. and E. Morgan, 'Market Structure and Economic Performance in the United Kingdom' *Journal of Industrial Economics* 26(2) (December 1977): 177–93, and Clarke, R. 'Profit Margins and Market Concentration in UK

Manufacturing Industry: 1970–6' *Applied Economics* 16(1) (February 1984): 57–71.

3. A crucial change in the relatively uncritical acceptance of this methodology was signalled by the article of Phillips, A. 'A Critique of Empirical Studies of Relations between Market Structure and Profitability' *Journal of Industrial Economics* 24(4) (June 1976): 241–9; see as well the series of articles in that journal for June 1984.

4. Bain, J. 'Relation of Profit Rate to Industry Concentration: American Manufacturing 1936–1940' *Quarterly Journal of Economics* 65(3) (August 1951): 293–324.

5. See for instance Brannman, L., J. D. Klein and L. Weiss 'The Price Effects of Increased Competition in Auction Markets' *Review of Economics and Statistics* 69(1) (February 1987): 24–32.

6. See for instance Dalton, J. and D. Penn 'The Concentration-Profitability Relationship: Is There a Critical Concentration Ratio?' *Journal of Industrial Economics* 25(2) (December 1976): 133–41.

7. Bothwell, J., T. Cooley and T. Hall 'A New View of the Market Structure–Performance Debate' *Journal of Industrial Economics* 32(4) (June 1984): 397–417.

8. In a recent study [Leitzinger, J. and K. Taylor 'Foreign Competition and Antitrust Law' *Journal of Law and Economics* 26(1) (April 1983): 87–102] industry profitability was used as a criterion to distinguish between concentration measures.

9. Manke, R. 'Causes of Interfirm Profitability Differences: A New Interpretation of the Evidence' *Quarterly Journal of Economics* 88(2) (May 1974): 181–91.

10. These examples are taken from industries used in the tests by Hart and Morgan (note 2).

11. Phillips (note 3).

12. See Breshnahan, T. and R. Schmalensee 'The Empirical Renaissance in Industrial Economics: An Overview' *Journal of Industrial Economics* 35(4) (June 1987): 371–7.

13. See Ravenscraft, D. 'Structure–Profit Relationships at the Line of Business and Industry Level' *Review of Economics and Statistics* 65(1) (February 1983): 22–31. There exists as well a UK PIMS data set.

14. See, for instance, Demsetz, H. 'Industry Structure, Market Rivalry and Public Policy' *Journal of Law and Economics* 16 (April 1973): 1–9 as well as his 'Two Systems of Belief About Monopoly' in Goldschmid, H. (ed.) *Industrial Concentration* Little, Brown 1974, pp. 175–81 and Smirlock, M., T. Gilligan, and W. Marshall 'Tobin's q and the Structure-Performance Relationship' *American Economic Review* 74(5) (December 1984): 1051–60.

15. Nickell, S. and D. Metcalf 'Monopolistic Industries and Monopoly Profits or, Are Kellogg's Cornflakes Overpriced?' *Economic Journal* 88 (June 1978): 254–68.

16. Porter, M. *Competitive Strategy* Free Press 1980 and Porter, M. 'The Structure within Industries and Companies' Performance' *Review of Economics and Statistics* 61 (May 1979): 214–27, which is the basis for the present discussion.

17. Support for the existence of firm-specific strategies even in a relatively homogeneous sector is found in Hatten, K. and P. Schendel 'Heterogeneity within an Industry: Firm Conduct in the US Brewing Industry 1952–71' *Journal of Industrial Economics* 26(2) (December 1977): 97–113. The

heterogeneity of experience of firms within 'industry' groupings is also reported in Cubbin, J. and P. Geroski 'The Convergence of Profits in the Long Run: Inter-Firm and Inter-Industry Comparisons' *Journal of Industrial Economics* 35(4) (June 1987): 427–42.

18. Cheung, S. 'The Contractual Nature of the Firm' *Journal of Law and Economics* 26(1) (April 1983): 1–21.
19. 'Burton Dodges CGT with £100m Off – Balance Sheet Deal' *Accountancy Age* 16 October 1986.
20. On Japan, see Yamamura, K. 'Entrepreneurship, Ownership and Management in Japan' in Mathias, P. and M. Postan (eds) *Cambridge Economic History of Europe* vol. VII part 2 Cambridge University 1978, ch. 3, Allen, G. *The Japanese Economy* Weidenfeld and Nicolson 1981, chs 7 and 8 and Clark, R. *The Japanese Company* Yale University 1979, chs 3 and 4.
21. A typical example is the study of profit margins by R. Clarke (note 2). The complete description of the profitability variable is as follows: 'Profitability: The profit margin was taken as net output minus operative and other wages and salaries divided by net output and expressed as a percentage.'
22. Hicks, J. *Value and Capital* second edition Oxford University 1946, p. 172.
23. This distinction is related to but not identical with the distinction between *ex ante* and *ex post* income in ibid., pp. 178–9.
24. Edey, H. 'The Nature of Profit' *Accounting and Business Research* 1(Winter 1970): 50–5.
25. Lippman, S. and R. Rumelt 'Uncertain Liability: An Analysis of Interfirm Differences in Efficiency Under Competition' *The Bell Journal of Economics* 13(2) (Autumn 1982): 418–38.
26. See Eatwell, J. 'Growth, Profitability and Size: The Empirical Evidence' in Marris, R. and A. Wood (eds) *The Corporate Economy* Macmillan 1970 appendix A; the debate seemed to have been initiated in Stigler, G. *Capital and Rates of Return in Manufacturing Industry* Princeton University 1963, though the origins of the controversy reach to fundamental and unresolved questions on the nature of normal profits.
27. See Lamberton, D. *The Theory of Profit* Basil Blackwell 1965, ch. 1.
28. Foster, G. *Financial Statement Analysis* Prentice-Hall 1978, p. 33.
29. See Phillips (note 3).
30. Fisher, F. and J. McGowan 'On the Misuse of Accounting Rates of Return to Infer Monopoly Profits' *American Economic Review* 73(1) (March 1983): 82–97. See also Manke (note 9).
31. Kay, J. 'Accountants Too Could be Happy in a Golden Age: The Accountant's Rate of Profit and the Internal Rate of Return' *Oxford Economic Papers* 3 (November 1976): 447–60, and Peasnell, K. 'Some Formal Connections between Economic Values and Yields and Accounting Numbers' *Journal of Business, Finance and Accounting* 9(3) (1982): 361–81.
32. Higson, C. 'What do Accounting Rates of Return Mean?' Kingston Polytechnic (manuscript).
33. Holland, D. Introduction and summary to Holland, D. *Measuring Profitability and Capital Costs* D. C. Heath 1982, p. 2.
34. Solomon, W. 'Alternative Rate of Return Concepts and their Implications for Utility Regulation' *Bell Journal of Economics and Management Science* 1(1) (Spring 1970): 65–81.
35. Beaver, W. and R. Dukes 'Tax Allocation and δ Depreciation Methods' *The Accounting Review* 48(3) (July 1973): 549–59, and Dukes, R. 'An

Investigation of the Effects of Expensing Research and Development Costs on Security Prices' in Schiff, M. and G. Sorter (eds) *Proceedings of the Conference on Topical Research in Accounting* New York University 1976, pp. 147–93.

36. Even cash flow is subject to manipulation. For instance, the complications of 'income recognition' – how payment is accounted for in different stages of a sale (on order, on shipment, on installation etc.) – can distort the timing of cash flow statistics as usually calculated. See Griffiths, I. *Creative Accounting* Sidgwick & Jackson 1986, ch. 2.

37. This identity is close to Hicks's definition of *ex post* income (note 22), pp. 178–9.

38. Holland (note 33), pp. 1–2.

39. An early discussion of this point in the context of a static test may be found in Thomadakes, S. 'A Value-Based Test of Profitability and Market Structure' *Review of Economics and Statistics* 59(2) (May 1977): 179–85.

40. Different taxation regimes can also affect the levels of q and marginal q. See Edwards, J. and M. Keen 'Taxes, Investment and Q' *Review of Economic Studies* 52 (October 1985): 665–79 and the references cited therein.

41. Yoshikawa, H. 'On the "q" Theory of Investment' *American Economic Review* 70(4) (September 1980): 739–43.

42. Lindenberg, E. and S. Ross 'Tobin's q Ratio and Industrial Organization' *Journal of Business* 54(1) (January 1981): 1–32 and Brainard, W., J. Shoven and L. Weiss 'The Financial Valuation of the Return on Capital' *Brookings Papers on Economic Activity* (2) 1980: 453–511. See as well the appendix to von Furstenberg, G., B. Malkiel and H. Watson 'The Distribution of Investment Between Industries: A Microeconomic Application of the "q" Ratio' in von Furstenberg, G. (ed.) *Capital, Efficiency and Growth* Ballinger 1980, pp. 395–459.

43. This is not true if one's central concern is with the absolute level of q (as opposed to its relative value between firms), in which case the difficult questions surrounding the after-tax return to a 'typical' investor cannot be ignored. For present purposes the taxation regime is of little importance unless it changes in such a way as to cause distortions in the observed time path of convergence of qs between firms.

44. Sandilands, F. (Chairman) *Inflation Accounting* Report of the Inflation Accounting Committee Cmnd 6245 1975, p. 58.

45. Ciccolo, J. and G. Fromm '"q" and the Theory of Investment' *Journal of Finance* 34(2) (May 1979): 535–49.

46. Lindenberg and Ross (note 42).

47. Little, I. 'Higgledy Piggledy Growth' *Bulletin of the Oxford Institute of Economics and Statistics* 24(4) (November 1962): 387–412 and Little, I. and A. Raynor *Higgledy Piggledy Growth Again* Basil Blackwell 1966.

48. See Foster (note 28), ch. 3. The first edition is more detailed on these matters than the second edition of 1986.

49. Mueller, D. 'The Persistence of Profits Above the Norm' *Economica* 44 (November 1977): 369–80. A recent application of this methodology is to be found in Odagri, H. and H. Yamawaki 'A Study of Company Profit-Rate Time Series – Japan and the United States' *International Journal of Industrial Organization* 4 (1986): 1–23.

50. The question of survival biases is discussed in Ball, R. and R. Watts 'Some Additional Evidence on Survival Biases' *Journal of Finance* 34(1) (March 1979): 197–206.

51. Lindenberg and Ross (note 42).
52. Few studies have explicitly dealt with the influence of macroeconomic fluctuations on invisible hand equalisation, an exception being Ehrbar, H. and M. Glick 'Structural Change in Profit Differentials: The Post World War Two Economy' *British Review of Economic Issues* 10(22) (Spring 1988): 81–102.
53. von Furstenberg et al. (note 42).
54. As was done, for example in Mueller, D. *Profits in the Long Run* Cambridge 1986. For this reason we have concentrated on his earlier study.
55. The literature on firm turnover is not extensive; see for instance Hymer, S. and P. Pashigian 'Turnover of Firms as a Measure of Market Behaviour' *Review of Economics and Statistics* 44(1) (February 1962): 82–7, and Caves, R. and M. Porter 'Market Structure, Oligopoly and Stability of Market Shares' *Journal of Industrial Economics* 26(4) (June 1978): 289–313, and the bibliographies therein.
56. Edey (note 24).

5

The Managerial Revolution

The Managerial Revolution and Economic Theory

The Empirical Premises of Managerialism

The emergence of giant firms based on limited liability in the first part of the twentieth century has caused many commentators to question the relevance of traditional views of business organisation and behaviour. The most popular alternative approach among academic economists has been to emphasize and extend the analysis of monopolistic market structures, since the growth of the latter in place of 'competition' was the most readily comprehensible meaning which could be imposed upon these great events within the context of the Marshallian methodology. As we have seen in chapter 2, these attempts to construct an alternative to (perfect) competition were ultimately unsuccessful. However, the empirical presumption that industrial trends associated with the growth of large firms may be characterised as a movement from competitive to monopolistic structures has been of continuing influence.

Mainstream literature at the turn of the century found almost nothing of interest to say about the emergence of giant, as opposed to monopolistic firms, a fact reflected in part in the unsatisfactory nature of the discussions concerning the determination of firm size. We thus find writers such as Frank Knight still accounting for the size of firms on the basis of 'personality and historical accident rather than intelligible general principles'.[1] The silence of the orthodox methodology in this regard is unsurprising given its concomitant failure on the question of limited liability. Marshall's representative firm was dominated by a profit-seeking owner–entrepreneur and even in later editions of his text the joint stock company is treated somewhat exceptionally.[2]

There was a great deal of discussion of these issues away from the centres of academic economics, especially in the US. Political writers, Congressional committees and dissident economists such as Veblen gave a great deal of attention to the newly dominant corporate form[3] but, ironically, their emphasis upon double-dealing and stock market speculation tended to re-inforce the tendency for economists and others to use the traditional firm as a norm of behaviour.

A crucial event in the analysis of the corporation was the publication in 1932 of *The Modern Corporation and Private Property* by Adolf Berle and Gardiner Means, a lawyer and an economist respectively. The book made the first systematic attempt to assess the level of aggregate concentration – as measured by the share of assets held by the top 200 non-financial corporations – and was thereby a statistical documentation of the eruption of giant firms that had taken place at the turn of the century in the US and of their increasing importance through to the year 1929. For the authors, the emergence of these corporations represented a change qualitatively as significant as the industrial revolution itself. As the trend towards a growing influence of the largest firms seemed to be a continuing one, the book's impact upon public opinion and economists partially centred upon the question of whether these firms had an unfair advantage in product and, most especially, capital markets.[4]

The major concern of their book, however, was not upon these economic considerations but upon the legal proposition that the traditional system of private property relations was under threat due to the wide dispersal of equity ownership in these giant firms, which left them under the control of professional managers who were responsible to no-one but themselves.[5] As a result of the focus of this tremendously influential book, subsequent empirical research into the nature of the modern corporation has been indelibly linked with the phrase 'the separation of ownership and control', as has the mainstream theoretical writing in this area.

There are two distinct problems to be confronted in any empirical investigation of this separation. First, the ownership of company shares must be documented. While the laws on disclosure have caused more detail on large shareholdings to be revealed as the century has progressed, the parallel development of personal income taxes has given ever more incentive to wealthy individuals to disguise and understate the value of their possessions.

Secondly there is the problem of corporate 'control'. As Berle and Means suggest 'control . . . like sovereignty, its counterpart in the political field . . . is an elusive concept, for power can rarely be sharply segregated or clearly defined'.[6] Dogmatic views in this area would seem possible: since ultimate control always (except in cases of extreme financial difficulty) resides in the hands of equity owners, the case for their continuing power can be argued from a legal perspective. The contrary or proximate view is that corporate managers control (most) large modern companies since it is they who make the day-to-day decisions on company policy. Most research in this area, however, has adopted the intermediate perspective put forth by Berle and Means:

> Since the direction over the activities of a corporation is exercised through the board of directors, we may say for practical purposes that control lies in the hands of the individual or group who have the actual power to select the board of directors, (or its majority), either by mobilizing the legal right to choose them – 'controlling' a majority of the votes directly or through some legal device – or by exerting pressure which influences their choice'.[7]

This general view is dominant in subsequent studies, including the definitive one by Edward Herman.[8]

Several questions have arisen about the operational measure used to measure control. Berle and Means's conclusion was that as of the year 1930, of the 200 largest companies (42 railroads, 52 public utilities and 106 industrials), 44 per cent were under management control, and that while this process has progressed least far in the case of industrials, 'even in this field the separation had assumed considerable importance'. Much significance has been attached to Means's cut-off of 20 per cent as the portion of shares which must be held by an individual or compact group, below which the firm would be declared to be under the control of its managers. While this was the basic criterion used by Means, he claims that in no cases were companies classed under management control where the dominant stock interest was known to be greater than 5 per cent of the voting stock. In fact, the classifications were not produced solely on the basis of arbitrary statistical criteria, but were supplemented with an examination of all available information about the internal workings of these firms. Even the basic statistical data often had to be culled from such publicly available sources as the financial pages of the *New York Times* and the *Wall Street Journal*, and companies were sometimes classified on the basis of general 'street knowledge'. The best data available were for the public utilities and railroads, since they were subject to regulation, and were least accurate in the case of industrials.[9]

Thus Berle and Means's case was weakest in the crucial sphere of industrials, and most decisive in the peculiar area of regulated public utilities and in railroads, which were subject to a long-term decline in importance. More critical was the fact that since 'management control' was used more or less as a residual category, any limitations on the gathering of information about centres of control were biased in its favour, and indeed the TNEC monograph number 29, prepared by the Securities and Exchange Commission in 1940, found substantially more centres of ownership than did Berle and Means.

Few empirical studies followed in subsequent years in the US, though the notion that a managerial revolution had indeed taken place was proceeding apace in the theoretical literature. This presupposition eventually received reinforcement with Robert Larner's study confirming the 'completion' of the managerial revolution in the US. His research, along with that of P. Sargant Florence for the UK, which used a similar methodology and reached comparable conclusions represent the high water mark of managerialism in empirical work. In subsequent years these conclusions were questioned in the US by writers such as Phillip Burch who, using publicly available sources such as articles in *Fortune* magazine, pointed to centres of ownership control which were not revealed by the Securities and Exchange Commission disclosure requirements (the data used by Larner), while others used the Congressional report of the Patman Committee in an attempt to demonstrate a resurgence of financial control of companies.[10]

The empirical question of corporate control in the US rested somewhat indecisively until the publication in 1981 of Edward Herman's study *Corporate Control, Corporate Power*. Herman's most important achievement has been to underline the real-life complexities involved in the overall concept of control and the difficulties inherent in identifying the locus of power even within the bounds of such a concept. Herman makes use of share holding statistics as basic data, the fundamental rule for declaring a firm subject to managerial control being that no group be found with 5 per cent of the company's shares. The overall approach to the question of control is similar to that used by Means, as can be seen in the discussion centring upon the influence in the US of financial institutions (bank trust departments, insurance companies, etc.). Two criteria were used to establish control:

1 Do these institutions use their voting powers, directly or by threat, in a collective manner, designed to influence the selection of boards of directors?
2 Does their use or threat of use of the power to buy or sell stock on a collective basis (whether tacit or explicit) allow them to exercise a decisive or substantial influence over corporate decision making?

The answer to the first question on voting power is decisively negative; the answer to the second is that groups of owning institutions rarely work together to discipline managements, but they do think alike and emulate one another and their behaviour does exercise a real influence. This form of influence, however, is more accurately described as a form of constraint than control.[11]

Herman's distinction between 'control' and 'constraint' will be crucial to our argument below on the relevance (or irrelevance) of this enormous managerial revolution literature. But first, we shall summarise Herman's findings. In the process of replicating past results he corrected several misconceptions which had grown up in this area. The wider dispersion of share holdings over time does not imply that control may be exercised by ever smaller percentages of shares as argued by Larner and others, thereby reducing over time the relevant cut-off for management control – it merely enhances the power of whomever controls the firm's proxy machinery, which may indeed be the management itself. Furthermore, the tradition stemming from Berle and Means of regarding a firm as under management control if the firm dominating it is so classified is seen to be quite irrelevant from an economic point of view since

> a management-dominated firm that is in control of another firm would hardly encourage 'expense preference' [a form of managerial abuse] by the controlled management, even if the management of the parent engages in such behavior itself, and it might plausibly be expected to fix maximization rules such as large firms impose on their divisions and profit centers. In short, intercorporate ownership control may elicit behavior similar to that sought by owners, whatever the form of ultimate control.

Finally, with the addition of a specific category for 'financial control' which previously had been subsumed under the rather vague one of 'control by a legal device', Herman was able to replicate the Berle and Means study for 1929, and concluded that managerial control was present in 40.5 per cent of the companies, as opposed to Means's figure of 44.3 per cent. More significant are Herman's conclusions concerning the long-term secular trend:

> [The] principal fact . . . is the steady increase in management control, as opposed to the two other major potential bases of control – ownership and credit. . . . Ultimate management control accounted for 82.5 per cent of the number and 85.4 per cent of the assets of the 200 largest non-financials and 78 per cent of the number and 80 per cent of the assets of the 100 largest industrials in the mid-1970s. That this is a fundamental trend is indicated [by the fact that] in 1900–1901, ultimate management control accounted for 23.8 per cent by number of a sample of very large companies, rising to 40.5 per cent in 1929. It also appears that the shift toward management control *since 1929* has been as dramatic as the shift between 1900 and 1929.[12]

By contrast, a recent study for the UK is that by Nyman and Silbertson, who deny that there is any tendency at all towards a growth of managerial control as a result of a case-by-case analysis of the top 250 firms (by turnover) in the UK.[13] A justification for a continued interest in the managerial phenomenon even in Britain is first, that the striking similarities between the structure of company law and the financing of companies in the US and UK are such that we may wish to regard the differences as merely reflecting sluggish company growth and the consequent slow dispersal of new shares in the UK, with the American trend representing the underlying tendency of the common 'system' in the two countries. Furthermore, even with their grave doubts about the significance of managerial control, Nyman and Silbertson still place 43.75 per cent of the 224 firms out of the top 250 for which they have sufficient information for 1975 in the category of firms for which no centre of ownership or institutional control could be found and which may, therefore, be deemed to be management controlled in the conventional terminology.

For Berle and Means the managerial mode of control has had the most profound implications for private property relations, while in academic work this issue has occupied a large part of the theoretical work on the mode of operation and the significance of the large company for the last forty years. Why then is a company which is managerially controlled considered to be so special?

Managerialism: Theoretical Considerations

The question of managerialism confronts us with an even more fundamental issue: why for so long were the internal workings and decision-making processes of the firm ignored in economic theory? At one level it is sufficient to note that earlier writers referred to the profit-seeking, profit maximising 'entrepreneur' in an unquestioning way – that is to say, they proceeded on the basis of an implicitly understood empirical assumption about the organisation of business activity. Such an explanation avoids, however, the methodological presuppositions underlying the traditional analysis. Managerialism, by changing the focus of analysis away from the external constraints imposed upon the firm, did more than simply introduce the 'separation of ownership and control'. 'The firm' had never been central to the neo-classical tradition, and has no real existence in the pure general equilibrium framework: the very existence of the firm is considered a major conundrum in orthodox theory. In the Marshallian branch of this tradition, it has been argued that:

> the firm in that theory is not, as so many writers believe, designed to serve to explain and predict the behavior of real firms; instead, it is designed to explain and predict changes in observed prices (quoted, paid, received) as effects of particular changes in conditions (wage rates, interest rates, import duties, excise taxes, technology, etc.). In this causal connection the firm is only a theoretical link, a mental construct helping to explain how one gets from the cause to the effect. This is altogether different from explaining the behavior of a firm. As the philosopher of science warns, we ought not to confuse the *explanans* with the *explanandum*.[14]

This passage may be taken as a fair stylisation of the reasoning implicit in the minds of most mainstream economists at the turn of the century and for many years subsequently, and largely accounts for the long-term failure of orthodox economists to devote much effort to analysing the basic structure of the internal organisation (much less the detailed workings) of the firm. The pointed growth of aggregate concentration, with its consequent focus upon the activities of individual giants made the above 'black-box' approach unsustainable for many economists, but there have remained many persistently unreformed defenders of this methodology to the present day.

An alternative, but related explanation for the by-passing of the internal workings of the firm may be found in the Social Darwinist approach of Alchian discussed in chapter 3: for many economists, the existence of a competitive environment made questions of individual entrepreneurial propensities quite irrelevant. It is thus not coincidental that Tibor Scitovsky's seminal article[15] calling into question the necessity for profit maximisation cites articles on monopoly and on imperfect competition in the first paragraph. In his exposition, represented in figure 5.1, an owner–entrepreneur, exhibiting a 'normal' trade-off between income and leisure in the indifference curves for his entrepreneurial labour will maximise utility at b, trading off some profits for the sake of leisure. Scitovsky suggested that, as a matter of fact, the psychology of the entrepreneur is closer to that illustrated by indifference curve 'U_z', in which case since the entrepreneur exhibits zero income elasticity of supply of entrepreneurship, the outcome closely approximates the traditional assumption of profit maximisation at point a. Nevertheless, Scitovsky had posed the possibility that there might exist a conflict between the standard presumption that the behaviour of economic participants would be based on self-interest, and the maximisation of firm profits.

Scitovsky's particular formulation of this conflict between differing self interests has not enjoyed great popularity in the literature, one reason being that contemporary theory suggests that in a world of smoothly functioning capital (and labour) markets, the 'rational' owner–entrepreneur will find it in his or her own best interest to maximise profits in the firm and

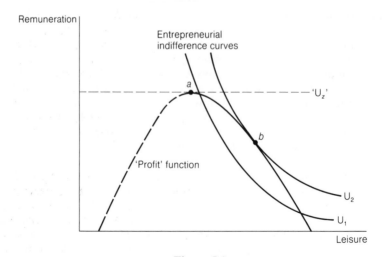

Figure 5.1

pursue leisure/consumption in other spheres.[16] Scitovsky's model, however, already possesses, with minor changes, the essential elements of the managerial literature which flowered in the 1960s.[17] The conflict in this literature is between the owner–rentier, who wishes to maximise profits at a, and a professional manager who, quite naturally will have interests different from those of the owner, and will be willing to trade off some of the owner's profits for the sake of 'something else' – leisure, emoluments, security, or whatever else enters into his or her utility function. It was not long before the professional journals were full of articles trying to detect higher profitability on the part of owner-controlled firms than firms deemed to be managerially controlled.[18]

While most of the literature in this area developed in fairly abstract, analytical terms, lurking behind it was the implicit, but fairly strong perspective on the industrial history of the twentieth century as a movement from small firms directed by profit maximising owner–entrepreneurs to large (presumably monopolistic) enterprises run by professional managers who were maximising 'something else'. An enormous literature also developed concerning the implications of this change for society as a whole, which conflated quite conveniently with Schumpeter's late pronouncements on the death-knell of entrepreneurial capitalism.[19]

The managerial model represented a departure for neo-classical theory by emphasizing the individual firm and its internal workings. In another sense, however, it fits well into the mainstream tradition of conflict models stretching as far back as Edgeworth – in this case the battle is posed between an owner–rentier who, like the owner–entrepreneur would like to maximise profits, and the professional manager who has other interests. For this model to be of any interest as a perspective on the economic history of the twentieth century there is a host of assumptions implicit in the analysis which have to be satisfied, two of which concern the 'utility functions' of the participants:

1 Have owner–rentiers in fact desired to maximise either firm profits or the value of the firm? Has this behaviour remained roughly invariant throughout the twentieth century? Are the goals of an owner–entrepreneur identical with those of an owner–rentier?
2 What forces have actually motivated the professional manager, and in what direction have these motivations been evolving?

and two which concern their ability to exercise their desires:

3 What assumptions are appropriate with regard to the capacity of the owner–rentier to monitor the firm and its professional managers, and do we presume that this ability has been unchanged throughout the century?
4 Must we assume that the professional manager is neither more nor less competent than the owner–entrepreneur, i.e. that both operate along the frontier of an identical profit function (figure 5.1)? Alternatively,

must we assume that any gap in capability between the two groups has remained constant over time?

These four points embody the issues we wish to discuss with regard to the separation of ownership from control, but a blunt statement about our own position is in order. It is our contention that the elaborate literature surrounding the managerial revolution is not only fallacious, but to a substantial extent the opposite of the truth. The last several decades of corporate development have not been significant because of a progressive separation of ownership and control. On the contrary, successive decades have evidenced the increasing ability of property owners to monitor their corporate wealth holdings and to proceed in an efficacious manner to maximise the value of this wealth. Furthermore, and of greater significance for the evolution of the competitive process, the masters of the modern corporation, far from being the dull bureaucrats of Schumpeterian stereotype, are demonstrably more systematic and wide-ranging in the pursuit of profits than their relatively rough-hewn predecessors.

All this is not meant to contest the possibility that, *ceteris paribus* (and at a given moment of historical development), the handing over of the firm's assets to its managers or employees might in many cases result in an increase in firm value: the current spate of managerial buy-outs are interesting experiments in this direction, even if the increased leverage of these firms complicates any evaluation of the effects of buy-outs. Any such experiments, however, have little to do with the long-term historical processes we are examining. Many twentieth century economists have contended that increasing 'managerialism' in firms, by causing a decline in entrepreneurship and in the desire to maximise profits, has contributed to a secular tendency for the economy to deviate from a state of competitiveness which had formerly existed. On the contrary, the important changes which have taken place in the internal management of firms in the twentieth century have been of a very different kind, and are linked with a long-term tendency for competitiveness to increase in the economy. Much of the argument presented here is, we suspect, far less controversial than it would have been only a few years ago as a result of developments within the literature of economics, economic history and other fields. There is reason to believe that a more coherent approach to the 'managerial revolution' is in the process of formation.

The Transformation of Business Management in Economic History

An Overall Perspective
The standard approach to managerialism may be re-exposited as follows: 'If a wholly owned firm is managed by the owner, he will make operating decisions which maximize his utility . . . as the manager's ownership claim falls, his incentive to devote significant effort to creative activities such as searching out profitable ventures falls . . . [this and similar effects] can be

limited (but probably not eliminated) by the expenditure of resources on monitoring activities by the outside stockholders'.[20] The terminology of 'monitoring costs' is useful and extremely suggestive: one way of summarising our own view of the historical development of firm control is that the costs to owners of monitoring firm performance have had a long-term tendency to fall, as have the costs to managers of monitoring the firm's internal activities and its external environment. Such terminology must, however, be adopted with reservations, since costs in mainstream economics are invariably conceived of as external constraints imposed upon economic actors with given behavioural parameters, while here we shall be suggesting that the most significant mechanism lowering, for instance, the monitoring costs of managers has been an increase in their own efficaciousness and knowledgeability – a transformation *in the behavioural function itself*.

It would be difficult to argue that present-day shareholders find it easy to exercise a precise monitoring of managerial activity, or that fairly obvious abuses of managerial position are not to be found. But as a long-term tendency the constraints imposed upon managers by stockholders have increased and the monitoring of managerial and firm activity has improved. These developments, coupled with a long-term transformation in the nature and quality of managerial activity, implies that the modern corporation is, relatively speaking, more directed towards maximising profits than ever before.

Our own perspective may be indicated in answer to the questions posed at the end of the previous section: the desires of the owner–rentier have been evolving in the twentieth centry in significant ways. The assumption of contemporary orthodox theory that these desires may always be identified with maximisation of the firm's value develops a particle of plausibility only in relatively recent times, and is inconceivable in the absence of a complex process of sociological and intellectual development. Furthermore, value maximisation is also an incomplete description of the historical behaviour of the owner–entrepreneur. It is indubitable that managers' desires will not necessarily prove identical with those of owner–rentiers, but a precise characterisation of the nature and development of managerial motivation over the century is a matter of sociology and history, and may not be deduced from the principle of utility.

More significant, however, than changes in 'utility functions' is the transformation in the *abilities* of participants. The ability of the owner–rentier to monitor the firm has improved dramatically over the century, while the development of the skills of professional managers is gradually being recognised in the academic literature as being of such great consequence as to make changes in ownership structure *per se* of relatively little consequence. In the context of figure 5.1, the shape and level of the profit function itself has been dictated by developments in this actual, substantive 'managerial revolution' – any trade-off *vis-à-vis* some mythical owner–entrepreneur is quite irrelevant in an historical context. We now proceed to explore these questions in detail.

Owners and Company Control

One reason for a certain a priori suspicion about the premise of managerialism regarding a growing separation of ownership and control is its historical implausibility: can one really accept the notion that the possessors of the corporate wealth – a compact and relatively knowledge-able section of the population – would permit the development of a set of institutions in which their ability to monitor their own wealth was *progressively* degraded? As is usual in these matters, deductive logic is not really sufficient and the historical record is complex and contradictory.

A method of approaching this issue is to return to the original Berle and Means classic. When read in the context of the year of its publication (1932), what they (specifically Berle) are describing is not some subtle deviation between the utility functions of property owners and managers, but *a crisis in property relations* as the laws, regulations and conventions developed in earlier times no longer seemed sufficient to protect the owner–rentier under the new conditions of the emergent giant corporate structures. What has been forgotten, or ignored, is that the Berle and Means book was written in the wake of the frauds and stock market manipulations of the 1920s and *before* the passage of the Securities and Exchange Commission (SEC) Acts and other New Deal legislation initiated in 1933. Most of the manipulative practices described in book two of the text have either disappeared through legislative fiat or stock market regulation, while other possibilities portended, such as the pervasive issuance of non-voting stock by managements, have simply failed to materialise.[21] Despite the great success of the book and its vast influence, much of the original text, most especially that which can be attributed to Berle, became obsolete within a decade. It is possible to detect a certain embarrassment in Berle's 1968 footnote to the original text of book three – *Property in the Stock Markets*:

> This book, describing property in the stock markets, became the foundation for the Federal legislation begun in 1933 and further developed later, regulating stock markets and the rights of security holders which prevailed in 1968. These laws are popularly referred to as the 'Securities and Exchange Acts'. . . . They have been further amplified by regulations of the Securities and Exchange Commission, and by an immense number of decisions of the United States courts and of the Securities and Exchange Commission. . . .
> The Securities and Exchange Laws, the regulations and decisions thereunder, and the practice of stock markets and bankers have carried to reality, and in some cases gone beyond, the conceptions expressed in this book.[22]

What emerges from a careful reading of the original text is Berle's concern with the public accountability of the corporation. This was manifested not only in a general way, but specifically with regard to the standards of financial reporting to which firms should be subject. In a paper presented to the American Institute of Accountants in 1933, four months after the passage of the initial SEC Act, he emphasized the growing importance of accounting in the economy:

> 'It becomes plain', Berle said, 'that accounting is rapidly ceasing to be in any sense of the word a private matter'. He then raised questions about several accounting practices . . . which might distort comparisons.
> He stressed the desirability of comparisons of the results of one company with others in the same industry.
> He continued, 'How then should we handle the consistent development of principles of accounting, bearing in mind that these are likely to be subjected to the test of public opinion and public desirability as well as to their effectiveness in specified private transactions? For accountancy is now coming of age; there is no mistake about it.' Mr. Berle suggested that the first approach must be made by accountants themselves, acting through such organizations as the American Institute. But he questioned whether individual accountants could maintain completely impartial minds when under the instructions of a client. He predicted that a bureau would be set up, presumably in the Department of Commerce, to standardize accounting practices in various industries. The speech was something of a shock to the Institute audience.[23]

The disclosure of accounting information was thus seen to be of critical importance for the control of the firm.

Of all the mechanisms mentioned earlier which promote the ability of owners to monitor their wealth, the one to which we attach the greatest weight is the expansion in the quality and quantity of the publicly available information issued by companies. This expansion is due to the incremental effect of improvements in accounting practices and, discontinuously, to changes in legal requirements and the disclosure standards dictated by other regulatory bodies such as the Stock Exchange. Thus, it may be true in the US, as in the UK,[24] that the influence of individual shareholders is rather feeble at annual meetings. But the SEC's 1970 requirement that firms make interim reports on a quarterly basis is still likely to have had an important impact upon shareholders' decisions through investment advisory services (their most important source of information),[25] even though these reports are not required to be sent to individual shareholders.

Historically, professional investment analysts have been an important force promoting the quality and quantity of information disclosed by companies.[26] The importance of the legislated constraints on the behaviour of companies as well as the legal and institutional imposition of disclosure requirements is that they impose restrictions on the behaviour of managements, in the first case directly and, in the second, by increasing the quality and quantity of information available to shareholders. The latter change in the environment means that, even in the absence of direct participation in firm decision-making, shareholders can use what even Berle and Means concede is a powerful weapon of control – the actual or threatened sales of their shares[27] – in an ever more discriminating and informed way.

The growing sophistication and aggressiveness of shareholders is reinforced by the progressive development over the century of financial control of large share holdings by institutions.[28] These institutions, furthermore, have shown an ever greater willingness to be flexible in their holdings in the search for maximum returns:

> [An] important recent development is that private sector institutions in a number of major countries are ... embarking on an inter-nationalisation of their portfolios. ... Improvements in communications technology are breaking down many of the barriers that have isolated markets from each other in the past. Banks and securities firms are setting up global networks, and having developed global products they are pulling out the stops to persuade investors to buy them'.[29]

While it would be difficult to contend – much less to prove – that in some absolute sense managements have become the responsive tools of owner–rentiers, or that managerial self-interest is of no significance, it is hard to conceive that any contemporary writer on corporate management, even in the wake of recent scandals, could write as below – one of many similar paragraphs to be found in *The Modern Corporation and Private Property*:

> there are numerous ... ways in which at least part of the profits of a corporation can be diverted for the benefit of those in control. Profits may be shifted from a parent corporation to a subsidiary in which the controlling group has a large interest. Particularly profit-able business may be diverted to a second corporation largely owned by the controlling group. In many other ways it is possible to divert profits which would otherwise be made by the corporation into the hands of the group in control. When it comes to the question of distributing such profits as are made, self-seeking control may strive to divert profits from one class of stock to another if, as frequently occurs, it holds interests in the latter issue. In market operations such control may use 'inside information' to buy low from present stockholders and sell high to future stockholders. It may have slight interest in maintaining conditions in which a reasonable market price is established. On the contrary, it may issue financial statements of a misleading character or distribute informal news items which further its own market manipulators. We must conclude, therefore, that the interests of ownership and control are

in large measure opposed if the interests of the latter grow primarily out of the desire for personal monetary gain.[30]

Why should enforced disclosure be necessary? Voluntary improvements in corporate reporting are not unknown, and could conceivably lead to a higher valuation of the firm's assets by the public compared with companies which were otherwise equivalent but had failed to disclose as much information. Greater disclosure has in fact usually been resisted by managements, often under the claim that valuable information will be passed on to competitors, implying that such information has 'public good' characteristics. There is little question that more information has been brought forth than would have been disclosed voluntarily.[31] Uniformly enforced practices may well promote a certain mediocrity, but it may well be so that 'because they foster comparability between firms, standards help analysts and potential investors; there is even something to be said for the view that it is better if all firms issue second-rate figures on the same bases, than first-rate figures on conflicting bases'.[32]

In the broader context of economic history, the development of accounting technique cannot merely be assumed to have been adequate or 'good enough' for the problems with which it was confronted, since this very aspect of behaviour shaped the environment in which firms functioned and acted as a constraint both on the magnitude and the extent of their activities. For those confirmed in the view of the existence of an earlier, golden age of entrepreneurial capitalism when entrepreneurs maximised the value of the firm, it may be disconcerting to note for instance that 'even in the late eighteenth century and early nineteenth century many substantial partnerships did not use the double-entry system. The widespread adoption of double entry in England was a feature of the nineteenth century, probably the latter part of it. The development of the accounting profession was a major influence in its adoption'.[33]

The general aspects of nineteenth century accounting in Britain may be summarised as follows:

a lack of provision or systematic procedure to deal with depreciation and contingencies

the publication of a balance sheet without a profit statement and without a professional audit

the failure to provide copies of the audited balance sheet to shareholders (these being offered for inspection only at the Annual General Meeting)

the failure to require that holding companies present consolidated financial statements.

These basic characteristics were re-affirmed by the Companies Act of 1907.[34] Despite the slow accretion of professional accounting and auditing practices in Britain and the US, it can be said with little exaggeration that until the passage of the Companies Act of 1948 (the comparable date in the US was 1933) the state of the company's financial health was fundamentally the affair of those who ran it. Indeed, until the Royal Mail case of 1931 in Britain (to be discussed below), very little meaning could be attached to a firm's profitability figures:

> Provided it was done in good faith and in the interests of the company, the director could, within wide limits, present final accounts embodying deliberate and material deviations from the application of the accounting conventions. In appropriate circumstances the profits, and hence net assets, could be under-stated, for example by depreciating assets faster than was necessary, by treating capital expenditures as current revenue expenditures, and by providing excessively for contingencies. In this way smaller profits could be disclosed, without shareholders being made aware of the approximate magnitude of the undisclosed reserves; and the reinvestment of profits could be made easier. [Note: a prominent company chairman in the 1930s (the late Mr. Arthur Chamberlain) said: 'it is better not to show more (profit) and run the risk of exciting appetites'.][35]

In inter-war Britain, a company chairman could state that he was bringing to the accounts 'just as much … as will enable us to pay dividends we recommend and placing to general reserve or adding to carry forward just as much as will make a pretty balance sheet'.[36] It was not until the 1948 Act that the profit and loss account had to be attached to the balance sheet and auditor's report (which were available to all shareholders since 1908) and thus distributed to all shareholders, and not only to those in attendance at the general meeting.[37] Even the 1948 Act, a watershed in twentieth century UK company legislation, remained vague on such questions as a consistent approach to depreciation.[38] In Britain and in the US disclosure requirements have been gradually extended since the passage of their respective legislation, professional accounting bodies have made increasing demands for uniformity and precision (though the continued level of controversy indicates that these are far from settled matters), with the disclosure demands of the Stock Exchange in both countries greater than those to be found in the company law.

There can be little doubt that the long-term growth of professionalism of the accounting profession, coupled with the imposition of legal and institutional demands for firm disclosure, have been important in giving owners a progressively greater ability to monitor their wealth holdings. The crisis depicted by Berle and Means in 1932 was real enough, reflecting an atavism in the response of legal and professional institutions to the emergence of the large, widely-held company. The subsequent half-century's development reflects systematic attempts at its alleviation.

In this section we have so far implicitly conceded that the monitoring of managers by owners is due to a conflict of goals between these two groups. But can we say anything about the key actors in the conflict, besides the rather uninteresting statement that they proceed to maximise their respective utilities? A common assumption about the owner–entrepreneur and the owner–rentier is that they would both be desirous of maximising the wealth–value of their share of the firm. The owner–entrepreneur, while numerically an insignificant figure in the largest corporations in contemporary life, retains a symbolic importance in economic theory by illustrating how a firm's behaviour would be different if it *were* run by such a figure, as opposed to a professional manager.

There is little reason to doubt that individuals can be found who fit well into the mould of the (long-term) profit maximising entrepreneur.[39] The overall historical record is, however, discouraging with regard to this hypothesis. For nineteenth century Britain it has commonly been argued that the existence of the family firm structure of ownership set limits to the pace of economic development; on the continent, family firms are said to have been reluctant to invest in new capital equipment because of the risks it would entail for the family fortune.[40] For the US at the turn of the century Chandler reports that 'the few firms among those studied here that have remained family held have tended to be slower in changing both structure and strategy than the others'; similar conclusions have been reached for firms in the post-war UK.[41]

In general terms, owner–entrepreneurial firms seem to reflect the background and propensities of their owners. Firms such as Du Pont and Polaroid (Edward Land) are widely thought to have 'over invested' in research and development from a wealth maximisation point of view due to the technical orientation of the founders: the freedom of the owner to indulge whimsicalities, eccentricities and obsessions is less likely to be present with a professional manager. Henry Ford's continuing devotion in the 1920s to the Model T and his defeat by GM's professional manager Alfred Sloan perhaps suggests a replacement of Schumpeter's view of twentieth century capitalism as a movement from control by the creative, dynamic entrepreneur to the dull, bureaucratised manager with the alternative perspective, admittedly also simplistic, of the amateurish (albeit inspired) owner being replaced by the systematic wealth maximising professional.

Ultimately, the aspirations and actions of the owner–entrepreneur, like those of the owner–rentier, are questions of empirical observation and not of deduction. With regard to the passive wealth holder, it is possible to argue that he or she attempts to pursue a (risk constrained) wealth maximisation strategy in the contemporary world. But to what point in the past does this become a reasonable presumption? It must be remembered that, for instance, the formal derivation of the price of a share under the assumption of a fixed growth in dividends was popularised in the *professional* literature only relatively recently.[42] If there be any tendency for Life to imitate Art (with, presumably, a long and variable lag) then even the most greedy shareholder of a relatively short time ago was without the conceptual framework necessary for value maximisation.

But were shareholders desirous of maximising value? There is some evidence to suggest that the traditional strategy of the 'rational' shareholder until fairly recently was to try to maximise, not the value of the share, but the current dividends emanating from those shares. Whether or not there existed sufficient wealth-maximising shareholders at the margin to compensate for such an attitude is uncertain, but it is clear that managements took their shareholders' dividend obsession very seriously indeed. This may have been a key motivating factor for the holding of secret reserve accounts in Britain. Until what is popularly known as the Kylsant or Royal Mail case of 1931, the use of secret reserve accounts in order to stabilise profits for dividend purposes was generally accepted accounting practice.[43] The following exchange took place when Lord Kylsant's defence attorney cross-examined a witness in court:

> Are there not many cases in which a reserve of this kind is made into the credit of the year's profit and loss, and no mention is made that reserves have been called upon?
> *There are such cases.*
> Is it done by firms of the very highest repute?
> *Yes.*
> Is it your view that no exception can be taken to that practice?
> *As a principle, no exception could be taken.*[44]

Now, what are we to make of all this? At one level it may be argued that, even if secret reserve accounts are out of the question at the present day, it has continued to be a common practice for changes in dividends to be more sluggish than movements in overall profitability. This phenomenon is usually explained by the long-term signalling role that dividends play in the external assessment of firm performance. Furthermore, cynics may argue that contemporary managements can approximate the effect of these secret reserve accounts by failing to revalue assets fully.[45] In this view, little has really changed.

Here, however, we suggest that a continuous transformation has been taking place in the attitudes of individuals involved in the operation of companies. The modern enterprise, whether dominated by owner–entrepreneurs, professional managers, or owner–rentiers is the product of a business culture that puts a well-defined and explicit emphasis on the maximisation of the value of the firm: any separation of ownership from control will therefore be of progressively less significance. But even if all participants were to share this common goal, there would still be an asymmetry of time rate of discount and of access to company information among economic actors. Since managers differ inevitably from rentiers both in the commitment of their human capital and in their access to insider information, a divergence of attitudes is likely to remain. But what form is this divergence likely to take?

Our discussion so far would seem to indicate that, at least for earlier times, there might have been some validity to the stereotype of a conflict between the owner–rentier, desirous of maximising wealth, and the rapacious manager, in pursuit of personal reward, to the detriment of the value of the firm. It is possible, however, to put a different interpretation upon at least one aspect of this conflict:

> For salaried managers the continuing existence of their enterprises was essential to their lifetime careers. Their primary goal was to assure continuing use of and, therefore, continuing flow of material to their facilities. They were far more willing than were the owners (the stockholders) to reduce or even forego current dividends in order to maintain long term viability of their organisations.[46]

Thus, according to Chandler, in many cases professional managers were carrying on a 'heroic' attempt to maximise the long-term profitability of the firm, i.e. the value of the firm, all the while fending off myopic, dividend hungry owner–rentiers, eager to do nothing other than fleece the firm. From one perspective, that of the Miller–Modigliani theorem,[47] the level of firm dividends should have no effect on firm value. If, however, we accept for the moment the more commonly held presumption that the level of dividend payout *is* of consequence and that the phenomenon described above was not untypical, how shall we interpret it? In the past owner–manager conflicts have been seen as confirmation of the notion that managerially-dominated firms emphasise(d) sales or growth maximisation to the detriment of the owners, who wanted to maximise firm value. But is it not at least possible to consider Chandler's proposition? We have no powerful reasons for asserting here a strong belief in his hypothesis as opposed to its alternative. In neo-classical analysis however, with its invariant assumption that individuals are the best judges of their own interests, it is not possible even to consider the proposition that professional managers have tried to maximise the wealth of owners *despite* the impediments imposed by the latter. (We return to this question in chapter 6.)

But what indeed can we say about the goals of managers? There is some evidence to suggest that the sociology of management has been moving in the direction of an internalisation of maximisation of the value of the firm or the individual project as a personal goal,[48] which is consistent with its ever more explicit and precise emphasis in the business texts used to train managers. More straightforwardly, remuneration of executives in the US has become progressively more linked to firm performance. (This has been somewhat less true in the UK.)[49]

What emerges from the historical literature is that differences between the psychology, sociology and propensities of managers, on the one hand, and owner–entrepreneurs on the other, and the changes in these differences over time were of relatively little consequence compared with the question of the evolution of the technical facility of the executants.

Railroads in the US in the 1850s were under great pressure to innovate and develop new business practices such as cost accounting, but their success at these tasks was due in no little extent to the existence of a pool of technically sophisticated personnel needed to facilitate these developments, a group whose technical and analytical skills few other industries could match.[50] Similarly, those individuals to whom Chandler gives the most credit as organisational innovators are indifferently a collection of professional managers and owner–entrepreneurs, but what most of them had in common was either engineering or some other form of technical training.[51] What was rare then has become progressively more commonplace.

The real managerial revolution has little to do with a developing separation of ownership and control, but rather with the continuous transformation of the technical competence and overall facility of the individuals involved in the direction of companies. As such skills become more interchangeable and widespread, it becomes ever more likely that the market for managerial talent will be such that any differences in behaviour between managers of 'managerially controlled' and 'owner-controlled' firms will tend to disappear.[52]

It is difficult, however, within the domain of neo-classical theory to deal with the more significant aspects of the evolution of managerial competence and facility. Usually these skills are considered to be 'sufficient' for the environment in which actors find themselves operating, and developments take place in terms of conflicts and their resolution in the context of that environment. It is in this sense that the managerial literature depicted in figure 5.1 is well within Edgeworth's neo-classical focus on conflicts and their resolution: *at no point does it consider whether the very constraints in which the conflict takes place (represented here by the 'profit' function) might be transformed by the change in ownership structure*. We contend, on the contrary, that changes in the ability of actors to deal with their environment has had a major effect in shaping it: this real, and continuing managerial revolution has been a crucial factor in the development and evolution of the competitive process, and its role cannot be explained within the purview of orthodox theory.

Competition and the Managerial Revolution

'Profit Maximisation' and the Evolution of Professional Skills

The most important factors affecting the evolution of the business environment are changes in the propensities and capacities of those individuals who control and administer the affairs of firms, complemented by parallel developments in transportation, communication and in the quality and accessibility of information relevant to business activity. We shall be bringing together these various aspects in chapter 9, but here we shall deal with the effect of the transformation of business management on these developments. The almost inexorable tendency for the technical facility of management to increase over time, both in terms of the level of relevant skills and the number of individuals so trained implies a secular tendency for the rate of competitiveness to increase in the capitalist market economy. Such an hypothesis is incapable of meaningful formulation in the context of mainstream economics, which is largely concerned with the adaptation of individuals to a given, exogenously specified environment, one not shaped by the behaviour of its participants.

There is a further, rather curious aspect of mainstream economics which militates against the above hypothesis, which is its Hegelian, almost mystical tendency to treat much of economic history *as if it were a branch of the history of economic thought*. A truly remarkable example of this phenomenon may be found in the reception given by economists to Hall and Hitch's 1939 study, documenting the widespread use of full cost or average cost pricing by firms.[53] Coming as it did at the end of a decade largely devoted to attacks upon perfect competition and, consequently, upon the rule of setting price equal to marginal cost, the study was taken as confirmation of a drift away from competitive practices (which *surely* must have existed in Marshall's day) and towards non-competitive practices. The Hall and Hitch study was far from being a confirmation of the development of imperfectly competitive practices from an earlier period in which firms competitively set price equal to marginal cost. It was in fact a documentation of the partial progress that had been made up to that date in Britain towards the creation and diffusion of accounting procedures which contained even a minimal level of uniformity and comparability between firms. For the first time there was the possibility of even a modicum of resemblance to the 'rational' cost and revenue calculations outlined in neo-classical theory.

Pity the poor accountant – decades of Promethean effort, only to be told by the economist that he was aiding and abetting non-competitive behaviour and that, in any case, he did not understand the concepts of marginal or opportunity cost! This view differs radically from that which emerges from business history. Despite Charles Babbage's famous plea in 1832 for the importance of knowing 'the precise expense of every process' and of having 'a correct analysis of the expense of the several processes of any manufacture',[54] early accounting texts were capable of giving rules for the recording of transactions, but simple cost calculations, much less their allocation in complex situations, are not to be found.[55]

In the US much of the pioneering work in cost accounting, including the allocation of direct and indirect costs took place in the mid-nineteenth century among the railroads. It emerged in this sector for two reasons. First, it contained a relative plentitude of technically expert people and secondly, a naive approach to marginal cost pricing here would be especially deceptive and indeed treacherous. With the emergence of giant firms, interest in the problems of costing increased with the growing scale and complexity of business, the ever greater importance of overheads in total costs and the need for a method for setting prices in heavy goods sectors such as engineering.[56] The latter issue was one of major significance. Since nineteenth century firms almost invariably did not account for depreciation, it was possible for firms systematically to underestimate their consumption of capital:

> If a firm's revenues were sufficient to cover interest payments and taxes, but not the depreciation of its capital, it might not even realize it was operating at a loss. As officers of the International Paper Company [in the US] admitted in 1908 'There is no queston in our minds that it was a mistake not to have charged off depreciation. Had such charge been made, paper would never have sold at the prices for which we have sold it'.[57]

In Britain in 1899, an authority could write of 'the marvellous absence of really useful and practical knowledge as to the cost of an article produced',[58] and in the US modern costing practices did not begin to be diffused until after 1900.[59] As a general practice, firms paid dividends out of profit calculated gross of depreciation, unaware they might be operating at a loss. The latter practice, as might be imagined often resulted in serious problems when capital had to be replaced.[60] Well into the century the giant meat packers Armour and Swift could not estimate their assets, costs and rate of return on capital.[61] The evolution and implementation of procedures to calculate costs and, therefore, profits in any but the simplest operations were long and arduous.

The developments in cost accounting at the turn of the century were part of a broader movement in the direction of the scientific management of firms – a movement which was designed to make firms behave in a more efficacious manner, thereby transforming the competitive environment in which these firms functioned. In a paper delivered in 1895, Fredrick W. Taylor criticised earlier schemes which based costs on past experience. Instead, he believed that norms should result from standard time and output, to be determined scientifically through careful job analyses and time and motion studies of the work involved.[62] Taylor's famous interventions into the work process were clearly not based on an Alchian-like presumption that norms of efficiency had already been established by the external (competitive) environment. On the contrary, new norms could be created by acts of imagination and will from the entrepreneur or company manager, these acts constrained only by the facts of nature and the obduracy of the labour force.

These developments were mirrored in the field of cost accounting. The late nineteenth century was dominated by procedures for calculating actual cost – the total of direct wages, materials costs and overheads. For the purpose of using costs as a *control mechanism* for the firm, such procedures had many inadequacies – how does one deal with interest on capital, plant obsolescence, the allocation of overheads and the burden of unused capacity, or materials bought at different prices? The main lines of advance in this period were a refinement in the apportionment of overheads, the development of methods used to isolate the effect on costs of changes in the scale of output and of techniques for attempting to separate out the different factors which determine costs.

But such developments were far from sufficient for the needs of scientific management. What was needed was a concept of standard costs – a measure which could be used to enforce a *normative*, cost control view of the firm's budget, rather than a positive, retrospective view of the firm's costs. The comparison of the firm's costs with outside values 'seems to be the nearest that the nineteenth century came to standard costing as we know it'.[63]

The development in parallel of standard costing and of scientific management in the twentieth century was not fortuitous. The new costing procedures were a necessary prerequisite for the operationalising of the new schemes of scientific management, and 'standard costs mean little without standard processes and standard operating times, such as F. W. Taylor and his followers developed'.[64] It may well be that the simpler practices of earlier times were on the whole 'adequate' for the purposes to which they were put – most especially in small, closely held firms,[65] and that the new tools did not emerge until there was a 'need' for them. But such an approach verges on the tautological. The development of standard costing, combined with advancements in the mechanized means of keeping cost records, the growing integration of costing and production control, the application of costing to the selling and distribution functions and the diffusion of these techniques over the century have been crucial for the 'rational' control of businesses and the evolution of the competitive environment.

This interaction between the quality of a firm's accounting procedures and its internal processes of control continues to the present day. Current best practice in manufacturing planning and control (MPC) systems takes as a prerequisite data that are 'appropriate, consistent and accurate', with the benefit from a good MPC system deriving largely from a substitution of information for organisational slack. The creation of an integrated database 'provides new avenues for cooperation in strategic planning, budgeting and control ... the establishment of financial budgets and strategic plans become integrated with the data base, its operations, its maintenance and its accounting performance measurement'. But the cost accounting system only yields usable information from normative control if it is 'accurately reporting every detailed transaction as materials move in and out of stockrooms through various production conversion steps'[66] in the context of the MPC system itself: a 'rational' manufacturing system and its associated system of accounting must develop together. Thus it has recently been argued that contemporary cost accounting, with its emphasis on direct labour costs is inadequate for measuring the impact of the new 'just-in-time' manufacturing procedures (to be described in chapter 8), with their savings in materials and overheads.[67]

A factor contributing to the emergence of modern managerial practices has been the development and the universalisation of the literature used to train managers. Vague notions of acceptable rates of return and payback periods have been replaced with more 'exact' techniques such as net present value and the explicit consideration of risk in the evaluation of projects. There can be no question that texts in such fields as business finance, operations research and accounting have grown incomparably more sophisticated over time, and show a continuing attempt to professionalise the subject and raise its analytical level. There is substantial evidence that while the use of these techniques in business practice is greater in the US than in the UK, in both countries their dispersal has continued to increase rapidly in the 1970s and 1980s.[68] Even observers who are most cynical about the efficacy of such techniques or who doubt their superiority in practical situations to rules of thumb[69] may be willing to concede the unifying effect upon the sociology of business of clearly defined goals of value maximisation. The demands made in contemporary business courses may also act as a screening device – attracting analytically inclined, technically competent individuals, and siphoning out many who were formerly the standard output of business programmes.

Until the emergence of modern business practices and a large body of individuals available to administer them, there were severe constraints upon the size of firm and its sphere of activity, both in geographical terms and in the range and complexity of its operations. While there is no presumption that these problems have been 'solved' in the present day,[70] we can at least partially identify rational and competitive firm behaviour with an ability to calculate the relation between revenues and costs in its *own* operations and then make estimates of *potential* revenues and costs in *alternative* spheres. The development of cost accounting then plays no small part in the evolution of the competitive process.

Business Management and the Growth of Competition

The inexorable increase in the quantity of business information, the improvement of the quality and comparability of business data with the development of the accounting profession and the adoption of standards of reporting and the general improvement in communication of all kinds – all these factors, coupled with the progressive professionalisation of management have generated a long-term tendency for competitiveness to increase in the capitalist market economy. These factors in the context of mainstream Marshallian analysis might be thought to inhibit the development of competitive practices. In a given (market) environment, factors such as a growing uniformity of accounting standards and an expansion in publicly available information might be thought to make tacit co-ordination less difficult between firms, and there are undoubtedly specific historical situations (especially when activity in the overall economy or in a particular sphere is stagnant) when such an analysis is relevant. We believe, however, that events in the long-term must be evaluated *not* in the context of a given environment, but by how this environment is shaped and affected by the factors mentioned above, most especially the *behaviour* of the participants in that environment. The managerialist stereotype is of an historical evolution from the competitive entrepreneur to the bureaucratic, managerial oligopolist. We may counterpoise it with another one:

> Formerly, men in, say, the cement business knew exactly what to do with their profits: pay out part of them to stockholders and reinvest most of the balance in cement plants. But anyone who sets out to clarify his ultimate objective comes, fairly rapidly, to the proposition that his main objective is maximizing the return on his capital and, thereby, raising the value of his stock. And when he gets to *that*, he proceeds inexorably to the thought that alternative investments may yield higher pay-offs than cement. When he gets used to the idea that alternative investments are not only legal and moral, but profitable he is pretty far along the road to becoming a conglomerator.[71]

Without necessarily agreeing with all aspects of the above quotation, or pre-empting our discussion in chapter 8, it is hard to deny its essential point: the historical identification of firms with specific industries was not an externally imposed constraint, but one which was due to *the behaviour of the individuals in control of those firms*. In inter-war Britain, 'While some managers undoubtedly transferred to new industries, management still tended to be industry specific, and the "steelmen" or "cotton men" who transferred did not take with them more than very basic skills.'[72] If they stayed within a specific sphere of activity either out of personal propensity or because of plain ignorance of the opportunities which loomed elsewhere, such behaviour would have a dampening effect on the rate of equalisation of profits and the process of competition.

It is quite possible, of course, that our cement manufacturer was right not to cross into another sphere – that his or her traditional way of doing business was so specialised, so idiosyncratic even down to the way the company books were kept – that it would have been impossible to cross over industry boundaries successfully. Modern managements, however, will tend to be less inhibited about moving into alternative spheres of activity, and are likely to have better information on profitable opportunities. Furthermore, techniques of doing business such as accounting and finance have become much more standardised and professionalised, so that new entrants to a sector are less likely to have some of the problems which might have befallen our cement maker.

To the extent that these managerial differential rents have fallen between spheres of activity, the process of equalisation has accelerated. Of course, apologists for conglomeration have claimed that there are no problems in running any sphere in this age of scientific management. As we shall see, while there is more than a little evidence to the contrary, it is hard to deny that the very existence of the conglomerate phenomenon is striking evidence of the development of managerial technique and of the extension of its sphere of vision.

In a similar way, the emergence of the multinational is a powerful indication of the evolution of management skills and of the expansion in their perception of the relevant domain of their activity. Such a phenomenon would be impossible without the evolution of a very high level of organisational competence, a great expansion of the information available to the firm on a world-wide scale and even some sociological evolution of at least part of the managerial class in a less parochial direction. While the explosion of multinationals took place only after the Second World War for specific historical reasons, the above mentioned factors which act as essential prerequisites are so obvious that they sometimes escape mention. And yet they are central to the expansion of the geographical domain of economic activity and of competition onto a world-wide scale.

The evolution of management activity has been extending the domain of competition by breaking down barriers between markets and by expanding their geographical extent. It has also resulted in an acceleration of the *speed* of the equalisation process, with a growth in the information available about profitable opportunities and the growing rapidity and flexibility of managerial response to such possibilities. These changes may not in any way be identified solely with the largest companies: the small company may be just as modern in its business techniques as the large company, as these techniques have become commonplace. Thus, the development of the information industry and of sophisticated management techniques have permitted the creation of large, viable decentralised organisations, but also work in favour of increased competitive activity from small firms.

As these management skills have been cheapened and dispersed, they have permitted the development not only of modern small firms, but of new firms located far away from the origins of market capitalism. Journalists have discovered that not only is there a Protestant Ethic, but Confucian, Shinto and other 'Ethics' which seem at least as powerful as the original force. This dispersion of modern business practices and attitudes, coupled with other, related developments such as the continuing improvements in the availability of information and the speed and quality of transport point to a secular tendency for competitiveness to increase in market capitalist society.

We proceed now to examine the meaning of this managerial revolution in greater depth.

Notes

1. Knight, F. *Risk, Uncertainty and Profit* London School of Economics – Scarce Tracts in Economics and Political Science 1933, p. xxi.
2. Marshall, A. *Principles of Economics* Macmillan 8th edn 1920, book IV, ch. 12.
3. See Herman, E. *Corporate Control, Corporate Power* Cambridge University

1981, p. 7 for a discussion of the famous Pujo Committee report of 1913, and Veblen, T. *The Theory of Business Enterprise* Transaction Books 1978; reprint of the 1904 edn.

4. Ch. 3 of Berle, A. and G. Means *The Modern Corporation and Private Property* Harcourt, Brace and World revised edn 1968. A recent issue of the *Journal of Law and Economics* – June 1983 – was devoted to this book. The contributors included George Stigler, Eugene Fama and Gardner Means.

5. Berle and Means (note 4), chs 4 and 5.

6. Ibid., p. 66.

7. Ibid., p. 66.

8. Herman (note 3); his study will be discussed in detail below.

9. Berle and Means (note 4), pp. 85–110.

10. Larner, R. *Management Control and the Large Corporation* Dunellen 1970, p. 22; Florence, P. *Ownership, Control and Success of Large Companies* Sweet and Maxwell 1961; Burch, P. *The Managerial Revolution Reassessed: Family Control in America's Large Corporations* Lexington Books 1972; Fitch, R. and M. Oppenheimer 'Who Rules the Corporations?' *Socialist Revolution* July–August 1970 and September-October 1970; Kotz, D. *Bank Control of Large Corporations in the United States* University of California, Berkeley 1978 and other works cited by Herman in chs 1 to 4.

11. Herman (note 3), pp. 17–18.

12. Ibid., pp. 53–66.

13. Nyman, S. and A. Silberston, 'The Ownership and Control of Industry' *Oxford Economic Papers* new series 30(1) (March 1978): 74–101.

14. Machlup, F. 'Theories of the Firm: Marginalist, Behavioral, Managerial' *The American Economic Review* 57 (March 1967): 1–33. Footnote omitted.

15. Scitovsky, T. 'A Note on Profit Maximization and its Implications' *The Review of Economic Studies* 11(1) (Winter 1943): 57–60.

16. Gravelle, H. and R. Rees *Microeconomics* Longman 1981, p. 341, though an alternative view of the matter is posed in Jensen, M. and W. Meckling 'Theories of the Firm: Managerial Behavior, Agency Costs and Ownership Structure' *Journal of Financial Economics* 3(4) (October 1976): 305–60.

17. Prominent examples are Monsen, R. and A. Downs 'A Theory of Large Managerial Firms' *Journal of Political Economy* 73(3) (June 1965): 221–36 and Williamson, O. 'Managerial Discretion and Business Behavior' *American Economic Review* 53(5) (December 1963): 1032–57. This, of course, was written before Williamson met the Two Alfreds (Sloan and Chandler) on the road to Damascus (see ch. 6).

18. A minor example of which was perpetrated by the author: Auerbach, P. and J. Siegfried 'Executive Compensation and Corporation Control' *Nebraska Journal of Economics and Business* 13(3) (Summer 1974): 3–16.

19. See, for example, Hacker, A. (ed.) *The Corporation Takeover* Anchor Books 1965; the most popular exposition is in Schumpeter, J. *Capitalism, Socialism and Democracy* Harper and Row third edn 1950; first edn 1942.

20. Jensen and Meckling (note 16). This article will be discussed in detail in ch. 6.

21. Herman dismisses these aspects of the Berle and Means study and he (certainly no apologist for the corporation) makes it clear that manifestations of fraudulent behaviour are relatively minor compared with the good old days (p. 157). Recently in the US, there has been controversy over the revival of the issuance of shares with differential voting power.

22. Berle and Means (note 4), p. 253.
23. Carey, J. 'The Origins of Modern Financial Reporting' in Lee, T. and R. Parker (eds) *The Evolution of Corporate Financial Reporting* Nelson 1979, pp. 241–64.
24. See Midgley, K. 'How Much Control do Shareholders Exercise?' *Lloyds Bank Review* 114 (October 1974): 28–41.
25. Baker, H. and J. Haslem 'Information Needs of Individual Investors' *Journal of Accounting* 136 (November 1973): 64–9.
26. Edey, H. and P. Panitpakdi 'British Company Accounting and the Law 1844–1900' in Littleton, A.C. and B.S. Yamey (eds) *Studies in the History of Accounting* Sweet and Maxwell 1956, pp. 356–379.
27. Berle and Means (note 4), p. 247.
28. For the UK, see Nyman and Silberston (note 13), and Minns, R. and C. Hird 'The Concentration of Corporate Power' *New Statesman* 24 October 1980. For the US see Herman (note 3), ch. 4. By the mid-1980s institutions (including companies, government and others) controlled almost 40 per cent of shares in the US and almost 80 per cent in the UK – see the chart p. 23 in the *Economist* survey *International Banking* 16 March 1985.
29. 'More Aggression Shown on a Broader Front' *Financial Times* survey *International Fund Management* 18 November 1985.
30. Berle and Means (note 4), p. 115.
31. Leftwich, R., R. Watts and J. Zimmerman 'Voluntary Corporate Disclosure: the Case of Interim Reporting' *Journal of Accounting Research* 19 supplement (1981): 50–6. The role of legislation in enforcing disclosure will be discussed further in ch. 6.
32. Baxter, W. 'Accounting Standards – Boon or Curse?' *Accounting and Business Research* 12(45) (Winter 1981): 3–10.
33. Yamey, B. 'Some Topics in the History of Financial Accounting in England, 1500–1900' in Baxter, W. and S. Davidson (eds) *Studies in Accounting* The Institute of Chartered Accountants in England and Wales 1977 (footnote omitted), pp. 11–34. An extensive bibliography on the history of accounting may be found in Parker, R. *Management Accounting: An Historical Perspective* Macmillan 1969, pp. 75–122.
34. Lee and Parker (note 23) introduction, pp. 3–4 and Lee, T. *Company Financial Statements* Nelson 1976, ch. 2.
35. Yamey (note 33).
36. Quoted in Hannah, L. 'Takeover Bids in Britain Before 1950: An Exercise in Business "Pre-History"' *Business History* 16(1) (1974): 65–77.
37. Marriner, S. 'Company Financial Statements as Source Material for Business Historians' *Business History* 22(2)(1980): 203–35.
38. Ibid.; Edey, H. ['Company Accounting in the Nineteenth and Twentieth Centuries' in Lee and Parker (note 23) pp. 222–30] suggests that the 1929 Companies Act in the UK already went a substantial way in the direction of presenting the form and contents of the balance sheet.
39. Examples of (small) firms which seem to adhere to textbook notions of rationality may be found in Barback, R. *The Pricing of Manufactures* Macmillan 1964 and Early, J. 'Marginal Policies of Excellently Managed Companies' *American Economic Review* 46(1) (March 1946): 44–70.
40. Pollard, S. *The Genesis of Modern Management* Harvard University 1965, chs 1 and 2, Landes, D. *The Unbound Prometheus* Cambridge University 1969, ch. 3.

41. Chandler, A. *Strategy and Structure* MIT 1962, p. 380 and Channon, D. *The Strategy and Structure of British Enterprise* Macmillan 1971, ch. 4.
42. The share price derivation was first given in Gordon, M. and M. Shapiro 'Capital Equipment Analysis: The Required Rate of Profit' *Management Science* 3 (October 1956): 102–10.
43. Lee, T. 'Company Financial Statements' in Lee and Parker (note 26) and Marriner (note 37), pp. 15–39.
44. Hastings, P. 'The Case of the Royal Mail' in Baxter and Davidson (note 33), pp. 339–46.
45. See Griffiths, I. *Creative Accounting* Sidgwick and Jackson 1986, ch. 9. Griffiths (p. 5) also describes less subtle contemporary versions of secret reserves: 'There is a well known British company, a constituent of the *Financial Times* 30 index [whose] finance director has what he calls his bottom drawer in which he keeps the fruits of his creative accounting – be they profits or losses – which he feeds out in order to ensure that the share price is kept within closely defined bands which reflect the company's genuine worth at a given moment'.
46. Chandler, A. *The Visible Hand* Harvard University 1977, p. 10; see also pp. 146, 387.
47. Miller, M. and F. Modigliani 'Dividend Policy, Growth, and the Valuation of Shares' *Journal of Business* 34(4) (October 1961): 411–33.
48. Nichols, T. *Ownership, Control and Ideology* George Allen 1969, chs 9–11 and Useem, M. 'Classwide Rationality in the Politics of Managers and Directors of Large Corporations in the US and Great Britain' *Administrative Science Quarterly* 27(2) (June 1982): 199–226.
49. For the US, the classic study is Lewellen, W. *The Ownership Income of Management* Columbia University 1971. For the UK, see Pratten, C. *The Management of Operating Businesses by Large Companies* Gower 1986, ch. 10.
50. Chandler (note 46), ch. 3.
51. Chandler (note 41), p. 317.
52. Fama, E. 'Agency Problems and the Theory of the Firm' *Journal of Political Economy* 88(2) (April 1980): 288–307. What we have described is the implicit historical development which stands as a prerequisite to this article's conclusions.
53. Hall, R. and C. Hitch 'Price Theory and Business Behaviour' *Oxford Economic Papers* 2 (May 1939): 12–45.
54. As quoted in Solomons, D., 'The Historical Development of Costing' in Solomons, D. (ed.) *Studies in Cost Analyis* Sweet and Maxwell 1968, pp. 3–49. Solomons notes that Babbage did not give any guidance in his book as to how industrialists were to achieve these objectives.
55. Chandler (note 46), p. 39.
56. Solomons (note 54).
57. Lamoreaux, N. *The Great Merger Movement in American Business 1895–1904* Cambridge University 1985, pp. 53–4. Footnote omitted.
58. Quoted in Solomons (note 54).
59. Chandler (note 46), p. 278.
60. See Brief, R. 'The Origin and Evolution of 19th-century Asset Accounting' *Business History Review* 40 (Spring 1966): 1–23 and Lamoreaux (note 57), pp. 53–5.
61. Chandler (note 46), p. 397.

62. Chandler, A. 'The United States: Evolution of Enterprise' in Mathias, P. and M. Postan (eds) *The Cambridge History of Europe* vol. VII part 2 Cambridge University 1978, pp. 70–133.

63. Solomons (note 54).

64. Ibid.

65. See Yamey (note 33) and Yamey, B. 'Accounting and the Rise of Capitalism: Further Notes on a Theme by Sombart' *Journal of Accounting Research* 2 (Autumn 1964): 117–36; an alternative interpretation of the role of accounting may be found in McKendrick, J. 'Josiah Wedgewood and Cost Accounting in the Industrial Revolution' *Economic History Review* 23 (1970): 45–67.

66. Vollmann, T., W. Berry and D. C. Whybark *Manufacturing Planning and Control Systems* Richard D. Irwin 1984, p. 85.

67. 'Old Practices that Distort Decisions' *Financial Times* 1 July 1987.

68. The dissemination of the techniques of project evaluation is extensively discussed in Parker (note 33). The most recent study is Pike, R. and M. Wolfe 'A Review of Capital Investment Trends in Larger Companies' *University of Bradford Management Centre* Occasional Paper No. 8701–8702 March 1987.

69. Baumol, W. and R. Quandt 'Rules of Thumb and Optimally Imperfect Decisions' *American Economic Review* 54 (March 1964): 23–46.

70. '"We usually didn't know until about a year after a car went out of production whether we actually made money on it", laments one former high level GM official. Adds a manufacturing consultant working for GM: "It's obvious GM has a problem determining where its true costs are."' 'General Motors: What Went Wrong' *Business Week* 16 March 1987.

71. Editors of *Fortune* 'The Case for Conglomerates' in *The Conglomerate Commotion* Viking 1970, p. 7.

72. Hannah, L. *The Rise of the Corporate Economy* Methuen second edn 1983, p. 106.

6

Contrasting Views of the Corporation

Foundations of a Paradigm

Coase and the Existence of the Firm

It is with some trepidation that the question of the existence of the firm is posed here. For economists suffering from insecurity of a psychological or professional kind, there is a certain hesitancy in announcing to the outside world that two of the profession's central concerns in recent decades have been the need to demonstrate the existence of firms and the existence of money. The former problem, however, has become a crucial issue as a result of the influence of an article by Ronald Coase from 1937:[1] its subsequent role in both the principal–agent and the markets–hierarchies approach should become self evident.

Why do firms exist? demanded Coase: '... in view of the fact that it is usually argued that co-ordination will be done by the price mechanism, why is such organisation necessary? Why are there "islands of conscious power"?' His answer is that there are costs of organising production through the price mechanism, namely those of

1 discovering what the relevant prices are,
2 the costs of negotiating and concluding a separate contract for each exchange transaction, and
3 it may be desired to make a long-term contract for the supply of some article or service.

Coase deduces that 'a firm is likely therefore to emerge in those cases where a very short term contract would be unsatisfactory'.

In an extremely influential article, Alchian and Demsetz[2] follow Coase in trying to explain the existence of firms, but reject his emphasis on its link to long-term agreements: 'I have no contract to continue to purchase from the grocer and neither the employer nor the employee is bound by any contractual obligations to continue their relationship. Long term contracts are not the essence of the firm'. For them, the firm exists:

1 for the proper metering of team productive processes, so that rewards can be apportioned according to productivity, and shirking can be minimised. Team production i.e. a firm, will be used if the extra product yielded by the group working together (compared to their separate efforts) is more than enough to cover the cost of organising and disciplining the team members, and
2 because the central party in the firm (the employer) finds the firm more efficient than the market for acquiring information about a large set of specific inputs.

This second point is quite close to Coase's cost of 'discovering what the right prices are', and the question of proper metering fits nicely with the principal and agent approach. Alchian and Demsetz's rather vague specification of the nature of firm organisation has retained popularity among those who prefer to think of the firm as a 'team', as opposed to any more conflictual interpretation. Williamson's synthesis, however, united the Alchian and Demsetz modifications of Coase, the essential aspects of principal and agent analysis and a dash of organisation theory, but *linked all these elements to a series of specific institutional developments* first analysed by the historian Chandler. In this sense, whatever the actual chronology, all this literature seems as if it were feeding into Williamson's *tour de force*.

But let us return to Coase. While it is certainly true, as Alchian and Demsetz point out, that it is close to tautology to say that firms are formed when the benefits of using the market are exceeded by the costs, even this is far from a trivial statement. On the contrary, it is a powerful way of structuring our analysis of business and its evolution: the market and the price mechanism exist, and exist ubiquitously – why then are there firms? It is like overhearing a 25th century conversation between robots who want to know why *homines sapientes* exist(ed). The question here is not just one of history, but of conceptual priority: can a rich array of markets exist without organisations to generate them?

Historically, the evolution and development of markets – of their extent and their depth – has been contingent on the actions pursued by traders:

> The shopkeeper, as we have seen, makes the market continuous in time, by being ready to do business on any day, not just market days. He may also do something to make it continuous in space, if he goes forth, or sends his agents to go forth, to fetch from neighbouring centres things he can profitably sell in his own centre, and for which

he can offer in return things that are available in his own place. In this way trade can grow.[3]

Firms have been *at the same time* devices for the avoidance of the market mechanism *as well as for* its extension. The option of avoiding internal organisation by the use of the market is only possible if *other* entities have been organised in sufficient depth that a 'market' appears for the service at hand. This is not the case for Coase's Robinson Crusoe trader. In Coase's article, the strong implication exists that the economy is so naturally endowed with markets that their use at a finite price is always a viable alternative to internal production:

> the operation of a market costs something and by forming an organisation and allowing some authority (an 'entrepreneur') to direct the resources, certain marketing costs are saved. The entrepreneur has to carry out his function at less cost, taking into account the fact that he may get factors of production at a lower price *than the market transactions which he superseded, because, it is always possible to revert to the open market if he fails to do this*. (italics added)

Such a position, however, is not peculiar to Coase. Indeed, it seems to have become the commonplace approach to the role of organisations in economic analysis. For Kenneth Arrow 'organisations are a means of achieving the benefit of collective action in situations in which the price system fails'.[4] But is it really coherent to speak of a price system prior to a discussion of the nature of the organisations that generate this system?

This one-sided approach, this presupposition of the existence of markets and the failure to see the role of firms in the *making* of markets informs Coase's analysis and that of his followers. It further distorts his treatment of the extent of the firm (to be examined below). One aspect of his argument will reinforce our critique:

> Changes like the telephone and telegraph which tend to reduce the cost of organising spacially will tend to increase the size of firm [unless, as Coase suggests in a footnote, they have an even greater effect in reducing the cost of using the price mechanism]. *All changes which improve managerial technique will tend to increase the size of firm*. (italics added)

Once again, markets are fully in place, so that increases in managerial technique will substitute for *already existing markets*. There is no place in this analysis for the possibility that improvements in managerial technique which are of special benefit to relatively smaller entities (e.g. inexpensive desktop computers) might cause the *creation* of markets *where none had heretofore existed*, and vertical disintegration. For Alchian and Demsetz, 'The mark of a capitalist society is that resources are owned and allocated by such nongovernmental organizations as firms, households and *markets'*. (italics added)

But whatever difficulties we have in defining firms and households, they *exist – they are entities*. Markets, on the other hand, are largely figures of speech in economics. Of the enormous number of transactions in an economy, only a tiny fraction of them take place in what may literally be described as a market. The term 'market' is a reification of a set of behavioural relations which exist between participants – a *market is not a thing but a behavioural relation*. The danger of this process of reification is that to see markets as ubiquitous, and to conceptualise them *as entities which invariably exist as alternatives to internal organisation* is to miss the interaction – in both directions – between market and organisation which is explored in chapter 8 and is central to capitalist development and its present evolution.

The Managerial Approach Extended

Principal and agent analysis, along with the markets and hierarchies paradigm have now largely displaced the 1960s managerialist literature which emerged in the wake of the Berle and Means controversy as theoretical structures for the study of the control and behaviour of the modern firm. The most distinctive contribution from this period was that of Robin Marris.[5] In his exposition, managerial utility is linked to the growth rate of the firm, which is a proxy for income, power and prestige. Unconstrained pursuit of growth is limited by the latter's negative effect on the share price of the firm, which then makes the firm more susceptible to takeover raids.

Marris's belief is that the takeover constraint is less than fully binding, so that the modern managerial firm will deviate in distinctive ways from a share price maximising firm. (It will be questioned below whether share price and value maximisation are the same thing, but for the moment the two terms will be used interchangeably.) In fact, the mechanism of takeovers is much more complex – much odder than is here implied, and it is not clear that in any consistent way it functions to punish or to punish exclusively inefficient or deviant managements. On the other hand, critics[6] of Marris who claim his model is indistinguishable from one of value maximisation because it responds in similar ways to changes in factor prices, excise taxes, etc., ignore the most powerful stylised fact in its favour: large firms have consistently expended enormous energy in the direction of merger, totally out of proportion with its indifferent effects on firm valuation. While these and other manifestations of managerial volition should not distract us from other, more fundamental tendencies in the control of the firm, it would seem difficult to argue that there have not been significant deviations from value maximisation in firm behaviour, some of which indeed may be managerial in origin.

There is little question that Marris's work, and other managerialist analysis of the owner–manager conflict have lost vogue in favour of the principal and agent paradigm. The reason for this shift is quite comprehensible in the context of the logic of contemporary theory. Marris and other managerial theorists had posed what was essentially a standard neo-classical conflict of interest problem. Owners, who wish to maximise the value of the firm (which is identified with its share price) are in conflict with managers who desire 'something else'. All participants are aware of what is taking place, and yet somehow the desires of the shareholder are thwarted. But, ask Jensen and Meckling,[7] what is so peculiar about the contract between an owner and a manager? Is it not merely a subclass of the more general problem of the monitoring of behaviour in a contractual relation?

> In an agency relationship, the principal(s) engage other parties (agents) to perform some service on their behalf. If both parties are utility maximisers, the principal will have to engage in monitoring and bonding activities to limit the divergence between the agent's decisions and the welfare of the principal. Even when these activities are undertaken, divergence is likely to result in an additional, residual loss to the principal, since the pursuit of these activities is not costless. Agency costs are thus the sum of the monitoring, bonding costs and the residual loss. The kinds of contracts which will be written between a principal and an agent (for instance between an owner and a manager) are contingent on the relative costs to the principal of monitoring and bonding and the benefits to the agent of deviating from the principal's wishes.

The firm is thus a legal fiction, and ultimately the focal point of a multitude of complex contracts between individuals: the extent of the firm becomes ambiguous. In this more general formulation, unlike the older literature, there is no need to idealise the wealth maximising potential of the owner–entrepreneur of chapter 5. If there are no costs of agency, the firm exhibits optimum wealth maximising behaviour on behalf of the owner even when ownership and management are separated.

One of the reasons for the great popularity of this approach is its apparent applicability outside the owner–manager conflict. If the examples are deftly chosen, it begins to appear as if all social relations can be reduced to (neo-classical) problems of agency. For example, until the turn of the century in Britain, management often subcontracted jobs to master workmen on the 'butty system'. These workmen hired their own labour, negotiated the price of each job with management, and organised their own work.[8] It would be unsurprising in the agency context to find that such arrangements were especially prevalent in those industries such as ship-building, in which management found it difficult to calculate the cost of complicated jobs in advance, so that it was willing to expend a great deal on bonding costs (the high price of subcontracting) to minimise sub-sequent monitoring costs.

Two problems with this kind of analysis should be mentioned in passing. First, it can have a rather *ex post* quality, so that any given arrangement between, for instance, workers and managers may be analysed as optimal after the fact. It may tell us little about the underlying historical dynamic of these relationships: the butty system began to decline in the 1890s and was replaced by wage labour as accounting techniques improved and permitted management to calculate the costs of complicated jobs in advance. Agency analysis is capable of explaining both the existence of the butty system in terms of the high costs of the monitoring of workers, as well as explaining the existence of the successor system of wage labour. But it gives us little insight into how we might go about understanding or predicting the transition from one system to another – in this framework, the accounting system and other costs of monitoring are taken as exogeneous parameters which are not under the control of management. The dynamics of change, of the development of new management (or in other contexts worker) techniques to change the parameters of the conflict between these groups are not really part of this framework. This restriction to *ex post* explanation, however, may be the best we can do in many circumstances, and so perhaps we should not consider this to be a severe flaw. We may be satisfied by what little enlightenment is offered by this theoretical structure.

A second, and more serious criticism is the restriction of this approach to purely utilitarian formulations. We believe there are many factors which determine the nature of relationships between economic groups which do not fit easily into the utilitarian framework. In the case of the butty system, one of its non-pecuniary costs which management found it worth while to eliminate was the disruptive effect upon the discipline of other workers of the example of this proud, independent group of men. Coherent explanations of economic motivation do not cease to be relevant because one chooses to label them 'sociology'.

A central difficulty with the principal–agent paradigm, a problem which it shares with traditional managerial approaches is its treatment of the question of time and uncertainty. This problem manifests itself most significantly in the conflict between owners and managers. Thus Jensen and Meckling chide Herbert Simon for his iterative 'satisficing' approach: they believe that problems involving choice with limited information are best dealt with in terms of maximisation subject to the costs of information and decision making. But to know the cost of acquiring information – to know how much you don't know – is profound knowledge indeed. What the possession of such knowledge would imply in this context is that all disputes between owners and managers are conflicts over self-interest – all participants perceive the same maximum share price (which is taken to be identical with maximum firm value), and conflict is over the division of wealth. Owner ignorance about the company (the extent of which they know) can be eliminated at a known and finite price.

Thus, according to Jensen and Meckling, companies will voluntarily make public issue of company accounts and engage independent auditors, because this will raise the share price by reducing the shareholding public's monitoring costs. There is clearly an element of truth here, since companies have on occasion released information voluntarily but, fragmentary evidence to the contrary,[9] the great, discontinuous expansions in company knowledge took place through government fiat:[10] companies could previously (and still do) claim their unwillingness to reveal information to competitors. Furthermore changes in the legal environment have their effect upon the habits and practices of day-to-day business behaviour:

> The immediate effect of the Kylsant case [discussed in chapter 5] so far as our profession is concerned, was that auditors decided that, if secret reserves were to be drawn up to bolster current earnings, this fact would have to be disclosed in the accounts. Following the Kylsant case, several companies immediately proceeded to redesign the form of presentation of their accounts in the light of lessons to be learnt from that case.[11]

Improvements in information, as they are wont to do, merely inform people about the extent of their ignorance, and whet the appetite for more. It is dangerous to treat knowledge as a commodity.

A more profound kind of ignorance is about the future. Let us put aside disputes either between shareholders and managers, or those between shareholders which result, for instance, from the fact that different groups may discount earnings at different rates because of the nature of the taxation regime. All disputes between shareholders and managers in the principal and agent analysis are over the distribution of wealth, because in this model *conflicts over the correct perception of the value of the firm cannot arise*. The managers in the Kylsant case claimed that their secret reserve accounts were for the benefit of the shareholders. Now while one might well suspect this not to be the case, and in principle one would be loath to admit that individuals are better off in a state of ignorance, *the claim is a perfectly meaningful one*.

The key to understanding this issue is to see that the very wide applicability of the principal–agent analysis is due to its strict correspondence to the transactions-conflict relation to be found in an Edgeworth Box. In the latter context, each participant is the best judge of his or her own best interests, which are defined by the choices which they reveal. It is meaningless to say here that B knows better than A what are A's best interests. But for the firm, even if we assume that all participants wish to discount cash flow at the same rate, it is *meaningful* to suggest that managers know the best interests of the shareholders better than the latter do themselves, if we assume shareholders want to maximise their wealth, and if the method shareholders are using for valuing the firm is incorrect. Disputes between owners and managers may then be not merely conflicts of *interest*, but conflicts of *perception* as well.

Such a critique may not come across as particularly elegant, but it is central to the writings of Chandler and Schumpeter and to a whole popular debate on firm finance. The intimate relation between banks and companies in Japan and other countries is often seen as a secret of success, since firms are in a position to plan long term without the day-by-day constraints of the stock market. Thus, according to the managing director of the UK microelectronics firm Ferranti:

> [Ferranti] is constrained from taking an adventurous approach by the need to maintain the loyalty of its shareholders. Partly, no doubt, to deter takeover bids, the company sets itself [strict] financial targets . . . These call for a 25 per cent annual return on investment and a 25 per cent a year increase in pre-tax profits.

The article continues 'Plenty of people in the UK electronics industry sympathise with Ferranti's problem of reconciling the needs of a voraciously capital intensive risk business with the stock market's emphasis on short term results.'[12]

On the other hand, to paraphrase a famous British philosopher 'that's what they *would* say, isn't it?'[13] The derailing of companies' long-term plans by 'money managers'[14] could very well be management's latest excuse for lack of success. For D. C. Mueller, in fact, over investment of a kind by mature companies takes place, a fact which is taken to be strong confirmation of the 'managerial discretion' hypothesis: such firms have large internal cash flows relative to the quantity of new investment that can be undertaken at rates of return in excess of the returns stockholders can earn elsewhere.[15] For such firms, it is possible that managements, as in the case of the Royal Mail, convince themselves that its shareholders are overly 'impatient'. Furthermore, contrary cases can be read in the financial press where management 'became so entranced with far horizons that they failed to notice until too late the black smoke billowing from the engine room'.[16] Lastly, it has not proved easy to establish that the stock market is in fact myopic in its treatment of company expenditures on capital investment and investment in research and development.

This last point, however, underlines our essential criticism of the principal and agent paradigm. It may well be that greater shareholder control will push the value of the firm to its maximum level, but this is ultimately an *empirical* question. The principal and agent analysis *assumes* this problem away. It is not even coherent *to ask the question* whether a Japanese shareholder's wealth is greater under existing institutional arrangements than it would have been under American style shareholding and takeover arrangements. Note, however, that the structure of the principal–agent model *strongly hints* that the latter arrangements are invariably preferable.

And how could it not be so? Except for the problems brought about by the existence of agency costs themselves, firms for Jensen and Meckling exist in a Fisherian equilibrium, Modigliani–Miller world (to be explored in chapter 7) in which efficient financial markets correctly evaluate changes in company behaviour: the value of the firm is *strictly identified* with its current share price, the choice between dividends and retained earnings has no effect upon this share price and there is a cost of capital for the firm as a whole: risky projects are financed no differently from safe projects.

However, there is (unsurprising) evidence that the market differentiates between methods of finance and demands a higher rate of return on projects financed from new share issue than from retained earnings. Furthermore, retained earnings may well appear to management as a cheap form of finance, given the market's conventional expectations about dividends: earnings above a conventional level are taken to belong to the firm and are available for reinvestment. Retained earnings may also be cheap in the further sense that a company's investment plans with these funds are subject to less scrutiny than a new issue would be, so that long-term projects are not revealed in detail to competitors. Japanese firms, besides being the recipients of cheap debt in a literal sense, may find it possible to base long-term plans on debt funding, since much of the debt is held by insiders who are linked to the company. Otherwise equivalent Anglo-Saxon firms, whose indebtedness contracts are more at arm's length may find such arrangements impossible. It may well be that non-market forms of finance – retained earnings for Anglo-Saxon firms, as well as the nominally external but intimate forms of finance available to Japanese firms, are more conducive to long-term planning than market forms of finance, due to this public good aspect of long-term planning.

The principal and agent paradigm is thus guilty on several charges. First, it *assumes* the existence of this knowledgeable, rational principal, and therefore cannot readily deal with the historical changes in the perception and 'monitoring power' of principals discussed in chapter 5 which have altered attitudes to company ownership. Secondly, by *identifying* maximum firm value with the share price which would exist for a firm totally constrained by its owners, it is unable to distinguish between Marris's and Mueller's self-indulgent managerial firm and the proverbial giant Japanese firm with its long-term horizon and manifest success. If there is a possibility that this latter phenomenon in fact exists, can we be satisfied with a paradigm which excludes *in principle* the existence of such a firm? In a world in which it appears that the transformation of financial markets dictates that perhaps even the largest companies are subject to takeover, it would seem important to explore the effects of such changes on company behaviour rather than deduce them by tautology.

For Oliver Williamson, an early contributor to the literature on owner–manager conflict, the tools of the principal–agent analysis – costs of monitoring, etc. are indeed appropriate. Under the powerful influence of the historian Alfred Chandler, however, the most interesting problem to which they are applied is not the battle for overall control of the firm, but to a consideration of its internal structure and organisation. It is to that development which we now turn.

Markets and Hierarchies

Chandler and Firm Integration

The writings of Alfred Chandler[17] have had an influence on mainstream economic theory which is without precedent for a business historian. On the face of it, Chandler is reporting a simple chronology of the development of American enterprise. In the first phase, until the 1840s, the expansion of the market encouraged manufacturing, distribution, and finance to specialise in the manner of Adam Smith's theorem. In the second phase, lasting until the First World War, new technologies transformed the processes of transportation, production and distribution and encouraged the use of the modern integrated multi-unit business enterprise. The distinctive feature of the large modern industrial enterprise, which first appeared suddenly and dramatically in the 1880s, is that it integrated mass production with mass distribution. The final phase, from the 1920s to the present, is marked by the spreading predominance of the multi-unit enterprise in nearly all sectors of the economy. Growth by these enterprises through diversification into new product lines and new overseas markets, in both manufacturing and distribution is a direct consequence of the transformation which took place in the second phase in the running of the multi-unit enterprise. The vital phase is clearly the second:

While in the first phase, expanding markets with the resultant tendency towards specialisation had been dominant, in the second, the prime influence became that of the new technologies. These technologies used a new energy source – steam, underpinned by the expansion of coal. As coal was making possible a great expansion in the production of goods, the revolution in transportation and communication lowered the cost and increased the speed of distribution, thereby facilitating high volume production and marketing. The new technologies led to the integration of many specialised units within the enterprise as a whole, and by revolutionising the processes of transportation, distribution and production greatly increased the speed and volume of the output of goods and services. The new speed and volume required, in turn, an increase in the numbers of managers to plan and supervise the new processes. This increase in the velocity of activity also demanded the development of new organisational procedures and designs to permit the more efficient use of the much larger amounts of materials, men and machines used in the processes of production and distribution.

The widespread mergers and consolidations which took place round the turn of the century were in part to fulfil this new strategy of integrated production and distribution. Having consummated these combinations, for the salaried executives heading the new managerial enterprises the first and most pressing task was the creation of an organisational design through which their consolidated properties were to be managed. In other words, the necessity was to create organisational structures which would accommodate the new-found strategy of integration.

The widely adopted, and successful solution was an extension of the line and staff organisational structure of 'America's First Big Business' – the railroads. The key distinction here was between line and staff responsibilities. The managers of the line of authority 'handled *men*' – they were given power to order the movements of trains and traffic (that is, freight and passengers) as well as any emergency maintenance of equipment and roadbed. The executives in the other functional departments (maintenance of way, maintenance of equipment, and finance) became designated as staff officers – they 'handled *things*'. While the line executives ordered when and where the maintenance crews carried out their work and when the repair shops had to complete their duties, the staff officers set standards and evaluated, promoted, hired and fired managers in their departments, but they could not give orders concerning the movements of men and track.

The senior executives in the new consolidated enterprises had to transform an agglomeration of widely scattered, hitherto competing manufacturing units and sales firms into a single manageable whole. Their task included the building both of the functional departments (finance, sales, production, etc.) and of a central office to co-ordinate, appraise, and plan the work of the departments and of the enterprise as a whole. In creating these functional departments, the executives of the new managerial enterprises pioneered in developing methods and procedures of modern general management.

The executive committee evaluated, co-ordinated and planned the work of the departments and of the corporation as a whole. Appraisal became relatively routine, based on comparative statistics developed by the finance department. Co-ordination became systematised by means of interdepartmental co-operation in the scheduling of flows through the enterprise's many units. Long-term planning soon became the executive committee's most difficult task, and the one that took up most of its time. By the First World War, the newly centralised, functionally departmentalised structure of the modern industrial enterprise (Williamson's U-form) was not only being perfected in manufacturing industries but was also being adopted by the large retailing enterprises.

Two major modifications took place in this structure after the First World War:

The sharp post-war recession of 1920–1 and the resultant inventory crisis caused GM and other firms to tie all broad-based activities – the scheduling of purchasing, production, employment, deliveries of finished goods and the setting of prices – to annual forecasts of demand adjusted periodically to reports of actual sales.

Secondly, firms such as Du Pont which were highly innovative in research proceeded to adopt a strategy of diversification. GM on the other hand had already been serendipitously 'diversified' – it was a shambolic collection of enterprises thrown together by its pioneer entrepreneur Billy

Durant. Du Pont moved towards a more decentralised structure (Williamson's M-form) to meet the requirements of this strategy, while GM approached it from the other direction through the creation of a central office. The adoption of this structure facilitated movements from one industry to another and the co-ordination of heterogeneous groups of products. Each autonomous division handled all the functions involved in the production and distribution of a single major line of products (e.g. GM was organised into autonomous divisions such as Chevrolet, Buick, etc.). The internal organisation of each of these divisions was similar to that of independent (U-form) enterprises, but they were expected to co-ordinate with each other on purchasing, manufacturing and marketing, and thus preserve the benefits of mass production and mass distribution.

The general office consisted of a few top executives and large advisory and financial staffs, usually functionally defined. It appraised regularly and continually the performance of the divisions, using as criteria the change in market share in addition to the rate of return on investment. The general office concentrated even more than in the earlier system on long-term planning – how the enterprise's resources were to be allocated among the divisions and in what functions, products and regions the enterprise should contract or expand its operations.

It is the creation of the general office which was the great achievement of the modern business enterprise. As Chandler never ceases to remind us, company structure follows strategy, and the technology which brought about the strategy of integrated production led to a company structure whose centrepiece was the creation of the general office. The general office was necessary for several reasons:

1 It acted to co-ordinate in a coherent way the different aspects of production and distribution in the integrated enterprise, so that all the benefits of mass production and purchasing were reaped by the large firm. For Sloan of GM this central office was a necessary mechanism for rationalising the Durant collection of enterprises.
2 The central office could use modern statistical techniques to predict demand conditions, as opposed to the 'guesses' which had formerly been made.

It is with Chandler's third reason that he departs from the canons of economic orthodoxy:

3 Salaried managers in the central office could plan long term, not only because the structure of the firm frees managers from day-to-day running of business affairs, but because it permits the over-riding of the short-term desire of shareholders for returns.

To repeat, for Chandler, it is the building of the general office, and not the creation of the M-form structure *per se* which was the critical event in modern business organisation. In the case of companies like GM, the building of an M-form structure meant a process of centralisation, with the creation of a central office on top of an already decentralised collection of enterprises. M-form is a specific structure brought about to deal with a strategy of diversification. It is purposefully and inherently ambiguous, attempting to capture the advantages of planning and co-ordination in the U-form, while preserving at the same time the benefits of decentralisation.

There are a few other elements in Chandler's approach which are worth observing. Note, however, that the theory embodied in an historian's work takes a different form from that put forth by an economist. The latter's notion of a theoretical structure, especially in the contemporary world, is uniquely defined by the formal propositions embodied in the model and the predictions which accrue from it. For the historian, much of the relevant theory, even among analytically aware practitioners such as Chandler, is inevitably embodied in the historical narrative itself.

Thus, in Chandler's treatment of the creation of giant firms at the turn of the century, two issues – the creation of monopoly and the separation of ownership from control – are more or less ignored as irrelevant. Indeed, in the latter case, the separation, to the extent that it was important at all, actually promoted the development of a professional managerial class. But a far more significant example of the historian's approach is the extensive time that Chandler devotes to the discussion of the education of specialists and company infrastructure of all kinds, the evolution of cost accounting and the techniques of monitoring of performance. For him, these developments at the managerial level hold the same significance as the emergence of scientific management (Taylorism, etc.) at the shop floor level. These developments are central to Chandler's narrative, and their lack of emphasis by analytically inclined economists is crucial to their misunderstanding of Chandler's thesis and the nature of these historical developments.

The Williamsonian Synthesis

For Williamson,[18] the crucial event in the development of the management of the modern firm was the last phase in Chandler's process of development – the creation of the M-form structure. This structure has for Williamson such inherently advantageous control properties as to be analogous to the 'design for a brain' put forth by W. Ross Ashby. The essential aspects of this markets and hierarchies paradigm may be put forth as follows:

1   Viable modes of organisation (market, quasi-market or internal) are those which economise on transaction costs. We assume that economic actors proceed with *bounded rationality* (rationality less complete than that which would be necessary for writing contracts in the present for all contingent circumstances) and *opportunism* (self-interest seeking with guile – actors will take advantage of loopholes in contracts). Under these conditions, the critical dimensions for describing transactions are

a uncertainty

b the frequency with which transactions recur, and

c the degree to which durable transaction-specific investments are required to realise least cost supply. This last condition is particularly crucial where there are idiosyncratic transactions – those in which the specific identity of the parties has important cost bearing consequences.

2   In the choice between the use of markets and internal organisation, we find that the latter is well suited to transactions that involve recurrent exchange in the face of a non-trivial degree of uncertainty, and that involve transaction-specific investments. As these conditions would seem to be widely applicable, it is clear that we can explain, in this Coase-like framework, the existence of the firm. But there are costs to using a highly centralised, hierarchical (U-form) structure, especially as enterprises grow in size and diversity. These costs are of three kinds:

a Attempts to achieve unnnecessary co-ordination generate overhead costs.

b Forced interdependencies give rise to congestion and other spillover costs.

c Opportunistic sub-goal pursuit is more difficult to detect and control as the degree of interconnectedness increases.

3   Operating cost increases thus arise out of a failure to recognise 'essential decomposibility', that is to say, situations in which sub-units could (best) operate semi-autonomously. Furthermore, U-form also served to confuse organisational purpose by its failure to separate strategic from operating decision-making. The organisational change from U-form to M-form served both to economise on bounded rationality by relieving top executives of the more routine operational activities and simultaneously to reduce sub-goal pursuit, which is the manifestation of opportunism.

The benefits of M-form involve not merely an assignment of semi-autonomous standing to natural sub-units within the firm. For the investment of resources to be assigned to high yield uses, it was necessary to have a general office which

a had a sense of direction,

b was able to evaluate the merits of investment proposals originated by the operating divisions and

c had the capacity to audit and assess operating division performance.

Removing top management from the operating affairs of the enterprise meant that, whereas bureaucratic control processes had governed previously, operating divisions were now governed in a quasi-market fashion. Thus divisions were assigned the status of quasi-firms, and the central office assumed functions of review and resource allocation ordinarily associated with the capital market. As a consequence of these changes the goal confusion (or incongruence) that had previously reigned was supplanted by sub-goal clarity that was meaningfully related to enterprise objectives. The self-interest seeking that, when coupled with goal incongruence, had once drained the energies of the enterprise were now turned to productive purposes.

Williamson thus managed to synthesize an enormous body of thought – organisation theory, with its emphasis on the limits to human perception and rationality, Coase's choice between internal organisation and the market, and the principal–agent paradigm, with its analysis of agency costs. Williamson's real coup, however, was that unlike the earlier formulations, which dealt with these problems in fairly general terms, he linked his analysis to a specific organisational form – the M-form – which emerged historically in the US in the period after the First World War.

There are several important ways, however, in which Williamson's approach differs significantly from that of Chandler. Oliver Williamson has chided Chandler for underplaying the decisive role of 'organisational innovation' in the emergence of the modern enterprise.[19] As is so often the case in such situations the historian appears ambiguous and indecisive to the economist because he or she is presenting an interconnected series of historical developments which do not fit neatly with the economist's model, with its neat lines of causation. In Chandler's work it is far from clear that the adoption of an M-form structure is the unique and decisive factor affecting the destinies of the firms under consideration. On the contrary, a devil's advocate counter-argument to Williamson might be made: M-form structures, far from being decisive innovations in their own right, predictably emerged from the developments in cost accounting and infrastructure discussed in chapter 5.

It is these developments which were crucial for the emergence of the modern firm, since they provided the bases for the rational calculation of first, interdivisional transfer prices and, secondly, of the profitability/rate of return for a firm consisting of heterogeneous entities and of separate divisions. Without these developments, M-form structures would never have been feasible.[20] In fact, this 'devil's advocate' argument somewhat distorts the historical case in the opposite direction, since the introduction of M-form structures gave great impetus to further innovations in accounting technique. But if a crucial and permanent aspect of the evolution of the modern firm is to be chosen between these two factors, we must turn to the incremental development of accounting and related management techniques rather than to the discontinuous innovation of M-form structures.

If the analogy is to be made with technological change, the true focus of, for instance the industrial revolution, would not be upon individual inventions, but upon the long-term development through the late Middle Ages of the techniques of metal working, casting and agriculture which made the later, more spectacular innovations possible. Similarly, the continuing transformation in the way business is done is due less to any specific organisational innovation than to a continuous refinement of techniques of operation, complemented by an improvement in the general education, professional qualifications and skills of the firm's personnel.

Furthermore, while Chandler concurs with Williamson that M-form structures are now ubiquitous in the US, for him it is a reflection of their adherence to a strategy of diversification, both domestic and international. Williamson suggests that the widespread use of the M-form organisational structure is due to its inherent characteristics as a control mechanism, rather than it being a specific stage in an historical evolution which is contingent, among other things, on the strategy pursued by firms. This perspective has two distinctive implications:

First, that the introduction of M-form structures into large firms can bring about exogenous improvements[21] to firm performance, without specific reference to the strategy being pursued by the firm. There is no indication from Williamson of the possibility of multiple lines of causation between firm success, strategy and structure. Thus, the adoption of M-form structure in the UK appears to have taken place most distinctively among sophisticated, progressive firms who were in any case more receptive to new ideas of all kinds (in this case those of US management consultant firms) than were tradition bound (often family owned) firms in slow growing industries.[22]

Secondly, M-form emerges in Williamson's analysis as a higher stage in managerial evolution. In support of this proposition Williamson cites Lawrence Franko as confirming a rapid movement among continental companies towards M-form structures.[23] On the contrary, however, there is little indication that continental firms have in the past or even at present approached the level of use of divisionalised structures to be found in the US,[24] but this has not proved a major obstacle to their superior post-war performance. From Chandler's perspective – that of structure following strategy – the less diversified and non-multinational nature of continental compared with US firms would put less pressure on them to proceed with decentralised structures. One might hazard a guess that even within the slow growing UK, the adoption of this 'higher' form of organisation has proved more popular than on the continent due to the very high concentration in the UK of large multinationalised firms, as well as the powerful influence of the latest American fashions.

Franko, in fact, is part of a present-day chorus of denunciation of highly divisionalised procedures, invidiously comparing them to unified, integrated Japanese approaches in which their centralised, certainly non-divisionalised[25] form of governance encourages a broader view of firm control than is to be found in the West:

> Western firms often had a much narrower conception than did their Japanese competitors of what product it was they were producing. ... Even when Western firms have not been conglomerates *per se*, the management of their corporate structures has forced managers of related divisions or business units to compete with each other, rather than cross-fertilize each others' technological and market

development. Indeed, during the past decade, the product visions of Western managers have often become progressively narrower, as finer and finer compartmentalizations of responsibility for strategic business units came in some circles to replace broader product divisions as an organizational principal. In contrast, successful Japanese – and Western – firms have structured these activities in organically related, vertically integrated chains, *especially in activities where product definitions and product and process technologies are rapidly changing*.[26] (italics added)

For other analysts, the main weakness of the highly divisionalised form compared with the more centralised, integrated Japanese approach is that it inhibits long-term strategies of cross subsidisation for breaking into a new market.[27] Even in the citadel of divisionalisation, GM, there are indications that the developing strategies of firm integration are leading to revisions of the Sloan structure to encourage integration. Thus contemporary tendencies may be moving in the direction of a re-centralisation of control in many enterprises – perhaps even an abandonment of M-form structures. What will not be abandoned is the heightened level of sophistication in day-to-day operations which has been evolving in firms throughout the century.

It is not our place here to pronounce on the relative merits of different kinds of managerial structures for Western firms, or even for GM. It seems self evident that gigantic, multinational enterprises could never be run efficiently from totally centralised, U-form structures, and that something approximating M-form divisionalisation would have to exist. Within this rubric however, could fall a multitude of alternative levels of centralisation: even if the organisation charts of ITT in the late 1960s and IBM were both indicating a *de jure* M-form structure, it is hard to conceive that the latter *de facto* was not far more of a centralised organisation due to the integrated nature of its business strategy compared with that of the ITT conglomerate.

The implications of the view of Chandler's managerial revolution presented here are that the vast increases in trained personnel and the widespread development of techniques of monitoring and measurement permitted, at one juncture of economic history, the creation of the modern, large corporation at a viable level of decentralisation. But with the passage of time, the identification of modern techniques of business practice with this small group of large firms has become ever less plausible. These business-like techniques, once the province of the largest firms, have now become universalised: the sociology of value maximisation – clearly, precisely, and analytically defined – is now all pervasive, and not limited to a small vanguard of managers in the largest companies quintessentially represented by Alfred Sloan at GM in the 1920s.

If, indeed, the correct explanation for Chandler's managerial revolution is that it was a reflection of fundamental sociological changes accompanied by a diffusion of the new techniques of management, we may well expect that, as this process continues, it will act against the hegemony of the largest and most established firms, both within national economies and in the world at large.

The real question is whether this M-form structure is an accommodation to a stage in corporate development, or a decisive, 'Pareto efficient' innovation, as suggested by Williamson. The M-form structure, far from being an unambiguous advance, is a very clever and successful compromise between total decentralisation and complete centralisation. In situations where integration facilitates change and development, there is an obvious cost to any form of decentralisation. This does not make it a bad, or unworkable structure, but indicates that its utility must be judged in the context of substantive situations, and not merely on the a priori characteristics of the model.

If indeed the Williamson model is of limited use in explaining the success of firms or the growth of economies, what accounts for its current popularity? As will be noted in chapter 8, there are specific situations which seem well accounted for by this formulation, and furthermore, like the principal and agent analysis, it appears to have wide applicability outside the domain of firm control.[28]

Its real strength, however, is that, like the principal and agent analysis, it deftly skirts the bounds of orthodoxy. It is an attempt to demonstrate that the *historical* process of corporate development can be reduced to an *analytical* description of the performance characteristics of different kinds of control regimes. Indeed, while the descriptions of the disadvantages of the over-centralised U-form structure are very convincing, the weakest part of Williamson's argument is why the M-form firm should be at all superior to an equivalent collection of firms united by the capital market. For Chandler, there are unambiguous positive benefits to integration and to long-term planning – the ability of the central office to ward off the 'impatient' shareholder yields benefits to the firm in both the U-form and M-form managerial structures. Thus Chandler, when invidiously comparing UK to US corporate practices notes that

> the basic contrast in the operation of the multidivisional form in the two nations has come in the makeup and the functions of the general office ... overall control and planning has been less extensive and less sophisticated in British than in American multidivisional enterprises. By 1970 few British firms had gone beyond financial performance as the criterion used in monitoring and evaluating the performance of divisions. ... Forecasting was still not widely employed for short term adjustment of flow or long term capital allocation. ... Relatively few firms had formal planning offices and fewer had offices that concentrated on management development.[29]

Williamson, however, straying only slightly from the canons of orthodoxy, specifies the advantages of the internal capital market in rather negative terms: because of information impactedness, the general management, which enjoys an internal relationship to the divisions 'might be prepared to assume risks that an external investor ought properly to decline'.[30] As suggested earlier, 'differential information' is part of a coherent explanation of the advantages of inside, as opposed to capital market finance, but it is far removed from Chandler's emphasis on the *positive* benefits to long-term planning and co-ordination. Since Williamson stays well within the rational choice and Coasian frameworks, the ever present question is – why not use the market? It is unsurprising, therefore, that his discussion of vertical integration (see chapter 8) is in terms of 'market failure': a more positive approach to integration and planning – planning as an active constituent in the making of markets – is not really possible here.

The growth and development of the firm, however, cannot be explained within a limited set of postulates about rational actors. It is an historical process, whose nature can be most clearly grasped by reviewing the earlier debates on the extent of the firm.

The Extent of the Firm

The Debate
Much of the literature of the previous two sections emerged in the wake of an earlier debate on the determinants of the size of the firm. For some economists the issue does not exist: theorists of pure general equilibrium have dispensed with the firm altogether by ignoring the existence of this awkward entity: goods are produced, brought to the market and sold. The problem of the extent of the firm is thus eliminated by this touch of medieval imagery, just as the problem of commodity delineation in general equilibrium is 'solved' by a guild-like separation between goods.

The Marshallian tradition has always had a more difficult path to follow.[31] It would be convenient if the empirically dubious but widely accepted short run law of diminishing returns could be adopted to explain the size of the firm in the long run. If this were the case, a *physical* reason for a determinate size of firm could be placed alongside the 'objective' and qualitative delineation made between commodities: for Marshall himself and most of his followers, there is almost a complete identification between the firm and the plant producing a single commodity. This is not simply for the sake of analytical or expository clarity: as firms become more flexible and diversified in production, the supply side gaps between different commodities become less pronounced and the integrity of the individual commodity breaks down as firms can freely substitute between the production of different commodities. In a similar way, firm diversification leaves little room for a law of diminishing returns as a constraint on the firm's *total* output.

Marshall's earlier well-known solution to the problem of a determinate size of firm was to tie it to the life-cycle of the entrepreneur and the entrepreneurial family. With the manifest rise of the joint-stock company, this approach had to be abandoned and Marshall could give no well-defined reason why monopoly should not be a normal industry outcome. The universally accepted solution emerged from two publications in 1931: from Jacob Viner[32] came a clear exposition of the distinction between the Marshallian short run, where diminishing returns were prevalent and a long run, in which a determinate size of firm was dictated by the minimum point on the long run average cost curve (the curve's shape being determined by the resolution of the firm's economies and diseconomies of scale). The latter phenomenon was the one in need of explanation, and out of E. A. G. Robinson's detailed discussion,[33] it was his brief exposition on the managerial problems of the co-ordination of large units which has been appropriated as part of the standard literature on diseconomies of scale.

It has not been always appreciated that this *deus ex machina* of managerial co-ordination is a major break from neo-classical analysis. The Marshallian tradition now had many questions to ask itself – if the extent of the firm and long run costs are significantly affected by managerial factors, do not costs cease to be rooted wholly in production? Will not changes in relative prices result as much from managerial as technological innovation? Will not the supply-side gap between commodities be linked as much to managerial flexibility as to technological substitutability? Lastly, if managerial co-ordination is crucial to the market outcome, why has the tradition dealt with the firm as if it were a black box?

We have seen in chapter 5 how the tradition confronted the challenge of the internal management of the firm. The issue of the size or extent of the firm, however, was followed up by Kaldor,[34] but the next work of real significance (with the exception of Coase, to be discussed below) was not until 1959 with the publication of Edith Penrose's *The Theory of the Growth of the Firm*. For Penrose, like Kaldor, the decisive role of managerial co-ordination is not in the static determination of the size of firm, but a dynamic one:

> In an unchanging environment ... an established firm that had succeeded in creating optimum administrative procedures and framing an optimum set of policies could operate successfully without any overt acts of 'central management' at all; even new appointments could conceivably be made according to established regulations.[35]

The real challenge to a firm's administration, and its *raison d'être* is its ability to adapt to change of both a long and short run nature. It is the rate of growth of the firm and not its absolute size which is both determined and constrained by the quality of management and its capacity to plan for the future. No wonder that Alfred Chandler thought so highly of the book:[36] the current literatures of both the principal–agent and the markets–hierarchies variety seem retrograde by comparison, with their static and rather apologetic emphases on the role of administration as a device for overcoming the costs of using the market place.

Two Marshallian elements in Penrose's view of the firm weaken it as an analysis of the evolution of the corporate economy. The first problem is that according to Penrose, the primary economic function of an industrial firm 'is to make use of productive resources for the purpose of supplying goods and services to the economy in accordance with plans developed and put into effect within the firm'.[37] On the contrary, the firm's only reason for existence, as Thorstein Veblen has emphasized[38] is to make money, not to supply goods. Dr. Marx has reminded us that the capitalist advances money – M – to produce commodities – C, but all for the purpose of gaining M' where M' > M. The distinction between making goods and making money is not a frivolous or polemical one. The view of the firm emerging from Marshall was a generalisation of the experience of late nineteenth century British enterprise, but it was an unimaginative one. On the one hand, Marshall postulated a strong tendency towards competitive equalisation and on the other presumed that firms were tied to an industry producing a specific commodity, for reasons which were never adequately explained.

But as the experience of the twentieth century has revealed, increasingly sophisticated management, by viewing the affairs of the firm less from a production and more from an abstract, that is to say financial perspective, have not felt the need to contain themselves within the bounds of narrowly defined products. As profitable opportunities outside the 'industry' have been perceived, there has been an ever greater likelihood that the firm will pursue them. *The Edwardian firm observed and described by Marshall was restricted in its domain of activities largely because of its own managerial limitations*. These very limitations inhibited the process of competitive equalisation. Marshall, by presenting a picture of firms restricted for unspecified reasons in their domain of activity and yet existing in an environment of competitive equalisation greatly contributed to the present day confusions which exist on the nature of the competitive process.

Product diversification is an important part of Penrose's framework, but the emphasis on a 'production' approach to the role of management precludes an understanding of the substantial energies directed by the modern firm in financial spheres: one pound sterling saved in cash inventories is viewed identically by management with an equivalent cash saving in physical inventories. Equally, money advanced in a speculative takeover is an 'investment' as much as the building of a steel mill; expansion by industrial firms such as General Electric into the realm of financial intermediation (see chapter 7) can only be understood by the greater *abstractness* which management now uses to conceptualise the potential domain of the firm's activities. Penrose's definition seems to exclude the possibility of this kind of development. The emphasis on production also implies a kinship with the classical dichotomy: the expansion of the firm and limitations to that expansion in Penrose's analysis are largely determined by real factors. For her, as for Chandler[40] even conglomerate acquisition is largely explicable in terms of the managerial and entrepreneurial benefits accruing to the combination. Only passing reference is made to the substantial and ever changing role played by the capital market in constraining and shaping the growth of firms.

The second 'traditional' element in the analysis is even more pronouncedly Marshallian – an emphasis on partial equilibrium:

> the development and dissemination of the techniques of decentralised managerial organisation, *the rise of a professional management class*, government actions (especially tax policy) which create favourable conditions for acquisition, the *extensive development of industrial research* and the consequent widening range of knowledge of chemistry, mechanics, electronics, and other fundamental aspects of industrial science which create within the industrial firm an industrial technology suitable for a broad range of products, *will all tend to raise the growth rate of firms*.[41] (italics added)

Despite a subsequent promise (p. 197) to correct the bias, the clear implication remains that the effect of such changes on trends in the size distribution of firms and on the use of internal organisation versus market forces for the economy as a whole can be analysed in this partial manner. But while a more widespread professional management class and the development of industrial research may *ceteris paribus* increase the growth of a (large) firm, it is inappropriate to hold other things equal. Such factors will affect not only the large firm, but other firms as well in the environment in which the large firm operates. Earlier Coase had performed a similar exercise and made a similar error:

> Other things equal, a firm will tend to be larger
> (a) the less the costs of organising and the slower these costs rise with an increase in the transactions organised.
> (b) the less likely the entrepreneur is to make mistakes and the smaller the increase in mistakes with the increase in transactions organised.
> (c) the greater the lowering (or the less the rise) in the supply price of factors of production to firms of larger size.[42]

If Coase's arguments are interpreted as explanations for changes in the size of firms over time, with growing sophistication in firm organisation, factors (a) and perhaps (b) will lead to increases in firm size. Since for Coase the market exists irrespective of any such developments, a lessening in the 'costs of organising' can only be of benefit to the firm, as opposed to the market. In reality, the lowering of, for instance, the costs of organising can *increase* the role of market transactions, if the new developments permit an expansion in the number of firms participating in the market.

For both Coase and Penrose, changes which promote firm organisation are analysed in terms of their effect *upon the growth of individual firms*. But improvements in managerial technique set up countervailing tendencies simultaneously. On the one hand, they make administrative co-ordination more attractive. Contrarily, by expanding the potential number of individual participants and their capacity to compete, these improvements may increase the role of market forces, a development which can restrict the growth of the large firm either by offering direct competition or by encouraging vertical disintegration. The resolution of these real factors, however, is mediated through the capital market, whose own structure and behaviour evolves over time. How these conflicting tendencies resolve themselves must be analysed in an historical context.

The Gerschenkron Hypothesis and the Evolution of the Firm

Alexander Gerschenkron's thesis on industrialisation was largely concerned to explain the use on the continent, most especially in Germany of industrial investment banking:

> The industrialization of England had proceeded without any substantial utilization of banking for long term investment purposes. . . .
> By contrast, in a relatively backward country capital is scarce and diffused, the distrust of industrial activities is considerable, and finally there is greater pressure for bigness because of the scope of the industrialization movement, the larger the average size of plant, and the concentration of industrial processes on branches of relatively high ratios of capital to output. To these should be added the scarcity of entrepreneurial talent in a backward country.[43]

Gerschenkron's thesis has been extended to other spheres.[44] Late developing economies are likely to use highly centralised structures in order to compensate for the lack of a well-developed infrastructure (e.g. a smoothly working market for inputs)[45] and for the absence of a large pool of highly skilled personnel who could be trusted to perform efficaciously in the peripheries. Like the proverbial nineteenth century director of schools in Paris who knew by looking at his pocket watch what lesson was being conducted in any district of France, including rural ones, turn of the century Russian steel magnates trusted few decisions to be made out of their control and constructed few plants, but each of enormous size so that central direction could be maintained.

Historians and economists who have found Gerschenkron's explanation convincing for much of European economic development have been troubled by the fact that in the most highly developed economy of all, that of the US, the emergence of modern business practices also seemed coincident with a high degree of centralisation. Chandler's studies indicate that the structures which emerged usually necessitated a high degree of decentralisation within the organisation. The great innovations documented by Chandler were made possible through the development of new techniques of monitoring and management (e.g. cost accounting) and the training of whole generations to the new profession of management to accommodate the needs of companies. With growing sophistication, it became possible for firms to abandon the centralised forms of control described by the Gerschenkron hypothesis and to use more flexible structures such as the M-form.

Thus Chandler's research seems to give a convincing solution to the seeming paradox of the growth of non-market forms in the US. The new technologies emerging in the late nineteenth century facilitated the development of integrated, co-ordinated production. The US, more than any other country, was in a position to exploit these technologies partially because it succeeded in developing administrative structures through which these enterprises could be managed efficiently. An important concomitant of these developments was the existence of procedures and personnel for the monitoring and transmitting of information within and through the firms. The absence, or perceived absence of such personnel was an obstacle to entry into this new world. In inter-war Britain

> even amongst the industrialists who supported the principle of rationalization and were convinced that through it firms could gain access to important scale economies, there were many who were prey to doubts about the personal capacities of the men available to run large-scale enterprise. 'The most difficult thing at present', the Macmillan Committee were told by a banker, 'is to find a man who can control 10,000,000 spindles. Find that man and I think you will find five or six positions clamouring for him'.[46]

The U-form centralised structures could not avoid the problems and disadvantages of such centralisation, especially in the US, where the expanding horizons of management moved the firm in the direction of diversification. In other countries, such as Germany, there was far less sophistication: 'At the top of large firms before the First World War and later there was an intricate mixture of system and improvisation, bureaucratic and personal methods, fixed order and flexibility.'[47] In the United States, a more bold solution was attempted – the development of the M-form structure.

The M-form structure was facilitated by the richness in administrative skills and personnel in the US, which benefited both the centralising and decentralising aspects of the structure. On the one hand, the high level of administrative sophistication from 'the top' meant that monitoring procedures for units lower down could be installed efficiently, but the richness in the number of high quality managers at lower levels compared with other countries meant that semi-autonomy to sub-units was a viable procedure. M-form may have been an analytical triumph, but its development had as a prerequisite specific infrastructural and institutional developments in the US which were present after the First World War.

As so described, it may appear as if differences between Williamson's analysis of M-form and the interpretation of Chandler's ideas presented here are merely questions of emphasis. But the two approaches lead to different substantive predictions about the future development of the industrial economy. For Williamson, the fundamental importance of M-form is its possession of unique properties as a control system. The prediction emerging from this perspective is that, among large firms at least, the M-form's ubiquitousness should continue, and will spread to domains where it is not yet fully dominant.

There is a contrary possibility, based on the perception of M-form as a compromise between market and centralised forms of organisation which has emerged in specific historical circumstances. There are reasons to believe that contemporary developments are squeezing this structure in favour of, on the one hand, highly marketised arrangements, and highly integrated, almost U-form structures on the other. M-form was a structure developed to facilitate the strategy of large firms which were diversifying their activities. In some cases, this diversification took the form of making products which were part of their main activity, i.e. an aspect of vertical integration. GM made many parts for its cars which might otherwise have been bought in simply because such markets for these commodities did not always exist, i.e. the middle managers in GM's subdivisions were capable of supplying these goods more efficiently than any smaller enterprises in a 'market'. This factor (as suggested above by Chandler and Penrose) may have contributed to the conglomerate's ability to exist: its middle managers running a subdivision specialising in, for instance, car hire were able to compete successfully against independent enterprises simply because they were superior in management and organisation. Both of these forms of diversification are now coming under increasing pressure, as skilled management and best practice techniques spread to the smaller entities which make up the markets for these commodities. With pressure on these forms of diversification, there is less need for the M-form compromise.

From the contrary direction, there is pressure on large firms, especially in highly dynamic sectors to have integrated strategies for dealing with the future, in other words to proceed with *planning* – an activity whose continued centrality to the operation of business and to the competitive process is often hidden in the static conceptualisations of orthodoxy. Planning is:

a complex process which, in addition to intellectual activities of perception and analysis, involves this social process of implementing formulated policies by means of organizational structure, systems of measurement and allocation, and systems for reward and punishment, and finally, involves a dynamic process of revising policy as shifts in organizational resources and the environment change the context of the original planning problem.[48]

Just as the wider dispersion of managerial skills pulls M-form from below in the direction of the market, so the expansion of top management's perception of its domain of control pulls from above in the direction of planning: the present ideals of good management, such as IBM and the large Japanese firms are based on their 'holistic', integrated conceptions of their activities. IBM has under its own control all of the main parameters – from integrated circuits to research and development and marketing – which may affect its ability to respond to changing circumstances. Corresponding to this strategy of integration and co-ordination of activities is likely to be a more centralised, less divisionalised structure than is typical of many other firms. Whether or not the actual organisation charts of the large firms change, actual control is likely to emanate progressively from the centre as integration rather than divisionalisation becomes a new catchword.

Thus the development and progressive dispersion of management skills implies that the bipolar pattern of the electronics industry – firms which are either highly integrated giants with convergent strategies, such as IBM, or which are small and highly specialised, and thus highly marketised – will become the norm. Large M-form entities with divergent strategies, a type of enterprise which evolved, when, paradoxically, both the forces of 'planning' and of 'the market' were weaker than they are today, are likely to go into decline. If such a pattern should emerge, it might be taken as suggestive verification of an historical, evolutionary approach to firm structure, as opposed to one based on the analytical properties of a control system.

These developments do not, however, take place in an institutional vacuum. The role of government has shaped the path of industrial development; a more purely economic force has been played by the capital market. Its segmented nature has had, in John Blair's felicitous terminology, a centripetal effect on the evolution of the industrial structure, very likely subduing somewhat the real factors we have outlined above which have progressively heightened the level of competitiveness. As, however, the managerial revolution has spread to the financial sphere, there may well be a tendency for the layers of the capital market to be 'squeezed'.

A second aspect of the 'distorting' effects of the capital market can be seen in its interaction with macroeconomic factors. It is periods of recession which seem most obviously competitive, since it is in such periods that we observe those price-cutting wars which neo-classical theory would point to as the most distinctive manifestations of such an environment. On the contrary, it is periods of substantial economic growth which are most threatening to established firms in a dynamic context, since it is then that the creation of new capital takes place, this being perhaps the most fundamental aspect of the process of competition.

(This new capital may later manifest itself as excess capacity during a recession.) But why should it necessarily be true that established firms are relatively more secure in recessions? In a world of capital markets corresponding to those to be found in neo-classical theory, little sense can be made of such a statement. To understand the evolution of the industrial structure and of competition we must proceed to examine the theoretical, historical and institutional aspects of the financing of business activity.

Notes

1. Coase, R. 'The Nature of the Firm' *Economica* new series 4 (1937): 386–405.
2. Alchian, A. and H. Demsetz 'Production, Information Costs, and Economic Organization' *American Economic Review* 62 (December 1972): 772–95.
3. Hicks, J. *A Theory of Economic History* Oxford University 1969, p. 29.
4. Arrow, K. *The Limits of Organization* W. W. Norton 1974, p. 33.
5. Marris, R. *The Economic Theory of Managerial Capitalism* Free Press 1964; and see Marris, R. and D. Mueller 'The Corporation, Competition and the Invisible Hand' *Journal of Economic* Literature 18 (March 1980): 32–63.
6. Solow, R. 'Some Implications of Alternative Criteria for the Firm' in Marris, R. and A. Wood (eds) *The Corporate Economy* Macmillan 1971, pp. 318–42.
7. Jensen, M. and W. Meckling 'Theories of the Firm: Managerial Behavior, Agency Costs, and Ownership Structure' *Journal of Financial Economics* 3(4) (October 1976): 305–60. Other important articles in this paradigm include Fama, E. 'Agency Problems and the Theory of the Firm' *Journal of Political Economy* 88(2) (April 1980): 288–307, and Fama, E. and M. Jensen 'Separation of Ownership from Control' and 'Agency Problems and Residual Claims', both in *Journal of Law and Economics* 26(2) (June 1983): 301–26 and 327–50. The summary below of the principal–agent theory is adapted from the Jensen and Meckling article.
8. Landes, D. *The Unbound Prometheus* Cambridge University 1969, ch. 5.
9. Watts, R. and J. Zimmerman 'Agency Problems and the Theory of the Firm: Some Evidence' *Journal of Law and Economics* 26(3) (October 1983): 613–33.
10. See, for the UK, Edwards, J. R. and K. Webb 'The Influence of Company Law on Corporate Reporting Procedures, 1865–1929: An Exemplification' *Business History* 24(3) (Nov. 1982): 259–79 and for the US, Burton, J. 'SEC Enforcement and Professional Accountants: Philosophy, Objectives and Approach' in Previts, G. (ed.) *The Development of SEC Accounting* Addison-Wesley 1981, pp. 240–7. For a contrary view on disclosure to the one expressed here see Benston, G. *Corporate Financial Disclosure in the UK and the USA* Saxon House 1976. A general survey of company disclosure may be found in Foster, G. *Financial Statement Analysis* Prentice-Hall second edn 1986, ch. 2.
11. De Paula, F. R. M. *Developments in Accounting* Sir Isaac Pitman and Sons 1948, pp. 36–7; from a paper delivered in 1946.
12. 'How Ferranti's World Lead Slipped Away' *Financial Times* 2 September 1985.
13. Mandy Rice-Davies reportedly said this during the Profumo affair.
14. 'Will Money Managers Wreck the Economy?' *Business Week* 13 August 1984.

15. Mueller, D. 'Further Reflections on the Invisible Hand Theorem' in Wiles, P. and G. Routh (eds) *Economics in Disarray* Basil Blackwell 1984, pp. 159–82.
16. 'When Companies Plan Long Term' Lombard column *Financial Times* 15 August 1985.
17. Alfred Chandler's extensive writings include *Strategy and Structure* MIT 1962; 'The Development of Modern Management Structure in the US and UK' in Hannah, L. (ed.) *Management Strategy and Business Development* Macmillan, 1976, ch. 1; *The Visible Hand* Harvard University 1977; 'The United States: Evolution of Enterprise', ch. 2 of Mathias, P. and M. Postan (eds) *The Cambridge Economic History of Europe* vol. VII part 2 Cambridge University 1978; 'The Growth of the Transnational Industrial Firms in the United States and the United Kingdom: A Comparative Analysis' *Economic History Review* second series 33 (1980): 396–410; 'The United States: Seedbed of Managerial Capitalism' in Chandler, A. and H. Daems (eds) *Managerial Hierarchies* Harvard University 1980. The paper 'The M-Form: Industrial Groups, American Style' *European Economic Review* 19(1) (September 1982): 3–23 contains the most 'Williamsonian' interpretation of his ideas to date. The stylised summary of his ideas below was drawn mostly from the *Cambridge Economic History*.
18. Oliver Williamson's writings since his conversion (see ch. 5) include 'Managerial Discretion, Organizational Form and the Multi-division Hypothesis' in Marris, R. and A. Wood (eds) *The Corporate Economy* Macmillan 1971, ch. 11; *Markets and Hierarchies* Collier Macmillan 1975; 'Emergence of the Visible Hand' in Chandler and Daems (note 17), ch. 6; 'The Modern Corporation: Origins, Evolution, Attributes' *Journal of Economic Literature* 19 (December 1981): 1537–68; 'The Markets and Hierarchies Programme of Research: Origins, Implications, Prospects' (with W. Ouchi) in Francis, A., J. Turk and P. Willman (eds) *Power, Efficiency and Institutions* Heinemann 1983 and 'Organizational Form, Residual Claimants and Corporate Control' *Journal of Law and Economics* 26(2) (June 1983): 351–66. The stylised summary of his ideas below is largely from the article in Francis et al.
19. Williamson 'Emergence of the Visible Hand' (note 18).
20. On the application of accounting principles to these problems, see Solomons, D. *Divisional Performance: Measurement and Control* Markus Weiner 1965.
21. Williamson in Francis et al. (note 18) favourably cites Steer, P. and J. Cable 'Internal Organization and Profit: An Empirical Analysis of Large UK Companies' *Journal of Industrial Economics* 27(1) (September 1978): 13–30, in which organisational form is used as an exogenous variable.
22. See Channon, D. *The Strategy and Structure of British Enterprise* Macmillan 1973, especially chs 3, 5 and 7.
23. Williamson 'The Modern Corporation' (note 18).
24. See Levy-Léboyer, M. 'The Large Corporation in Modern France' in Chandler and Daems (note 17), ch. 4; Prais, S. *Productivity and Industrial Structure* Cambridge 1981, ch. 5 (Germany) and Franko, L. *The European Multinationals* Harper and Row 1976, ch. 8.
25. See Clark, R. *The Japanese Company* Yale University 1979, ch. 4.
26. Franko, L. *The Threat of Japanese Multinationals* Croom Helm 1981, p. 128.
27. Hamel, G. and M. Prahalad 'Do you Really Have a Global Strategy?' *Harvard Business Review* 4 (July–August 1985): 139–48.
28. See, for instance, the articles in Francis et al. (note 18).
29. Chandler 'The Development of Modern Management Structure' (note 17).

30. Williamson *Markets and Hierarchies* (note 18), p. 144.
31. The discussion of the early historical development was aided by the reading of Williams, P. *The Emergence of the Theory of the Firm* Macmillan 1978, chs 4 and 5, and Shackle, G. *Years of High Theory* Cambridge University 1967, chs 1–6.
32. Viner, J. 'Cost Curves and Supply Curves' *Zeitschrift für Nationalökonomie* 3 (1931): 23–46.
33. Robinson, E. A. G. *The Structure of Competitive Industry* Cambridge original edn 1931, revised 1935. The 'problem of co-ordination' is discussed on pp. 44–8.
34. Kaldor, N. 'The Equilibrium of the Firm' *Economic Journal* 44 (March 1934): 60–76, and E. A. G. Robinson's response 'The Problem of Management and the Size of Firms' in the same volume, pp. 242–57.
35. Penrose, E. *Theory of the Growth of the Firm* Basil Blackwell 1959, p. 17.
36. See Chandler *Strategy and Structure* (note 17), p. 453. A neglected book along similar lines is Bower, J. *Managing the Resource Allocation Process* Harvard University 1970.
37. Penrose (note 35), p. 15.
38. Veblen, T. *The Theory of Business Enterprise* Transaction Books 1978; originally published in 1904.
39. Penrose (note 35), p. 20.
40. Ibid., ch. 8, and Chandler *Visible Hand* (note 17), p. 481.
41. Penrose (note 35), p. 151.
42. Coase (note 1).
43. Gerschenkron, A. 'Economic Backwardness in Historical Perspective', ch. 1 in *Economic Backwardness in Historical Perspective* Harvard University 1962. The thesis with regard to finance is discussed in many places in Kindleberger, C. *A Financial History of Western Europe* George Allen and Unwin 1984.
44. See the excellent if unfelicitously titled book by D. Granick *Soviet Metal Fabricating and Economic Development* University of Wisconsin 1967 and Sutcliffe, R. *Industry and Underdevelopment* Addison-Wesley 1971.
45. Hannah, L. 'Visible and Invisible Hands in Great Britain' in Chandler and Daems *Managerial Hierarchies* (note 17) explains the slow development of 'visible hand' administrative hierarchies in Great Britain by the efficient working of markets and middlemen.
46. Hannah, L. 'Managerial Innovation and the Rise of the Large Scale Company in Interwar Britain' *Economic History Review* second series 27 (1974): 252–70.
47. Kocka, J. 'Entrepreneurs and Managers in German Industrialization' in Mathias, P. and M. Postan (eds) *The Cambridge Economic History of Europe* vol. VII part 1 Cambridge University 1978, pp. 492–589.
48. Bower, J. 'Planning Within the Firm' *American Economic Association Papers and Proceedings* 60(2) (1970): 186–94.

7

Capital Markets, Finance and the Structure of Industry

Introduction

In this chapter we engage in a critical review of the neo-classical theory of finance and its present role in industrial economics. Our rationale is as follows:

1   We have already rejected the notion that a typology of firms can be usefully constructed which characterises them as belonging either to competitive or monopolistic market structures. Neo-classical economics attaches little or no significance to the absolute size of firms. Is there, then, in the famous Galbraithian phrase, no difference between General Motors (or a great conglomerate) and the corner grocery? If analysis of competition between firms in different size classes – in different capital market layers is to be meaningful, the relationship between the firm and the capital market, and the inadequacies of the neo-classical approach to finance must be confronted explicitly.

2   From the orthodox perspective only real factors generate changes in the industrial structure. A consideration of financial questions is therefore important for verification or refutation of some of the mainstream theory's central propositions on industrial evolution.

3   The mainstream theory of finance is largely derived from normative optimisation theory. We have several objections here:

   a   When closely examined, the theory makes much stronger assumptions about human rationality and indeed the nature of the universe than would first appear. These assumptions are not usually made as prominent as they might be for a full consideration of their plausibility.

b The central conclusions of orthodoxy are in serious contradiction to the enormous body of side information relating to firm and capital market behaviour. The perspective of most texts in microeconomics would lead one to think that considerations of finance, indebtedness and liquidity were of no more significance to the director of a typical capitalist enterprise than to a Soviet plant manager – an intriguing but hardly convincing notion.

c Most significantly, the standard methodology does not lend itself to an analysis of processes of historical *change*. For our purposes, rather than ask *whether or not* a particular financial market is efficient in processing available information, it is more relevant to compare the quality of financial information in the present with that available in the past and to observe *the change in the speed of response* of financial markets. Rooted as the static theory is in questions of optimisation within a *given* environment, it is not readily adaptable to such modes of dynamic analysis.

Thus a consideration of the theory of finance – its place in industrial economics and the theory of the firm – is unavoidable. We proceed first to examine the role of finance in twentieth century industrial evolution.

The Evolution of Giant Firms

The Stylised Facts of 'Anglo-Saxon' Economies
The fact of a long-term rise in aggregate concentration in the US and UK in the twentieth century would seem indubitable:[1]
There are difficulties both practical and conceptual with the measurement of aggregate concentration[2] but they are trivial compared with those to be found with the concept of market concentration. However, there is little in the way of theory or reasoned argument which permits strong conclusions to be derived from this evidence. The most well-known advocate of the notion that bigness has a distinctive – and malevolent – effect on the operation of industry is Corwin Edwards:

> [A large firm] may possess power in a particular market not only by virtue of its place in the organization of that market but also by virtue of the scope and character of its activities elsewhere. It may be able to exploit, extend or defend its power by tactics other than those that are traditionally associated with the idea of monopoly.

What then is the source of the large firm's power?

> An enterprise that is big . . . obtains from its bigness a special kind of power based upon the fact that it can spend money in large amounts.

Table 7.1

Share of the hundred largest enterprises in manufacturing net output (%)

	1909	1924	1928	1935	1947	1949	1953	1954	1958	1963	1967	1968	1970	1976	1977
United Kingdom	16	22		24		22	27		32	37	41	41	41	42	
United States	22		25	26	23			30	30	33	33		33		33

Sources: Prais, S. *The Evolution of Giant Firms in Britain* Cambridge University second edn 1981, pp. xv, 4 and 213; Weiss L. 'The Extent and Effects of Aggregate Concentration' *Journal of Law and Economics* 26(2) (June 1983): 429–53 and Scherer, F. M. *Industrial Market Structure and Economic Performance* Rand McNally second edn 1980, ch. 3.

If such a concern finds itself matching expenditures or losses, dollar for dollar, with a substantially smaller firm, the length of its purse assures it of victory.[3]

Critics have been quick to point out that since such strategies, if they are to be successful must presuppose the existence of substantial *market power* in particular sectors, and it is the latter which should be the subject of public scrutiny: the large conglomerate operating in many perfectly competitive markets is not to be feared. It is, however, the second aspect of the problem – the source of the big firm's power – which is of interest here. The 'deep pocket' approach as postulated above suggests that, for instance, a large firm may succeed in repelling or preventing the entry of a small(er) firm into a lucrative market by setting (or threatening to set) a price at a loss-making level, financing this operation from cash reserves or activities in other markets.

The orthodox response is that such a strategy is a priori unworkable: the large firm will only consider such action if the present discounted value of the future stream of excess returns is sufficient to compensate for short-term losses from this predatory strategy. In the absence of any displacement[4] or contrived excess capacity barrier to entry the future returns to a suitable entrant – of whatever size – are likely to be substantially above the rate at which such a firm *could raise funds on the capital market* and therefore no advantage accrues to the big firm's possession of a cash reserve in any struggle with the smaller firm. In the kind of capital market ordinarily postulated in economic theory there is neither advantage to the possession of cash *per se* nor to absolute size.

There is broad consensus that the emergence of giant firms in the US and the UK in the early part of the century was due to real factors, despite such financial aberrations as the creation of US Steel (see chapter 9). In recent years, especially under the influence of the writings of Alfred Chandler, the weight of emphasis among these real factors has shifted away from any monopolistic advantages of large firms to technological advantages, combined with the managerial revolution of those years. But what can be said about the dramatic post-war developments in aggregate concentration, in two decades doubling in the UK and in the US rising by 50 per cent?

For the UK, Prais's study concluded that it would be difficult to account for the rise in aggregate concentration by any dramatic increase in the efficient scale of operation of firms due to rises in plant or multi-plant economies.[5] Of the remaining efficiency factors, the most significant would seem to be the dynamic advantages of size – the capacity of large firms to innovate technologically and – more importantly here – to take successful advantage of the fruits of new technology. There is little evidence of a statistical kind in the contemporary literature on the relationship between technical progress and the size of firm[6] to account for the dramatic rise in aggregate concentration which took place both in the UK and the US between the late 1940s and 1970. As for marketing and distribution economies, it appears that, especially in the case of advertising, the advantages in favour of the largest firms have continued to increase up to the present day.[7] But the development in recent decades of well-developed 'markets' in advertising and distribution services may have countervailed against this tendency, so that smaller non-integrated firms now find they can purchase these services without the need for an elaborate 'do-it-yourself' infrastructure.

Ultimately, however, despite the impressive armoury of statistical analysis brought to bear by Prais on these questions, his conclusions are not wholly convincing. A large part of the UK merger movement would seem explicable by old-fashioned merger for monopoly and/or (sometimes government inspired) rationalisation of industry capacity in response to an increasingly competitive world environment, with three-quarters of the mergers between 1965 and 1977 taking the form of horizontal integration.[8] (Their apparent lack of success, however, raises doubts about the sufficiency of such an explanation.)

In the US, where so much of the growth of large firms has been of a highly diversified form, a stronger suspicion is present that the post-war increase in aggregate concentration has largely taken place for other than real reasons. In the 1960s and 1970s in the US only 20 per cent of mergers by value of assets were classified as either horizontal or vertical, while pure conglomerate mergers (those neither product extension nor market extension) comprised between one-third and one-half the total.[9] The remaining real factors[10] – process economies and synergy are those which are most relevant for consideration of firm growth outside its original sector. The former relates to technical gains from vertical integration, which on available evidence has not been increasing in recent decades (see chapter 8), while the latter is best discussed in the context of mergers.

Mergers and Acquisitions

In orthodox theory in the absence of real advantages or disadvantages – managerial, monopolistic, synergistic or otherwise – the market's evaluation of a bundle of assets (physical, human and organisational) should be identical whether they are collected together in an independent entity or as a subdivision of another firm. If, however, we should find that industrial evolution is crucially contingent upon the institutional arrangements governing finance and the disposition of property, we may call into question not only the mainstream theory's approach to finance, but much of its essential message with regard to the structure and organisation of the firm and the evolution of industry as well. An obvious manifestation of any such anomalies should be present in the ubiquitous and public (and therefore somewhat observable) phenomenon of mergers.

The case here may seem self-evident. Mergers have long been identified in the public mind with financial manipulation and boardroom drama. Large exchanges of property rights invariably have a financial dimension, but it is conceivable that real considerations ultimately predominate, despite the veil of financial considerations on the timing and form of events. It is our contention, however, that financial factors affect not only the timing and form of mergers, but are crucial to an understanding of the whole phenomenon – its genesis, magnitude and direction in the economy.

The overall effect of mergers on the growth of large firms is substantial, accounting in the UK in the 1960s for half the rise in aggregate concentration on some calculations and for over 100 per cent on others.[11] Mergers also accounted for comparable shares of the expenditure in gross investment[12] (reaching the extraordinary peak of 104 per cent in 1968) for the largest companies. For quoted companies as a whole, one-third of the total uses of funds was devoted to acquiring subsidiaries in the remarkable year of 1968. A large percentage of the post-war increase in US aggregate concentration would also seem to be accounted for by mergers, with the absolute values of the takeovers even more awe inspiring.[13]

A precise calculation of the role of mergers in the growth of the influence of large firms is, however, problematic. Of the various measurement difficulties encountered,[14] the most fundamental is the counterfactual nature of any such calculation: the pool of acquirors from the top one hundred firms is likely to change over the sample period and, more significantly, some assumption must be made about what growth rate *would* have taken place in the assets acquired if the merger had never been consummated. The overall conclusion is, however, uncontested: mergers had a major impact on the growth of post-war aggregate concentration in the UK and the US.

But the relationship between these phenomena is complex. The post-war rises in aggregate concentration in both countries were not coincident with great merger waves, and furthermore great waves often did not result in rises in aggregate concentration. Mergers are of especial interest because they represent public and in principle measurable manifestations of large firm financial advantage. Thus consider, for example, the effect upon the supply of loanable funds to smaller companies if mergers had been blocked in the UK in 1968. In the absence of perceived profitable alternatives to the mergers as investment opportunities, the largest firms might have made fewer demands for external finance upon the capital markets, and some additional part of their retained earnings, redistributed as dividends may have become available for small firm expansion. Managerial theories of mergers accurately reflect this desire of managers to avoid deterioration in the relative size of their companies, but such theories may also be congruent with approaches which emphasize the existence of imperfections in the capital market.

In the UK and the US the stylised facts of mergers are at variance with the standard theory's picture of events in three respects:

1 They do not seem capable of sufficient explanation by real advantages accruing to the firms involved.
2 There has been a systematic tendency for big firms to take over small ones and not vice versa.
3 Mergers take place in waves or cycles that seem financial in origin.

While some remarkable events in recent years call some of these points into question, any satisfying theory of the historical record of mergers should account for, or at least consider these factors.

The real advantages of mergers accruing to firms would seem, in many cases, quite limited, and the more distant from the acquiring firm's central sphere of activity, the more dubious they become. In the case of the pure conglomerate merger, the dominant firm in individual cases may be able to offer improvements in management technique to the smaller entity, but it is highly questionable as a systematic tendency. In fact, in the UK there are instances where mergers have failed even in closely linked spheres of activity due to 'managerial diseconomies' in the new combination.[15]

The possibility of synergy – a net gain in value due to real advantages when heterogeneous entities are conjoined, are severely discounted in the US literature. In a survey of executives on their opinion of the degree of importance of various sorts of synergy in conglomerate mergers, marketing, technology and production advantages scored 58, 20 and 32 marks out of 100 respectively, while advantages of a financial kind – the resultant availability of additional capital and the lowering of borrowing costs – scored 100.[16] The burden of proof would seem to lie with those who detect significant and pervasive synergistic benefits from the conglomeration of highly disparate activities.

The second stylised fact is an intriguing one, because to most people the idea that 'big fishes eat little fishes' and not the other way around is rather unsurprising. One of the more distinctive and interesting conclusions of neo-classical analysis is that in the absence of real economies, there is no significance to absolute size. Why, then, the blatant size difference historically between acquirer and acquiree?[17] In specific instances, various proximate explanations may be offered, but why the overwhelming tendency? An answer consistent with 'rational' behaviour on the part of all concerned, but in the context of capital market imperfections, would be as follows: the assets – physical and human of the smaller firm – are perceived by the larger company to have a valuation greater than that given by the market place. The large firm would then view the earnings potential of the smaller one as if the latter had access to the former's financial resources, and not as if it were subject to the financial limitations of a firm in its size class, which is how the market values it. If the gap between a (small) firm's expected returns and its ability to raise finance tends to widen at a particular phase in the credit cycle due to asymmetries in access to the capital market, it may help account for the last piece in the puzzle, which is the tendency for mergers to come in waves which seem roughly synchronised both with the business cycle and with stock market prices.[18] In the US especially, it has been suggested that the relationship is somewhat closer with stock prices than with general business activity, the implication being that mergers are synchronised with bull markets which fuel (and are fueled by) the efforts of promoters who make quick gains by paying with paper rather than cash when markets are bouyant.[19] But these and other statistics, including interest rates, move closely enough together to make discrimination of hypotheses on the basis of R^2 races a perilous pursuit. The fact that mergers seem to be synchronised with stock market movements even in West Germany, where the market has little direct role to play in mergers, may serve to suggest that share price movements may in some cases only be a reflection rather than a central cause of merger waves.[20]

Two versions of the speculative hypothesis reinforce the idea that the link to stock prices is more than a fortuitous one. Within the academic literature, Michael Gort[21] has suggested that economic disturbances associated with rapid movements in stock prices would have a greater effect upon the (more volatile) expectations of outsiders than of existing owners, thereby making for differences in their respective valuations of the firm and thus promoting changes in ownership. Not surprisingly, Gort believed most mergers to be unsuccessful, since they were the result of violently fluctuating expectations.[22] An implication of this theory is that rapidly falling stock prices should generate mergers no less than rising prices: clearly this is not the case.[23] Overall, Gort's explanation is within the broad purview of orthodoxy, with its emphasis on the dominance of real factors as the ultimate determinant of merger success, but it is in strong contradiction to the orthodox presumptions of capital market efficiency and symmetrical access to information.

There is indeed impressive evidence that waves of merger activity are often accompanied by hysteria and stupidity. G. Newbould[24] examined most of the important mergers in the UK in 1967 and 1968, and for 53 of the 242 mergers the growth rate per annum in the earnings of the acquired assets had to be less than 3 per cent – less than the rate of inflation – to achieve a 10 per cent rate of return on the acquisition. Clearly, some acquisitions were good bargains. But for 85 of the takeovers, the required growth rate was over 20 per cent per annum, and of these, *there were 22 mergers where the growth rate in earnings would have to be over 50 per cent per annum to gain a 10 per cent rate of return on the cost of the acquisition*. Veblen would have laughed.

The second version of the speculative hypothesis emphasizes not a generalised irrationality, but a cold-blooded attempt by acquiring groups to hoodwink the public. This version, which we may dub the Briloff[25] approach suggests that much of the impetus to the 'go-go' conglomerate wave in the late 1960s in the US came from dubious accounting practices. A company using, for instance, pooling-of-interest accounting could generate 'magical' increases in reported earnings and earnings per share (at the expense of an actual deterioration in cash flow as tax allowances for depreciation were lost on the undervalued assets) by taking assets of the acquired company on board at low nominal values instead of market (purchase price) values. This practice, combined with the market's tendency to capitalise all earnings at the acquiring firms' (higher) price-earnings ratio, was conducive to explosive, but meaningless growth in a binge of acquisition. It would be difficult to evaluate this analysis in terms of its objective validity as a scientific hypothesis due to the strong

'Heisenberg uncertainty' effect: Briloff and others succeeded in alerting the financial markets to this supposed abuse, but down to the present and it would seem *ad infinitum* new generations of promoters emerge with new schemes – opposed by new Briloffs, who will reintroduce these issues at ever higher levels of sophistication.

In general, it is impossible to dismiss the speculative element in mergers, but there is a danger of attributing too much importance to this explanation of such a pervasive phenomenon. Conglomerate firms do not appear to have had distinctively high price-earnings ratios in the heyday of the earlier US conglomerate merger wave,[26] and furthermore, the timing of mergers does not seem to be right to maximise advantages of this kind: Newbould[27] notes that the price of the victim firms' shares were at a 10–15 per cent discount four weeks before the first bid compared to the year's high while the discount for the acquiring firm was only 7–8 per cent. But while it is undoubtedly true that in an immediate sense acquiring firms seek the lowest possible price for a desirable acquisition, we would expect that, if this were a dominant consideration, mergers would be definitively out of phase with stock market prices, since price volatility of shares is inversely related to firm size:[28] the best bargains are to be had in a depressed market.

The most significant objection to a purely speculative explanation, however, is that we would expect the combinations to result overwhelmingly in failure, and the evidence on these questions is ambiguous. As we observed earlier with Newbould's data, while some of the acquisitions were apparently absurd decisions, a fair percentage appeared to be good investments. In the US and UK many large conglomerates – the products of recent binges of acquisition – seem capable of respectable performance as profit-making entities. The key result for the UK, however, is the study by Meeks,[29] which shows marriages by firms to be 'disappointing' when he examined the profitability of a sample of 233 UK mergers representing over a third of the total between quoted companies from 1964 to 1972. Similar results have been found in other studies for the profitability of mergers in the US and UK.[30]

Criticisms have been made of the methodology used in Meeks's work and in similiar studies, most significantly that post-merger profitability will tend to fall merely because there tends to be a downward bias in accounting rates of return whenever company results are grouped together under present accounting conventions.[31] If one believes that the latter problem is a substantial one, but that financial markets have the capability of seeing past accounting conventions to the underlying value of the firm, then merger success might better be measured using changes in firm valuation as a standard.

The results of valuation studies which have been undertaken for mergers in the US are more ambiguous. There is one school which suggests that merger behaviour is indeed consistent with value maximising behaviour on the part of the bidding firm,[32] though most find that the bulk of the benefits accrue to the shareholders of the target firm.[33] D. C.

Mueller, on the other hand finds that mergers generally fail to be successful in value terms.[34] For him, this evidence stands as a potent refutation of the neo-classical notion that firms are invariably guided by considerations of value maximisation, as opposed to a managerially-based growth maximisation strategy.[35]

Events in recent years in the US seem to shed light on Mueller's hypothesis of a managerial motivation for mergers, as well as some of the issues discussed earlier. The present wave of megamergers[36] began in the US in about 1974, and at least in its earliest stages it was not coincident with a booming stock market. This is not to suggest the absence of an important speculative component in these mergers. On the contrary, these events have re-inforced the old belief that promoters' profits play an important part in mergers, with the promoter's role often played today by an investment banker: 'In the not-so-old days an investment banker could wait for a golf buddy or a squash partner to drop a deal in his lap. Now bankers themselves come up with most of the ideas and persuade chief executives to go along.'[37]

But financial institutions have not just been functioning as promoters. They have shown their willingness to support takeover artists such as T. Boone Pickens and Carl Icahn in their raids on giant firms with money borrowed by consortia of banks and by the taking on of low-rated 'junk bonds'. While these acts *per se* contradict the notion developed below that the increasing competitiveness of financial institutions is having a de-concentrating effect on the industrial structure, in one sense they serve to illustrate the point very well: historically, as we have noted, 'big fishes eat little ones', and this fact seemed to be important confirmation of the existence of capital market layers. But in mergers since the mid 1970s there have consistently been cases in which smaller firms or independent financiers with the help of sophisticated outside financing arrangements have either taken over larger firms or have made credible threats to do so. There is a strong feeling that the special role of the giant firm in the hierarchy of enterprises is a thing of the past. 'What company is safe from the next wave of raiding? Answers Pickens: only Exxon.'[38] Such statements may contain a certain element of hyperbole, but do reflect what appears to be a significant departure from one of the major stylised facts about mergers.

In other ways, these mergers represent a discontinuity from earlier waves in the US. A far higher percentage of them have been of a horizontal variety, reflecting first and most significantly (after 1980) a more lenient attitude from the Justice Department, a prejudice developed by the stock market from earlier waves against combinations without an economic rationale behind them and, lastly the special circumstances existing in industries like oil and steel. It would be difficult to prove conclusively that these mergers have reflected goals for the firm other than value maximisation. It would seem, however, that these mergers have illustrated Mueller's presumption that managers finding themselves with large pools of cash in this period have used the money to purchase[39] other firms because they would rather do almost *anything* with the firm's resources than redistribute them to the owners. For many firms 'The choice of a target is a decision of lesser importance than the initial decision to acquire.'[40]

These managerial motives for merger invariably exist in the context of conditions in the capital market very different from those portrayed in the neo-classical picture, as may be seen in the case of the McDermott Corporation, which became involved in the bidding contest for Babcock & Wilcox in 1977 because it had a great deal of cash and didn't want to become a takeover target itself.[41] Thus, while shareholder control over firms is relatively speaking tighter than at any time in the past, the present merger wave may be evidence of how much residual managerial slack still exists.

We conclude that mergers are a complex and contradictory phenomenon. If the decision processes seem to display greater elements of irrationality than preconceptions based on standard theory would have led us to believe, it may be simply that, compared with other investment decisions of the firm, mergers are more subject to public scrutiny, and that such irrationality is typical of firms' decision processes. On the other hand, important systematic tendencies have historically existed, with big firms consistently setting a higher valuation upon smaller firms' assets than does the market, all this taking place in phase with cyclical activity.

How does this discussion integrate with the stylised fact of an increase in aggregate concentration, and what is the relationship between this increase and the change in the level of competitiveness in the economy? Until now, we have identified movements in aggregate concentration with the destiny of the largest firms, when it is just as concerned with the growth and creation of firms at the other end of the spectrum. For all the furore in the US in the late 1960s and early 1970s about conglomerate mergers, aggregate concentration *did not increase at all in this period*. We think it not accidental that this tendency was manifest in the faster growing US, rather than in the UK, and that, for both countries, the period of most significant deconcentration coincided with the period of the Second World War – a *period of rapid growth in both economies which was combined with inhibition on merger activity*.

The growing predominance of large over small firms in the post-war world does not represent any inevitable technological wave of the future. This assertion is based not only on the statistical evidence presented above, but as well on a strong intuitive feeling derived from the observation that this predominance is most evident in the slow growing UK, while in the US, but especially in rapidly growing and dynamic economies such as Japan and Italy, the small firm sector is far stronger.[42]

Thus, there is heuristic evidence of both a cross-sectional and time series kind to suggest that economic growth is, at least in the twentieth century; inherently deconcentrating, a fact somewhat disguised and neutralised by the countervailing force of mergers. The significance of changes in aggregate concentration for overall competitiveness will be pursued in chapter 9, but what becomes manifest is that despite improved information and growing sophistication of financial markets in the twentieth century, the growth of these giant entities makes unconvincing the picture derived from standard theory of all firms having equal and symmetrical access in a perfect capital market.

The Neo-classical Theory of Finance

The World of Finance from a Neo-classical Perspective

The 'problem' of time has always presented itself as an obstacle of particular difficulty in economic theory. One might suppose that the special needs of the mainstream theory – convergent, harmonious results all derived from simple, rational axioms of choice – would make this an area of extreme contentiousness in economics. Indeed, in the sphere of macroeconomics time and its related aspects remain substantive issues in the debates surrounding the Keynesian revolution. But curiously, in microeconomics such controversy is remarkably attenuated. The over-whelming dominance of the orthodox theory of finance upon mainstream microeconomic theory has been a major obstacle to the development of industrial economics and to an accurate perception of the evolution of business activity.

Perhaps the best testimony to the pervasiveness of the real factors hypothesis is in Marshallian textbook theory, where its role as an hypothesis – an empirical statement capable of disproof – is never really clarified, let alone debated. Thus consider the following propositions:

1 *The cost curve is derived only from real factors of production.* The firm's cost curve is invariably derived from a production function whose inputs include only real factors – land, labour and capital, along with the market prices of these inputs. The role of cost as regularly used in a colloquial and business sense to include the cost of finance is ignored or relegated to a separate discussion on investment appraisal. It is these real cost curves which, when combined with demand, are used to determine relative prices.

2 *Only real factors determine firm size.* A corollary of proposition 1 is the strong prediction that in competitive environments the size of the typical firm will be shaped by the countervailing forces of (technological) economies of scale and managerial diseconomies – the familiar minimum point on the long run average cost curve. *If we knew all the real factors impingeing upon firms we could predict their average size.* Broadly under-stood, this prediction would apply to firms in non-competitive environ-ments as well, in which case the relevant real factors are those affecting both cost and demand.

3 *Firms never fail for financial reasons.* The standard presentation contains a prediction of firm failure. Firms go out of business in the short run because revenues fall below variable costs and in the long run because

they fall below total costs. Firm survival then is a matter of income and not liquidity. They will not go out of business simply because they have the wrong mix of assets (e.g. not enough cash).

4   *A firm's decisions concerning real investment are totally independent of how these decisions are to be financed.* There is a cost of capital for the firm as a whole, and there is no reason why methods of finance should be tailored to different kinds of projects or to different kinds of assets. It is not evident from the theory why firms in capital intensive sectors, such as steel and railways, compared with textile firms should traditionally have been financed with greater proportions of fixed obligations – long-term debt for instance, as opposed to variable short-term bank loans linked to turnover.

5   *The possession of cash is not a consideration in deciding whether or not to undertake a project.* As a corollary of 4, in evaluating an investment project (e.g. a merger) the only consideration will be the net present value of the future stream of earnings to be derived from that project. The question of the possession of cash to be able to afford the project is irrelevant. Furthermore, cash is irrelevant to the evaluation of an invest-ment in another sense: two firms, for instance, will not set different valuations on the income stream of a potential takeover rich in liquid assets simply because one of the potential acquirers is short of cash. More generally, in the absence of real synergistic effects, all firms will use the same rate of discount in evaluating projects or, at the very least, there should be no systematic biases in any such evaluation connected, for instance, with capital market advantages due to firm size. The only relevant calculation for *any* firm is the present value of the future stream of earnings, evaluated with the universal market rate of discount and an appropriate consideration of any real sector or business risk that might be present, but none for any intrinsically financial (e.g. liquidity) aspects of the decision.

Two clarifications must be made here: first, the propositions are to be viewed from a positive, predictive perspective: whatever their good sense as normative decision rules, for instance, proposition 4, our only concern is whether they are good descriptions of reality. Secondly, note that these 'predictions' had to be culled from the standard textbook expositions, in which context they are usually presented as if indistinguishable from such statements as 'firms maximise profits at a level of output where marginal cost equals marginal revenue', which are tautologies.

Assumptions about the nature of the capital market thus have crucial implications for standard microeconomics, as can be seen from the following example. In figure 7.1, a monopolist faces demand curve DD´ and has costs represented by AC (= MC). Profit maximisation, given the 'fact' that the market is monopolised will take place at a price of P_M, with output of Q_M. In the Marshallian conception, P_M may be identified not only with profit maximisation in a single period (the 'rational' profit maximising monopolist), but with the intertemporal *wealth* maximising

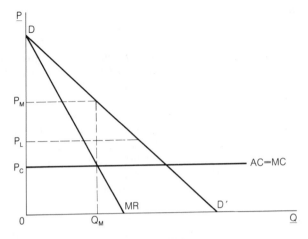

Figure 7.1

monopolist as well. *Once the possibility exists that there are barriers to entry into an industry which are less than blockaded, it is not necessarily true that static profit maximisation may be identified with the 'rational' wealth maximising entrepreneur.*

It is sometimes suggested that P_L, the entry limiting price (which, presumably, is known with certainty) will invariably be set by the monopolist. But why? It may well be worth while for the wealth maximising monopolist to 'take the money and run'. This will be dependent (in no simple way) upon the interaction of:

1   the level of the entry barrier (symbolically repesented by the difference between P_L, the average costs of a potential entrant, and AC, the average costs of the monopolist),
2   the time dimension involved in entering the industry. (It may be easy to enter the natural rubber industry, but may still take seven years to produce a crop), and
3   the subjective rate of discount of the monopolist. *Unless we make some very powerful assumptions about the nature of the capital market so that the rate of discount is universal and exogenous, it will be a decision variable for the firm.*

These conditions break with the traditional view that static profit maximisation models may be identified with, and used as, surrogates for models of wealth maximisation, since the two may well diverge unless profit maximisation is proposed, rather tautologically, to take place over a 'long run demand function' incorporating the possibility of entry.[43] In such a case, the demand curve is being used to disguise the uncertain nature of the environment which faces a monopolist. Instead of a simple static profit maximisation problem, the monopolist faces a complex intertemporal problem in which the current and expected future market demand curve interacts with the uncertain behaviour of potential rivals who *may* choose to enter. But even if we put aside the problems of an uncertain environment, *the simple Marshallian solution only holds if the monopolist's subjective rate of time preference has no influence on the price which is set*.

Underlying this proposition and the others listed above is a theory of the capital market which permits us to examine the real influences on business activity behind the veil of financial flows and institutional structures. The characteristics of such a market are broadly analogous to those found in a conventional (static) perfect market. The conditions facing individual traders are such that the market and the prices within it are:

1 *Symmetric*. All participants in the market face the same (unique) rate of interest. In the strongest formulation there is not even a gap between the borrowing and lending rate.
2 *Anonymous*. No special qualities are attached to individual traders (i.e. borrowers and lenders) in the derivation of the market outcome.
3 *Parametric*. At the going rate of interest individual borrowers and lenders are unconstrained, and not subject to credit limitations or restrictions of any kind. Allocation of credit is determined purely by its 'price', and not by any quantitative limitation.

When such a capital market exists, we may derive the famous Fisherian Separation Theorem which decisively distinguishes real from financial decisions:[44]

In figure 7.2, an individual or firm has an initial endowment of Y_0 consumption in the present and Y_1 in the future which yields a level of satisfaction U_1 and a present value (wealth) of $0W_0^Y$, based on the gradient $-(1+r)$ of the capital market line MM. The individual could improve utility and wealth by moving along the productive opportunities surface PP', sacrificing present for future consumption. In the absence of capital market opportunities, the outcome in the real economy – the point R chosen on the production locus PP' – would be a reflection of the personal trade-off between present and future consumption of the individual given the state of production possibilities.

With a capital market, however, outcomes in the real sector will be separated from individual preferences about the mix between present and future consumption. All individuals will use their wealth in the combination dictated by point K, the tangency between the capital market line and the productive opportunities set. If individuals desire a different mix between present and future consumption from that dictated by point K, they can move along the capital market line on which K lies to point C, which clearly dominates the point R.

Individual subjective preferences have no effect upon real outcomes, and the production decision is unrelated to an individual's or firm's

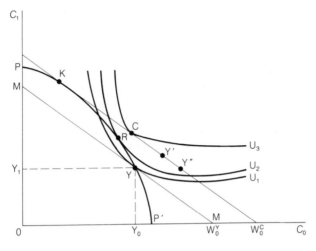

Figure 7.2

subjective rate of discount. Even a company wholly owned by Bertie Wooster would never produce at point Y, no matter how 'impatient' he was: it would be easy for his loyal servant Jeeves (no problem of owner-manager conflict here!) to convince him that production should proceed to point K *no matter what his personal preferences*, which Wooster could, if he chose, then transform into personal consumption streams such as C, or into Y′, which has the same proportions of present and future consumption as does Y but in greater amounts, or even to Y″, where all of the gains are taken as present consumption. There is another interesting conclusion here: the individual's starting point on the PP′ curve – the initial endowment depicted by point Y – has no effect on the final outcome. Even if Wooster's endowment had been a firm whose wealth is completely in terms of claims on future revenue, such as patents (a point on the PP′ curve to the left of K), the move to production point K and then on to the desired mix of present and future consumption at C, Y′ or Y″ would take place in the same way: the initial possession of wealth in a particular form – such as cash – is of no significance here.

Thus, it has long been implicit that the adoption of Fisherian capital market theory makes ordinary business topics such as working capital management an irrelevancy in the orthodox microeconomic theory of the firm. The only internally generated measure necessary for the calculation of the value of the firm is its flow of income (net earnings) represented in the static framework by the difference between revenue and costs. But the absolute irrelevance of the firm's financial structure to its value was not made explicit until the publication of the famous article of Modigliani and Miller in 1958 which, ironically, was highly dissident and controversial in the context of the traditional view of finance held by business practitioners and business academics.

In the traditional view, as may be seen in figure 7.3, there is an optimal ratio of debt to equity (X*) which the firm must determine in order to minimise the cost of capital and (other things equal) maximise the value of the firm. (As we shall see below, the implicit presumption that there is a cost of capital for the firm as a whole and not one specific to individual projects has been questioned empirically.) Cheap debt causes the average cost of capital to decline, until this effect is counteracted by the increasing riskiness of the firm due to its greater indebtedness.

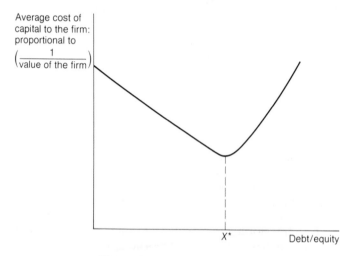

Figure 7.3 The 'traditional view'

The argument from Modigliani–Miller in figure 7.4, however, is that two firms with the same earnings profile and the same level of business (i.e. 'real' – cost and demand determined) risk[45] cannot differ in value simply because their assets are financed by different proportions of debt and equity:

> a firm cannot reduce the cost of capital, i.e. increase the market value of the stream it generates – by securing part of its capital through the sale of bonds, even though debt money appears to be cheaper. This assertion is equivalent to the proposition that, under perfect markets, a dairy farmer cannot in general earn more for the milk he produces by skimming some of the butter fat and selling it separately, even though butter fat per unit weight sells for more than whole milk. The advantage from skimming the milk rather than selling whole milk would be purely illusory; for what would be

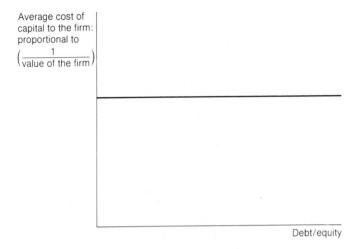

Figure 7.4   The Modigliani – Miller view

gained from selling the high-priced butter fat would be lost in selling the low-priced residue of thinned milk.[46]

The mechanism postulated by Modigliani–Miller to bring about this result is as follows: any individual investor, *able to borrow and lend at the going rate of interest* can reproduce through 'home-made leverage (gearing)' the proportions of debt and equity which exist in any company, and therefore the only criterion used for the valuation of a company by a wealth holder would be its stream of earnings. There is no reason why the market should evaluate a company issuing debt any differently from an all equity company if both have an equivalent earnings stream. These results have been extended to suggest that other aspects of firm finance, such as the dividend policy, are also irrelevant.[47]

In summary, the standard theory of the firm contains a host of implicit predictions about business activity which derive from the Fisherian separation of real from financial activity in a perfect capital market, many of which appear to be sharply at variance with behaviour ordinarily observed of firms, such as the contention made explicit in the Modigliani–Miller theorem that the value of the firm is unaffected by the structure of its financial claims. A further serious problem for the theory is that the initial derivation by Fisher of a perfect capital market is not strictly analogous to that for a static market for a commodity, since it takes place in a world of *certainty about the future*. In such a context, the Modigliani–Miller theorem on the irrelevance of a firm's mix of financial assets between 'risky' debt and 'safe' equity becomes trivial, since the distinction between bonds and equity has no meaning – it was only in the context of the possibility of disappointed expectations on the part of wealth-holders that the Modigliani–Miller theorem seemed so wildly counter-intuitive. The questions to be posed are as follows: how does the mainstream theory transfer its essential conclusions to a world of less than perfect certainty and is this adaptation successful?

Risk and Uncertainty in Capital Markets

The mainstream theory gains its greatest prestige as a *global* theory of finance (as opposed to, say, its practical application in the prediction of stock market prices) due to its origins in the rational theory of choice. As in the theory of competition, there is a split in the orthodox theory of finance between the exposition to be found in the literature of general equilibrium and that of more practical approaches. In the former presentation commodities are delineated qualitatively, in space and also in time. An inter-temporal general equilibrium is brought about when all markets, including futures markets and a complete set of contingent futures markets covering all possible states of nature, are cleared simultaneously. A complete set of commodity prices then emerge which embody not only exchange relations in the present, but time-weighted values in the future.[48]

There are two reactions to the conclusions reached in this model which, curiously, do not seem to be mutually exclusive. First, that they are a *per se* demonstration of the impossibility of a coherent solution to the 'problem' of time in the context of decentralised market decisions, since the notion of futures markets ranging over all contingencies is inconceivable and empirically non-existent. A common response to this breach of faith in free markets is wonderfully Panglossian: such markets would exist if people 'wanted' them, and their non-existence is not a sign of anything suboptimal in a Paretian sense. In this static framework it is quite impossible to deal with institutional changes resulting from alterations in habits, attitudes and perceptions. Does the present explosion of financial futures markets imply that the world was formerly suboptimal, or have they come into existence because the benefits now exceed the costs, where before they were 'obviously' unnecessary? We come perilously close to theology with such arguments.

It is the second reaction to the results of the general equilibrium theory which has proved more important: there *is* a solution to the 'problem' of time in the context of rational choice theory, in which the only primitive data necessary concern individual preferences and the state of nature. In other words, these real factors alone determine economic outcomes, without regard to finance or to institutional setting. But general equilibrium theory, with its focus on non-existent contingent futures markets distracts attention from the central problems of risk and uncertainty highlighted in the more practical approaches to finance, and it is to these which we now turn.

The mainstream theory of finance attempts to re-create a perfect capital market in a world of less than perfect certainty. It makes the key assumption that *the gap between the theory of the capital market under perfect certainty and the real world of uncertainty may be bridged by modelling individual behaviour (and the world itself) on a foundation of risk-based parameters.* Since this assumption is a crucial prerequisite to the (re)construction of a perfect capital market, it brings into question the common usage of the latter term, which implies a strict analogy with the static case: it is one thing to suggest that the static market for a particular commodity, say steel, would be 'perfect' by the usual criteria in the absence of government restrictions, tariffs, etc., and quite another to say that the capital market would be perfect but for the fact that the Almighty designed the Universe to be Uncertain rather than Risky!

The overall intention of the neo-classical procedure is clear: a global theory of the capital market may be constructed if to every asset in the economy can be linked one additional parameter – a measurable amount of its risk. In a world of risk-averse individuals the asset would suffer a finite and well-defined reduction from its certain value depending on the market valuation of this risk. *The gap between the world of certainty and that of uncertainty is bridged by a mere readjustment in the relative prices of assets.*

It is not our purpose here to criticise these decision rules, or to suggest improved alternatives. Indeed, the essentially operationalist origin of the risk-based approaches has such a dominant influence in this literature that the existence of a parametric rate of interest available to borrowers and lenders is a common incidental presumption of these models. But the question is precisely whether such a parametric rate can exist at all in a world of less than perfect certainty: the significance of this body of theory here is its implicit role in mainstream analysis as a viable *description* of the pricing of *every asset* in the economy. This model is used to legitimate the fundamental conclusions of the Fisherian view of the capital market and the related Modigliani–Miller theorem, with their segregation of real from financial outcomes.

The risk-based theory of finance gains its greatest prestige from the fact that its rules of behaviour may be derived from a set of axioms of choice superficially very similar to those found in the static theory of consumer choice, with the necessity for comparability and transitivity for individuals no longer defined over commodities but over 'prospects'.[49] The axiom which for our purposes crucially distinguishes it from those of static consumer theory suggests that we can use finite probability measures to put a 'price' on the uncertainty attached to various prospects. Thus, if X, Y and Z are outcomes such that the preference ordering is as follows:

$$X > Y \geqslant Z \text{ or } X \geqslant Y > Z,$$

then there exists a unique α (a probability) such that an individual will be indifferent between Y and a gamble between X and Z with probability α:

$$Y \sim G(X, Z; \alpha)$$

Thus, he or she is willing to attach a finite value to the risk attached to any outcome. This assumption permits us to use probability measures to derive finite, consistent and cardinally ranked inter-temporal trade-offs in a world of 'uncertainty'.

The most prominent model of capital market pricing which has been developed using the above axioms has been the Capital Asset Pricing Model (CAPM).[50] The model constructs a frontier of efficient portfolios – the envelope of portfolios with minimum risk for a given level of expected return for every participant in the market, as illustrated in figure 7.5, with points 1 and 2 for individuals A and B respectively.

The only part of a security's risk that has to be considered for its incorporation in an efficient portfolio is that which is correlated with other securities in the portfolio (the systematic risk), since by the assumptions of the model all other risk can be diversified away. Note that our use of the term 'security' mimics the terminology in the CAPM literature, where the focus is upon its application to public security exchanges. But to be valid as a view of the price of any asset, there must be such a price of risk applicable to *every* asset – marketed and non-marketed – in the economy, and not just those listed on a specific exchange. In equilibrium the only risk a security has is its systematic covariance with the market portfolio (a portfolio containing all assets in the proportions held by the market as a whole), its β risk, since its residual (unsystematic risk) can be diversified away. Low β investments will demand a lower expected return than high ones (in a risk-averse world).

The efficient frontier of portfolios gives us a market trade-off between risk and return as in figure 7.5. However, the 'price of risk' will not be

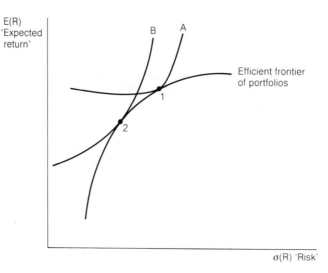

Figure 7.5

unique, since the trade-off between risk and return will differ between individuals depending upon the point of tangency between their highest indifference curve and the efficient frontier. The solution to this problem is a new separation theorem. An unsurprising equilibrium condition for the model is that the market portfolio is on the efficient frontier, the slope of which at any point (in mean–variance analysis) will be a constant. Then, as can be seen in figure 7.6, *the slope of the efficient frontier at the market portfolio point gives us a clear and universal measure of the appropriate trade-off between risk and return – the market price for risk*.

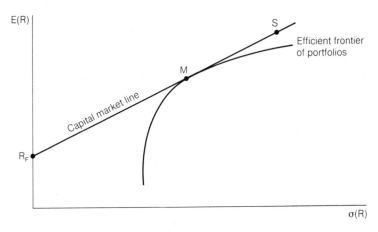

Figure 7.6

In figure 7.6 the efficient frontier is now extended out to R_F, the rate of return on a riskless asset,[51] M, the market portfolio and since short selling is possible in the model, a portfolio such as S. The new separation theorem states that efficient portfolios will consist only of combinations of the market portfolio and the riskless asset. It is now clear that *any* asset in the economy can be priced using the market price for risk. For asset i,

$$E\ (R_i) = R_F + \beta_i\ [E(R_M) - R_F]$$

where β_i is a measure of the systematic relation between the return on the market portfolio (R_M) and on asset i:

$$\frac{\mathrm{cov}\ (R_i, R_M)}{\sigma^2\ (R_M)}$$

Thus, if the returns on asset i were totally uncorrelated with those in the market portfolio ($\beta_i = 0$), it would only have to yield the riskless rate of return R_F. If $\beta_i = 1$, i.e. fluctuations in its returns perfectly parallel those of the market portfolio, and asset i would have to yield an expected return of R_M. All asset prices can then be modified in moving from a certain to a risky world, with the market portfolio as a norm, assets having values of β < 1 being adjusted upwards in price and those with values of β > 1 being adjusted downwards. It is then possible to re-derive the essential conclusions of neo-classical theory such as the Modigliani–Miller theorem in a model in which 'uncertainty' has been explicitly incorporated.[52] There is then nothing special about the 'problem' of time, and both in principle and in practice questions surrounding the existence of uncertainty can be integrated into the theory of relative prices.

What meaning can be attached to this solution, and does it form the basis of a viable general approach to asset pricing? It is often asserted that disputes over the use of risk-based decision rules purely concern their role as an accurate description of human behaviour[53] and that, while there is no question of these rules being realistic, they serve to generate a wide variety of testable hypotheses, and thus pass muster as part of a viable scientific research programme.

It is the nature of this class of models that, in order to be operationalised, these risk-based beliefs must correspond to some aspects of objective reality, and therefore, the model is implicitly imposing a specific structure on events in the real world. Let us return to figure 7.6. Note that prices in the capital market emerge from a maintained equilibrium, with the market portfolio always on the efficient frontier. Furthermore, the CAPM is invariably estimated statistically on the assumption that returns follow a fair game pattern, whereby expected values are taken to be the best predictor of the results that actually emerge in the market: on average, expectations are an unbiased estimate of the future.

The strongest hint about the meaning to be attached to this model of market equilibrium (note that such hints are usually all we can expect from such models, since the question of the substantiality of the equilibrium – is it instantaneous or to last for all time? – is open-ended in static frameworks) concerns the question of the convergence of expectations of participants. In pure general equilibrium models with simultaneous clearing of all markets, present and future, the results are unaffected whether all individuals hold heterogeneous expectations or identical, homogeneous-equivalent average expectations.[54]

However, in the capital market models developed in the theory of finance, such as the CAPM, the construction of the efficient frontier is ordinarily done on the assumption that investors have homogeneous expectations about the expected return and variance of securities: an explicit derivation of market prices from models in which investors have heterogeneous expectations can only be done as part of a simultaneous solution, since such models have to take into consideration individual investors' marginal rates of substitution between expected return and variance. But marginal rates of substitution are in general a function of wealth and therefore prices. This implies that market prices themselves are needed to determine individual investors' trade-offs, which are then used to determine market prices. To avoid this problem of simultaneity operational models seem to demand homogeneous expectations,[55] which has been interpreted to mean that market investors converge around certain average values.[56]

The congruence of the assumptions of convergence of expectations of investors with the existence of capital market equilibrium is not fortuitous. While in a formal sense the investor may construct subjective estimates using any set of (consistent) criteria, there is a strong implication in the theory that, *if the convergent expectations that consistently emerge are not to be the result of accident or psychological uniformity, investors must be using a methodology rooted in classical probability theory, and the maintenance of this equilibrium over time implies that the world is reasonably modelled in this manner.* The efficient frontier of portfolios of figure 7.4 then represents not merely the market's conventional or subjective opinion on the relationship between the return and risk of every asset, but depicts results *emanating from an objectively correct decision rule.*

It is just conceivable that there have been enough repeatable events and a well-defined enough model in the minds of investors to give coherent, risk-based discounts to the relative valuation of, for instance, shares in companies producing baby foods versus those in capital goods or, perhaps, government securities at different ends of the term structure. But could such a mechanism be relevant to *every* asset in the economy, marketed and non-marketed (including those containing large amounts of so-called human capital), even as a first approximation, with this equilibrium constantly maintained or renewed? The question involved is not simply one of lack of information about all these assets, but whether the world, as a first approximation, is so uniform, so lacking in discontinuity and unforeseen events as to make this approach viable:

> We should not conclude from this that everything depends on waves of irrational psychology. On the contrary, the state of long term expectation is often steady, and even when it is not, the other factors exert their compensating effects. We are merely reminding ourselves that human decisions affecting the future, whether personal or political or economic, cannot depend on strict mathematical expectation, *since the basis for making such calculations does not exist*; and that it is our innate urge to activity which makes the wheels go round, our rational selves choosing between the alternatives as best we are able, calculating where we can, but falling back for our motive on whim or sentiment or chance.[57] (italics added)

Recently, it has been suggested that prices on the New York Stock Exchange have varied much more widely over the last several decades than could possibly be explained by a simple pricing rule using *ex post* dividends.[58] While this has been taken as evidence against the idea that the stock market is efficient, it seems even more relevant to the question of one's 'feel' about the capital market: if prices on a sophisticated exchange such as the stock market move about erratically, what about the market for *all* assets? Can we take as a first approximation a model which presupposes globally rational risk-based behaviour which, furthermore, must be rooted in an objectively correct understanding (implicit or explicit) of how outcomes are generated in the real world?

We shall be attempting below to raise the outlines of a descriptively accurate picture of the capital market. Such a procedure may seem unexceptional to readers from other social sciences or indeed, other sciences, but within the rigid framework of contemporary economic orthodoxy it borders on pure heresy. It is, therefore, incumbent upon us first to divert the reader from more substantive questions to the murky depths of methodological disputation.

Firm Finance and the Capital Market – An Empirical Approach

A Methodological Detour

Finance is a fitting and particularly intriguing setting for a consideration of the conjuncture between theory and practice in economics. On the one hand, in no other area has the application of advanced microeconomic theory reached such a wide and receptive audience,[59] while, at the same time, there are consistent indications that even sophisticated financial analysts proceed to deal with practical issues as if neo-classical theory never existed: 'A company [such as Bendix] that owns so much money is also a mouth-watering takeover target, which means Agee must look to his defences as often as he scours the horizon for fresh conquests ... a potential acquirer would only have to put up $600m because he could finance the rest of the deal with Bendix's own cash'.[60] In the academic literature, two alternative approaches have been posed to the neo-Fisherian orthodoxy, the 'potential surprise' theory of George Shackle,[61] and the attempts to supplement the standard theory with more realistic assumptions.

Shackle's purpose is to create normative rules which more closely adhere to our intuitive notions of decisions under uncertainty than do the usual risk-based criteria. Attempts to operationalise Shackle's theory into a fully fledged alternative to neo-classical theory have not been successful. This failure is hardly surprising, as any movement in the direction of pure uncertainty is bound to make the derivation of decision rules even more difficult, unless restrictions are imposed upon the model which may, in the end, seem no less arbitrary than the risk-based criteria of the standard theory. Our own view is that while it may be desirable and possible to construct (presumably rather complex) normative decision rules which mirror actual behaviour in this world of non-certainty more accurately than do present risk-based approaches, it would be wrong to suspend the construction of a detailed picture of how in fact firms and others finance themselves while awaiting this development. Botany may not be classical physics, but it is a real science with substantive accomplishments, and economists should not balk at such a comparison.

An institutionalist approach to finance would certainly be contested by the second alternative to the neo-Fisherian school, whose attitude is best summarised in a discussion by Harry Johnson on the correct approach to floating exchange rates:

> The difference can be encapsulated in the proposition that whereas the older generation of economists is inclined to say 'the floating rate system does not work the way I expected, therefore the theory is wrong' . . . the younger generation is inclined to say 'the floating rate system is a system that should be expected to operate rationally, like most markets; if it does not seem to work rationally by my standards, my understanding of how it ought to work is probably defective; and I must work harder at the theory of rational maximizing behavior and the empirical consequences of it if I am to achieve understanding'.[62]

As Charles Kindleberger comments on the above passage, rationality is thus an a priori assumption rather than a description of the world. There is a phrase from contemporary British politics that also seems appropriate in characterising this attitude: the Resolute Approach, with its ever abiding corollary, TINA.[63] We shall record here our astonishment at the ever increasing tendency to identify the domain of rational approaches to economic and, indeed, all social and historical questions with that of utilitarian, transactions-based approaches rooted in general equilibrium methodology.

An enlightened and, in many ways, productive example of this attitude may be noted in an article by George Akerloff. He writes that 'a major challenge . . . *to economic theory* . . . [is] to construct an individualistic theory in which income and resource allocation reflect, to some extent, the divisions of society as described by the sociologists'.[64] As an example he notes that after the American Civil War the share cropping system had to vie with wage payments in the South and that the former eventually won out because for landlords it alleviated the burden of monitoring their tenants' efforts.

Akerloff's explanation may indeed be the correct one, but do we believe it co-extensive with *economic* or even coherent responses to the problem? The model implicitly assumes an unchanging adversarial relationship between landlord and tenant, with the sharecropping 'experiment' ultimately winning out as a result of its greater technical efficiency from the landlord's perspective. An alternative hypothesis is that landlords, with their extensive experience as slave owners and, predominantly, with small numbers of tenants, were relatively unconcerned with monitoring costs, and that the most significant reason for the growth of the semi-feudal relationship was that, for black people, a free market in labour or any form of civil protection progressively ceased to exist in the South with the decline of Reconstruction governments and the imposition of racist terror symbolised by the Ku Klux Klan. Thus share-cropping was simply the vehicle for increased exploitation of the former slaves. Some may consider such an explanation less convincing than Akerloff's, but is it outside the boundaries of rational or even economic discourse?

The methodology of utility maximisation has been rapidly spreading to other domains.[65] Should economists impose upon themselves the constraints of this methodology? If conditions in the capital market cannot be explained with reference to any well-defined model of inter-temporal utility maximisation, should economists continue to use such an approach because it represents the only possible course, or should they abandon any discussion of the topic until an 'economic' explanation is found?

In recent years, several attempts at an augmented neo-classical approach have been made in the literature, and the results have been suggestive. The practice by banks of screening and non-price rationing of borrowers certainly violates the Fisherian picture of a capital market which is symmetric, anonymous and parametric. But screening can be made consistent with rational maximising behaviour in a world of imperfect information, as can non-price rationing when higher interest rates would increase the riskiness of the banks' portfolio.[66] In a similar vein, the existence of agency and monitoring costs in the context of the separation of ownership from control in the modern corporation has been used to explain 'real life deviations from Fisherian conclusions while preserving . . . the fundamental principle of maximising behaviour . . . on the part of all individuals'.[67] The existence of information and agency costs, combined with the Chicago School's somewhat wistful observation that legal obstacles exist to a free market in human capital (i.e. laws against endenturing and slavery), seem to be at the centre of contemporary attempts to preserve traditional neo-classical methodology with non neo-classical conclusions.

What reservations do we have to these new-found attempts at realism?

1   In the past, models constructed on the basis of individual maximisation behaviour have been far from convergent in their conclusions – the Modigliani–Miller theorem is a prominent example: small changes in assumptions, each one of which may seem inherently reasonable (e.g. the introduction of corporate taxes), can cause the model to generate radically different results. This new literature, with its attempt to respond to real world anomalies in the theory seems to be incorporating a hidden methodology of science: models are acceptable if they offer satisfactory *ex post* explanations or rationalisations for one specific aspect of objective reality (e.g. credit rationing) which violates the conclusions of the general theory, but these models must be generated from a framework of individual utility maximisation in which the broader aspects of the theory are not brought into question. There is no obvious convergence towards an alternative general theory which can deal simul-

taneously with the *multiple* anomalies of the existing approach to the capital market and which offers a coherent and believable picture of its mode of operation.

2   Is there a sense in which these models will be seen as mere *ad hoc* adjustments to the pure free market approach without, however, the latter's elegance, simplicity and decisiveness? If, within the economics profession there is an inherent tendency to focus on the central 'frictionless' paradigm in all theories generated from individual maximising behaviour, all attempts at modification may continue to rest on the peripheries of the discipline. Kierkegaard once suggested that while most philosophers wrote in order to simplify understanding of the world, his goal was to make it more complicated. Analogously, if all maximisation models ultimately reduce to a perfect capital market as a norm from which all else is seen as mere deviation, may we not be forced to abandon this simple methodology for a more disorderly institutional approach in which such a temptation is not present?

3   The implication exists in these new approaches that, in the absence of these costs of information and agency, there is not much to question in the initial Fisherian conception. We believe there are inherent limits to inter-temporal rational decision making, and a residual magnitude of 'imperfections' would continue to exist even in relatively 'frictionless' environments. The size of this residual is, perhaps, inherently uncertain!

4   Lastly, we have what are not objections but some cautionary admonitions in the form of questions. We have earlier noted the Hegelian tendency among economic theorists to conceive economic history as a branch of the history of economic thought. Now that theoretical constructs exist to describe the existence of monitoring and information costs, will the implicit presumption develop that these phenomena now exist though formerly they did not, when in fact an important aspect of modern financial evolution is the substantial lowering of these costs? Furthermore, will it ever be possible to orient these static frameworks away from their traditional obsessions with *whether or not* a market is efficient in some absolute sense and towards a time-based consideration of changes in the financial environment?

To summarise, our methodological discourse reduces down to a plea for a recognition of the existence of an objective reality whose character must be explained, and not just explained away. They may have to give way to a less elegant but scientifically more secure approach.

An Institutional Approach to Firm Finance

What is the logical connection between the concept of an invisible hand process of competition and that of a perfect capital market? At one level, they would seem to have little to do with each other. If say, seventeenth century British landowners tend to recommit resources to an area in proportion to past received remuneration, there might well be a close approximation to an equalisation process without the need for a well-functioning capital market to shift surplus returns between areas of investment.[68]

There are two important exceptions to this statement. The first is that the remuneration may be linked to an asset or situation which is non-reproducible, for instance, the accidental discovery of water on a piece of land. Such rents are not good signals for re-investment and are not conducive to a process of equalisation. However, the presence in an economy of a predominance of such non-reproducible wealth bearing assets would be inconsistent not only with a perfect capital market, but with even the minimal valuation calculus necessary for the functioning of the invisible hand: rents, as we have seen in chapter 4, may exist in a market economy only as an exceptional case, amidst a sea of wealth bearing assets capable of replication.

The second, and more significant exception is the possibility of the emergence of a gap between the existent (high) average rates of return available to the assets of our landowner and the even higher returns from new investment possibilities in the incipient industrial sector. If the landowner shows the flexibility, managerial skill and inclination (moral and otherwise) necessary to enter into this sphere, there may be once again little need for elaborate mechanisms shifting capital from saver to investor. As the complexity of industrial processes increases there is progressively more need for specialised skills and full-time activity in this sector, with the consequent demand for financial markets to reallocate passively committed landowners' surplus to industry.

In Britain, as in many other European countries, an intermediary existed in the form of the merchant – providing not only commercial competence, but also the large amounts of cash needed to finance the progressively greater capital demands initiated with Arkwright's machinery in the latter half of the eighteenth century. The pattern which emerges in this period seems to possess a remarkable continuity with the present: compared with the rest of Europe, Britain had, despite the restrictions posed by the Bubble Act, a more widespread use of shares than any other country.[69]

On the other hand, while the emergence of a rich and complex set of financial institutions and mechanisms gave broad access to short-term finance and working capital to early industrial firms (in spite of the constraints of the usury law) there was little provision for long-term loans to finance fixed capital, especially for new firms. Furthermore, despite the presence of industrial banks – started by industrialists to satisfy their own requirements, the separation of finance from industry was well established in this period. While such lines of delineation – between short and long-term credit and between finance and industry were never unambiguous, they were significant enough to exclude skilled but relatively impecunious artisans from entrepreneurial activity in those areas that involved relatively large amounts of fixed capital; the practice of discounting bills of exchange probably made the rolling over of short-term debt more difficult than the later overdraft system.

The major innovation in early nineteenth century Britain was the joint stock bank, already widespread in eighteenth century Scotland, which greatly extended the capacity of the banking system. The picture which emerges from the early industrial revolution is of fixed capital formation (still a very small proportion of company assets compared with later developments) being financed initially by the owners' own wealth and then almost exclusively from retained earnings. Working capital, on the other hand, had a rich diversity of sources – trade credit from other manufacturers supplying inputs, merchants, wholesalers and the developing banking system.

This period of industrialisation up to mid nineteenth century did not generate the need for but a fraction of the fixed capital expenditure to be seen subsequently.[70] For our purposes, an interesting question is whether capital formation could have proceeded as it did in the latter part of the century without the reforms in the laws on limited liability (incorporation) of 1855 to 1862, so that capital could '... be advanced by respectable persons to a sufficient extent'[71] to answer the needs of progressively larger undertakings. The emergence of modern forms of capital financing proceeded slowly, with issues from limited companies being at first taken up from an area within a few miles of the company's registered office. The London market of the 1870s was geared for a small body of very large issues, mostly government bonds and railway securities, the latter being, until the First World War, the only quoted securities which were fully marketable. Debenture issues emerged only slowly in the later nineteenth century, and no specialist financial press existed until the 1880s. And this was the most highly developed financial environment in the world.

The other great Anglo-Saxon economy developed institutions which possess remarkable similarity to those of the older country. This is not solely due to cultural parallelism, but was a reflection of British financial investment in the US. In western regions British investment was more significant than the flow of funds from financial centres on the eastern seaboard, in part because of inhibitions imposed by (especially ante bellum) restrictions on inter-state banking activities. Perhaps as a result of these restrictions, there developed even before the Civil War a widespread market in commercial paper (a definite innovation when compared with developments in Britain) in addition to a rich assortment of trade credit and forms of commercial bank borrowing. But these diverse sources were, as in Britain, all for short-term finance. What long-term finance existed was local until well after the Civil War (except of course for the railroads), embodying presumably the high monitoring costs attached to long-term loans in this period.

In the US, the second half of the century apparently marked an increase in investment not only in absolute terms, as in the UK, but as a proportion of national income as well,[72] and therefore the question of financial provision becomes even more vital. The legal inhibitions on the institution of limited liability were not as serious as in Britain. But the market in company shares remained thin throughout most of the nineteenth century, limited before the Civil War to a few hundred individuals within the state of issuance on a particular offering. Both before and after the Civil War, the overwhelming share of funds for new investment came from internal sources (retained earnings and the wealth of owners). It would be difficult indeed to separate out the role of these capital market imperfections from the effects of technology on scale economies in the dramatic growth of industrial concentration in this period.[73]

By the beginning of the twentieth century most contemporary aspects of corporate finance and the capital market in both countries were already in place, excepting only those which relate to financial institution regulation and company disclosure. Change has left institutional structures intact, but has been significant enough to make earlier phenomena almost unrecognisable, especially in the equities market. In Britain before the passage of legislation in 1929, brokerage commissions on new shares came to 25 per cent of the nominal value of the shares even for the best companies, and could go up as high as 50 per cent, while as of the 1930s whole sectors of enterprise as important as food and retailing were still almost totally unrepresented in the quoted sector. Introductions to the stock market of (newly public) ordinary shares had to pay discounts averaging over 35 per cent of their market value for the privilege.[74]

The existence of such conditions poses some important questions about the meaning we should attach to the 'indubitable fact' that the first part of the century has witnessed a dramatic rise in aggregate industrial concentration. We have already indicated that growth in aggregate concentration is only meaningful in the context of the problem of capital market access. If this growth has been accompanied by an increasing fluidity and flexibility in capital market institutions, it is conceivable that the 'small firm – large firm' distinction has lessened, or at least not increased in extent, despite growth in the skewness of the distribution of firm size.

The capital market which emerged in the post-war world has been undergoing a process of continuous transformation, but a summary of its essential contemporary characteristics may be highlighted by contrasting them with the presumptive perfect market alternative:

1 *The capital market is layered.*
   Firms of different size classes seem to live in qualitatively contrasting capital market 'universes', confronted by different spectra of servicing institutions and opportunities for finance. This appears in sharp contrast to the ideal of a unified capital market.
2 *The capital market is not impersonal.*
   Firms are subject to highly personal and specific forms of monitoring. As a result, rationing is often done on a quantitative, non-price basis and is certainly not parametric in the sense that firms could borrow without restriction at a given price.
3 *There is no clear separation of real and financial decisions.*
   The lack of impersonality in the capital market would not be troublesome for the standard theory if it were restricted to so-called business

risk, but institutional monitoring of business firms is equally concerned with their financial structure. 'Real' decisions by firms are not merely constrained by an exogenously specified cost of capital: outcomes in financial markets shape the structure of a firm's assets in un-neo-classical ways.

In attempting to describe this first characteristic, numerous contradictions are likely to be encountered, since some small units, especially those in fashionable sectors, may have better capital market access than certain firms which are nominally in more elevated size classifications. Further-more, present trends in the evolution of the financial system may be undermining the basis of many traditional perspectives on the capital market. Lastly, a major obstacle to an evaluation of these questions is that the issue of small firms and the capital market evokes such partisan, emotional responses (both self-interested and otherwise) as to make one fear that a disinterested discussion is about as likely to come about as one between opera devotees on the relative merits of the tessiture of Galli-Curci and Tetrazzini. With these caveats in mind, we may proceed.

Of the approximately two million business enterprises of one kind or another in the UK, about 300,000 are active companies (incorporated enterprises in US terminology), and only a fraction of these companies – about 16,000 – are permitted to sell securities directly to the public. Of these only about 2,500 are quoted on the London Stock Exchange. (The New York Stock Exchange lists about 2,000 stocks.) It is from within this small group of quoted firms that our giant enterprises can be found.

Trying to define and locate the small firm, on the other hand, is far more difficult. There is no developed methodology for defining the small firm, a fact reflected in the range of definitions offered up in official studies.[75] If we stretch our purview to include the great sea of unincorporated enterprises, we can feel the weightiness of the assumption that in the Modigliani–Miller Republic of Equals all firms and individuals have symmetrical access with the largest firms in a unified capital market. The point is merely academic, because hard evidence is only available for companies, and we must presume that if capital market segmentation exists within this subsample, it must be present *a fortiori* in a broader group containing all enterprises and individuals.

If there are substantial differences in the cost of equity flotations on the basis of size of issue even among the few thousand firms actually or potentially involved in share issue, any doubts about capital market symmetry would be substantially reinforced. Conditions in the capital market in the mid-1980s are undergoing rapid change, but the formal requirements of the Stock Exchange in terms of fees, disclosure and minimum market value of firm substantively exclude small firms by any definition. Small firms have also been disadvantaged by the substantial fixed costs on new issuance which impose an inevitable structure of scale economies, and by the greater market price discount they are compelled to offer.[76] Stock market listing is not a magical route to raising firm value[77] but the important point here is that public offerings of securities, be they debt or equity have not been an option symmetrically open to firms of all size classes.

Thus it is to be expected that the company accounts of small firms will differ greatly from those of larger ones.[78] Existing evidence confirms this presupposition, though superficial analysis of balance sheet variables does not do so in any spectacular way. Balance sheets of small firms reveal a higher ratio of short to long-term liabilities than for large firms. This may be due to the smaller share of fixed assets in the balance sheets of small firms, since in practice, if not within the theory of finance, the 'rule' of an approximate balance between the relative length of assets and liabilities is observed, if not precisely followed. As a percentage of total assets, trade credit (both debtors and creditors) liquid assets and bank overdrafts seemed more important for the smaller units, and they had lower gearing than large companies and much lower dividend distribution as a percentage of net profits, though difficulties of interpretation are raised by the level of directors' remuneration. While issues of ordinary shares, preference shares and of long-term loans made for a higher percentage of the total generation of funds than for large firms, it seems unlikely that much of this represents external market sources of funds: at least half of the funds raised from long-term loans were in the form of loans from directors; a fair proportion of the issues of ordinary shares must similarly have been taken up by the existing proprietors of the businesses.

Clearly, such generalisations about the length of liability structure disguise much significant detail about the nature of firm finance – the rich diversity of sources of funds available to the largest firms, including cross-subsidisation from highly disparate activities which make each of these firms a kind of self-contained capital market,[79] and the fact that for many small firms the observed balance sheets may be as much a product of a disinclination to borrow or dilute equity as any externally imposed constraint.[80] Problems of measurement may be significant in this area, including the existence of off-balance sheet forms of financing such as leasing, the tendency for larger firms to revalue their assets more frequently than do small firms and the ambiguity attached to the length of bank loan liability, with the possibility of almost perpetual rolling-over of short-term debt.

The most significant difficulty of interpretation, however, concerns the problem which we have already confronted in other contexts: the need to use *ex post* data in the verification of *ex ante* behavioural hypotheses. The balance sheets which we observe both for small and large firms represent the presumptive resolution of each company's optimal balance between internal finance, public issuance, credit from financial institutions and with other firms (trade credit, etc.). Substantial economies exist for larger firms, as we have seen, for the public issuance of long-term debt and equity, and similar advantages accrue for short-term issuances. To the extent that these phenomena imply an improved bargaining position with banks and other institutions on the part of a large firm compared with smaller entities, the potentiality for public issuance may not necessarily reflect itself in a larger percentage of public issuance *per se*, but in the price and conditions of availability of credit from financial institutions.

The consequences for a large firm of a potential for the public issuance of short-term credit may be reflected, for instance, in an exceptionally low level of liquid assets if a promise to cover liquidity embarrassments, even in periods of tight money,[81] has been extracted from a bank. In such periods an increase in the variability of a small firm's profits could take place which has nothing to do with its pure business risk, as the small firm, with fewer alternative sources of finance faces discontinuous cancellations of projects, illiquidity and even bankruptcy as a result of the credit squeeze. Even expected profitability of the firm might be adversely affected if, for instance, disproportionately large cash balances are held by the firm as a precautionary motive.[82] Thus the common assertion that small firms suffer from capital market restrictions because they are riskier already presumes the existence of a classical dichotomy in which real and financial outcomes can be separated: the latter presupposes a perfect capital market in which discrimination is impossible.

A second characteristic which emerges from observation of contemporary capital market institutions is that it is not impersonal. Upon examining the large number of financial institutions which service firms, it would be easy to suggest that the traditionally specialised nature of these institutions is in obvious contradiction to the vision of a unified capital market. Neo-classical analysts would be quick to point out that such institutions often exhibit more flexibility than first appears – short-term lenders even include life insurance companies in times of high interest rates and in contemporary conditions such barriers are continuing to be reduced.

But, if we look carefully at the activities of these financial institutions, we note that a characteristic aspect of present practice is the need for precise monitoring of firms through the setting up of specialist divisions and careful analysis of the whole spectrum of firm behaviour. It would be no violation of the spirit of neo-classical analysis if this monitoring were limited to firms' business risk, but contemporary practice on the part of financial institutions is also oriented towards an intense examination of the liquidity and gearing ratios of customers. If banks are concerned about a firm's present fixed interest commitment and use it as a criterion to decide on future loans, it is not surprising that they will use quantity rationing techniques to allocate finance,[83] and not simply rely on higher interest rates to do the job for them. There seems little doubt that analysis of 'both sides of the balance sheet' is standard procedure in trade credit management, the (US) market for commercial paper and other forms of inter-company finance. The demands for such information are increasing rather than diminishing in the context of the commodification of firm finance and an increasingly frantic search by financial institutions for competitive returns.

The monitoring of firms' financial structure in addition to the real side of its performance is indicative of what is considered to be best practice, with a common rule being a rough balancing of the length of assets to the length of liabilities. Such a practice means that the Marshallian distinction between fixed and variable assets will be largely reflected in financial terms in the firm's structure of costs, but only under conditions which violate the Fisherian basis of the Marshallian model, which excludes the possibility of any interaction of real and financial decisions. In the real world, there is no simple correspondence between a firm's fixed costs and its capital intensity: heavy equipment may be leased, computer time may be purchased and, depending on the form of contract, a whole range of different possible cost structures may emerge from a given set of combinations of real inputs. If, however, the pervasively observed link between asset and liability structures is to be preserved as a first approximation of the manner in which firms actually function, then the abandonment of the Marshallian attachment to the classical dichotomy would seem a necessity in the absence of *ad hoc* adjustments to orthodox theory.

A third characteristic of the contemporary capital market is that there is no clear separation of real from financial decisions on the part of firms. A widely quoted study[84] based on a statistical analysis of US company data suggests that the rate of return on new equity capital is very much higher than either the rate of return on retained earnings or new debt, the implication being that these different rates reflect the differing costs of these forms of finance. This conclusion is in sharp contrast to the perspective of all orthodox approaches to finance, where the calculation of the overall cost of capital for a firm is separated from the real investment decision, but it is consistent with the descriptions of financial practices given by even reputedly well-run companies of their own methods.[85] It would appear that firms link decisions to issue 'expensive' equity finance to projects which are expected to yield exceptionally high rates of return, thereby violating the alleged separation of real and financial decisions.

One must approach with care the effects on real investment decisions of events in the financial sphere. But if the source of finance affects the real decisions of firms, it is obvious that the economic effects of alternative financial arrangements cannot be ignored. Dramatic changes in the relationship between financial institutions and industrial firms appear to be taking place at the present time throughout the world. Are these developments to be ignored as well, because the wall of separation of orthodox theory divests them of any possible significance in the evolution of the structure of industry?

Our discusion of firm finance has created an almost caste-like structure of firms on the basis of size. The main difficulty with this notion of a segmented capital market is its overly static nature. In other spheres of economic activity, we have suggested that changes in behaviour within business entities have resulted in increasing competitiveness. May not a similar phenomenon be present in the financial sphere? This question will be considered below, but to complete our picture of the financial sector we must consider the ubiquitous phenomena of bankruptcy and financial panics, and make some international comparisons.

Other Institutional Considerations: Bankruptcy and Financial Panics; International Comparisons

Bankruptcy and panics are not usually treated as central questions in mainstream economics, and can easily be avoided by students of economics who are likely to confront them either as applied, institutional topics or else as esoteric paradoxes in advanced theory. This is no accident, but a logical development from neo-classical theory, which, especially in its straightforward Marshallian manifestations, has a strong predisposition towards ignoring such phenomena.

The textbooks tell us that firms go out of business when $P < AC$. (The so-called short run conclusion that firms will cease to exist when $P < AVC$ is excluded from consideration since the fixed cost-variable cost distinction cannot be formulated consistently in a Marshallian world.) Therefore, the only variable relevant to the survival of a firm is its net income – a strong prediction, if it is taken as such. Firms, then, do not go out of business because of a lack of cash, and apparent preoccupations with liquidity, the timing of cash flow and other such financial hazards (such as increased gearing) reflect either misapprehension on the part of economic actors of their true situation or are a surrogate for concerns which ultimately devolve to net income. Little meaning in orthodox terms can be attributed to the following quotation from the financial press on the causes of bankruptcy: 'Too often people concentrate on whether they are making a profit, but if this profit is tied up in debtors or work in progress and there is not enough to pay the bills then the profit is not much use',[86] which is essentially criticising people for being too neo-classical in their approach to firm valuation.

Similarly, it is within the spirit of neo-classical theory to suggest that, for instance, construction firms are more likely than others to fail because of their greater business risk (large β) over the cycle, but not if their greater risk of failure is due to their (supposed) greater financial exposure, which makes them more subject than other firms to fluctuations in the price of credit.

On the basis of the largely US literature on financial distress, there is limited confirmation of the neo-classical emphasis on net income surrogates as the key indicator of firm survival.[87] Somewhat contrarily, a recent study of UK bankruptcy from a macroeconomic perspective has pointed to the role of changes in money supply and interest rate variables in explaining the level of firm bankruptcies.[88] These alternative hypotheses are distinctive enough to be made explicit as empirical hypotheses – capable of disproof – even to introductory students in economics, and not buried away as part of a general – and presumptively uncontroversial – exposition of the theory of the firm.

Similarly, the standard theory has little room for a theory of financial panics. We have seen that the mainstream theory deals with risk most felicitously when there is unanimity among participants about the mean value and variance of assets and this, oddly enough, resembles the Keynes–Minsky–Kindleberger[89] herd instinct approach to financial markets. The crucial distinction is this: the neo-classical financial market has a collective opinion that seems to be rooted in an *objectively correct* decision rule, and discontinuous changes in this (these) opinion(s) would undoubtedly emanate from movements in the underlying objective reality. If, as in the alternative view, collective opinion is largely conventional in nature and is at least sometimes irrational in its opinions, then discontinuous changes in collective opinion may well take the form of panics. Not surprisingly, a discipline bent on proving rational, convergent models of (collective) behaviour has a disinclination for discussing such phenomena. But can an empirically based subject afford to ignore such an important part of the history and present reality of the institutions being studied? Since, however, only preliminary work, either theoretical or empirical has been pursued on this fundamental question, we shall for once adhere to Wittgenstein's admonition.

There is only a very limited academic literature on the topic of international comparisons of capital market institutions and their effect upon industrial structure. Given our earlier discussion, the reticence of orthodox economics should be unsurprising. Academic writings emerge from the standard paradigm, in which the conditions facing individual traders are such that the market and the prices within it are symmetric, anonymous and parametric, with a consequent separation of the real and financial sectors. It is inevitable that neo-classical explanations of industrial evolution or of economic growth give almost exclusive consideration to real efficiency factors (inputs of capital, labour, technical change, etc.) as explanatory variables.

The usual presentation of the Fisherian view of the capital market is highly formalised. It is not a coincidence, however, that it emanates largely from the Anglo-Saxon world, where the traditional arms length relationship between banks and firms, accompanied by a freely floating stock market, give this view a modicum of plausibility. But what about countries such as Japan and West Germany? Decades ago, many would have dismissed their alternative capital market structures as representing nothing other than immaturity, malformation and atavism, but few today in the Anglo-Saxon world would have the confidence to make such blanket pronouncements. Indeed, there is a fairly substantial literature from outside academic economics which searches for the secret of the success of these non Anglo-Saxon countries in their financial arrangements.

In Japan, bank involvement in industry was practically unknown as late as the 1880s.[90] The emergent predominance from the late nineteenth century until 1945 of the gigantic merchant, industrial and financial entities – the *zaibatsu*, and the *shinko-zaibatsu* signal an economic development which has no parallel in the Anglo-Saxon world, with the large industrial companies forming part of the *zaibatsu* using the banks within the group to satisfy their requirements for fixed and working capital. The most common interpretation put upon this fact is congruent with the hypothesis of Gerschenkron – this direct, administered method of finance developed by default because of the primitive nature of the capital and money markets. The post-war dissolution of the *zaibatsu* temporarily put an end to these arrangements, but the subsequent reintegration of banks and industry has also been attributed to the inability of the relatively under-developed capital markets to deal adequately with the financial demands of the period of rapid economic growth.[91] Similarly in Germany we may observe strong, if less formalised linkages emerging somewhat earlier, a significant difference being that in the German case the conspicuous role of the state as a planner and co-ordinator of industrial activity did not continue into the post-war world.[92]

In the present period, the distinctive aspects of German financial arrangements are the very substantial share holdings by banks, especially by the 'big three' (the Deutsche, Dresdner and Commerz banks) often amounting to over 25 per cent of a firm's equity,[93] with a universal banking service 'offered' to the firm in the form of working capital and industrial loans, as well as merchant bank and stockbroking services. Furthermore, through the two-tier system of control existent in Germany, banks would appear to have a far more powerful set of institutionalised mechanisms for the exercise of influence on firm behaviour than is to be found in the UK or the US.

The contemporary arrangements in Japan are in even greater contrast to those in the UK or the US than those in Germany, and with the spectacular success of the Japanese economy have been subject to even more intense scrutiny. The *keiretsu* (groups of firms integrated in a hierarchical structure, including substantial finance for associated firms) and the *sogo shosha* (general trading companies) have no western, let alone Anglo-Saxon parallel. In the latter category, as an example, Mitsubishi appears as a gigantic, diversified industrial and trading conglomerate which also functions as a bank and financial organ of vast proportions.

The most important result which has been attributed to the financial arrangements in the latter two countries compared with the arm's length situation in the Anglo-Saxon world has been the appearance of much larger ratios of external (especially debt) financing to internal (cash flow) sources in Japan and West Germany; this is said to be one of the secrets of their success.[94] There are many reasons to be cautious about this notion. A rising ratio of external (including debt) finance to internal sources is common even within the Anglo-Saxon world during the upswing of a business cycle, so it would be easy to reverse the direction of causation observed between high gearing and rapid growth in these economies: successful firms always find it easier to borrow than unsuccessful firms. Secondly, there are severe measurement difficulties even in registering the stylised facts of firm financing. In the Japanese case, for instance, traditional accounting methods often leave assets at (very!) historic values rather than revalue them, thereby accentuating the differences in gearing (leverage) compared with British and American companies.[95]

In approaching these questions from a normative perspective, the crucial issue of contention is whether the intimate links between industry and financial institutions to be found in countries such as West Germany and Japan are to be thought of in a Gerschenkron sense – as having taken place by default in the absence of viable capital market institutions – or alternatively, to be considered from a Chandler perspective. In the latter view the substitution of the visible hand of administrative co-ordination in place of the arm's length capital market relation represents an innovation and a superior set of arrangements. But in Japan one 'secret' of post-war economic growth was the apparently high savings propensity of the population which facilitated the strong 'encouragement' given to banks by the government to take up bonds at a low rate of interest. Such a practice says nothing about the efficiency with which these savings were used – the point at issue.

If one were to attempt to formulate efficiency arguments in favour of financial participation, they would be of two kinds. First, it has been suggested that financial institutions, when acting as insiders, do not have that 'Fatal Fascination with the Short Run'[96] – an obsession with growth in earnings per share or dividend payout, which might conflict with (long-term) maximisation of firm value. Insiders, it is argued see matters from the same perspective as, say, the directors in the Royal Mail case of 1931 (see chapter 5), or of a value maximising owner–entrepreneur, and not from the short-sighted, limited perspective of the passive equity holder. The latter, and through them the stock market, may put an overly low valuation on firms pursuing projects which appear, individually, to possess an insufficiently low internal rate of return, but which insiders can perceive as having significant positive externalities for the firm as a whole. Secondly, since the lenders are also substantial equity participants (in the West German case), the management of the firm does not have to be responsive to a substantial constituency of debt holders who are asymmetrically concerned only with the repayment of a fixed annuity, and not the maximisation of firm value.

In recent years, the business and financial press has been giving these ideas a somewhat less enthusiastic reception than heretofore. West Germany especially, with a decline in that country's formerly 'miraculous' economic growth, has had to face a more cynical attitude to its economic institutions, including its financial structure: 'All this pious talk about the German banks' deep and searching knowledge of the needs of industry is so much hogwash. It is a damned good device the banks have invented for tying industry to their apron strings. What they do is get a company borrowed up to the eyeballs, and put a man on the Board to ensure they grab all future borrowings.'[97] Furthermore, it is now common to read reports that the bank-dominated West German financial sector is staid, and either unable to identify or unwilling to supply capital to new, high-technology venture capital sectors of the economy.

There are complaints as well that the bank-dominated stock market of West Germany is 'A Primitive Way to Raise Cash'.[98] Japan's continued high growth has shielded its financial system from such harsh re-evaluation, but pressure to reform due to the general internationalisation of finance and Japan's desire to invest in other countries has generated a more critical view. Not surprisingly, the oil shock of 1973–4 has brought into question the unmitigated virtue of Japanese firms' high gearing ratios, and the priority of loans to the largest firms at the expense of smaller ones during the period of crisis has led to questions about the bank–industry linkages. The stock market is often viewed by many individuals as highly speculative and increasingly dominated by financial institutions and companies; poor disclosure requirements are presumed to give an exceptional differential advantage to the insider knowledge of these institutions.[99] Other procedures, such as Japanese banks' requirement that firms hold a substantial proportion of their available funds in bank deposits in the form of compensating balances (to be discussed below), are viewed as rather old-fashioned, and in other countries such as the US have largely disappeared.

In terms of the positive predictions yielded by alternative financial structures, a central neo-classical hypothesis concerns the limits of the size of firms, which is fundamentally a real factors explanation, stylised by the bowl-shaped long run average cost curve. In the Anglo-Saxon world, the development of the industrial structure and the size and activities of individual firms have been dramatically affected by waves of merger activity. It would appear that these phenomena have not been replicated in Japan and Germany or, to our knowledge, in other non Anglo-Saxon economies,[100] leading one to suppose that the differences in financial arrangements between countries have had an important effect on industrial evolution.

Japan, as we have noted, has long had a type of conglomerate organisation of its own, while Germany, despite a relatively advanced level of diversification early in the century,[101] has few firms one could call conglomerate. But in both cases, the pronounced Anglo-Saxon tendency in recent decades for combination, whether conglomerate or otherwise, has been absent. It has been contended that in these countries substantial control of shares by a financial institution or a link within a group inhibits takeovers, especially contested ones,[102] and that the aforementioned weakness of the stock market acts as a further inhibition of the use of this vehicle as a device for financing a merger. It is further possible that, in the Anglo-Saxon world, equity participation in a new enterprise is a natural form of investment of the surplus funds of firms, especially when profitable projects in the existing spheres of activity are seen to be exhausted. Such a decision may well register itself in the form of a merger. In a situation where, on the contrary, there is substantial equity participation by financial institutions, the accrued surplus may take the form of loan finance to a new firm from the financial institution, so that no merger or change in industrial structure takes place.

If these presumptions have any validity, they pose the possibility that the evolution of the industrial structure and mergers themselves are crucially affected by institutional considerations – a doctrine hard to reconcile with mainstream theory. In conclusion, international comparisons of financial institutions certainly do not lead one to the conclusion that finance is just a veil over the real factors in these economies. The institutions of a country and the substantive differences in institutions between countries cannot be ignored in the analysis of the evolution of industrial structure.

Financial Evolution

Efficient Markets and Financial Change
It would be anomalous indeed to suggest that a dynamically evolving industrial environment could exist in the context of a rigid layering of firms determined by an unchanging capital market and its institutions. The critique of such an approach from an imaginary Chicago economist might be something like the following: 'This layering effect, if it is to mean anything at all, must imply a mispricing of assets in the capital market, and most especially a systematic underpricing of those connected to smaller enterprises. It is hard to believe that any such differentials would not be eliminated in an efficient market, as profitable opportunities are seized by market participants.' Part of our response to this comment is implicit in earlier sections: there is no good reason to draw a strict parallel between the arbitrage and pricing procedures of a static market and those of a capital market, since the latter are inextricably associated with valuation in an uncertain future. Furthermore, whatever the a priori arguments, there is much evidence to suggest that such layering exists.

Orthodox theory has tended to deal with these issues in recent years by posing the question of whether or not the capital market is efficient. As we shall see, the concept of efficiency as it is used in this literature is far more limited and narrowly defined than is at first apparent. Furthermore, this analysis of the capital market has the same difficulties that we have attributed to orthodox theory in general in its attempts to deal with the concept of the market: it poses in a static framework the question of whether an anonymous market is or is not efficient, when the real question here, as in the case of product markets, is how changes in the behaviour of participants affect the structure and mode of operation of these markets over time. Since financial markets and institutions are undergoing a dramatic process of transformation, we shall make some conjectures about the effects of these changes upon the industrial structure: orthodox theory, it would seem, does not provide a framework in which such questions can even be discussed.

The literature on the existence of efficient markets (which has largely concentrated on prices in the stock market) is an impressive demonstration of the power of contemporary econometric methodology in applied work.[103] Capital market efficiency in its *weak form* implies that it is not possible to make abnormal trading gains by analysing past patterns of security prices, so that, for instance, there are no mechanical trading rules which can be used to predict share prices successfully (i.e. profitably). Despite occasional embarrassments (or 'anomalies', as they are called in the literature) such as the 'weekend effect',[104] studies of weak form efficiency have done a highly successful demolition job on the whole subculture of 'technical analysis' or 'chartism' which divines exploitable patterns in stock price movements. *Strong form* efficiency, on the other hand, would suggest that abnormal gains on the stock market are never possible, even for those possessed with insider information. Not surprisingly, few researchers have been willing to claim that the stock market is efficient in this sense.

Most interesting from our point of view is the concept of *semi-strong form* efficiency, whereby all publicly available information is embodied fully and immediately in share prices. The market is apparently not deceived, for instance, by the adoption of alternative regimes of accounting depreciation by firms,[105] and is capable of making a correct evaluation of the meaning of a stock split (scrip or capitalisation issue) for the future of the firm, a 'two for one' issue merely halving the price of each share unless the split is also communicating what proves to be correct information about increases in future dividends.[106]

From our perspective, the problematic aspect of semi-strong efficiency is neither the existence of examples of entities such as the Value Line Survey which seem capable of making above average returns on a long-term basis using publicly available information, nor the problems posed by Shiller's analysis of stock market volatility,[107] but of the very question embodied in the definition of the term: when is information 'publicly available'? The work of Abraham Briloff, whom we have already met in our discussion of mergers, is the object of examination in an article by George Foster.[108] He notes that companies whose accounting practices are criticised in print by Briloff suffer an immediate and permanent drop in share price. The speed of the market's response to Briloff's revelations is consistent with an efficient market, but can the same be said for the revelations themselves, since Briloff bases them almost exclusively on readily available information?

A capital market is efficient, in Eugene Fama's terminology, if security prices 'fully reflect' all the information in time t. Thus,

$$f\left(P_{t+1} / \phi_t\right) = f_m\left(P_{t+1} / \phi_t^m\right)$$

where

$f(\ )$ = the 'true' conditional probability distribution of security prices in period $t + 1$.

ϕ_t = the information set available in period t.

$f_m(\ ) =$ the market-assessed conditional probability distribution based on ϕ_t^m

$\phi_t^m =$ the information set used by the market in period t.

As Foster notes, the equation does not specify what would constitute evidence consistent (or inconsistent) with capital market efficiency. '*It is necessary to assume something about the information set* ϕ_t. ... If we assume the information provided by Briloff is already costlessly available to all market participants, then capital market efficiency implies there should be no price reaction to Briloff's articles.' According to Foster we do not have here an airtight refutation of the semi-strong hypothesis, because an alternative exists – the 'superior insight' explanation: Briloff possesses superior skills and can (if he chooses) earn a more than competitive return from using these skills. Thus the observed results are not inconsistent with the efficient markets hypothesis.

In Foster's words, 'Once one recognizes that individuals can earn economic rents from their information production activities, tests of capital market efficiency become more difficult to undertake.' In the end, Foster reaches the agnostic conclusion that he is unable (given existing data) to determine whether the magnitude of the price reaction is consistent with the capital market inefficiency explanation or the superior insight explanation, and ruefully quotes another source, who suggests that it is not clear that any real world data are available for attacking these problems.

If a non-specified and changeable skill factor is introduced, the concept of efficiency reduces to the statement that individual traders *try* to maximise their returns, but this is neither interesting nor testable until constraints are specified. Thus, it is reported that Meshulam Riklis, an early 'conglomerator', was astounded to discover as a student of finance that the stock market frequently placed a lower value on a firm than the value of its *liquid* assets:[109] constrastingly in the mid-1980s 'program trading' has come into being – highly sophisticated mathematical techniques and computer programs have been used to make hitherto unexploited (relatively riskless) arbitrage profits between the stock market index and the corresponding futures prices (which now have their own market) on that index. Would we still classify financial markets in the earlier period as having been 'efficient', since these individuals had to exercise 'superior insight' given the lower level of technique of financial analysis generally available and the poorer quality of publicly available information?

In the context of this methodology, it may well be that capital markets have been 'efficient' *since the seventeenth century*. The efficiency notion does not provide us with a meaningful framework in which to discuss changes in the efficacy and speed with which the capital market responds to profitable opportunities as the behaviour of its participants evolves over time. The concept is defined conditionally on exactly those features whose evolution is at issue.

The Changing Boundaries of Financial Institutions – the Compression of Capital Market Layers?

To judge from the literature current in the financial and business press, the capital market world-wide, and especially in the Anglo-Saxon world, is going through a series of changes quite as monumental as any to be found in the industrial sector. We have seen that orthodox approaches to these problems leave us bereft of any coherent way of understanding these events. It is unsurprising, therefore, that the symptomatic manifestations of these changes (e.g. the 'Big Bang' reforms on the London Stock Exchange of 1986) have been met with a general bewilderment or have been attributed to specific and proximate causes – to the introduction of new technology, or to the deregulation of financial institutions. In fact these processes are more organic and more inexorable than such explanations would indicate: the events of the past few years are, to a great extent the continuation of post-war tendencies, and are essentially manifestations in the financial sector of the managerial revolution phenomena discussed in chapter 5. All these phenomena are intimately connected, but for the sake of exposition they will be broken down into three elements:

1 There has been a transformation in the ways of doing business by banks and other financial institutions – an increased aggressiveness compared with former practices. As a direct consequence of this change in behaviour, the boundaries formerly separating financial institutions are breaking down, with the new entities emerging each offering a full spectrum of financial services. There has been, furthermore an outbreak of substantial amounts of new competition from non-financial corporations.
2 Both a cause and effect of the above changes has been the progressive commodification of financial services – the substitution of marketable securities for bank loans, and the distancing and the 'unbundling' of the relationship between firms and financial institutions; firms choose – and pay for – only those services which they actually desire from the financial institution.
3 Finance has been internationalised to a hitherto unprecedented extent, both with the development of Euromarkets, swap markets and international equity markets, as well as the movements internationally of the great financial institutions. In the wake of these developments attempts by nation-states to regulate their financial markets at a national level have been progressively collapsing.

Let us proceed with each of these phenomena in turn:

1 *The increased aggressiveness of financial institutions.* In both the US and the UK (commercial and clearing) banks have traditionally held an overwhelming predominance in the process of lending to business because, as recipients of the deposits of firms and the general public,

'that's where the money is', in the felicitous words of the estimable banking expert Willie Sutton.[110] In the post-war world there has been a long-term tendency for the banks to expand away from their traditional arrangements in which there was a liability base in demand deposits, and in which loans to business were limited to short-term lending in support of working capital requirements. On the liability side there have been moves in the direction of attracting longer term deposits in competition with other depository institutions, while in the case of bank assets loans have been lengthened in term and 'lowered' in quality in the direction of activities such as hire purchase lending (both consumer and commercial), personal mortgages and long-term leasing – activities far removed from traditional banking practice.

In recent years, the activities of banks have taken a more radical form. As of the mid-1980s, 2,000 banks in the US offer brokerage services, and they have been pushing past the legal requirements limiting them to individual states through the use of such devices as (one) bank holding companies and Edge Act corporations (the Edge Act (1919) authorised the setting up of interstate outlets to facilitate international banking activity).

Most significantly, US banks are attempting to free themselves of the restrictions of the Glass–Steagall Act of 1933, which separated commercial from investment banking (a similiar provision exists in Japan as Article 65 of the Securities and Exchange Law; the only thing inhibiting British clearing banks from these activities has been tradition). This act has been the greatest single constraint on the activities of American banks, since they are unable to act as principals in the underwriting of securities by taking them on their own books and are limited to acting as agents. This legal restraint continues to be of significance in the context of an increasingly commodified financial environment and the collapsing boundaries between types of financial institutions, but American and Japanese banks with their vast depository resources are finding various ways around this restriction against direct competition with the investment banks, whom they now face as close rivals.

At the same time that banks in the US have moved 'long term', they have had to consider the increased competition which they are now facing in their own domain from other kinds of depository institutions. As of the 1980s many of these institutions can offer the equivalent of chequing services (for instance the NOW account of Savings and Loan Associations) to depositors. The convergence of the services offered by a host of depository financial institutions – *all* of whom now claim to offer a full range of financial services to both depositors and borrowers – was recognized in the Depository Institutions Deregulation and Monetary Control Act of 1980, where approximate uniformity of treatment was imposed on the activities of these formerly disparate institutions.

New competition has also emerged from non-financial corporations such as General Electric, which has expanded far beyond its traditional role in extending consumer and commercial credit to become a significant source of funds for industry. An even more direct challenge to the depository institutions has emerged from the fully-fledged 'financial supermarkets' such as American Express (incorporating the investment bankers Shearson Lehman) and Sears (including its brokerage firm Dean Witter). Sears, helped by interstate restrictions on banks, has been able to offer a broad range of services – life insurance, broking, estate agency and even a widely used credit card. The general impression is that Sears and other financial conglomerates have not been very successful, but there have been other threats from non-financial corporations as well. An example is the challenge by the electronic funds transfer systems of IBM, which banks in the UK have been making a strenuous effort to keep under control. IBM has also entered into a joint venture with the financial conglomerate Merrill Lynch to provide information to business customers; the entry of non-financial companies – Reuters, McGraw-Hill and others into the 'information business' threatens to attack the very source of financial companies' remaining commercial advantage.

2 *The commodification of financial services.* The initial impetus for many of the changes now observed in the behaviour of financial institutions has been the progressive commodification of financial services. (The word commonly used in this field is 'securitisation', but we wish here to emphasize the parallel between events in the financial market and those in other spheres, where the progressive substitution of marketable commodities for existing 'in-house' services is an unexceptional development.) A fundamental transformation is taking place in the way banks and other financial institutions view their asset portfolios, as for instance mortgage and consumer loans are re-packaged and sold as tradeable securities. While such practices may yet have profound effects on the functioning of financial markets, we wish to focus here on those changes which have a direct effect on the industrial sector.

In the US the high interest rate periods of the 1960s and 1970s developed into crises of 'disintermediation' for the banks, since Regulation Q restrictions on the interest rates which banks could offer meant that large amounts of money were syphoned away from bank deposits and into the higher returns offered by money market mutual funds. A more permanent threat (Regulation Q was withdrawn in 1984), and more typical of the problems faced by the banks has been the growth of the market for short-term commercial paper, which by 1987 stood at well over $300 billion. The increasing internationalisation of capital markets has meant that, in the 1980s, for the first time, a few large British companies could take advantage of the low (relative to US bank and money market) short-term rates available on the US commercial paper market where, acting through investment banks, notes are sold directly to financial institutions or other corporations. In this case, the only role for a bank (besides buying the paper for returns substantially lower than bank notes) is the rather lowly one of writing letters of credit for those issuers unable, or unwilling to obtain the appropriate Standard and Poor's or Moody's credit rating. European versions of this market are now developing in the form of the Euronote, Euro commercial paper and sterling commercial paper markets, though as yet they remain only a tenth the size of the US market.

Other financial institutions such as investment banks are facing competition from direct dealings between companies and 'the market', and are forced to accommodate to the new arrangements and make themselves as attractive as possible. Thus, there is less need for the services of the investment banker as an underwriter with the development of the Eurobond market, so the skills of the investment banker have been devoted to making sure that the offering is tailor made to the needs of borrowers and lenders. In the US, the Securities and Exchange Commission Rule 415 of 1982 permits a 'shelf-registration' procedure by which a company indicates the amount of capital it is likely to sell within the next two years. It can then take all or part of an issue 'off the shelf' at any time and dispose of it in a variety of ways. The threat which this poses to traditional investment banking practices is clear, and it is not surprising that the 1980s witnessed the unthinkable – the outbreak of price competition of an explicit kind in underwriting fees. In the UK, stock market reforms promise a more competitive environment among brokers, especially with the substantial entry of foreign, especially US and Japanese securities houses.

The key to this upheaval has been the pressure emanating from the industrial sector. Large industrial firms have been forcing an unbundling of the services which financial institutions offer, as they proceed to take only those services which they want from them. These corporate customers – far more sophisticated than their predecessors – have their own corporate finance departments and do not *need* investment banks to design an issue for them – what they need are their skills in distribution. Businesses (and other rich and sophisticated clients) are proceeding to pick and choose exactly what services they want, putting an end, for instance, to 'free' research from brokerage houses.

In the banking sector the monetisation of services is evidenced by the tendency, especially in the US, to charge explicit fees for the use of credit cards and chequing accounts. In the industrial sector, this monetisation of bank activities is of great significance as banks find it progressively more difficult to tie up firms in relationships that extend beyond the length of a loan: indicative of this tendency is the phasing out in the US of the traditional rather cosy practice of 'compensating balances',[111] by which borrowers were required to maintain minimum balances in their checking accounts, this being an implicit and rather imprecise additional cost to the loan and, more importantly, a device by which the firm was linked to the bank and excluded from competitive sources of finance. Firms are also having more 'transactional' relations with investment banks: 'Corporate treasurers, with their business school degrees, have clear ideas of what transactions they want to do, and they will do them not with their old golfing pals [golf again!] but with the bank which offers the most attractive terms.'[112]

Commodification has clearly had a profound effect on the nature of relationships in the capital market. But just as we have seen in chapter 3 that the full effect of international competition cannot be measured by the *ex post* level of imports into a market, so too the impact of commodification is not fully measured by the relative decline of bank loans *vis-à-vis* commercial paper: 'Banks are offering a bewildering array of new financial arrangements that are more like securities than bank loans. . . . In 1985, for example, banks underwrote nearly $50 billion of standby credit tied to so-called Euronotes, vs. $3.3 billion just two years ago. Until credit is used, none of it appears on balance sheets.'[113] For banks, one advantage of these commodified relationships – most especially swaps – is that (in the absence of any changes imposed by regulators) they are not charged against the balance sheet of the banks,[114] and this desire to escape regulation is both a key motivation for financial institutions and a problem for the regulators. The international arena has been crucial in the manifestation of these problems.

3 *The internationalisation of finance*. It may seem odd to speak about the internationalisation of finance when an important international dimension has been present in that arena for half a millenium. But contemporary events have no precedent. While the Euronote market, including the Euro commercial paper market is only one-tenth that of the US commercial paper market (though the latter now includes some overseas borrowers), in 1985 the volume on the Eurobond market surpassed that in New York for the first time. These Eurobonds are at present outside of any regulatory authority (which might impose withholding taxes, etc.), and can be tailor made by investment banks to suit the needs of clients, so that firms retain tremendous flexibility in their financial arrangements. A prime borrower like IBM can raise money more cheaply than the US Treasury, without the need for formal underwriting procedures – instead of underwriting and syndication, the bank whose bid is successful takes the whole issue in a 'bought deal' and then sells it off.

Another and rather spectacular manifestation of this process of internationalisation has been the development of an international equity market, with the claim of 'firm' prices for over 200 (non UK) stocks through the Stock Exchange Automated Quotations (SEAQ) international system in 1987. However, the opposition of British institutional shareholders to the floating of new equity overseas, as well as regulatory and disclosure differences between countries put brakes on these developments.[115] We are still quite a distance from an international market in equities: 'The big test for the bold new world of global equities, in which over half the business in ICI shares is said to be in New York and over half Sears Roebuck trades in Japan, will come however when stock markets around the world turn downwards.'[116]

Of greater significance at the moment than the development of international equity markets is the phenomenon of swap arrangements. Eighty per cent of European bond issues are now linked to swaps of some kind, be they currency or interest rate swaps, so that borrowing anywhere in the world is possible, even from a country (and in a currency) where the borrower is not known. In an interest rate swap (the market for which reached $313 billion at the end of 1986),[117] a high grade borrower of fixed rate funds can exchange with a lower grade borrower of floating rate funds, who then pays a premium to the high grade borrower, both of whom gain through arbitrage. 'In addition to cost advantages, interest rate swaps also provide an excellent mechanism for entities effectively to access markets which are otherwise closed to them – whether by reason of credit quality, lack of familiarity or excessive use.'[118] It takes no great imagination to conceive what a great headache swaps can make for national regulators intent on constraining 'inappropriate' forms of lending. Such problems would be accentuated by present attempts towards the standardisation and the marketing of swaps, developments which are piously opposed by the financial institutions which act as marriage brokers in these arrangements.

Just as the development of commodified arrangements within the US capital market was a central cause of the change in the behaviour of financial institutions, a similiar phenomenon can be observed internationally. The extension into the international domain of all major financial institutions and the process of consolidation of financial institutions of all kinds to permit participation in international dealings has been going on for several years, this international participation being the most significant aspect of the Big Bang events in London in the Autumn of 1986. The international-isation of finance is putting enormous pressure on the idiosyncratic aspects of national capital markets, and it remains to be seen how much will be left in a few years of our earlier description of the distinctive aspects of the Japanese and West German capital markets.

* * * * *

It is one thing to describe these changes, and quite another to interpret them. In general, any specific tendency in the direction of the breaking down of barriers between financial institutions, or of commodification or internationalisation could reverse itself in the face of economic or financial perturbations or alterations in the regulatory environment (including taxation regimes). But the underlying factors which these tendencies represent seem irreversible.

We have earlier noted a predisposition in economic orthodoxy to avoid questions concerning the evolution of financial markets and to concentrate on the static question of whether or not they are efficient. But some explana-tions of economic change are, however, more congruent than others with neo-classical methodology, and for our purposes this delineation is a con-venient one. Thus, for John Lintner, the increasing illiquidity and higher debt ratios in the post-war corporate sector (complementing the lengthen-ing of the assets position of financial institutions) is not to be thought of as speculative, 'Ponziesque' activity, in Minsky's colourful terminology, but as first, a wringing out of redundant positions with the increasingly effective methods of cash management and new technology in the context of post-war stability and, secondly, as a response to the (largely unanticipated) inflation of the 1960s and 1970s.[119]

Technological change can be taken as a suitably exogenous force upon financial institutions, and if we forget the aforementioned fact that some of the new-found competition for financial institutions is coming from the *creators* of new technology such as IBM, the new ways of doing business brought about by technological change – techniques of cash management, of funds transfer and a vast assortment of financial services hitherto impossible – may be taken as illustrations of 'exogenous change in the constrained optimization of the firm that stimulates a search for new policy tools.'[120] The new technology has also facilitated the process of commodification, permitting the creation of an enormous array of small denomination debt instruments and the very existence of these new telephone–electronic markets themselves. Commodification is then due to 'the exogenous shift which has taken place ... in the hardware and software that is available to run markets in financial instruments.'[121]

Technological change is thus a legitimate neo-classical explanation for financial evolution, and changes resulting from the lifting of regulatory constraints would be an even more orthodox candidate. The latter is certainly of significance, but first in the US and then in the international arena financial institutions have anticipated deregulation by finding loopholes in existing laws, prompted by an environment that was already becoming increasingly competitive. Much of the deregulation that has come about – for instance the lowering of national boundaries to the operation of other countries' financial institutions – has been a ratification of the emerging state of affairs.

But exogenous change in the context of a given set of behavioural parameters is not sufficient to explain events in the financial markets. Change has interacted with and been reinforced by evolution in the – dare we say it? – sociology of financial institutions, resulting in what seem to be irrevocable alterations in attitudes and ways of doing business. Economists will be relieved to hear that much of what we attribute to the traditional behaviour patterns of (commercial) banks can be given an economic rationale: the asymmetry of rewards – fixed interest loans (restricted by convention and regulation to relatively short-term offerings) which are either repaid or are not cultivate a mentality by which 'bankers are not supposed to be smart; they are supposed to be safe.'[122] One of the changes associated with banks trying to become 'financial supermarkets' is that they are having to consider offering remuneration comparable to that traditionally associated with investment banks and other financial institutions; in the past, it has been the lack of cunning of the commercial banks as much as any Glass–Steagall restrictions (witness the British case) which has permitted the investment banks, with their vastly inferior resources to build up a key role in the financing of firms.

This push for change has clearly been engendered by the aforementioned exogenous factors such as technological change, deregulation and inflation, but the banks' constituency has also been transformed. Depositors have, in recent years become more knowledgeable and sophisticated, and are more able and willing than ever to go to the market directly if the bank return is not competitive. Of greater significance has been the necessity for banks and other financial institutions to respond to changes in the practices of borrowers, as corporations have refined their techniques of cash management and for financing projects at minimum cost. The development of these more precise techniques in the corporate sector has been encouraged by inflation and made possible by technological change, but it also reflects a longer term evolution of techniques, attitudes and available infrastructure. Financial institutions live in the same world as do companies, and they naturally respond both to the new pressures put upon them by firms and to the new-found opportunities which confront them.

The movement towards the 'financial supermarket' and the erosion of Glass–Steagall constraints has caused some commentators to compare contemporary events with those described by the turn of the century German economist Ruldolph Hilferding.[123] But the situation described by him is one in which banks dominate industry, with an uncompetitive tying up of a firm to a financial institution. However, at least one historian has suggested that the very powerful links discussed by Hilferding were loosening even as he wrote about them, as industrial firms became more powerful and self-assertive.[124] It is evident, contrary to this 'finance capital' school, that contemporary events are the outcome of a progressively more competitive environment.

The present relationships evolving between banks and firms, far from signalling a growing dominance of financial institutions represent a precisely contrary development. They result from the efforts of financial institutions to accommodate themselves to a far more insecure environment, one made insecure by the activities of financial institutions in competition with each other and by the ever more stringent demands made upon them by their clients, especially their business customers. Thus in contrast with the traditional practice of compensating balances, in which the maintenance of funds in the bank was part of the price extracted from even the largest firms for the granting of a loan, both holders and users of funds now have a wide variety of alternative sources which formerly did not exist. On the other hand, there may be an element of truth in the finance capital doctrine in the situation we see emerging before us: if indeed banks are in the process of seeking returns higher than they could traditionally receive on 'self-liquidating' loans, can they proceed in this direction without – implicitly or explicitly – gaining an equity stake in the company and can they, and will they still desire to maintain their traditional *laissez-faire* attitude towards the running of company affairs?

A further question of interest raised by these events is whether the commodification of finance which has been developing signals a departure from the traditional analysis performed by financial institutions on borrowers, most especially their analysis of the firm's financial (gearing and liquidity) risk. The failure to have a precise rating system may have in fact inhibited the development of some of these markets, as indicated by the fact that the US commercial paper market with its formal credit rating system for firms is still ten times the size of its (by necessity) more name conscious equivalent in the Euro markets.

On the other hand, it has been suggested that one of the great advantages of swaps is that 'The ability to obtain the benefits of markets without the need to comply with the prospectus disclosures, credit ratings and other formal requirements provides an additional benefit especially for private companies.'[125] Outsiders may well query what such developments imply for the future stability of the financial system. A further effect of commodification could be, in the manner suggested earlier, on the time horizon used by firms in their investment decisions. As Robin Leigh-Pemberton, Governor of the Bank of England has suggested 'If markets are driven by traders, long-term credit may be taken on the basis of short-term market opportunities.'[126] It could however be argued that public fluctuations in the prices of a firm's securities are a powerful and more objective constraint on its behaviour than the private strictures imposed on it by a bank: 'With bank loans increasingly taking the form of marketable paper there can be no more fudging when countries or companies run into trouble: the market will rapidly reflect changes in credit status by ranking paper to a discount.'[127] In either case, commodification is likely to have important consequences for firm behaviour.

A last issue concerns whether these changes in the financial environment will have the effect of accentuating or squeezing the layers of the capital market. New competition in the financial environment could work to the detriment of small firms if banks find their margins squeezed in their dealings with big firms and try to make up for these shortfalls in their dealings with smaller firms, which have fewer alternative sources. Thus 'Mr. Alan Jones, the assistant general manager for advances at Nat West, notes that the new instruments are still largely confined to the top end of the market, and that loan margins are still more attractive for banks in the middle and small-sized company market.'[128] In a world of limited finance, recent events may have accentuated the gap in the bargaining power of large firms *vis-à-vis* the banks, thereby increasing the layering effect of the capital market.

In a contrary direction, the increasingly competitive financial environment may act to squeeze the layers of the capital market. One mechanism is the intervention of financial institutions in the area of so-called venture capital. In the US, the traditional source of venture capital for 'high risk, high return' new businesses, often (and mistakenly) exclusively associated with high technology, was extremely wealthy families. In recent years, partially as a result of tax concessions, there has been an upsurge of interest from institutions such as pension funds, insurance companies and others – a conspicuous example being Merrill Lynch's creation of a public venture capital partnership ML Venture Partners. Other countries have attempted to emulate what is taken to be an extremely successful element in the American economy, especially in its ability to encourage 'silicon valley' high technology enterprises. The UK has been the most prominent follower, with an explosion of venture capital funding since 1980 resulting in a pool of funds almost a quarter that of the US,[129] much of which has been used to finance managerial buy-outs.

Of perhaps greater significance is the growing ease with which firms may market their equity. In the US, this tendency has been aided not only by the shelf-registration rule, but by the continued development in the breadth and depth of the over the counter and regional markets. The over the counter markets especially have benefited from the introduction in 1971 of the National Association of Securities Dealers Automated Quotations (NASDAQ) system, a sophisticated computer-based communications network which stores information on 4,700 companies. In the UK, the launching in 1980 of the Unlisted Securities Market has been a success, with over 400 companies having been listed, and in 1987 a third tier market was initiated. It appears that the new found freedom in equity issue, when coupled with the greater aggressiveness of financial institutions in searching for highest possible returns, acts as a centrifugal force, or at least as one neutralising the centripetal effects of the capital market – squeezing the distances between the capital market layers and tending to narrow any unfair advantages to large firms or those with special access to the capital market.

The direct effect of the changed attitude and behaviour of financial institutions on the evolution of the industrial structure is an important issue. A first suggestion discussed earlier is that a force encouraging mergers is the new-found aggressiveness on the part of financial institutions, especially investment banks for whom merger fees are a key source of remuneration. But the very aggressiveness of investment bankers like Drexel Burnham Lambert which has promoted mergers has also moved in the direction of creating – to paraphrase the syntax of the US Constitution – a 'more perfect' capital market. Junk bonds – those less than 'investment grade' (at a rating of BB+ or less at Standard and Poor's, or Ba1 or below at Moody's) have been used to finance takeover raids. But at the same time the success that Drexel Burnham Lambert's Mike Milken has had in convincing blue chip investors that junk bonds were underpriced on the basis of academic evidence on their risk-return profiles (Life imitating Art again) has permitted low grade companies to be freed from strict dependence on bank loans. Only 675 American companies earn investment grade ratings from the two agencies, which has meant that 19,000 American companies with total assets of over $25 billion have had virtually no access to the bond market.[130] If alterations in the financial environment from increased aggressiveness by institutions are squeezing the capital market layers, they may be mitigating the long-term tendency for mergers to reinforce increases in aggregate industrial concentration, even if at the same time they promote these mergers themselves.

A further effect of capital market changes is upon firms' internal organisation. If earlier diversification and merger often come about for financial as opposed to real reasons, then the present fashion for managerial buy-outs, asset redeployment and deconglomeration may not be a wholly transitory phenomenon. Rather it may be one which in part reflects an increased tendency for financial markets to allocate resources in the direction of their greatest perceived real value. This tendency is also present in improvements in the market for bankrupt firms or 'corporate losers'. Mergers may continue, but with a lessening tendency to form free-form conglomerates, and more in the direction of creating 'economically logical' companies in narrower, related fields which can be managed more knowledgeably. If this is the case, changes in the financial environment may have profound effects upon industrial structure, even if they are not reflected in the statistics documenting changes in aggregate concentration.

The conclusions which we draw about the effects of changes in the behaviour of participants in financial and capital markets on the industrial sector must remain agnostic: there is little sign that the development of financial conglomerates prefaces a Hilferding-like control over the industrial sector. Instead, the increased aggressiveness of financial institutions in search of the highest possible returns might involve greater equity participation, which could eventually necessitate departures from the hands off approach typically found in the relationship between financial institutions and firms. In addition the lack of monitoring implied by the commodification and the internationalisation of finance may engender financial instability or an emphasis on all sides in favour of short-term returns, while on the contrary the public nature of the contracts may be a more severe and more objective form of monitoring than the private relationships which have heretofore existed between firms and financial institutions. Lastly, the increased competitiveness of the capital market may improve the bargaining position of large firms in this sphere *vis-à-vis* small firms, or it may diminish it. But the failure here in this brief survey to draw decisive conclusions on the effects of these dramatic changes in behaviour does not justify ignoring these questions. To avoid these issues by focusing exclusively on static paradigms of the financial market is to court irrelevance for the sake of 'rigour'.

We turn now to examine restructuring in the 'real' sector of the economy.

Notes

1. This is strictly true only if we limit our measure to the manufacturing sector. In the early part of the century, the decline in the value added share of agriculture – a sector with few large enterprises – probably would have

reinforced the upward movement in manufacturing compared with economy-wide calculations of aggregate concentration. The rise of the so-called tertiary sector in recent decades might well have the opposite effect on economy-wide calculations, and, indeed, it is possible that our 'stylised fact' for manufacturing reverses itself when all sectors are considered: see White, L. 'What Has Been Happening to Aggregate Concentration in the United States?' *Journal of Industrial Economics* 39(3) (March 1981): 223–30. Ideally, aggregate concentration would be most meaningful for the economy as a whole, but for our purposes a restriction to manufacturing probably does little violence to the questions we are considering.

2. A discussion of these issues is to be found in Prais, S. *The Evolution of Giant Firms in Britain* Cambridge University second edn 1981, especially appendix E.

3. Edwards, C. 'Conglomerate Bigness as a Source of Power' in National Bureau of Economic Research (Introduction by G. Stigler) *Business Concentration and Price Policy* Princeton University 1955, pp. 331–59.

4. In its pure form, a displacement barrier may indicate that economies of scale are so substantial in a particular sector that a prospective entrant could not expect to earn an adequate return producing alongside (an) existing producer(s), despite the fact that the latter presently earn(s) at least 'normal' return. Such a barrier to entry could exist even in an otherwise 'perfect' market (see Stigler, G. *Theory of Price* Macmillan (US) 1966, ch. 12).

5. Prais (note 2), chs 3 and 4. The most extensive study of the question of multi-plant economies is Scherer, F. M., A. Beckenstein, E. Kaufer and R. D. Murphy *The Economics of Multi-Plant Operation* Harvard University 1975. It found important instances of multi-product, if not (static) multi-plant economies, but did not report changes over time in any such economies as having been of overwhelming significance. The latter question was, however, not confronted explicitly.

Friedman's well-known comments on the difficulty of observing static economies of scale statistically (comment on Smith, C. 'Survey of Empirical Evidence on Economies of Scale' in NBER (note 3) pp. 230–8) due to 'regression fallacy' problems are generally interpreted to mean that *ex ante* economies may exist which are not observed *ex post*. A bias, however, exists in the contrary direction which may show a small firm to be 'inefficient' when it is merely subject to capital market restrictions. Let us say a currently efficient small firm operating two plants is confronted with a new technology which doubles the minimum efficient scale of operations. If this firm is restricted from replacing these two now inefficient plants with a single efficient plant by virtue of 'arbitrary' capital market limitations against small firms, the observed outome may resemble that of a 'real' inefficiency on the part of a small firm. For an overall assessment of the empirical literature on static economies see the summary to be found in HMSO *A Review of Monopolies and Mergers Policy* ('The Green Paper') Cmnd 7198 1978 Annexe C, pp. 77–96.

6. Scherer, F. M. *Industrial Market Structure and Economic Performance* Rand McNally second edn 1980, ch. 15 has an exhaustive summary of the empirical literature, as does The Green Paper (note 5) Annexe E, pp. 113–22. It is not clear in this literature that a distinction has always been drawn between technologically based dynamic economies of size and those linked to the apparent financial advantages (e.g. the supposedly longer time

horizons on projects) which accrue to big firms, which might then facilitate the exploitation of innovations originating elsewhere.

7. See Blair, J. *Economic Concentration*, Harcourt Brace Jovanovich 1972, ch. 13. The following quotation is suggestive: "'Just take advertising alone," says John M. Diefenbach, president of Landor Associates, a San Francisco consulting firm. "Ten years ago, $5 million to $20 million could establish a brand. Today you are talking about a $50 million to $100 million annual investment."' 'P&G's Rusty Marketing Machine' *Business Week* 21 October 1985.

8. Green Paper (note 5), p. 110.

9. Scherer (note 6), p. 124.

10. Prais (note 2, ch. 2) gives a significant place to 'spontaneous drift' as a cause of the rise in aggregate concentration. Gibrat's law of proportionate growth demonstrates that even if growth is independent of firm size and firms' past growth histories, stochastic processes will generate long-term increases in concentration as long as the number of firms is fixed. The only really interesting insight that emerges from this approach is that increases in concentration are more likely in slow growing economies (that is, those with a relatively fixed number of firms) than in fast growing economies. This seems to be confirmed historically, as we shall see below. Otherwise, no clear meaning emerges from such an 'explanation'.

11. Aaronovitch, S. and M. Sawyer *Big Business* Macmillan 1975, p. 150, and Hannah, L. and Kay, J. *Concentration in Modern Industry* Macmillan 1976. In one study, McGowan, J. 'The Effect of Alternative Antimerger Policies on the Size Distribution of Firms' *Yale Economic Essays* 5(2) (Fall 1965): 423–76, it is contended that aggregate concentration in the US in manufacturing would have declined in the absence of mergers.

12. Meeks, G. *Disappointing Marriage* Cambridge University 1977, p. 4. This is for a sample of 893 of the largest companies.

13. Large acquisitions in manufacturing and mining from 1948 to 1968 consumed assets worth $53 billion: Federal Trade Commission *Economic Report on Corporate Mergers* US Government Printing Office 1969, p. 42. See also Blair (note 7), ch. 11, and Winslow, J. *Conglomerates Unlimited* Indiana University 1973.

14. See Aaronovitch and Sawyer (note 11) pp. 131–40, Briston, R. J. and D. G. Rhys 'Problems in the Analysis of Statistics Relating to Takeovers and Mergers' in Samuels, J. M. (ed.) *Readings on Mergers and Takeovers* Paul Elek 1972, pp. 77–93, Meeks (note 12) appendices A and B, and the discussion between Hannah L., and J. Kay in the *Journal of Industrial Economics* 29(3) (March 1981) with P. Hart and S. Prais, pp. 305–32.

15. Hart, P., M. Utton and G. Walshe *Mergers and Concentration in British Industry* Cambridge University 1973, ch. 7.

16. Kitching, J. 'Why Do Mergers Miscarry?' *Harvard Business Review* 45 (November–December 1967): 84–101.

17. Singh, A. *Takeovers* Cambridge University Press 1971 Meeks (note 12) pp. 20, 62; and Cosh, A., A. Hughes and A. Singh 'The Causes and Effects of Takeovers in the United Kingdom: An Empirical Analysis' in Mueller, D. C. (ed.) *The Determinants and Effects of Mergers* Oelgeschlager, Gunn & Haim 1980, pp. 227–70. This is true even within their populations of quoted firms. Data on acquisitions of unquoted firms can be found in Aaronovitch and Sawyer (note 11), pp. 133–8, and therein can also be found a listing of other

studies on this question. Similiar results are reported internationally in Mueller, D. 'A Cross-National Comparison of Results' in Mueller, D. (ed.)(this note), pp. 299–314.

18. Once again, see the assiduous Professor Scherer (note 6), pp. 123–154, 280–4, and Aaronovitch and Sawyer (note 11), pp. 123–54, 280–4.

19. The promoters' profits view of mergers and a discussion of the earlier literature may be found in Markham, J. 'Survey of the Evidence and Findings on Mergers' (with comments by G. Stocking and W. Adams) in NBER (note 3), pp. 141–212.

20. Cable, J., J. Palfrey and J. Runge 'Federal Republic of Germany 1962–74' in Mueller (note 17), pp. 99–132.

21. Gort, M. 'An Economic Disturbance Theory of Mergers' *Quarterly Journal of Economics* 83 (November 1969): 624–42.

22. Gort, M. and T. Hogarty 'New Evidence on Mergers' *Journal of Law and Economics* 13 (April, 1970): 167–84.

23. This point is made in Hughes, A., D. Mueller and A. Singh 'Hypotheses about Mergers' in Mueller (note 17), pp. 227–70.

24. Newbould, G. 'Implications of Financial Analyses of Takeovers' in Samuels (note 14), pp. 12–24.

25. Briloff, A. *Unaccountable Accounting* Harper and Row 1972. A review of these questions is to be found in Reinhart, U. 'Mergers and Consolidations: A Corporate Finance Approach' *General Learning Press* 1972.

26. Weston, J. and S. Mansinghka 'Tests of the Efficiency Performance of Conglomerate Firms' in Samuels (note 14), pp. 25–39.

27. Newbould (note 24).

28. Davis E. and K. Yeomans *Company Finance and the Capital Market* Cambridge University 1974, ch. 3.

29. Meeks (note 12).

30. Ibid., appendix C for a survey for the UK and US literature.

31. Appleyard, A. R. 'Takeovers: Accounting Policy, Financial Policy and the Case Against Accounting Measures of Performance' *Journal of Business Finance and Accounting* 7(4) (1980): 541–54.

32. Halpern, P. 'Corporate Acquisitions: A Theory of Special Cases? A Review of Event Studies Applied to Acquisitions' *Journal of Finance* 38 (2) (May 1983): 297–317.

33. Jensen, M. and R. Ruback 'The Market for Corporate Control: the Scientific Evidence' *Journal of Financial Economics* 11(1983): 5–50.

34. See Mueller, D. 'The Effects of Conglomerate Mergers: a Survey of the Empirical Evidence' *Journal of Banking and Finance* 1 (December 1977): 315–47 and his 'Further Reflections on the Invisible Hand Theorem' in Wiles, P. and G. Routh (eds) *Economics in Disarray* Basil Blackwell 1984, pp. 159–83.

35. Mueller, D. 'A Theory of Conglomerate Mergers' *Quarterly Journal of Economics* 83 (November 1969): 643–59.

36. A balanced discussion of these events can be found in Davidson, K. *Megamergers* Ballinger 1985.

37. 'A Hot New Star in the Merger Game' *Fortune* 17 February 1986.

38. 'What's Next for the Raiders' *Fortune* 11 November 1985.

39. A much higher percentage of takeovers were financed with cash in the late 1970s and the early 1980s compared with the late 1960s. See Davidson (note 36), table 6–5, p. 145.

40. Ibid., p. 147.
41. Ibid., p. 60.
42. See Small and Medium Enterprise Agency *Small Business in Japan* White Paper on Small and Medium Enterprises in Japan MITI 1986, and Ganguly, P. and G. Bannock *UK Small Business Statistics and International Comparisons* Harper and Row 1985.
43. For a survey of these approaches see Scherer (note 6), ch. 8.
44. See Hirshleifer, J. *Investment, Interest and Capital* Prentice-Hall 1970, chs 1–4.
45. Stiglitz, J. in 'A Re-examination of the Modigliani–Miller Theorem', *American Economic Review* 59(5) (December 1969): 784–93 demonstrates that in his version of the theorem the assumption of the existence of risk classes is not necessary, and that the conditions of capital market 'perfection' are somewhat weaker than we have indicated.
46. Modigliani, F. and M. Miller 'The Cost of Capital, Corporation Finance and the Theory of Investment' *American Economic Review* 48(3) (June 1958): 261–97.
47. The attempt to re-create the traditional view with the introduction of both corporate income taxes and costs of bankruptcy has been a failure, since bankruptcy costs do not sit well with the Modigliani–Miller assumptions of a perfect capital market. See Haugen, R. and L. Senbet 'The Insignificance of Bankruptcy Costs to the Theory of Optimal Capital Structure' *Journal of Finance* 33(2) (May 1978): 383–93.
48. Inter-temporal general equilibrium theory in the literature of finance falls under the rubric of 'state-preference' theory. For an exposition see Copeland, T. and J. F. Weston, *Financial Theory and Corporate Policy* Addison-Wesley 2nd edn 1983, ch. 5.
49. See Fama, E. and M. Miller *Theory of Finance* Dryden Press 1972, ch. 5.
50. The CAPM is now a basic topic in textbooks on finance. See Fama, E. *Foundations of Finance* Basic Books 1976, ch. 8. Rival, but closely related formulations are the Arbitrage Pricing Theory (see Copeland and Weston (note 48), ch. 7) and the Option Pricing Theory (see Elton, E. and M. Gruber *Modern Portfolio Theory and Investment Analysis* John Wiley 1981, ch. 17).
51. The existence of such an asset was postulated in the original development of the CAPM, but the latter has subsequently been derived without it (see Copeland and Weston (note 48), pp. 198–200).
52. See Copeland and Weston (note 48), pp. 410–18.
53. See Mossin, J. *Theory of Financial Markets* Prentice-Hall 1973, pp. 12–13.
54. See Stiglitz (note 45).
55. See Fama (note 50), p. 319.
56. Attempts to overcome this problem have still been forced to make strong assumptions about the convergence of investors' opinions. In one article, a capital market model is constructed in which investors hold different opinions about the mean and variance of assets, but even here all are unanimous on the level of what is essentially the 'systematic risk' embodied in each asset (Mayshar, J. 'On Divergence of Opinion and Imperfections in Capital Markets' *American Economic Review* 73(1) (March 1983): 114–28).
57. Keynes, J. M. *The General Theory of Employment, Interest and Money* Harcourt Brace 1964 (originally published 1936), pp. 162–3; italics added.

58. Shiller, R. J. 'Do Stock Prices Move Too Much to be Justified by Subsequent Changes in Dividends?' *American Economic Review* 71(3) (June 1981): 421–36.

59. See for instance Dimson, E. and P. Marsh, 'Use of Risk Measures for Calculating the Cost of Company's Capital' in *Financial Times* supplement *Corporation Finance* 18 May 1982.

60. 'Why Bendix is set on a Path of Constant Change' *Financial Times* 21 June 1982.

61. See for instance Shackle, G. *Decision, Order and Time in Human Affairs* Cambridge University 1961.

62. Johnson, H. as quoted in Kindleberger, C. *Manias, Panics and Crashes* Macmillan 1978, p. 26.

63. There Is No Alternative.

64. Akerloff, G. 'The Economics of Caste and of the Rat Race and Other Woeful Tales' *Quarterly Journal of Economics* 90(4) (November 1976): 599–617, italics added.

65. See for instance Posner, R. 'Anthropology and Economics' *Journal of Political Economy* 88(3) (June 1980): 608–16. Recent extensions of rational choice methodology to the animal kingdom (Battalio, R., J. Kagel and D. McDonald 'Animals' Choice Over Uncertain Outcomes' *American Economic Review* 75(4) (September 1985): 597–613) defy criticism or even satire. These general issues are discussed more fully in my 'Scientific Hypotheses and their Domain of Applicability: Comment on Coddington' *British Review of Economic Issues* 2(5) (November 1979): 61–9.

66. Stiglitz, J. and A. Weiss 'Credit Rationing with Imperfect Information' *American Economic Review* 71(3) (June 1981): 393–410.

67. Jensen, M. and W. Meckling. 'Theory of the Firm: Managerial Behavior, Agency Costs and Ownership Structure' *Journal of Financial Economics* 3(4) (October 1976): 305–60.

68. See Hill, C. *Reformation to Industrial Revolution* Weidenfeld and Nicolson 1967, ch. 3. It has been suggested, however, that even British landowners during the Industrial Revolution often invested in land connected industries (agriculture, brewing, milling and mining) when rates of return were near zero, while new industries were unable to acquire funds even at interest rates of twenty per cent; see Davis, L. 'Capital Mobility and American Growth' in Fogel, R. and S. Engermen (eds) *The Reinterpretation of American History* Harper and Row 1971, pp. 285–300.

69. Gille, B. 'Banking and Industrialisation in Europe 1730–1914' in Cipolla, C. (ed.) *Fontana Economic History of Europe* vol. 3 Fontana 1973, pp. 255–300.

70. See Feinstein, C. 'Capital Formation in Great Britain' in Mathias, P. and M. Postan (eds) *The Cambridge Economic History of Europe* vol. VII part 1 Cambridge University 1978, pp. 28–96, for estimates of capital formation in Britain till 1860.

71. Quoted in Cottrell, P. *Industrial Finance 1830–1914* Methuen 1980, p. 47.

72. Davis, L. and R. Gallman, 'Capital Formation in the United States in the Nineteenth Century' in Mathias, P. and M. Postan (eds) *The Cambridge Economic History of Europe* vol. VII part 2 Cambridge University 1978, pp. 1–69.

73. See Davis, L. 'The Capital Markets and Industrial Concentration: The US

and UK, A Comparative Study' *Economic History Review* second series 19(2) (1966): 255–72.

74. Thomas, W. A. *The Finance of British Industry 1918–1976* Methuen 1977, pp. 40, 43 and 86.

75. Report of the Committee of Inquiry on Small Firms ('Bolton Report') Cmnd. 4811, HMSO London 1971, pp. 1–3, and Jones, M. T. 'An Analysis of the Accounts of Small Companies' in Committee to Review the Functioning of Financial Institutions (Wilson Committee) *Studies of Small Firms' Financing* Research Report No. 3 Cmnd 7937 HMSO 1979.

76. Davis, E. and K. Yeomans *Company Finance and the Capital Market* Cambridge University 1974, chs 1–6. Tenders are relatively immune from the effects of these discounts, but are only ventured by those firms large and robust enough to brave the wrath of the City. None of these costs compare in order of magnitude with those earlier cited for the 1930s; conventional costs of issue have fallen by almost 50 per cent just in the period of Davis and Yeomans's study (1959–1971). US studies such as Faerber, L. 'The Cost of External Common Stock Equity Capital for Small Business: An Empirical Study of New Common Stock Offerings' *Journal of Finance* 19(4) (December 1964): 691–2 and Brigham, F. and K. Smith 'Cost of Capital to the Small Firm' *The Engineering Economist* 13(1) (Fall 1967): 1–26 also find cost economies on the basis of size. More recently it has been stated that 'the big name banks are not likely to handle a public offering unless it's at least $15 million to $20 million; any less, say the bankers is not economical for them': 'Timing is Everything When You Go Public' *Business Week* 3 November 1986.

77. See Van Horne, J. 'New Listings and Their Price Behavior' *Journal of Finance* 25(4) (September 1970): 783–94.

78. Our source here is Jones (note 75), which is restricted to public companies.

79. Committee to Review the Functioning of Financial Institutions (Wilson Committee) *Report* Cmnd 7937 HMSO 1981, p. 23.

80. 'Survey of Financing of Small Firms in the Service Industries' in Wilson (1979), (note 75) and Stanworth, J., J. Curran and J. Hough 'The Franchised Small Enterprise: Formal and Operational Dimensions of Independence' *UKSBTA Fifth Annual Small Business Research Conference* University of Glasgow September 1982.

81. See Galbraith, J. K. 'Market Structure and Stabilization Policy' *Review of Economics and Statistics* 34(2) (May 1957): 124–33.

82. This is an alternative explanation for the higher cash ratios of small firms to the 'economies of scale' explanation offered by Davis and Yeomans (note 76), p. 75.

83. Wilson (note 79), p. 25; for a theoretical discussion see Stiglitz and Weiss (note 66).

84. Baumol, W., P. Heim, B. Malkiel and R. Quandt 'Earnings Retention, New Capital and the Growth of the Firm' *Review of Economics and Statistics* 70(4) (November 1970): 345–55.

85. Unilever Submission to the Committee to Review the Functioning of UK Financial Institutions (Wilson Committee) (mimeo).

86. A quotation from a financial analyst in 'Why Companies Go Bust' in the *Financial Times* 8 March 1983.

87. See the survey in Foster, G. *Financial Statement Analysis* Prentice-Hall

second edn 1986, ch. 15. Note, however, that other variables, including firm (asset) size, seem to be of assistance in improving 'predictability'.

88. Desai, M. and D. Montes 'A Macroeconomic Model of Bankruptcies in the British Economy, 1945–1980' *British Review of Economic Issues* 4(10) (Spring 1983): 1–14.

89. For a discussion of these issues, see Kindleberger, C. and J. P. Laffargue (eds) *Financial Crises* Cambridge University 1982.

90. Yamamura, K. 'Entrepreneurship, Ownership and Management in Japan' in Mathias and Postan (note 72), pp. 215–64.

91. Elston, C. 'The Financing of Japanese Industry' *Bank of England Quarterly Bulletin* 21(4) (December 1981): 510–18.

92. Milward, A. and S. Saul *The Development of the Economies of Continental Europe 1850–1914* George Allen 1977, pp. 46–53, 318–23, Kocka, J. 'The Rise of the Modern Industrial Enterprise in Germany' in Chandler, A. and H. Daems (eds) *Managerial Hierarchies* Harvard University 1980, pp. 77–116 and Kocka, J. 'Entrepreneurs and Managers in German Industrialization' in Mathias and Postan (note 70), pp. 492–589.

93. In the past ten years there has apparently been a significant fall in West Germany in the number of companies in which bank shareholdings amount to more than 25 per cent of the firm's equity. See *Financial Times* survey *West German Banking* 6 July 1987.

94. Prominent writings arguing this case are Carrington, J. and G. Edwards *Financing Industrial Investment* Macmillan 1979 and Zysman, J. *Governments, Markets and Growth* Cornell University 1983.

95. See Elston (note 91) concerning this and other differences in accounting practice.

96. 'Fatal Fascination with the Short Run' *Business Week* 4 May 1981.

97. An overseas banker based in West Germany, quoted in 'Why Opinions Are Split on the Virtue of German Banking' *Financial Times* 14 March 1978.

98. 'A Primitive Way to Raise Cash' *Financial Times* 7 September 1983.

99. Elston (note 91).

100. See for instance the studies in Mueller (note 17).

101. Kocka in Chandler and Daems (note 92).

102. Prais (note 95) p. 40, Elston (note 91).

103. The standard exposition is Fama, E. 'Efficient Capital Markets: A Review of Theory and Empirical Work' *Journal of Finance* 25(2) (May 1970): 383–417, and a useful review is to be found in Foster (note 87), ch. 9.

104. Confirmation of the existence of a weekend effect can be found in Keim, D. and R. Stambaugh 'Further investigation of the Weekend Effect in Stock Returns' *Journal of Finance* 39(3) (July 1984): 819–35 and Jaffe, J. and R. Westerfield 'The Week-end Effect in Common Stock Returns: the International Evidence' *Journal of Finance* 40(2) (June 1985): 433–454.

105. Beaver, W. and R. Dukes, 'Tax Allocation and δDepreciation Methods', *Accounting Review* 48(3) (July 1973): 549–59.

106. Fama, E., L. Fisher, M. Jensen and R. Roll 'The Adjustment of Stock Prices to New Information' *International Economic Review* 10(1) (February 1969): 1–21. There is however substantial anecdotal evidence of the failure of the market to see through changes in accounting conventions. See for instance the story of the US firm Micro Focus in Griffiths, I. *Creative Accounting* Sidgewick and Jackson 1986, pp. 20–1.

107. There has been great controversy surrounding the Shiller findings (note 58);

see for example Mankin, N., D. Romer and M. Shapiro 'An Unbiased Reexamination of Stock Market Volatility' *Journal of Finance* 40(3) (July 1985): 677–87, and Shiller's comment pp. 688–9.

108. Foster, G. 'Briloff and the Capital Market' *Journal of Accounting Research* 17(1) (Spring 1979): 262–74; italics below added.
109. Grossack, I. introduction to Winslow (note 13), p. xi.
110. This was his answer to the question 'Why do you rob banks, Mr. Sutton?'.
111. See Hodgeman, D. *Commercial Bank Loan and Investment Policy* University of Illinois 1963.
112. *Economist* survey 16 March 1985.
113. 'Banks Seek a Life Beyond Lending' *Fortune* 3 March 1986 .
114. As of May 1986 the Bank of England makes a 50 per cent capital weighting to the underwriting commitments of UK banks.
115. 'The Rocky Road to a Global Village' *Financial Times* 27 May 1987.
116. 'Swiss Connection is Prominent' *Financial Times* survey *International Capital Markets* 17 March 1986.
117. 'Swaps – Regulators Take An Interest' *Financial Times* survey *Foreign Exchange* 3 June 1987.
118. *Euromoney* special supplement *Innovation in International Capital Markets* January 1986.
119. Lintner, J. discussion of papers by Minsky and others in Altman, E. and A. Sametz (eds) *Financial Crises* John Wiley 1977, pp. 204–5.
120. Silber, W. 'Towards a Theory of Financial Innovation' in Silber, W. (ed.) *Financial Innovation* Lexington Books 1975, pp. 65–6.
121. Cooper, I. 'Innovations: New Market Instruments' *Oxford Review of Economic Policy* 2(4)(Winter 1986): 1–17.
122. Unattributed quotation heading an article 'The New Shape of Banking' *Business Week* 18 June 1984.
123. Hilferding, R. *Finance Capital* Routledge Kegan Paul; English edn, 1981. Originally published in 1910.
124. Kocka in Chandler and Daems (note 92).
125. *Euromoney* (note 118).
126. Quoted in 'Money-Based Lending "Threat to Bank Decisions"' *Financial Times* 8 May 1986 .
127. 'Deregulation Gains That Add Up To Zero' *Financial Times* 29 August 1986.
128. 'The Overdraft Still Lives Despite Some New Ideas' *Financial Times* survey *Corporate Finance* 3 July 1986.
129. 'Stand By for Some Vertical Landings' *Financial Times* survey *Venture Capital* 8 December 1986.
130. *Economist* survey *Corporate Finance* 7 June 1986.

8

The Changing Patterns of Firm Organisation: Vertical Integration, Conglomerates and Multinationals

Vertical Integration

Measurement Problems and Conceptual Difficulties

The first of the three great changes in the organisation and structure of giant firms to be discussed here is the emergence of vertically integrated entities, i.e. (predominantly large) firms which have united several stages of the processes of production and distribution under common owner-ship. There are, however, difficulties in operationalising this definition. While it may appear obvious that a car firm which fabricates its own steel has united at least two separable activities, the question of where one stage stops and another begins is largely a matter of convention and perspective.

Even within steel fabrication or car manufacture, for example, the enumeration of stages is fairly arbitrary. But if, for the sake of argument, we were to treat each of these activities as an entity, and had never observed steel fabrication for any purpose but the making of cars, would we view car manufacture as the integration of two processes or simply as one? More graphically (and more fancifully) if steel fabrication had come down to us historically as a process uniquely linked to the manufacture of swords in which the fabricators forged their own steel and produced swords in a continuous flow, would not sword making and steel manu-facture be viewed as one process, until such time as other uses had been found for steel? These are ambiguities which exist on the supply side.[1]

On the demand side, the delineation of separate stages is also blurred in many cases, since substitution by the user is often a readily available possibility. For example, the question of the level of integration of firms competing in the computer industry is difficult to resolve unambiguously, since purchasers can, within limits, substitute between stages – input processing, storage, control and output of the full mainframe.[2] Furthermore, integration in the sense which is used here may develop in a direction contrary to the purely *technical* integration of processes. The emergence of the process plant contracting industry – the buying in of more or less complete plants from outside suppliers (largely in the chemical industry) had as a prerequisite a very advanced level of technical integration of processes *within* the plant.[3]

The problems of vertical integration and its conceptualisation have a family resemblance to those we have observed in the attempt to construct an objective delineation for the industry: whatever one's intuitive feeling about the intrinsic difference between one process (or product) or another, in the absence of a usable, principled criterion, there is always the danger that any delineation is largely arbitrary. The problem of industry delineation also intrudes itself more directly, since inter-industry comparisons of vertical integration will be affected by the (arbitrary) boundaries drawn around these industries – do we compare the level of vertical integration in the car industry with that in the television industry, or with the more broadly defined electronics industry? Conversely, the level of vertical integration is often critical in determining the relevant industry boundary. It was crucial to the US government's case against IBM to define the domain of competitiveness to include only those rivals who could fully match IBM's integration of production and service facilities in the mainframe computer industry. Was this specification too narrow? There are, as we have seen, no structural, a priori solutions to these problems.

In practice, the most commonly used procedure is to measure vertical integration by the firm's (or industry's) level of value added/sales, a technique which sidesteps the definition of vertical integration given above and with it the need for the counting of stages. A major difficulty with this measure can be illustrated with the following example:[4]

If we have an economy consisting solely of coal, steel and car industries, each with an equal (one-third) share of value added, where coal is sold exclusively to the steel industry, steel to the car industry and cars to final consumers, we have the following calculations for integration:

$$\text{COAL} = \frac{\text{VALUE ADDED (COAL)}}{\text{SALES (COAL)}} = \frac{\frac{1}{3}}{\frac{1}{3}} = 1$$

$$\text{STEEL} = \frac{\text{VALUE ADDED (STEEL)}}{\text{SALES (STEEL)}} = \frac{\frac{1}{3}}{\frac{2}{3}} = \frac{1}{2}$$

$$\text{CARS} = \frac{\text{VALUE ADDED (CARS)}}{\text{SALES (CARS)}} = \frac{\frac{1}{3}}{1} = \frac{1}{3}$$

where value added/sales is our measure. The economy-wide level of integration weighted by value-added shares is

$$\tfrac{1}{3}(1) + \tfrac{1}{3}\left(\tfrac{1}{2}\right) + \tfrac{1}{3}\left(\tfrac{1}{3}\right) = \tfrac{11}{18}.$$

If the steel and car industries merge we have, as levels of integration,

$$\text{COAL} = \frac{\tfrac{1}{3}}{\tfrac{1}{3}} = 1$$

$$\text{STEEL \& CARS} = \frac{\tfrac{2}{3}}{1} = \tfrac{2}{3}.$$

For the economy as a whole the index increases to

$$\tfrac{1}{3}(1) + \tfrac{2}{3}\left(\tfrac{2}{3}\right) = \tfrac{14}{18}.$$

On the other hand, a merger between the steel and coal industries will result in the following levels of integration:

$$\text{CARS} = \frac{\tfrac{1}{3}}{1} = \tfrac{1}{3}$$

$$\text{STEEL \& COAL} = \frac{\tfrac{2}{3}}{\tfrac{2}{3}} = 1.$$

For the economy as a whole the increase in the level of integration is, as before to

$$\tfrac{1}{3}\left(\tfrac{1}{3}\right) + \tfrac{2}{3}(1) = \tfrac{14}{18}.$$

The problem is clear. Our 'obvious' measure of vertical integration for an industry will depend not only on the magnitude of change in terms of value added, but its direction as well: the integration of steel and coal will not have the same effect on our measure as that of steel and cars. This problem makes industry and firm level comparisons of vertical integration deceptive and even unusable, both cross-sectionally and over time. Only for the economy as a whole does this problem tend to disappear.[5]

Other difficulties confront us. Of two firms, identical in the number of in-house stages of production, the more profitable one may appear more vertically integrated when using the index. This factor may explain the sudden fall in the indices of integration of US Steel in the early 1930s[6] which would imply a limited usefulness to this index in time series analysis. Furthermore, census data are constructed from plant (establishment) data, without regard to what company owns the plant and to what else that company produces. All measures of the index using the census data are thus of the extent of vertical integration *within* establishments, and only permit us to make generalisations about integration at the firm level under the uneasy assumption that 'non-within establishment vertical integration is empirically insignificant'.[7] On the basis of Scherer's interview evidence, many of the economies connected with multi-plant operation are associated with the (vertical) integration of firms' production and distribution activities.[8] With a secular tendency towards increasing multi-plant operation, increases in vertical integration may have taken place by this route that are unrecorded in the census data.

There are two additional considerations. First, the demarcation between an act of vertical integration and one of diversification is an ambiguous one. If a meat packing company takes up the manufacture of glue, it appears straightforwardly from a production perspective as an act of forward vertical integration. From management's point of view, however, this product brings them into a new market, confronting them with both problems and opportunities – it might well appear to them as an act of diversification. Contrarily, the purpose of GM's acquisition of a firm specialising in computer aided design is to facilitate the production of cars, but this act is likely to register as one of diversification on most objective indices: the line between such complementary diversification and vertical integration is a thin one. As these two phenomena, vertical integration and diversification are usually perceived to be quite distinct, the empirical and conceptual overlap between them is troublesome; for most purposes, classifications which emerge from the perspective of management's problems, attributes and limitations will be more useful than 'objective' measures derived from the delineation of physical stages in the production process.

The second consideration is the existence of vertical quasi-integration[9] – integration between firms which are not under common ownership. The primary reason for interest in vertical integration (aside from any anti-competitive implications) is that it appears to present instances in which the firm chooses to integrate different aspects of the production process by way of co-ordination and planning, and not through the mechanism of the market. A decisive upward trend in vertical integration might indicate a tendency to abandon market co-ordination and replace it with the visible hand of management. However, some of the most remarkable current instances of the by-passing of the market mechanism and its replacement by planning, co-ordination and control such as the arrangements between large Japanese car companies and their suppliers take place between companies which are (at least nominally) under separate ownership. Comparable Western instances of such integration will be discussed below, but they will not register statistically as vertical integration.

Detailed empirical evidence is available only for the US. In one study, the stages of production for 15 industry groups were counted and evidence was found, as would have been expected on the basis of Chandler's work of a decisive increase in the level of vertical integration from 1899 until 1929.[10] Subsequently, the data show further integration taking place into wholesaling, but no decisive trend towards forward integration into retailing or backward integration into raw materials. These results are consistent with Morris Adelman's findings of no clear trend in the ratio of value added to sales at the firm level in the steel industry, from the time these firms emerged as giant, integrated entities to 1952. Given the difficulties with firm level calculations of value added to sales, the most convincing evidence is at an economy-wide level, where no discernable trend in value-added to sales was found for the period 1929 to 1965, a result reinforced by the fact that the long-term fall in the relative prices of raw materials would put an upward bias on trends in (backward) vertical integration.[11] This conclusion has been confirmed at the industry and firm level for the periods 1954–1972 and 1953–1973 respectively.[12]

There remain several good reasons, as we have seen, why we may not wish to rest too securely with these results. But even well into the 1980s, it has remained apparent that even the largest and most sophisticated firms in many of the most dynamic industries make extensive use of the market mechanism: the market has not been by-passed by the New Industrial State's visible hand of management, despite the fact that turn of the century events seemed to be tending in that direction. How might we explain the halting of what many believed to be an inexorable tendency? To explore this question, we review first the different interpretations which have been offered for the phenomenon of vertical integration.

Causes and Conceptualisations
While the issue of vertical integration *per se* is of little moment to contemporary theorists, the approach taken to this problem reflects questions of more general significance. In orthodox theory, the firm is an island of administrative co-ordination, functioning in a sea of markets – its very reason for existence has therefore been subject to theoretical scrutiny. Vertical integration – the extension of the functional boundaries of the firm – is suspect for the same reason. The manner in which it is analysed tells us much about contemporary approaches to the firm.

Two classes of argument are available to explain the existence of vertical integration – one from the traditional industrial economics literature and another from the more recent writings on markets and hierarchies. In the traditional literature, the most obvious motive for vertical integration is the desire to gain an advantage through the creation of a barrier to entry. In the words of John Blair: 'When at the turn of the century US Steel acquired the iron ore deposits of the Mesabi Range, no elaborate analysis was needed to understand how ownership by one company of vast, low-cost resources could injure competition.'[13]

Few economists, however, would cite this factor as central to the development of vast, vertically integrated enterprises in the US at the turn of the century. On the contrary, current thinking puts relatively little stress on the monopolistic advantages gained by these giant firms (advantages most clearly associated with the wave of horizontal mergers) and instead emphasizes the increases in efficiency achieved relative to existing firms, especially that associated with the development of vertically integrated organisation. In Chandler's words 'horizontal combination rarely proved to be a viable long-term business strategy. The firms that grew large by taking the merger route remained profitable only if after consolidating, they then adopted a strategy of vertical integration.'[14]

In this period, vast economies were realised by the integration of complementary processes, most especially in continuous process industries. This transformation took place in an array of industries such as tobacco, matches, grain milling, canning, soap and photography.[15] Specific manifestations of this economy of co-ordination which have traditionally been thought important are the savings on the administrative costs surrounding purchasing and selling, and the facilitation of forward scheduling, so that economies associated with longer runs of production can be realised and inventory holdings can be economised.

Further advantages to integration can accrue at the level of distribution. At the turn of the century in the US integration took place in the direction of wholesaling both from large manufacturers and from large retailers. These groups often chose to avoid the wholesaler's commission, whose costs embodied services necessary to smaller firms and retailers, such as trade credit, merchanting advice and stockholding.[16] Manufacturing firms such as Kodak and Singer, concerned to control all aspects of the price and marketing decision including the provision of customer services, moved directly into retailing.

A last advantage to integration cited in the traditional literature is that it permits the buyer to avoid paying unnecessary profit to the supplier. As this motivation is often voiced by business practitioners, we are loath to ignore it. The problem for orthodox theory is that such a strategy only makes sense if the offending supplier is making above normal profits, which, if they are to persist, implies the existence of a barrier to entry into the supplying sector. If a barrier exists, why should an outsider imagine it will be profitable to integrate into this activity, all the while bearing the administrative costs of coping with a new domain? A similar problem is posed in the quotation from Blair cited above: it is no mystery why US Steel might want to integrate into the ore deposits of the Mesabi Range, but there is much to explain in the fact that these deposits are 'low cost'. Why didn't the purchase price of these deposits embody their potential gains? This and similar conundrums will be discussed below.

The recent literature also deals with the question of integration, but from the perspective of contracting and market failure. For Oliver Williamson 'The advantages of integration . . . are not that technological (flow process) economies are unavailable to non-integrated firms, but that integration harmonizes interests (or reconciles differences, often by fiat) and permits an efficient (adaptive, sequential) decision process to be utilized.' Thus, integration is likely to be profitable when 'it may be prohibitively costly, if not infeasible, to specify contractually the full range of contingencies and stipulate appropriate responses between stages'.[17] The problem is thus one of control and of conflict of interest between actors, rather than a purely technological one.

An historical example of this conflict is that between manufacturers and wholesalers. Chandler's suggestion is that one motivation for manufacturers to integrate into wholesaling was that wholesalers' activities were often less focused on increasing volume (a prime consideration for integrated manufacturers concerned with lowering unit costs) than with obtaining a satisfactory markup or commission.[18] In more recent times, contrarily, the chairman of Yardley & Co. Ltd has claimed that the reason for their integration into wholesaling was to control the indiscriminate distribution of their perfume to 'undesirable, badly kept shops'.[19] Firms may have found integration into wholesaling cheaper, for this reason alone, than the costs of monitoring wholesaler behaviour or of writing elaborate contracts specifying wholesaler behaviour in every contingent circumstance. In other market situations of even greater complexity, firms might well choose a hierarchical to a market solution.

We have presented the case for the defence before that of the prosecution, and must now proceed with the arguments against vertical integration. This literature is a bit more malleable for our purposes than the former, since the central argument presented by George Stigler deals with tendencies over time in vertical integration, which is the perspective from which we wish to consider this problem. His authority is Adam Smith: 'The Division of Labor is Limited by the Extent of the Market.'[20] Stigler's argument is encapsulated in his title. In a growing economy, we expect progressively greater specialisation and differentiation to take place at all levels, as within the famous pin factory. For an industry, growth should permit specialists to come forth and take advantage of scale economies, so that 'vertical disintegration is the typical development in growing industries, vertical integration in declining industries ... If one considers the full life of industries, the dominance of vertical disintegration is surely to be expected'. This is one part of Stigler's argument, and it is the part which is usually reproduced; a quite different justification for vertical disintegration is conflated in his exposition, and this second aspect will be discussed below.

There are other factors militating against vertical integration. Moving into a new sphere of activity brings with it many of the managerial difficulties associated with diversification; secondly, there are various kinds of inflexibility associated with vertical integration, one of which is summarised in the following well-known passage:

> The underlying assumption governing the entry [of Lever Brothers] into the raw material business – whether in the Congo, in West Africa, in the Solomons, or in the Antarctic whaling grounds – was that the possession of such resources might give Lever Brothers an advantage and at worst could not bring disadvantage since prices in

the oils and fats markets would always be the same for their competitors as for them; to them, in fact, would fall also the profits in times of raw material scarcity. . . . Lever Brothers, the soap makers and margarine makers, were now compelled to specialize in the use of West African oils and fats to the exclusion of other and possibly cheaper materials, in order to support their West African interests. . . . There was, it seemed, a darker side to the whole theory of 'vertical integration'. Instead of bringing independence, security and profit, it could bring bondage, insecurity and loss.[21]

It is for this reason that 'security of supply' has not traditionally been taken very seriously as a motive for vertical integration – any risk avoidance advantages would seem to be matched by the additional attendant risks of ownership; below it will be considered whether any meaningful interpretation can be given to the security of supply argument. Other forms of inflexibility have been associated with vertical integration – a productive inflexibility, so that Ford's decision in the 1920s to move away from the Model T was hampered by the ownership of plant which was geared at all levels to producing that specific model, and furthermore, managerial inflexibility, resulting from over-concentration on all the productive stages of a specific product, at the expense of managerial attention which might have been directed at the consideration of new products.[22]

Having presented the arguments for and against vertical integration, it would be tempting to suggest that the apparent stylised fact of no significant tendency towards further integration after the big push at the turn of the century is well explained by the mutually neutralising effect of the countervailing forces presented here. We find this comfortable explanation unconvincing. The arguments against vertical integration do not appear, on closer examination, to be powerful enough to reverse a trend which would otherwise have existed.

Dealing first with the Stigler argument in the truncated form in which we have presented it, it seems to possess limited explanatory power. Stigler suggests that, after an initial period of vertical integration, firms will tend to abandon stages of production and increase output in those areas in which they choose to specialise – the example given is that of the Lancashire textile industry in 1911, where firms engaged in both spinning and weaving had on average fewer spindles than those exclusively engaged in spinning. This example would seem to have little relevance to the characteristic type of giant firm which was emerging at that time in the US. These firms were themselves a large enough market to capture the static economies of scale for a whole variety of their inputs if they had chosen to manufacture them, so that no pressure towards disintegration was likely to result from suboptimal levels of production from the giant firms.

An exception to this general statement may not 'prove the rule', but should illustrate the point at hand. One major instance of vertical integration in the 1920s was Ford's decision to build its own steel mill. This, however, was in response to the monopolistic practices in the US steel industry, which were in part engendered by the high minimum efficient scale in that sector. As Scherer points out 'precisely because scale economies are so compelling, the number of disintegrated product sellers is likely to be small. ... From fewness of supply sources may follow monopolistic pricing of components. ... To avoid actual or feared monopolistic exploitation, users of high-scale-economy materials or components often decide to commence internal production even though they may incur a penalty in doing so'.[23] Thus, vertical integration, and not disintegration is a possible result in those exceptional cases where scale economies continue to exist for inputs even at the level of the large firm. In general, large firms continue to purchase a wide variety of inputs, but there exists no clear indication that these commodities are exceptionally produced under conditions of high minimum efficient scale.

The more static arguments against vertical integration are of even less weight in explaining a long-term countervailing force. The managerial difficulties of running highly diverse activities have lessened over time, in which case this particular inhibition to integration should be weaker than previously; the managerial inflexibility engendered by vertical integration can be a genuine problem for a firm if, as in some industries such as steel, it causes managerial focus to rest on the detailed processes of production, and not on the final product and alternative uses of the firm's resources. On the other hand, it has been argued that it was precisely the lack of vertical integration of the UK textile industry which made it incapable of responding with an integrated strategy to the challenges it faced in the twentieth century;[24] in recent times similar complaints have been voiced about the internal structure of the merchant semiconductor manufacturers in the US compared with their vertically integrated Japanese rivals.

Furthermore, for every such example in which vertical integration has been associated with managerial inflexibility, several can be offered where the contrary tendency is present. For IBM, full integration has extended the possibilities for firm development and greatly added to its flexibility. From the very beginning, the IBM-360 was a vertically integrated conception, both in terms of production and marketing: the innovatory SLT (Solid Logic Technology) components were devised and produced by IBM, as were all other parts of the computer. The final device was not only marketed by IBM at all stages, but *its genesis and production had at all stages taken place in the context of the marketing strategy which governed it*. The IBM launch of the 360 rests as much of a textbook example for marketing courses of a coherent, complete conception as does the battle strategy of the Red Army at Kursk in military academies.

We may observe a tendency towards integration even within specific manufacturing functions of the firm, for instance materials oriented decisions:

At one time, purchasing, production control, forecasting order entry, and physical distribution were managed independently. ...

The [result] was organizational slack: poor delivery performance, long lead times, overtime costs, the hidden costs of panic operations, and a lack of responsiveness to changes in the business environment ... In recent times, many firms have approached these issues by the creation of a new managerial position: the materials manager, who is responsible for purchasing, production control, physical storage, transaction processing, traffic and sometimes distribution. In a survey conducted in 1967, only 3 per cent of the firms had a materials manager. Eleven years later, nearly one half of the firms responding to a similar survey had a materials manager.[25]

This desire for integration has been extended to the firm's relationship with its vendors:

Many firms now work with their vendors to plan capacity for several years in the future. Old relationships based on fear of being committed to specific firms, or inflexible quantities are now being replaced with an understanding of the need for mutual ongoing relationships.[26]

Much of the interest in integration in recent years has emerged from the startling results achieved by Japanese companies, whose innovations have had a profound effect on other countries. We can isolate specific components of the Japanese innovations as follows. First, a changed attitude towards quality control, so that the costs to the company of mistakes in repairs and loss of custom are taken to be greater than those of improving quality – in the words of the American management consultant Philip Crosbie 'quality is free'. The dramatic quality improvements in Japan have come about in the actual process of manufacture on the factory floor and not by special provision for quality control. This strategy of quality control is linked with an apparently greater involvement by Japanese shop floor workers in the process of manufacture than would be forthcoming in the classic staff-line-worker hierarchy which emerged in the US at the turn of the century, and which has remained the standard managerial approach.

The second component is the treatment of inventories in large Japanese companies such as Toyota, where the turnover ratio of working assets has been ten times that of Western producers.[27] A key aspect of the Toyota production system which has been widely publicised is the just-in-time system, with its associated *kanban* technique for recording inventories. Just-in-time is but one part of the Toyota approach to smooth production flows:

The philosophical basis for [the] systems in Japan is substantially broader than material planning and control. The overall goal is to attempt to make continued improvements in the process or product. The production people at Toyota take as a desirable objective lot

sizes of one piece, finished just in time to be used on the next higher
level item. This would reduce in-process inventory to an absolute
minimum. . . . A great deal of management discipline, organizational
change and capital investment is required to carry out the improvements. Moreover, the *kanban* card control system is only suited to
very stable production schedules. (Toyota says plus or minus 10
percent.) Thus far, the applications of *kanban* have been in
repetitive manufacturing.[28]

These Japanese innovations are managerial and not technological, the
kanban being a simple card system for the registering of inventories. In
recent years a striking example of the managerial nature of these
innovations has been the greater efficiency of the traditionally equipped
GM New United Motor Manufacturing (NUMMI) plant in California, a
joint venture with Toyota (and run with Japanese practices), than all of
GM's newly equipped factories. The Japanese innovations thus have little
to do with technical change *per se*. Of far greater significance is Toyota's
relationship to its suppliers, many of which are treated as if they were work
centres within the Toyota plant, and who are often referred to as 'co-
producers.'[29]
   This treatment of suppliers was apparently inspired by the post-war
lectures given in Japan by the American management consultant W. E.
Deming, who recommended (somewhat contrary to the spirit of contemporary portfolio balance – risk aversion approaches) that companies
reduce the number of suppliers on the same item: 'You will be lucky to find
for any item one vendor that can furnish evidence of repeatable,
dependable quality, and that knows what his costs will be'.[30] The emphasis
is thus on the monitoring of (relatively few) suppliers, rather than on the
creation of a large portfolio of firms who supply from an arm's length
relationship. The characteristic quasi-integration by large Japanese firms
with their suppliers has permitted a remarkable level of co-ordination
between stages of production to take place, and unprecedently low levels
of inventories to be held. The maximum pressure upon and careful
monitoring of suppliers which the system has permitted has been a
prominent demonstration to many Western firms of the virtues of
carefully directed hierarchical, as opposed to market based forms of
control.
   Recently for instance GM in the US appears to have become significantly more aggressive in its attitude towards suppliers of steel. Until
1980, 'Thousands of tons of rejected steel piled up at many auto plants'
because of problems with quality and specification: 'At the same time GM
continued to pay suppliers' list prices even though it had the clout to
bargain.' GM's new strategy has been to announce that henceforth it
would require steel suppliers to bid against one another for its orders. By
itself, this would appear to represent the encroachment of a market-place
relationship where previously had existed a routinised, mechanical almost
pre-capitalist relationship. But 'Internal GM documents reveal a broad

range of criteria by which it is now judging steel companies ... quality, delivery, price ... financial strength, product size options ... facility modernization ... "management's philosophy and attitude in co-operating with GM at all times", and whether or not a company intends to remain a steelmaker'.[31] Though this particular instance will not result in any statistically observable increase in vertical integration, it illustrates once again the ever-increasing centrality of *control* to the aims and aspirations of the managers of the contemporary large corporation, a control which, other things equal, would be most easily exercised with common ownership.

Lastly, there is clearly a fashion for integration on the basis of its dynamic advantages. It is argued that integration can facilitate the process of turning ideas and inventions into successfully marketed products. Contemporary notions of managerial behaviour take as their *sine qua non* the domination of the marketing conception over production, and of the necessary integration between these spheres to promote innovation and flexibility. The key link between these two spheres is product design, and a decisive characteristic in America's best managed factories is taken to be 'Their success ... with tearing down the walls between product design and manufacturing.'[32] The goal of contemporary managerial approaches to the firm is to gain control and to integrate as many aspects of the behaviour of the firm as possible. Progressively, the flexible response of the large firm is identified with its ability to adapt all aspects of its marketing, design and manufacturing in a co-ordinated way to changing conditions. Once again, Japanese firms are the focal point of much attention, as the 'scrum and scramble' system found in Japan for getting engineers and specialists in marketing, industrial design and manufacturing to work together is thought to be at the forefront of these tendencies.[33]

The problem being posed is as follows. The managerial revolution described by Chandler was not a once and for all development which ended in the 1920s. On the contrary, only a few companies by that time had adopted the sophisticated form of multi-divisional structure which had been pioneered by GM and DuPont. The largest firms have not only expanded their share of net product in the economy since that period, but have continued to develop the tools and techniques of business calculation and control. Furthermore, they have widened their conception of the range and scope of the tasks – marketing, design and manufacturing – which have to be co-ordinated. All of these factors would seem conducive to the evolution of a Galbraithian vision of a new industrial state, in which would emerge large spheres of self-contained co-ordination and planning. And yet even with the substantial increases in aggregate concentration since the 1920s, we have not witnessed a parallel rise in vertical integration. How can we explain this paradox?

One way of approaching this problem is to return to Stigler's argument. After the sentence 'If one considers the full life of industries, the dominance of vertical disintegration is surely to be expected', the passage continues:

Young industries are often strangers to the established economic system. They require new kinds or qualities of materials and hence make their own; they must overcome technical problems in the use of their products and cannot wait for potential users to overcome them; they must persuade customers to abandon other commodities and find no specialized merchants to undertake this task. These young industries must design their specialized equipment and often manufacture it . . . When the industry has attained a certain size and prospects, many of the tasks are sufficiently important to be turned over to specialists. It becomes profitable for other firms to supply equipment and raw materials, to undertake the marketing of the product and the utilization of by-products, and even to train skilled labor.

Three separable reasons may be discerned in this passage to explain why a 'young' industry might tend towards a vertically integrated structure, and why disintegration should take place as the industry grows:

1 The aforementioned economies of scale argument, whereby a new industry cannot support specialisation.
2 A 'differential techniques' problem, whereby potential users and suppliers do not possess the full array of skills requisite to the successful production, delivery and use of the product, so that at least initially, it pays for the innovating firms to carry out these tasks themselves.
3 For a new industry, there does not exist a rich enough array of markets for supplying equipment and raw materials and for marketing the product.

We believe that Stigler's argument, even with the economies of scale aspect separated out, contains implicitly a suitable explanation for the problem at hand. The case is made in the context of a specific 'young industry' but is better generalised to the broad-based explosion of giant firms which took place in the US in the half century after 1880. These firms brought forth not only special skills and demands associated with their own particular industry, but a wholly unprecedented standard of precision, efficiency and business-like behaviour. Markets to service these large firms were inadequate because the groups on the peripheries of the large firms were incapable of matching the standards of efficiency found inside these firms.

As long as best practice technique remained the exclusive domain of a small number of giant firms, vertical integration was likely to increase. As the business techniques of the large modern corporation became more widely dispersed, the more the possibility emerged that smaller firms and markets could exercise their advantages of short run flexibility and learning by doing specialised knowledge.

Early in the century, the advantages of bigness (economies of scale) were often confused with best practice technique. With the ever wider dispersion of these techniques, small firms in the guise of market-based supply were often able to provision the needs of larger firms in a manner competitive with the internally based supply of large firms. The expansion of the richness and depth of markets in general has had an inhibiting effect on the growth of vertical integration and frequently in the contemporary world, firms are criticised for not making proper use of market-based supply: 'critics say Apple squandered millions developing disk drives, printers and other items it could have bought from suppliers.'[34]

In the British economy at the turn of the century, the development of vertically integrated hierarchy proceeded slowly, not only compared with the US but with the continent as well. This has been explained by the rich networks of middlemen – trading companies, wholesale and factoring houses, etc. which were available to manufacturing firms.[35] While these groups were undoubtedly efficient by the standards of the day, would they have looked so impressive if confronted by an array of leading firms as dynamic as those in the US? As Wilkins and Hill note:

> Even as early as 1885 a shrewd visitor to the United States [from Europe] remarked that 'the tools and processes we are inclined to consider unusual are the commonplace of the American shop'. . . .
> The automotive producer in the United States was also served by suppliers. He could turn to dozens of shops or plants (all like himself employing machine tools) that made tires, wheels, engines, forgings, transmissions and other parts, and stood ready to supply them in quantity at a low rate. The European car maker could call on few if any such firms.

The authors add 'Some of the disadvantages under which the European manufacturer labored need not have continued to handicap him. Unfortunately he was smugly satisfied with his hand wrought product.'[36] And yet it was the American, Henry Ford who, by 1908, had established a factory which made most of its own parts, all standardised. Even with its sophisticated subsidiary producers, the American car industry was the first to become fully integrated because of the *relative* dynamism of its emergent giant firms compared with its smaller rivals.

It took several decades for small producers to approach the levels of efficiency and precision of the emergent giant corporations, and for the benefits of market as opposed to hierarchical control to be manifest. For the large firms, growing precision in the calculation of the opportunity cost of intra-group purchases has made the efficient use of the firm's internal market a more viable proposition, but the progressive tendency to judge internal purchases against free market alternatives has been a powerful force ruling against the prejudice of the firm's engineers to 'do it yourself.'[37] Even in the present day it is not uncommon for large firms, for instance retailers to subject their suppliers to strict tutelage about the conduct of the latter's business – their finances and even their techniques of production, moving them along from the 'small time' to the most modern methods.[38] The provision of organisational and marketing skills by the centre seems to be an important component in the present day expansion of franchising, a form of quasi-integration otherwise difficult to explain.

The issue of the uneven development of skills embodies our central criticism of the markets and hierarchies paradigm as an approach to the historical development of vertical integration. 'Market failure' does not take place historically merely because of problems of moral hazard (the agents will cheat the principal unless the contract can specify all contingencies in detail), or because of high fixed costs or indivisibilities, etc.: it may fail simply because *markets do not exist* which can service the principal adequately. US Steel at the turn of the century may have been able to buy into the Mesabi Range cheaply, and firms may have had to integrate vertically in order to avoid paying monopoly profits and to guarantee security of supply, but all these events took place for the same reason – the poorly developed depth of existing markets relative to the needs of the newly expanding giant firms. By the 1980s, it is unlikely that many firms will encounter the kind of bargain US Steel came across in the Mesabi Range, but as consolation, security of raw materials supply can be guaranteed on the world's commodity markets not only for a whole host of current prices, but for futures prices as well. The perceptive remark by Dr. Lyon Playfair in mid-nineteenth century Britain is far more true today than when it was stated: 'Raw material, formerly our capital advantage over other nations, is gradually being equalised in price, and made available to all by improvements in locomotion, and Industry must in future be supported, not by a competition of local advantages, but by a competition of intellects.'[39]

There is clearly far less motivation than in earlier times for firms to integrate vertically simply to avoid a market imperfection in one of these traded commodities, and also less likelihood of gaining an easy bargain. While some of the integration pursued by firms in Chandler's account might be satisfactorily explained by agency problems (McCormick and Singer found they couldn't rely on commission agents so they hired their own salesmen),[40] in the overwhelming number of cases, the markets or what is the same thing, the personnel and organisation either supplying the firm or acting as its distributors, proved inadequate and vertical integration was overwhelmingly a defensive response to underdeveloped markets.[41]

The markets and hierarchies approach, by assuming that a well developed market always exists as an alternative to administrative co-ordination, misses the essential insight of Gerschenkron: administrative co-ordination and centralisation are often rational responses to a lack of skilled infrastructure, which in some contexts may manifest itself as a poorly developed set of markets. Centralisation may be a rational response when skilled personnel are a scarce resource. Central direction to avoid control loss is a necessity not only in the presence of moral hazard, but in order to promote uniformity of response when agents are not capable of operating independently at the same level of effectiveness as the principal.

The continued expansion of the depth and richness of the services provided by the market – advertising and marketing, financial management, etc. – has also dictated that specialised skills which once could only be embodied in the largest firms and were part of their economies of scale are now available to far smaller entities. The growing marketisation of services in business may not only militate against vertical integration, but may act as a force promoting competition and deconcentration: much of the defence of IBM in its anti-trust case was concerned with the enormous number of Lilliputians capable of providing and servicing parts of IBM's full line of business.[42]

The ability of outsiders to compete in many domains is obviously enhanced by the long-term tendency for the parameters of many goods to be expressed objectively and precisely, especially in the inter-industry sector, and for these components to have progressively greater uniformity and interchangeability. The growth and development of these markets, however, does not represent the replacement of conscious control by the objective, impersonal force of the market, but the introduction of a far larger number of entities which are capable of matching the giant firms in calculation, control and efficaciousness. If there is no longer a decisive secular tendency towards vertical integration, it is not because the forces impelling this development have ceased to be active: rather, the increasing average level (and the lowering of the dispersion) of technical and managerial skills has created an infrastructure which makes market solutions possible and thus counteracts the forces towards vertical integration.

There are thus two significant factors which have limited the rise of statistically observable vertical integration. First, the process of catching up with best practice technique by other firms servicing the giant companies has meant that market, as opposed to hierarchical solutions to the problems of input supply and distribution have become progressively more viable both for the giant firms and for others trying to survive in competition with them. Secondly, much of what in earlier times would have been conceived of, and will still be measured statistically as acts of broad-ranging diversification are now part of an integrated programme. The domain of firm planning has so widened that many kinds of diversified expansion now take place because of contemporary managements' extended vision of the number of stages which are relevant to a company in the production and distribution of their commodities. Thus, some of the trends in diversification to be discussed below are inseparable from the problems of vertical integration.

Diversification

The Conglomerate

We consider here the phenomenon of diversification and its most conspicuous fruit, the giant, highly conglomerated firm. We shall deal first with the explanations which have emerged for this development, and then only with the attendent problems of measurement. There are two reasons for so proceeding: first, unlike vertical integration, an upward movement in diversification is unquestioned, so that we may deal with explanations before we have evaluated measures of this trend. Secondly, the problems of measurement will lead directly to our own view that diversification is best conceptualised from the perspective of management: the diversified firm, like the multinational, is a manifestation of the expansion of the facility, horizons and aspirations of the modern firm; beside this, all other explanations rest as merely secondary and proximate.

There is little doubt that much of what passes for diversification is the manifestation of a fundamentally negative strategy. Thus, while US business managers appear more aggressive and wide-ranging than their British counterparts, the bias in the US in favour of conglomerate acquisition has been dictated primarily by the rigour of the anti-trust laws. Indeed, the temptation to indulge in more amenable horizontal combination has been heightened by the 'tolerant' atmosphere emanating from Washington in the 1980s: clearly, conglomerate mergers have been seen as second best solutions by acquiring firms because of the lack of market power advantages yielded by the new acquisition, but more importantly, because of the managerial problems of entering new sectors.

Many diversified acquisitions have taken place because a leading firm feels the market is saturated with its product, and/or because its market is mature. Acquisitions so motivated fuel the reputation of diversification activity as being without focus and haphazard. Mature firms and industries, awash with cash, take over firms in totally disparate spheres of activity. In many cases, they have little to offer the acquired firm in terms of advice, guidance, or managerial skills; indeed, management often has more than enough difficulty coping with the new-found problems of co-ordinating highly heterogeneous activities.

The supreme illustration of all the negative aspects of diversification would seem to be focused on the conglomerate company, as epitomised by ITT. This company was already a multinational giant in the world of telecommunications in the mid-1960s, when it was taken on a breathless joyride of acquisitions[43] by Harold Geneen. He explained before Congress:

> Each of these people [executives of acquired companies] lay out their own plans. . . . Their own plans are what they run against, their own performance is what we monitor with them and then we have this large central staff . . . which are there to aid and support them

when they get into any problems ... each of these people are essentially running their own companies with the support, the help, and monitoring, if you want to call it that, of the general staff.

'Strangely', John Winslow notes, 'the parent corporation is able to exercise more effective discipline over the two thousand executives than the discipline formerly required of them for survival as independent entrepreneurs.'[44] ITT, like many other 'go-go' conglomerates of this period, look today like nothing more than old-fashioned holding companies.[45] Curiously, Geneen seems to have been under the impression that the creation of such a structure was the great accomplishment of his hero Alfred Sloan.[46] On the contrary, Sloan's achievement was to set up a central office to co-ordinate the activities of the multifarious and chaotic divisions which already existed at GM: his accomplishment was not divisionalisation *per se*, but its unification and co-ordination with a centrally directed, coherent strategy.

For those with a strong moral sense, it is gratifying to learn that these corporate Don Giovannis did indeed receive their come-uppance. In recent years, ITT has been trying to deconglomerate – attempting a re-entry into the telecommunications industry financed by the selling off of assets not related to electronics technology. This tendency has been part of a whole trend of 'back to basics' by conglomerates: 'This riot of voluntary restructuring is something the US has never seen before. Many conglomerates jettisoned bad acquisitions in the early 1970s, but the current, far more pervasive sell-off spree is different. Rather than simply dumping dogs, companies are making moves to spin off and scale down healthy businesses to concentrate on what they do best.'[47]

Is there anything, then, to be said in defence of the conglomerate? We might say, as Samuel Johnson did about the dog standing on its hind legs[48] that the wonder is not whether they do well or ill, but whether they function at all. Given the apocalyptic pronouncements about conglomerates which came forth in the 1960s, we may note that as a group they appear to be a mediocre but acceptable group of performers by most criteria, containing some companies whose financial results are truly excellent. Their continued existence as an institution well into their second decade is clearly worth some consideration.

The modern conglomerate was earlier compared to the old-fashioned holding company. But while the latter disappeared as significant corporate entities in the 1920s, the firms emerging in the 1960s were more complex in structure, and much more far-flung in terms of product mix and geographical dispersion than the older entities. The fact that these conglomerates have survived and, in some cases, continued to prosper is a function not only of the skills and ambitions of the individuals running these companies, but of the further development of the managerial revolution which had begun earlier in the century.

The ability to monitor, co-ordinate and make even approximately rational decisions within these far-flung empires may be linked to the talents and energy of an individual such as Harold Geneen, but the pre-requisites for such decisions are an infrastructure of skilled personnel and a system of information flow that make rational decisions possible. These prerequisites include the existence of highly sophisticated data manage-ment and monitoring procedures for the making of commensurate evaluations between highly disparate activities. As noted in chapter 4, there are enormous difficulties even in conceptualising standards for such evaluations, whether between firms or between divisions of a single firm. It is thus worth while being dubious about any extravagant claims which are made for procedures for solving such problems. Compared with earlier times, however, the rapid and accurate flow of data through the company is a major organisational accomplishment. The very existence of the conglomerate is a reflection of the continuing development of manage-ment's ability to control large organisations: divisionalisation in some form of such enormous and heterogeneous entities is unquestionably needed for such control to be exercised successfully, but particular managerial forms *per se* explain little, and are a reflection of these more fundamental historical developments.

At the height of the conglomerate merger wave of the 1960s, there was some fear that certain practices such as cross-subsidisation between products and reciprocal buying between firms could be facilitated by the existence of highly conglomerated firms.[49] Little evidence has come forth to support this notion, and it seems reasonable to presume that the likely effect of conglomeration and diversification in general on the process of competition is to cause it to increase. As Gort has noted: 'The broadening of the investment horizon of individual firms is also likely to increase the sensitivity of capital flows to differences in profit rates between industries. To the extent that a wider range of investment projects is examined, capital funds generated in one sector of the economy are rendered more likely to move into other sectors where investment opportunities are more attrac-tive.'[50]

The pure conglomerate may be passing into history. Its impact on the US economy has not been overtly pernicious by conventional economic criteria, neither causing in its wake vast increases in aggregate concentra-tion nor having extended the realm of anti-competitive practices.[51] The continued interest here in the phenomenon is that as an abstraction, the conglomerate represents a firm unconstrained by managerial impedi-ments, so that it is extremely sensitive 'to differences in profit rates between industries'. Firms with this kind of potential help create an environment more competitive than that emerging from a Marshallian firm, bound to an individual industry, so that the phenomenon of diversification is intimately linked to the process of competition.

Diversification however, is not the same thing as conglomeration; while the conglomerate is an endangered, if not extinct, species diversification is still a continuing process for 'normal' large firms. Furthermore, while much diversification, especially of the most 'distant' kind, takes place as a result of merger, a good deal of the secular trend towards diversification has come about through the 'natural' expansion of firm activity. It seems, therefore, to be quite a fundamental and perhaps inexorable aspect of the growth of the large firm. How can this tendency be explained?

Explanations and Conjectures
Little has emerged in the orthodox literature to explain the continuous increase in diversification, which appears to be a stylised fact of modern capitalism. The Marris–D.C. Mueller approach discussed in chapter 6 finds the root of diversification in the managerialist imperative to grow, even if necessary beyond the constraints of traditional markets. It has much in common with the mature/saturated markets approach discussed earlier. But diversification has been a much richer, much more organic process than this, and has clearly been practised by successful firms in a manner far too coherent to indicate that they are merely escaping from their home market.

Probably the most venerable explanation for diversification is that it is a form of risk aversion: if the firm does not 'put all its eggs in one basket', the public's evaluation of the firm and its expected cash flows will be higher than it otherwise would be because the firm is less risky. While moderately convincing examples of this simple form of risk aversion can be given, these days arguments of this kind are served up largely for gullible investors and governmental inquiries. On grounds of economic orthodoxy the simple risk aversion argument makes little sense, since the individual investor could juggle his or her ownership of individual companies to create a diversified portfolio with a good deal less effort and expense than through the process of multiple merger by a firm.[52] More significantly, whatever the risk reducing possibilities of unsynchronised cash flows, they seem overwhelmed in the market's view by the dangers associated with entering into new spheres of activity.

Is there any sense that can be made of the risk aversion strategy? In the purely static portfolio choice conception, there is little. But with consideration of the expansion of managerial horizons, the concept of risk aversion develops a dynamic dimension, both with regard to products and to processes. Product diversification is not so much motivated by a desire for static mean-variance portfolio balance, but to maintain managerial flexibility in a world of uncertainty. If the commodities which are now offered to the public suffer unpopularity in the future, large enterprises hope they will have maintained enough residual skill and experience in different product lines to be able to switch without high costs of transition to the new activities. Thus, even firms now in the process of deconglomeration find themselves left with a repertoire of products and markets far wider than that traditionally associated with these firms only a few years ago: Kraft in the US, traditionally a specialist in cheese, has, after going through a substantial period of deconglomeration continued to expand into new food lines such as herb teas and ice cream.[53] Additional motivations for Kraft include the desire to exploit the production and marketing complementarities between these products and to make full capacity utilisation of its marketing division. There are also examples of firms in areas such as electronics (where the profitability of different sectors changes rapidly) who feel that diversification of the product line in the manner of IBM is the best way to avoid being caught with a single unprofitable product or market.

The second kind of dynamic risk aversion relates to processes, and somewhat resembles the arguments in development economics in favour of import substitution: while it may not make sense in static, comparative advantage terms to make certain commodities oneself, it is necessary to get 'into the business' for the sake of future development. Even a few years ago, process risk was conceived in terms of the challenges which might be forthcoming from a relatively narrow range of competitors, and the domain of technological change monitored and controlled by any particular company was within the confines of what it perceived to be the industry in which it operated, with all other developments thought to be exogenous and outside conscious control. Certain contemporary kinds of diversification into manufacturing processes (obviously not easily segregated from vertical integration) are a defensive response to changing technology, especially when the boundaries to this technology are undefined. A General Electric executive stated that 'We discovered to our chagrin that [we] were several years behind the leading edge of electronics technology . . . we found it difficult to be a smart user of electronics if we were not in the business itself [of designing and making microchips on a commercial scale]'.[54] Whether such strategies are in fact viable is another question. What is clear however is that the domain of what modern management conceives to be controllable risk has been expanding.

This domain of controllable technological change has a positive, as well as a risk averse dimension. As suggested above in the context of vertical integration, the number of processes which the modern corporation views as complementary to its own central activity has been greatly extended, the most highly publicised instance in recent times being the use of computer aided design by car manufacturers such as Chrysler (an in-house design in co-operation with large computer firms such as Control Data) and GM (with its acquisition in 1984 of Electronic Data Systems for $2.6 billion).

Nathan Rosenberg has stressed that complementarities are of such importance in innovation that it may be fruitful to view the latter process from a systems perspective. Success in the development of incandescent lighting rested with such innovators as Edison who considered the whole process – from the generation of electrical power to the production of the lamp – and were capable of developing all aspects of the process.[55] This tendency to view innovations from such an integrated perspective has greatly increased in recent decades. Once again, whether strategies of integration will ultimately succeed is another matter, and, as noted in chapter 7, there is a great deal of market cynicism about the possibility of synergy between highly conglomerated operations: most especially it is questioned whether such complementarity which does exist between the production of cars and contemporary electronics technology is most efficaciously exploited by taking the two under common ownership, as has GM, or by making market-based linkages, as has Chrysler. This expansion of horizon, however, seems to be part of a long-term, fundamental process, in whatever form current fashion dictates that it manifests itself.

The relative merits of the different methods of forging linkages between complementary aspects of business activity will be left an open question here, but clearly models of success such as IBM and its Japanese counterparts are notable for their 'holistic' approach to production and sales. Many firms feeling themselves weak in one end of their business find the need to compensate, sometimes by forming a joint venture ('AT & T has capital and technology, Olivetti is a superior sales machine'[56]) and other times by diversifying under a common ownership.

In summary, the enhancement of managerial technique has facilitated the holding together of highly disparate activities, while the expansion of management's aspirations has extended their horizons both to an attempt at long-term risk aversion and to increased aggressiveness in different markets. The managerial revolution discussed in chapter 5 is linked with a tendency for diversification to increase throughout the century. It is possible that the current developments in financial markets will force economically more 'logical' (presumably less conglomerated) mergers in the future, and that the market forces of specialisation which seem to have constrained the growth of vertical integration will have a similar effect on the process of diversification: all this remains to be seen.

Measurement and Conceptualisation
In chapter 3 we considered the limitations inherent in the concept of the industry as an exogenous constraint on business activity, but the existence of extensive firm diversification further separates the Marshallian paradigm from the contemporary realities of the corporate structure. In Marshallian theory, firm activity is constrained in the short run by production relations and/or by conditions of demand within a market; for a multi-product firm, these constraints are binding within each particular market.[57] But the greater the degree of diversification evidenced by firms, the more freedom firms appear to have in *choosing and initiating* activities in new spheres, the more convincing are alternative views of the corporation which emphasize either the financial or managerial limitations to firm expansion, and the less relevant the Marshallian emphasis on the limitations imposed by exogenous production cost and demand.

Unlike vertical integration, the measurement of firm diversification is not thought to present particular conceptual difficulties beyond those ordinarily involved in the use of the Standard Industrial Classification for the delineation of industry boundaries. But the practical problems are serious. Two difficulties are common to the main empirical studies for the UK and the US:[58] first, they are limited to manufacturing enterprises, thereby excluding one of the most characteristic and remarked upon aspects of recent firm behaviour – conglomeration between manufacturing and non-manufacturing enterprises. Secondly, such studies are unable to distinguish systematically between vertical integration and diversification. It may, however, be undesirable to distinguish mechanically between these two forms of expansion: the chairman of Exxon may not view his upstream activities in the exploration and production of oil and his downstream activities in refining as part of a strategy of achieving full integration in oil production. For him, the differential movements of rates of return between these activities may make them serviceable as part of a risk-averting diversification strategy.[59] The fact that this diversification takes place within the oil industry may merely be a function of managerial familiarity with this sector. To have management's subjective perception of its strategy as a sole criterion for distinguishing between vertical integration and diversification would be a dangerous path. It is vital to demonstrate, therefore, that a methodology for delineation exists somewhere between the mechanical use of industrial classification indices and a purely subjective approach.

Several kinds of biases are likely to be present in the use of classification indices. The elimination of non-manufacturing activities plausibly puts a downward bias on the rate of change of diversification; the confusion between measures of vertical integration and diversification on the whole biases the latter in an upward direction, since the number of activities which a firm is likely to consider complementary to its main activities and part of a unified, integrated process is secularly expanding. As a further distortion, the widening of management horizons has engendered activities in new markets which often do not register as (common ownership) diversification, such as Pilkington Brothers' venture capital funding of a small company manufacturing disks for computer disk drives. (This kind of activity is often difficult to segregate from the forms of extended vertical integration discussed earlier, since, for instance, Pilkington is interested in the disks for their own use in glass-making.)[60]

Techniques of measurement derived from industrial categories have also failed to solve some fundamental conundrums in the construction of diversification measures: using the UK Standard Industrial Classification System Michael Utton distinguishes between broad spectrum diversification (firm activity moving into one of the other 14 Industrial Orders) and narrow spectrum diversification (movement into another of the 120 Minimum List Headings within an Industrial Order).[61] But there are reasons to proceed with caution with this methodology. In chapter 3 the problematic and somewhat arbitrary nature of the classification system was noted. When the classification system is applied to the problem of diversification, additional issues arise: broad spectrum diversification, for instance, is meant to represent movement to activities remote from the firm's primary activity. Is this remoteness to be conceived and measured as an objective technological parameter confronting the firm (and thus an activity will measure an equal level of remoteness for any two firms possessing the same principal activity), or does it in principle embody the corporate strategy and the subjective propensities of the firm's managers, thereby giving a different measure of 'distance' for any given activity and firm?

These seemingly insoluble problems have been confronted directly in a series of studies issuing from what may be dubbed the Harvard Managerial school of diversification. The most famous of these is a study for the US by Richard Rumelt.[62] Rumelt begins by quoting Gort, who, echoing Stigler, poses the trend towards diversification as a paradox: 'notwithstanding the growth in markets and the increasing complexity of technology, the trend for companies seems to be toward greater diversification rather than toward specialization'. Rumelt's response is that the development of the multidivisional form has created a managerial environment which encourages rapid deployment of resources. This form has permitted 'the insulation of a set of business managers from the vicissitudes of the capital markets' (p. 2), once again posing the conflict often heard in practical circles between a free capital market and the development of rational long-term planning.

Strategy is the determination and the carrying out of the basic, long-term goals and objectives of an enterprise: there may exist financial arrangements which are more conducive to the carrying out of this strategy than those emerging from a free capital market. For Rumelt, 'the task of matching opportunity with corporate skills and strengths is the most important part of top management's responsibilities and may be taken as a primary component of diversification strategy' (p. 10).

It is then possible for Rumelt to *define* diversification in terms of managerial constraints:

> Using as a point of departure the range of skills possessed by a firm, a *diversification move* is taken to be an entry into a new product-market activity that requires or implies an appreciable increase in the available managerial competence of the firm. Thus, the essence of diversification is taken to be a 'reaching out' into new areas, requiring the development of new competences or the augmentation of existing ones. . . . *This definition identifies diversification in terms of the degree to which a new product-market activity taxes the ability of the firm's management, particularly its general management, together with the administrative structure it has created.* (pp. 10–11, latter italics added)

He adds, significantly, 'the fact that companies with operating skills in a given area can usually be purchased outright underlines the importance of management ability as one of the primary non-financial restrictions on entry into new business'. The half-hearted attempt of Marshallian theory to constrain the boundaries of the firm with productive or other objective limitations has ultimately given way even in the orthodox literature to a managerial view of the limits upon the size of the firm. But an objective production-oriented approach continues to hold sway both in the orthodox concepts of industry definition and structure, as well as in the attendent approaches to diversification: a 'productionist' approach to the industry and to diversification is as inappropriate as it is to the size of the firm, which is why Rumelt's managerially-based alternative is so significant.

To measure diversification, Rumelt uses a concept developed earlier, the specialisation ratio (SR) which is the proportion of the firm's annual revenues attributable to its largest discrete market activity (p. 11). It is the concept of a discrete business – one which could be managed independently of the firm's other activities – which is of particular interest to us. The criteria for the determination of discreteness involve making judgements about the interdependence between activities. We can thus outline demand related interdependencies, such as whether a firm can drop or add an activity without having an effect on the main activity (e.g. Ford could drop trucks, but not a passenger car line without affecting the price, quality and volume of its other passenger car lines), or whether the firm can change the price and quality of associated services (Xerox's paper business is clearly interdependent with its other lines).

Supply related interdependencies would include the decision to employ a different technology or process: 'A company, for example, that produces a wide variety of die castings for automobiles, aircraft, and industrial machinery, might find that a change to plastics in a few high volume items would not leave enough casting business to support the overhead costs of the facility.' By contrast, an auto-parts producer 'makes springs, batteries, valves and spark plugs, and necessarily employs a variety of production technologies. ... The decision to produce any of these products by a different method, would not strongly affect other activities. Thus the "diversified" casting company consists of a single discrete business, while the auto parts company may be divided into several distinct businesses (barring inseparabilities on the marketing end)' (pp. 12–14).

We have gone into the definition of the discrete business at length because Rumelt uses this concept to challenge the utility of 'objective' industry categories for his research:

> the standard lists of businesses, such as the Standard Industrial Classification categories, were not helpful. Each company had a unique history and had developed its own pattern of relationships among technologies, products and markets. *What was a discrete business for one firm was often an integral and non-separable part of a larger business in another firm*. (p. 13, italics added)

Thus the firm is the motive force of competitive behaviour. It is only by sheer coincidence that a sufficient symmetry of constraints, perceptions and opportunities will exist among a collection of firms so that they could be conceived as all operating in the same industry, *unless these firms are so bound by managerial constraints* (tradition, habit, ignorance) that all firms focus on the same narrow sphere in more or less the same manner. Rumelt continues:

Many researchers have commented on the failings of the SIC categories as definitions of 'businesses', but argue that such an approach is at least objective. We would argue, in turn, that even more 'objective' measures can be found, but they bear even less relation to the real issues under investigation. ... The arbitrary nature of the SIC classifications is [a] major source of inconsistency. A manufacturer of paper cups who adds a line of plastic cups is seen as entering into a new industry sector, according to the SIC system. The strategic category technique, while not having the degree of 'objectivity' generally accorded to the SIC system, permits the researcher to choose to ignore the difference between paper and plastic in this case and call the firm a Single Business Company. (pp. 17, 49)

The managerial perspective is thus quite different philosophically from that emerging from the use of 'objective' industry categories. In practical terms, Rumelt reports that there is over a 50 per cent misclassification between strategic categories and 2-digit (corresponding to UK orders) SIC categories (pp. 49–50), so the difference is not just one of principle.

We now give somewhat more detail on Rumelt's procedures. The breakdown of the firm's revenues by product area was used for the calculation of the SRs, and the richest source of these data proved to be firm prospectuses, since the legal requirement for the inclusion of the relevant information made them more revealing than annual reports. These data yield four major categories – single business (SR > 0.95), dominant business ($0.95 > $ SR > 0.7), related business (SR < 0.7, but with the related ratio RR – 'the proportion of revenues attributable to the largest group of businesses somehow related' > 0.7) and unrelated business (SR < 0.7, RR < 0.7) (pp. 29–32). Rumelt also has various sub-categories, including one for vertical integration. The qualitative information for the sub-categories 'was obtained by reading through twenty years of annual reports for each firm. In a few instances, the corporation's annual reports were so lacking in information or so abstract that books, newspapers, magazine articles and investors' surveys that dealt with the firm had to be consulted' (pp. 40–3).

Rumelt's use of such sources raises an important methodological point: 'subjective' analysis of firm behaviour necessitates and permits the use of a wider class of side information than would be permissible using 'objective' industry categories. When dealing with the domain of, for instance, the largest 500 firms, it should be possible in principle to have an exhaustive examination of every constituent of the population.

It is easy to come up with shortcomings in such an approach, but the existence of a coherent methodology from Rumelt for analysing diversification points to the possibility that these rich sources of data can be made reasonably commensurate. The alternative is that we continue to use the few sterile objective indicators which are conveniently available and fit onto our computer tape. In this and other areas of research, there is a decision to be made between a methodology which makes use of the *illusion* of scientific method ('objective indicators', statistical tests, computer packages) and an alternative – the exhaustive use and analysis of all relevant information, even if, at times, using traditional methods of scholarship and historical research, this analysis takes non-quantitative and inconvenient forms.

The results of Rumelt's sample of firms from the largest 500 industrial companies for 1949, 1959 and 1969 show significant increases in diversification, with a dramatic decline in the single business category complemented with a rise in unrelated businesses. The subcategory measuring firms whose strategy was linked to vertical integration remained unchanged (p. 51).

But much of the study was not simply concerned with trends in diversification *per se*, but its link to divisionalised management structures and economic success. Two sub-categories of failure in his sample are dominant vertical – mostly firms in traditional basic industries (e.g. steel) with non-divisionalised, functional form management structures and the unrelated-passive sub-category – firms which make acquisitions unrelated to their dominant business, but which are separated off from the acquisitive conglomerates. In both cases, Rumelt fails to draw glib conclusions about cause and effect relationships: he leaves open the question whether the steel industry is a poorer performer than the chemical industry because of 'inexorable economic laws' or because the strategy of vertical integration itself has helped to exclude steel firms from opportunities to apply their skills to new businesses based on other materials, markets or technologies (pp. 123, 100–1). He also notes the special role of science in promoting economically coherent diversification: 'The technologically advanced industries (chemicals, electrical and later electronic equipment and products based on the internal combustion engine) were not only science-based, but encompassed knowledge and techniques that were not related specifically to a single product, material or process. This special property of extensibility was and still is a key influence on the ease with which a firm can diversify' (p. 133).

With the emphasis here on the coherence of diversification, it might seem easy for Rumelt to explain the failure of firms in the unrelated-passive category (but not, we may add, the respectable performance of the acquisitive conglomerates), but here as well he points to the possibility of reverse causation: 'poorly performing companies ... may well elect to adopt linked or unrelated strategies of diversification, leaving behind those who remain successful. Therefore, controlled diversity is probably not the *cause* of high performance, it is rather that high performance eliminates the need for greater diversification' (pp. 124–5).

Lastly, Rumelt's unmechanistic approach to cause and effect relationships and his dynamic, rather than passive approach to diversification has much akin with the approach of Hayek, not least in its rejection of objectively defined products and markets:

the best defense against a declining market is not a new unrelated activity but a new product that is functionally related to the reasons for the declining sales or profitability of the old. Thus, the optimal response to a declining demand for, say, textbooks is not to emphasize fiction or to move into electronics but to create a product that should grow for the very reason textbooks are declining. If, for example, college instructors are making greater use of original sources, one might offer a scholarly reprint service along with collected excerpts from primary sources. This type of strategy, one of response rather than escape, requires two conditions: (1) *a strategy of defining one's business in terms of a function rather than a product*; and (2) the possession of sufficient managerial, technological, and marketing breadth and experience to permit rapid innovation and successful implementation of innovation. (italics added)

Returning to the measurement of trends in diversification, the empirical studies may be summarised as follows. Derek Channon, using a methodology similar to Rumelt's, finds a strong tendency in the direction of increased diversification in the UK for the period 1950–1970, though in absolute terms, Channon's sample of firms for 1970 was a good deal less diversified than Wrigley's US firms for 1967.[63] In the studies using industrial classification statistics, Charles Berry found that for 460 large corporations in the US the number of narrowly defined (4–digit) industries in which these companies operated increased by 40 per cent from 1960 to 1965, and 16 per cent at the broadly defined 2-digit level. When these activities were weighted by the percentage of the firm's sales in each of these industries using Herfindahl-type indices, the importance of the new activites fell, so that the increases ranged from 5 per cent at the 4-digit level to 10 per cent using 2-digit classifications.[64] These figures support the general consensus of a pronounced trend towards corporate diversification in the US, and have more power since they precede the great conglomerate merger wave of the late 1960s. They reinforce Gort's conclusion of an 'unmistakable trend' in the direction of diversification in the US from 1929 to 1954.[65]

For the UK, Utton weights activity by employment and uses a measure W which is derived from a cumulative diversification curve of the firm's activities in different industries.[66] Broad spectrum diversification using this index increased by 11 per cent between 1968 and 1972. The general conclusion is that 'diversification amongst manufacturing firms increased fairly persistently from 1935 to 1968. For the 200 largest enterprises this trend continued between 1968 and 1972 . . . the change in the importance of diversified enterprises in the five years 1958–63 was at least as great as that between 1935 and 1958'.[67] Studies in the UK and the US thus support a long-term trend towards firm diversification, but also assert their conviction that corporate specialisation remains a crucial aspect of firm behaviour, with the pure conglomerate 'holding company' still being a rarity.[68]

We now examine another, and equally remarkable form of firm expansion – the multinational.

The Multinational

An Overview

The multinational corporation is an embodiment and a representative of the continued development of the skills and range of vision contained within the modern business firm. The same forces which permitted, and the same motives which impelled the development of giant, integrated and then highly diversified firms were crucial in the transfer of business to overseas production. We summarise these ideas in the form of the following theses:

1   Developments in technique and organisation initiated by large firms have engendered integrated production and planning superior to that possible from the small firms in the markets surrounding them in their own country. These same developments also permitted large integrated firms to be pioneers who could assemble, market and finance the sale of their commodities in an alien environment; that very expansion of business horizon which caused firms to look beyond their immediate sphere of activity and to diversify also impelled them to examine possibilities overseas.

In many cases, international expansion took the form of exports, but with the increasing flexibility and sophistication of the giant firm, overseas production came to be seen as a viable alternative to exporting. The demonstration effect of early multinational firms and the positive externalities generated by these firms for subsequent entrants were accompanied by developments in the host countries and internationally which were conducive to the generation of a wave of multinational activity. While for many firms direct investment remained a second best alternative which was only resorted to because of tariffs or pressures from host countries, the choice for a firm between these two forms of international expansion became progressively a disinterested decision about the benefits and costs of these alternatives, where previously international production would have appeared for many firms as a dangerous and infeasible alternative to exporting.

2   Over time, we would expect to observe the expansion and diffusion of managerial technique and culture to host company businesses and others who were formerly limited to production within national if not regional boundaries. Initial expansion of production overseas has been generated by several factors, including the perceived differential advantages possessed by a particular firm over host company competitors, both actual and potential. Many of these advantages, both technological and managerial, have tended to dissipate over time, in part due to the demonstration

and behavioural (competitive) effects of multinational activity on domestic enterprise. In any specific instance, host company activity may be crushed or enlivened by the introduction of multinational activity, but the global tendency is indubitably towards an international diffusion of techniques and skills, a tendency which is reinforced by multinational activity.

3   With the growing interconnectedness of international business and the growth of institutions to service overseas business, the decision on whether to export or to produce abroad spreads from large vertically integrated pioneers to progressively less integrated, smaller firms. These smaller, less integrated enterprises use host country and international institutions to service their needs in those aspects of production, marketing and finance where they are not 'complete'. Firms which in the absence of some of these structures might have hesitated to indulge even in international trade now find themselves engaged in multinational production.

4   The major effect of the emergence of the multinational has been a more rapid diffusion of managerial and technical skills and of infrastructural business institutions (capital markets, etc.) than otherwise would have taken place, the influence of these changes being manifest not only within the host country, but throughout the international business environment. As a result, we observe a more rapid increase in world competitiveness than in the absence of international investment.

A difficulty with the above explanation of multinational growth is that neither the timing nor the rapidity of multinational activity after the Second World War is sufficiently explained by the demonstration and other economic effects described here. It is necessary to invoke specific political, institutional and historical developments from that period to deal with the phenomenon adequately. Otherwise, the emergence of multinational business is a straightforward extension of the general expansion of business activity.

The literature generated on the multinational firm has been enormous, in recent times dwarfing that of the other topics discussed in this chapter. Much of what has been written is consistent with the theses outlined above. However, the dominant analytical frameworks which have been adopted by economic orthodoxy to deal with the multinational company are inappropriate for explaining the growth and development of this phenomenon.

We now proceed with a brief reconstruction of multinational history and then confront these explanations in detail.

Historical Development

Our interest in the multinational is as a manifestation of the expansion and development of business enterprise. Various forms of international activity will be of relatively little concern to us here – for example, portfolio (financial) investment, in which enterprise control is not exercised, international expansion for the purpose of securing supplies of raw materials, tropical fruit, etc., and the special cases of US expansion into Canada and the growth and development of the international oil companies. The characteristic kind of modern transnational expansion of particular interest is overseas investment in manufacturing and service activity, in which foreign affiliates are set up by firms already functioning in their home countries. Within this category, special focus will be on the phenomenon of market-based investments between advanced countries who are potential trade rivals, for instance the US and Western Europe.

The period until 1914 was characterised by a broad series of advances in transportation and communications which made all kinds of international activity, especially trans-oceanic activity, more feasible; the development of foreign direct investment is a striking manifestation of these developments. Of the accumulated stock of foreign direct investment in 1914 almost half was accounted for by the UK and less than 20 per cent had its origins in the US. Of a stock of investment of some $14 billion for all countries, over half was devoted to resource-based and supply-related activities, and only 15 per cent to manufacturing;[69] for the US, only 18 per cent of foreign direct investment was in manufacturing, with the stock of investment in Mexico greater than that in all of Europe, east and west. These latter statistics are intended to dampen the impact of the fact that the ratio of the stock of US direct foreign investment to gross national product was the same in 1914 as in – 1966! (Inflation in the latter period contributes to this result, since the accumulated stock of investment compared with the Gross National Product is bound to be severely undervalued in historic cost data.)

Despite all caveats, US businesses showed an especial boldness in setting up what came to be recognised as genuine multinational enterprises, and the importance of US activity in later periods merits that we give it exceptional scrutiny. Myra Wilkins describes, in a now famous account, the development of 'the first American international business', the Singer Sewing Machine Company (as it came to be known) from its first involvement in international activity in the 1850s to full overseas production by 1867.[70] Wilkins stylises Singer's experience and that of similar companies as a series of stages. First, the firm sells abroad through a series of independent agents, such as an export man in New York. Secondly, the company appoints an export manager and/or acquires an existing export agency; the firm may also appoint independent agencies in foreign countries to represent it. Thirdly, the first stage that involves foreign investment: the company installs salaried representatives, a sales branch, or a distribution subsidiary abroad. In the last level, stage four, the firm introduces a finishing, assembling or manufacturing plant.

Clearly, caution is demanded with these categories. As Wilkins points out, firms sometimes bypass some or all of the first three stages; furthermore, a great deal of difference exists within these stages, so that, for instance, within stage four an assembly plant for 'knockdown' units shipped from the home country and a full-fledged manufacturing plant represent very different levels of overseas commitment. By 1920 for example Ford had car assembly plants in eight countries at various levels of complexity, but for many years subsequently had significant overseas production only in Britain. Lastly, and most importantly, one must avoid the temptation to interpret later stages of involvement as higher stages of international activity: the successive movement onto later stages often took place because of failures of market-based relations with agents, which were then replaced with ownership-based administrative relationships. But, even in subsequent periods highly sophisticated firms have continued to use lower stages to conduct business, often while they are engaged simultaneously in extensive stage four activity.

With the end of the First World War, the US emerged as the great creditor nation. This fact had permitted a doubling of the stock of US investment abroad between 1914 to 1919, from \$3.5 to \$7 billion, in which the foreign direct investment component rose from \$2.7 to \$3.9 billion, including a rise from \$200 to \$280 million in investment in European manufacturing. While the increase in foreign direct investment is exaggerated by wartime inflation, American business did indeed face the post-war world with great financial strength, and with confidence in the superiority of its enterprise.

The expansion of American economic power in the 1920s was enormous. Between 1919 and 1929, the stock of US foreign direct investment rose from \$3.9 to \$7.6 billion, but far more significant for the future was the rise in the American commitment to manufacturing in Europe from \$280 to \$637 million:

> In the *Economist*, the London *Herald*, *European Finance*, *Berliner Tageblatt*, *Die Boerse* and so forth, articles multiplied on the American invasion.... Ladwell Denny's *America Conquers Britain* (1930) included the activities of US direct investors. Britishers, Germans, Frenchmen and other Europeans had reason to be disquieted. In 1928–9, especially in the electrical, automobile, rubber tire, office machinery, and oil industry, as well as in public utilities, US direct investment plans burgeoned. By 1929, more than 1,300 companies or organizations in Europe were either owned or controlled ... by 1929–30, US direct foreign investments alone – \$7.5–7.8 billion – exceeded the direct and portfolio foreign investments of France, Holland and Germany combined.[71]

The US companies which expanded abroad with market-oriented, as opposed to supply-oriented investments were characteristically those which had already undergone a Chandlerian managerial revolution at home. They transferred abroad techniques for the marketing of widely advertised, trademarked or branded merchandise, or made use of technological leadership in product design, engineering and organisation of production. A quintessential example of the latter is the Ford Motor Company. But by the late 1920s even Ford was facing substantial rivalry in Europe not only from GM, but from European manufacturers who were adopting the Ford production techniques and designing vehicles particularly suited to local conditions.

These were, however, still early days for American business in foreign countries. Alcoa's president in the 1920s, A. V. Davis, explained the need for a specialised subsidiary to deal with foreign operations because most of Alcoa's personnel would rather not 'bother' with the relatively smaller quantities of sales abroad, very few of Alcoa's people could speak foreign languages, and there was 'incompetence' in dealing with foreign exchange. While similar complaints might well have been voiced by an American executive a half-century later, administrative problems of this kind were undoubtedly acute for many companies in those pioneering days.

US foreign direct investment collapsed with the Great Depression: many of the same forces which were constraining international trade – declining real income, currency fluctuations, political uncertainty, tariff and other governmental obstacles – were having the same effect on international investment. Furthermore, much capital fled Europe for the US in this period. As a result, there exists the extraordinary statistic of an apparent net *inflow* of capital to the US from 1933 to 1940, the first time this had happened since records had been kept at the turn of the century. The result was tremendously retrogressive from the perspective of American capital, and many great companies withdrew from international commitments, only to begin afresh in the post-war period.

The depression's interruption of the expansion of US foreign direct investment, when coupled with the vast increase in nominal (and real) GNP during the Second World War resulted in 1946 in a ratio of stock of foreign direct investment to GNP of 3.4 per cent – apparently the lowest of the century.[73] This statistic is offered as mild mitigation for the overwhelming effect of the *défi*, or better yet the *inondation américaine* which took place in the post-war world. At first, US investment was only moderate, net outflows averaging somewhat over half a billion dollars a year, and gradually rising to about three quarters of a billion dollars by the early 1950s. A dramatic jump took place in US outflow in 1956 originating largely from the oil companies, the average moving to over one and a half billion dollars a year. For the whole decade 1950–1960, the book value of direct investments rose by 170 per cent (by $20 billion in absolute terms).

In the subsequent decade, the US expansion was led by manufacturing investment, and the figures are even more impressive, since the percentage increases of the earlier decade were almost maintained, but the absolute increases were far greater: from 1960 to 1970, the book value of US direct investment rose almost 150 per cent (almost $50 billion in absolute terms), while US direct manufacturing in the EEC (with its 1957 membership) rose by over 190 per cent (over $20 billion in absolute terms).[74]

The movement to convertibility in Western Europe in the late 1950s was crucial to the flow of US investment to Europe. It has been convincingly demonstrated that traditionally the typical US multinational had a dichotomised view of overseas revenues and assets, viewing those denominated in foreign currencies as risky, while only dollar denominated returns were thought safe and 'real'. Convertibility was thus important because it meant that multinational profits could be converted into 'real' money and, at least potentially, brought home to the US. (Contrarily, Dunning has suggested that the very inability of Europeans to pay in dollars – the dollar shortage – was a motivation for US investment.[75])

The very factors which have been conducive to an increase in international trade such as convertibility have promoted, not deterred international investment. While for an individual firm at a given moment the two might seem to be alternatives, in an historical context both activities have developed together. Post-war multinational investment has been promoted not only by the currency stability of the Bretton Woods system and the rise in real incomes, but also by the fall of tariff and other barriers to trade when compared with the interwar period, despite the fact that *ceteris paribus* higher tariffs make direct investment more attractive for an individual firm. Trade and investment are complements within the system as a whole, and static choice theory based on individual firm decision is a deceptive guide to historical trends.

The situation in the late 1960s as it appeared to many was of a world dominated by US multinational corporations. Not only had US economic influence been extended in areas of traditional hegemony such as Latin America, but it appeared to be increasingly dominant in the manufacturing sector of what was then perceived to be its only significant commercial rival – Western Europe. In 1970, 300 US multinational corporations had 16 per cent of manufacturing output in the UK, 8 per cent in West Germany, and 6 per cent in France. Such figures however, significantly understate the central role of American firms in these countries in such key sectors as computers and cars. It seemed as if the American century might carry on for a millenium.

During the 1970s, however, there was a clear reversal of these tendencies, and by 1978 Lawrence Franko could write an article entitled 'Multinationals: the End of US Dominance'.[76] US foreign direct investment flows had made up two-thirds of the total among the top ten investing countries from 1961 to 1970, but this share fell to just over 50 per cent in the period 1971–75 and just under 50 per cent from 1976 to 1980. While over this period the shares of the UK and France stayed roughly steady at 14 and 5 per cent respectively and Italy's declined to less than 1 per cent, the real running was made by some of the strongest rivals of US business. West Germany doubled its share of foreign direct investment flows from 5 per cent in the early 1960s to over 10 per cent in the period 1976 to 1980, while the Japanese share in this period went from 1 to almost 7 per cent. Other dramatic increases came from the

Netherlands, which doubled its early 1960s share of 2 per cent, and Canada, which increased its early 1960s share of under 2 per cent to over 5 per cent. Furthermore, while developing countries have only increased their share of the stock of direct investment abroad from 1–2 per cent in the 1960s to 2–3 per cent in the 1970s, it is widely believed that there is a substantial potential for expansion of direct investment from these nations.[77]

The ratios of inward to outward foreign investment flows for the US rose from under 15 per cent for the 1960s to almost 30 per cent from 1972 to 1977 and almost 50 per cent in the period 1978–80. The high volatility of these ratios reminds us that foreign direct investment flows are subject to the vagaries of international finance, but these figures also correspond to substantive changes in the economic environment, including major West European and Japanese investment in the US. The Japanese have had to learn to face the problems of investing in underdeveloped countries:

> As NEC [of Japan] has discovered, going multinational can cause headaches. [The acquisition is not judged] to be up to Japanese quality standards yet. . . . Executives were appalled by the conditions they found when they took over Electronic Arrays. Workers at NEC's Kumamoto plant must change into special protective garments and pass through a forced-air 'shower' before entering the ultra-clean section where the most delicate part of the chip-making process is performed. 'But in California, people were wandering in wearing street clothes' according to one NEC manager.[78]

The above anecdote is not meant to indicate anything of significance about the overall standards of Japanese and American manufacture. It illustrates, however, the mechanism of the diffusion by the multinational of best practice technique, a process both more direct and perhaps more rapid than that emerging from firm responses to international competitive pressure. The substantial levels of direct foreign investment in the US in the 1980s mean there are now forces 'bringing it all back home'.

If we keep in mind Newton's Third Law of Journalism (every overreaction leads to an equal and opposite overreaction)[79] and note that among major investors, the US share in the stock of direct investment had only declined from 49 per cent in 1960 to 42 per cent in 1980 (perhaps even less, since inflation would have put a relatively greater underestimation in the latter years on the older American stock than others), American business abroad is still a force of overwhelming predominance. It is clear, however, that the US has entered into a more symmetrical role with other countries in the realm of foreign direct investment.

Interpretations
Much of the interpretation given by Charles Kindleberger to the rise of the multinational corporation is identical with that presented here:

Compare the growth of the international corporation in the 1950s and 1960s with the rise of the national corporation in the 1880s and 1890s in the United States . . . the national corporation emerging out of the growth of the local corporation and the regional corporation. . . . Prior to 1900, factor markets in the United States were less perfect than they are now. . . .

The rise of the national corporation provided a new institution alongside the imperfect factor markets . . . the national corporation provided an economic institution, unforeseen by classical economists which, while it carried the threat of monopoly, brought the United States closer to the classic competitive world.

Kindleberger continues with this analogy in a manner we do not think strictly precise:

The national corporation . . . was the product of the railroad, telegraph and telephone, which made it possible for a decision maker to operate over wide distances without too great cost. The jet air craft, the radio-telephone, and the rapid rate of growth in post war Europe have lifted the horizons of many national corporations to the world scene.

The 'operating' to which Kindleberger refers often involved a national corporation like GM 'exporting' its cars from Detroit to all over the United States, rather than investment 'abroad' from Detroit. In the post-war world, improvements in communications have clearly benefited all forms of international expansion, *both* trade and investment: improvements in, and lowering costs of transport are, relatively speaking, far more beneficial to the exporter than to the potential direct investor.

The main objection to Kindleberger's discussion is his emphasis on the need for market imperfections to exist for investment to take place, a point widely taken up in the literature:

in a world of perfect competition for goods and factors, direct investment cannot exist. . . . For direct investment to thrive there must be some imperfections in markets for goods or factors, including among the latter technology, or some interference in competition by governments which separates markets.[80]

But such a discussion of imperfections of goods and factor markets is uninteresting for explaining the post-war expansion of the multinational. On such a rationale, all investment, even within a country, is a sign of market imperfections – the process of competitive equalisation is thus a symptom of uncompetitiveness! Whatever imperfections have existed in the post-war world in some absolute sense, they have been far lower than inter-war imperfections in markets, with the political chaos, cartels and competitive devaluations of that period. The post-war establishment of currency stability, convertibility and of GATT, the elimination of legal cartels and the promotion of other devices for the expansion of trade – the removal of market imperfections – all signalled as well the growth of international investment. In the presence of perfect markets and no barriers to trade, perhaps all increases would have taken the form of trade, but we must seek elsewhere for the characteristic reasons for the post-war growth of the multinational.

Kindleberger's perspective on these problems may well have been influenced by his pupil Stephen Hymer. Hymer's view of multinational companies is usually identified with oligopolistic or market imperfections explanations for the existence of the multinational, but read in context his approach can be seen to have been dynamic and developmental, and hence far removed from static oligopoly theories. In a prescient article written (with Robert Rowthorn) for a seminar in 1969, the following ideas were presented about the 'non-American challenge'.[81]

> Europeans felt threatened because they saw US corporations gaining an increased share of the European market. They paid little attention to the fact that, in the world market as a whole, US corporations were themselves being threatened by the rapid growth of the Common Market and the Japanese economy, and required a rapid expansion of foreign investment to maintain their relative standing....
>
> To the short-sighted European firm, whose markets are mainly European, US investment seems to be an aggressive move to dominate Europe. To the long-sighted American firm, on the other hand, this investment appears to be a desperate attempt to defend its existing world share and keep up with the dynamic Europeans.

With mutual multinational investment between the key oligopolists in each other's home countries, it was suggested that a stable shares long run equilibrium could emerge, though Hymer believed that geo-political factors made this result unlikely. But even a tendency towards a stable economic equilibrium has not yet been forthcoming, and we believe it unlikely to be observed in the future. The ability of key oligopolists to control developments in the international economy is constrained by the generation of new multinationals from the US, Western Europe, Japan and from the newly developing countries, the continued expansion of international trade, intensified rivalry from host country enterprises and the continued legal and institutional inhibitions against overt carving up of spheres of influence. While violent economic and financial perturbations in the 1980s make long-term trends difficult to discern, there seems no tendency towards a stable equilibrium in the international economic area.

There can be little doubt, however, that, especially in the 1950s and 1960s or earlier, oligopolistic reaction can be crucial to the existence and direction of multinational activity, or to its absence in the form of mutual forebearance.[82] Statistical evidence of oligopolistic reaction has been offered by Fredrick Knickerbocker[83], who, in common with other studies, used the Harvard research project's sample of 187 US multinationals from 1948 to 1967 and found a statistically significant relationship between the US concentration indices for the industries in which these firms are represented and the bunching of investment in countries abroad within periods of three, five or seven years.

This result has been taken as evidence of the existence of oligopolies in which participants maintain market stability by mimicking each other's behaviour. Case-by-case analysis would clearly be needed to establish that this indeed was the motivation for bunched entry. The reader will already be familiar with our reservations about the use of concentration ratios in general, and there are further difficulties in drawing inferences from this 'extraordinary' group of enterprises, whose 'supergiantism' puts them in a class by themselves among the *Fortune* 500,[84] and which are far from being typical (despite their predominant share of total US foreign direct investment) of the population of multinationals. Knickerbocker notes that no relationship between concentration and bunching was found in another study for the petrochemical industry, the outcome seemingly contingent on Knickerbocker's use of broad two and three digit level SIC classifications, while the rival study used more narrowly defined five digit SIC industry codes. Problems and contradictory results of this kind are unsurprising, given the manipulations necessary on SIC categories to adapt them for statistical tests.[85]

Clearly, bunching may in some cases take place in order to control an oligopolistic arrangement – it may even resemble an exchange of hostages in warfare.[86] At other times it will function as a competitive response to the demonstration effect of the success of initial entrants, perhaps even taking advantage of the latter's creation of institutions and infrastructure. Bunching can then be seen to be a typical response in a competitive environment (as in Silicon Valley), and not as a manifestation of specifically oligopolistic behaviour. Thus, with regard to GM's tentative decision to locate its $5 billion Saturn project in Tennessee,

> The proximity of Nissan, say state officials ... must have weighed heavily in the decision. Since the Japanese company's arrival five years ago dozens of parts suppliers have sprung up, making everything from car seats to catalytic converters. Moreover, Nissan has helped acclimate Tennessee workers to the Japanese-style management and production techniques that Saturn will emulate.[87]

The dominant orthodox explanation for the existence and presumably the growth and development of the multinational (static theories, once again leave this relationship ambiguous) is the internalisation paradigm, which has close affinities with the markets and hierarchies model discussed in chapter 6. The internalisation paradigm emphasizes that vertical integration (multinational expansion, as opposed to exporting, licensing, or other market-type agreements) takes place, in a manner analogous to the Hymer-Kindleberger approach 'where international market imperfections would impose costs on firms using those markets'.[88] The multinational as a form of vertical integration

> has developed in response to exogenous government induced regulations and controls ... [and] to non-government market failure in areas such as information and knowledge. Here the [multinational] can use its firm specific advantage in knowledge and technology to service foreign markets by international production and marketing rather than through exporting or licensing. ... In general the [multinational] is in the business of bypassing externalities by creating an internal market to replace external markets.[89]

Thus, the creation of internal structures and the avoidance of markets permits the multinational to appropriate the full value of its knowledge and research, for which there exist only imperfect markets for license or sale, or which may be inextricably tied up with the firm's other processes. The motives and conditions for 'going multinational' directly correspond to those which explain why a firm might choose to manufacture a product itself, rather than to license its knowledge on the market-place.

The analogy is singularly inappropriate. Quite clearly, the best way to preserve knowledge internationally (or to maintain quality control, which is another motive cited for multinational expansion)[90] is to make the product yourself and then export it. Any other form of foreign expansion is likely to be more costly in the dissipation of knowledge. European firms, as we have seen, were stimulated by the presence of US car manufacturers during the inter-war period, and this process continued in the post-war years. In Japan, which has been the recipient of relatively little multinational activity, domestic firms have benefited from joint ventures with foreign enterprises in their own country: 'inscrutable Western systems, language, behavior, and motivational patterns, at least up to the level of middle and upper management, could be learned at home'.[91]

An emphasis in this literature on knowledge is due to its well-known public good characteristics which militate against purely market-type solutions, and the apparently high correlation found between research and development expenditures and multinational expansion by (predominantly) US firms.[92] We have already pointed out, however, that high levels of research and development activity are typical of diversified firms (such as these multinationals) since technology is a highly transferable (between products) resource, and often seems associated with outward-looking, ambitious management groups. It is therefore unsurprising to find international expansion of all kinds, including exports,[93] associated with research-oriented firms, although in the past, Japanese experience has been quite the opposite, since their traditional forms of supply-oriented international investment has involved the farming out of mature, 'low tech' industries.

High advertising expenditure also seems to be associated with multinational expansion (though not with exports),[94] and here we seem to reach an element of truth in the doctrine. Even in the inter-war period, American firms were motivated to invest abroad in order to customise consumer products to local tastes. American expansion in post-war Europe contained many consumer-oriented firms who relied heavily on their own advertising, marketing and distribution channels at home, and it was natural for these firms to have a 'presence' along with their commodities. By contrast, a country like Japan only creates market-oriented multinationals when forced to by outside pressure, since their comparative advantage has evolved in goods as opposed to services or service-oriented goods (the Japanese computer industry has traditionally been much better at producing hardware than software).

There are other elements of validity in the internalisation doctrine. Even at present, it is common to observe cases of moral hazard in international commerce, in which the firm integrates vertically to avoid using the market. When the new director of sales for BMW arrived in Tokyo, he immediately stopped selling through a local importer and set up a sales subsidiary. His reason was that 'If you really want to approach a market on a full-time basis, you can't rely on a local importer. He has a short-term profit orientation and doesn't have the financial strength to take the long-term view.'[95] Other advantages have been cited for multinational expansion as a form of vertical integration, such as the ability to internalise long-term contracts on purchases of raw materials, etc., the greater ease with which monopolistic exploitation can be pursued in sales and avoided in purchases and lastly, the economies of transfer pricing – the avoidance of *ad valorem* tariffs and the exploitation of differentials in rates of profit taxation.[96]

While each of these advantages may be relevant to a static decision to invest abroad, they do not seem very useful in explaining why a multinational explosion took place in the post-war world, and not at some other time. On the contrary, many of these factors would work against a post-war expansion of foreign direct investment as a vertically integrated alternative to exports. Thus, international markets for raw materials have been far more developed and less cartelised, transport costs have been reduced and tariffs and other barriers to trade have been much lower than in the inter-war period. (Franko suggests that while trade barriers have been an important motivation for European multinational expansion, this has been less so for US firms. But Wilkins and Hill remind us that for earlier times 'the only foreign country where government action did not, either by tariff or edict, spark Ford production was England'[97].) Furthermore, while advertising and distribution considerations were important in the decisions of post-war firms to 'go multinational' instead of exporting, it was undoubtedly easier for an American multinational to find good domestic advertising agencies and importers in post-war Western Europe than it would have been thirty years earlier.

The internalisation paradigm suggests why *ceteris paribus* a firm might decide to substitute multinational expansion for exports. But for the purposes of historical analysis, the relevant perspective is not from that of a 'substitution' effect but from an 'income' effect, in which international activity of all kinds has expanded significantly. Thus, between 1967 and 1980, the growth rate of both exports (including intra-multinational trade, which cannot be separated out on available statistics) and the stock of direct investment were significantly greater than GNP growth in developed countries.[98]

A strong implication of the internalisation literature is that the multinational represents a superior, a higher form of international activity. There is a sense in which this is true: modern multinational operation demands a breadth of vision and a level of administrative co-ordination which was possessed by few firms before the post-war period, and thus multinational expansion was not an option open to them. But the internalisation aproach is deceptive and distracts attention from fundamental factors in the development of the multinational. Multinational expansion and exporting are not always substitutes, but are often complementary activities. For a whole trading area, increased trade can finance direct investment: the significant growth of direct investment by EEC firms within the community has been for many a surprising result of the Treaty of Rome.

Furthermore, for an individual firm, the ambiguity of the term 'multinational expansion' can often hide situations in which a 'knockdown' assembly plant, or a marketing/sales division is set up to promote exports. From Japan at least as of the late 1970s (after which time foreign governmental pressure and fear of future restrictions may have induced more 'genuinely' multinational production) investment in Western Europe and the US has been overwhelmingly geared towards supporting the sale of goods actually produced in Japan or in the newly industrialising countries. The multinational, then, does not represent a higher stage of development in international economics.

If the multinational were to be analysed as a form of vertical integration, what predictions would follow on this for the future? John Dunning, one of the most careful advocates of this approach (as part of his 'eclectic' framework) suggests the following perspective: 'It is very likely that the concentration of international production in the hands of relatively few multinationals is witness to *the growing significance of hierarchical advantages* which themselves follow from the growth of foreign production prompted by market forces.'[99] On the contrary, we would suggest that, analogous with vertical integration in domestic environments, we shall be observing a rivalry between the growing sophistication of hierarchical structures and the increasing attractiveness of market-based solutions.

Thus, we are already seeing a greater use of joint ventures by multinationals, even by firms at the highest levels of integration and managerial sophistication such as Philips, AT&T and GM. In many cases, the motivation appears to be a desire to find complementary strengths in an increasingly competitive world environment, though an attempt to control 'excess' competition cannot be excluded as a possibility. However, the case history of the international link between Philips and Sony on the development and launch of the compact disc player, and the subsequent intense competition between these firms and dozens of others, indicates that successful cartelisation is far from being the invariable outcome of joint ventures.

In many instances, we would expect that the growing diffusion of managerial technique and related skills will make it progressively more economical for firms to use the market, just as in the domestic environment. In the future, with the continued development of marketing, financial and other infrastructure available for hire, we shall see progressively more vertically disintegrated and/or smaller firms who decide to 'go multinational' for tariff, cost of transport or other reasons. The exceptional ability of relatively small Japanese firms to export or to function multinationally is greatly aided by the provision of peripheral services by the *sogo shosha* – the great trading companies, and over time these services will be progressively offered to smaller Western firms by market-based institutions, a development which we already observe within domestic economies. If the analogy with the domestic market holds, there may be less reason in the future to identify the multinational with the large vertically integrated firm: in this sense, we offer a prediction which directly confronts the view of the multinational offered by the internalisation paradigm.

It would be a mistake, however, to underestimate the monumental significance of the multinational corporation both as a representative of an unprecedented level of managerial sophistication and as an initiator of increased international competition. Furthermore, the pace of these changes has not abated: in recent years, many multinationals have transformed their organisations from having 'truncated replicas'[100] abroad to country specialisation and rationalisation of subsidiaries, especially within large free trade areas such as the EEC. Companies have had to confront severe administrative problems in making the change from traditional decentralised structures to 'a transitional stage to global integration',[101] but in this sense only now do the full benefits of 'internalisation' have a potential for being realised.

Related transformations have been taking place in the marketing of products world-wide. Until a few years ago, there was a well-recognised product life cycle in international business, in which products, having reached maturity in, for instance, the US were then marketed in Europe.[102] It is now universally conceded that such an approach is no longer valid, since global views of company affairs are now dominant. The major controversy at present is between the choice of relatively uniform 'global product' strategy and of tailoring the product to the specialised needs of the host countries. The firm then has to adopt structures – relatively centralised in the global product case, and relatively decentralised (specialised divisions) in the latter case, to accomodate these strategies. Both approaches demonstrate a much more sophisticated, globalised view than the earlier product life cycle, in which mature products were simply hived off on foreigners. Current managerial thinking is demanding an even greater sophistication – products must be produced both as a part of a global strategy and yet customised to each individual nation or market.[103] But the fact that even a standardised global product can be considered as a serious possibility is breathtaking. It indicates a relative level of uniformity of standards, design parameters and even tastes throughout the world which would have been inconceivable only a few decades ago – a continuation of developments which had already taken place in the domestic environment of these countries, coupled with an unprecedented level of ambition, aggressiveness and managerial sophistication emanating from the multinationals.

The problems which these firms face are immense, not least being the intensely competitive global environment which they have helped engender for each other. But the effect of these developments is the creation of an environment in the 1980s where market forces are brought to bear globally with a speed that would have astounded such believers in the power of the invisible hand as Adam Smith, Karl Marx, or even the Milton Friedman of 30 years ago:

> Unions claim that multinationals are not only integrating production between countries, but becoming more sophisticated in their ability to shop around for cheap labour. American Airlines and Bank of America, for instance, ship cartons of data forms to Barbados and Brazil to be keyed into computer terminals, and then relayed to central records offices by satellite. Clerical workers cost $1.60 an hour in Barbados, compared with $9 an hour in New York.[104]

Notes

1. The ambiguities in delineating stages even in the relatively straightforward case of the aluminium industry are discussed in Stuckey, J. *Vertical Integration and Joint Ventures in the Aluminium Industry* Harvard University 1983, ch. 1.
2. Fisher, F., J. McGowan and J. Greenwood *Folded, Spindled and Mutilated* MIT 1983, ch. 3.
3. Barna, T. 'Process Plant Contracting: A Competitive New European Industry' in Shepherd, G., F. Duchêne and C. Saunders (eds) *Europe's Industries* Frances Pinter 1983, pp. 167–85.
4. This problem is described in Adelman, M. 'Concept and Statistical Measurement of Vertical Integration' (and comment by I. Barnes) in National Bureau of Economic Research *Business Concentration and Price Policy* Princeton University 1955, pp. 281–322. The use and the problems with the firm's ratio of inventory (stocks and work in progress) to sales as a measure of vertical integration is also discussed in this article.
5. See the appendix to this chapter.

6. See Barnes in Adelman (note 4).
7. Eckland, W. 'A Note on the Empirical Measurement of Vertical Integration' *Journal of Industrial Economics* 28(1) (September 1979): 105–7.
8. Scherer, F. M. *The Economics of Multi-Plant Operation* Harvard 1975, ch. 7.
9. Blois, K. 'Vertical Quasi-Integration' *Journal of Industrial Economics* 20(3) (July 1972): 253–70.
10. Livesay, H. and P. Porter 'Vertical Integration in American Manufacturing, 1899–1948' *Journal of Economic History* 29(3) (September 1969): 494–500.
11. Laffer, A. 'Vertical Integration by Corporations, 1929–1965' *Review of Economics and Statistics* 51(1) (February 1969): 91–3.
12. Tucker, I. and R. Wilder 'Trends in Vertical Integration in the US Manufacturing Sector' *Journal of Industrial Economics* 26(1) (September 1977): 81–94.
13. Blair, J. *Economic Concentration* Harcourt Brace Jovanovich 1972, p. 26.
14. Chandler, A. *The Visible Hand* Harvard University 1977, p. 315.
15. Ibid., ch. 9.
16. Sutton, C. *Economics and Corporate Strategy* Cambridge University 1980, p. 27 and Chandler (note 14), ch. 7.
17. Williamson, O. 'The Vertical Integration of Production: Market Failure Considerations' *American Economic Review* Papers and Proceedings 61(2) (May 1971): 112–23.
18. Chandler, A. *Strategy and Structure* MIT 1982, p. 31.
19. As quoted in Edwards, R. and H. Townsend *Business Enterprise* Macmillan 1967 (first edn 1958), p. 291.
20. Stigler, G. 'The Division of Labor is Limited by the Extent of the Market' *Journal of Political Economy* 59(3) (June 1951): 185–93.
21. Wilson, C. *The History of Unilever* vol. I Cassell 1954, p. 265.
22. Sutton (note 16), pp. 45–6.
23. Scherer, F. M. *Industrial Market Structure and Economic Performance* Rand McNally second edn 1980, p. 90.
24. Lazonick, W. 'Industrial Organization and Technological Change: The Decline of the British Cotton Industry' *Business History Review* 52(2) (Summer 1983): 195–236.
25. Vollmann, T., W. Berry and D. C. Whybark *Manufacturing Planning and Control Systems* Richard D. Irwin 1984, p. 194.
26. Ibid., p. 174.
27. Ibid., p. 308.
28. Ibid., pp. 709, 712.
29. Ibid., p. 713.
30. 'Japan: Quality Control & Innovation' (Special Advertising Section) *Business Week* 20 July 1981.
31. 'How Detroit is Reforming the Steelmakers' *Fortune* 16 May 1983.
32. 'America's Best-Managed Factories' *Fortune* 28 May 1984.
33. '"Scrum and Scramble" – the Japanese Style' *Financial Times* 19 July 1987.
34. 'Can John Scully Clean Up the Mess at Apple?' *Business Week* 29 July 1985.
35. Hannah, L. 'Visible and Invisible Hands in Great Britain' in Chandler, A. and H. Daems (eds) *Managerial Hierarchies* Harvard University 1980, pp. 41–76.

36. Wilkins, M. and F. Hill *American Business Abroad* Wayne State University 1964, pp. 10, 11, 36.
37. Edwards and Townsend (note 19), p. 255.
38. 'How to Deal with Big Fish: Pinneys Sells Salmon to Marks and Spencer' *Financial Times* 2 July 1985.
39. Dr. Lyon Playfair, quoted in Mathias, P. *The Transformation of England* Methuen 1979, p. 50.
40. Chandler (note 18), p. 26.
41. This argument is implicit in Chandler (note 18), ch. 1 and Chandler (note 14), ch. 9.
42. Fisher et al. (note 2) chs 1–3.
43. For a Leporellian list of conquests, see table 20, pp. 118–24 of Winslow, J. *Conglomerates Unlimited* Indiana University 1973.
44. Ibid., p. 126.
45. Chandler (note 18), ch. 3; on holding companies, see Bonbright, J. and G. Means *The Holding Company* Macmillan (US) 1932.
46. Sobel, R. *ITT* Sidgwick and Jackson 1982, p. 173; this also appears to be Sobel's view of Sloan's accomplishment.
47. 'Splitting Up' *Business Week* 1 July 1985.
48. This is not quite accurate but we must abjure out of cowardice from giving the correct context.
49. See Blair (note 13), chs 3 and 14.
50. Gort, M. *Diversification and Integration in American Industry* National Bureau of Economic Research 1962, p. 4.
51. This evaluation is confirmed in Utton, M. *Diversification and Competition* Cambridge University 1979, ch. 5.
52. Smith, K. and J. Schreiner 'A Portfolio Analysis of Conglomerate Diversification' *Journal of Finance* 24(3) (June 1969): 413–28.
53. 'Kraft, Minus Some Extra Baggage, Is Picking Up Speed' *Business Week* 9 March 1987.
54. 'Why GE is Bidding to Build the "Factory of the Future"' *Financial Times* 11 December 1981.
55. Rosenberg, N. *Inside the Black Box* Cambridge University 1982, ch. 3.
56. 'Olivetti and AT&T: An Odd Couple That's Flourishing' *Business Week* 4 March 1985.
57. See Patinkin, D. 'Multiple-Plant Firms, Cartels and Imperfect Competition' *Quarterly Journal of Economics* 61 (August 1947): 650–7.
58. Berry, C. *Corporate Growth and Diversification* Princeton 1975 and Utton (note 51).
59. 'Exxon: The Big Tests that Lie Ahead' *Financial Times* 3 July 1985.
60. 'Venture Capital: A Product of Partnership' *Financial Times* 9 August 1985.
61. Utton (note 51), ch. 1.
62. Rumelt, R. *Strategy, Structure and Economic Performance* Harvard 1974. Subsequent citations will be from this source.
63. Channon, D. *The Strategy and Structure of British Enterprise* Macmillan 1973, pp. 86–8.
64. Berry (note 58), pp. 61–6.
65. Gort (note 50), p. 7.
66. Utton (note 51), pp. 15–17 and appendix B.
67. Ibid., pp. 21, 80–1.
68. Utton (note 51), p. 19 and Berry (note 58), p. 73.

69. Dunning, J. 'Changes in the Level and Structure of International Production: the Last One Hundred Years' in Casson, M. (ed.) *The Growth of International Business* George Allen 1983, pp. 84–139.
70. Wilkins, M. *The Emergence of Multinational Enterprise* Harvard University 1970, pp. 37–46. In 1985 Singer sold its sewing and consumer products marketing operations in 11 European countries as part of a restructuring of business into high technology, aerospace and military products, as well as other consumer durables. 'Sewing Up Singer Sales in Europe' *Financial Times* 29 August 1985.
71. Wilkins, M. *The Maturing of Multinational Enterprise* Harvard University 1974, tables 1.2 and 1.3, pp. 30–1 and pp. 154–6.
72. Ibid., pp. 148–9.
73. Ibid., pp. 283–4.
74. Ibid., tables XIII.1–3, pp. 329–31. Problems with the use of these data are described in Stopford, J. and J. Dunning *Multinationals* Macmillan 1983, p. 5.
75. Gilman, M. *The Financing of Foreign Direct Investment* Frances Pinter 1981; Dunning (note 69).
76. Franko, L. 'Multinationals: the End of US Dominance' *Harvard Business Review* 56 (November–December) 1978: 93–101.
77. Ibid., table 1.3, p. 6; see Wells, L. *Third World Multinationals* MIT 1983 and Lall, S. *The New Multinationals* John Wiley 1983, who suggests (p. 250) that there are severe limitations to the data even for the countries (India, Hong Kong, Argentina and Brazil) within his sample.
78. 'Enter a Japanese Multinational' *Financial Times* 15 March 1982.
79. Franko (note 76).
80. Kindleberger, C. *American Investment Abroad* Yale University 1969, pp. 33–5, 11–14.
81. Hymer, S. and R. Rowthorn 'Multinational Corporations and International Oligopoly: the Non-American Challenge' in Kindleberger, C. (ed.) *The International Corporation* MIT 1980, pp. 57–91.
82. See Franko, L. *The European Multinationals* Harper and Row 1976, pp. 166–70.
83. Knickerbocker, F. *Oligopolistic Reaction and Multinational Enterprise* Harvard 1971. The severe problems which exist in aggregating up concentration data from lower (4 or 5 digits) to higher (2 or 3 digits) levels as Knickerbocker has done are discussed in Boyle, S. 'The Average Concentration Ratio: An Inappropriate Measure of Industry Structure' *Journal of Political Economy* 81(2) (1973): 414–26.
84. See Vernon, R. *Sovereignty At Bay* Penguin 1971, pp. 17–24.
85. Knickerbocker (note 83), pp. 50–1, and appendix C, pp. 213–18.
86. See Franko (note 82), p. 50.
87. 'Why a "Little Detroit" Could Rise in Tennessee' *Business Week* 12 August 1985.
88. Buckley, P. 'A Critical View of Theories of the Multinational Enterprise' in Buckley, P. and M. Casson (eds) *The Economic Theory of the Multinational Enterprise* Macmillan 1985, pp. 1–19; and see the discussion on multinationals contained in Williamson, O., 'The Modern Corporation: Origins, Evolution, Attributes' *Journal of Economic Literature* 19 (December 1981): 1537–68.
89. Rugman, A. *Inside the Multinationals* Croom Helm 1981, pp. 26–8.

90. Casson, M. Introduction to Casson (note 69), pp. 1–33.
91. Franko, L. *The Threat of Japanese Multinationals* John Wiley 1983, p. 60.
92. See Parker, J. *The Economics of Innovation* Longman 1974 and the review of the empirical literature in Caves, R. *Multinational Enterprise and Economic Analysis* Cambridge University 1982, pp. 8–12.
93. Bergsten, C., T. Horst and T. Moran *American Multinationals and American Interests* Brookings 1978 table 3.3, p. 81.
94. Ibid.
95. 'BMW's Japanese Driving Lesson' *Financial Times* 8 July 1985.
96. Casson (note 90).
97. Franko (note 82), pp. 76–84, 175–7; Wilkins and Hill (note 36), p. 401. Dunning (note 69) indicates that the avoidance of tariffs is an important motivation to US expansion in all periods.
98. Stopford and Dunning (note 74) figure 1.1, p. 8.
99. Dunning (note 69); italics added.
100. Ibid.
101. Doz, Y. 'Strategic Management in Multinational Companies' in Grub, P., F. Ghadar and D. Khambota (eds) *The Multinational Enterprise in Transition* Darwin second edn 1984, pp. 91–121.
102. Vernon (note 84), ch. 3.
103. See the articles in Porter, M. (ed.) *Competition in Global Industries* Harvard Business School 1987.
104. 'Multinationals Turn the Tables' *Financial Times* 12 March 1985.

Appendix

Let $a_1 \ldots a_i \ldots a_n$ be the shares of value added of the vertical chain

$$1 \Rightarrow 2 \Rightarrow \ldots i \ldots n$$

and assume

$$a_i = \frac{1}{n} \text{ for all } i.$$

For the integration index

$$I = \frac{1}{n} \sum_{i=1}^{n} \text{value added/sales} = \frac{1}{n} \sum_{i=1}^{n} a_i / (a_i \times i) = \frac{1}{n} \sum_{i=1}^{n} \frac{1}{i}$$

Compare (8.1) the effect of integration of i_0 and $i_0 + 1$ with

(8.2) the effect of integration of $i_0 - 1$ and i_0.

$$I_a = I - \frac{1}{n} \left(\frac{1}{i_0} + \frac{1}{i_0+1} \right) + \frac{2}{n} \times \frac{2}{i_0+1} \tag{8.1}$$

$$I_b = I - \frac{1}{n} \left(\frac{1}{i_0-1} + \frac{1}{i_0} \right) + \frac{2}{n} \times \frac{2}{i_0} \tag{8.2}$$

$$I_a - I_b = \frac{1}{n}\left(\frac{4}{i_0+1} - \frac{4}{i_0} + \frac{1}{i_0-1} + \frac{1}{i_0} - \frac{1}{i_0} - \frac{1}{i_0+1}\right)$$

$$= \frac{1}{n}\left(\frac{3}{i_0+1} - \frac{4}{i_0} + \frac{1}{i_0-1}\right)$$

Note that when $n = 3$, then $i_0 = 2$ and the term in brackets is equal to zero (the case in the text). In general $I_a - I_b \Rightarrow 0$ for $n \Rightarrow \infty$.

9

Trends in Competition over Time: the Historical Evolution of the Industrial Structure

I: GENERAL TENDENCIES

Introduction

Markets – the domains of competitive activity – cannot be understood apart from the mentality and behaviour of participants. The secular expansion of markets and the concomitant increasing competitiveness in the capitalist market economy are not simply due to the exogenous influences of reduced costs of transport and technological progress. On the contrary, changes in technology, transport and all other factors which create the competitive environment, including the techniques of business calculation, must be seen as part of a societal whole in which objective factors interact with the evolving consciousness of participants.

Outside the discipline of economics, such observations are commonplace. For Fernand Braudel and the *Annales* school of historians in France, a correct perception of any single aspect of a civilisation, such as its commercial life demands a knowledge of its totality – from the most mundane aspects of its material conditions to its cultural formations and intellectual activity. For other historians as well, it is impossible to view economic evolution separately from broader changes in the consciousness of actors. At the beginning of the Industrial Revolution in Britain, those very developments in attitudes and skills which engendered an entrepreneurial class and a financial infrastructure to service it also facilitated technological innovation, which in a general way was linked to the scientific revolution:

It was the same Western European society which saw both great advances in science and in technological change in the great sweep of time and region across the fifteenth to the nineteenth century. It would be carrying nihilism to the point of dogma to write this off as a mere accident, even though the case of China suggests that it is perfectly possible for sophisticated scientific and technological knowledge in some fields to produce a very small impetus towards lifting general levels of industrial technique ... both science and technology give evidence of a society increasingly curious, increasingly questing ... increasingly seeking to experiment, wanting to improve ... [In conclusion] the advances in science and in technical change should both be seen as characteristics of that society, not one being simply consequential upon the other.[1]

For sociologists as well, the development of a specific kind of mentality is an inherent part of a social system.[2] Werner Sombart believed that 'calculation forms an important element in the capitalist spirit ... calculation [is] the tendency, the habit, perhaps more, the capacity to think of the universe in terms of figures, and to transform these figures into a well-knit system of income and expenditure'.[3] Technological change facilitated this development, as well as cultivating business-like habits such as punctuality, even with developments which now seem as mundane as the perfection of clocks. New technology can spur the imagination to expand the range of what is possible in a business context.[4]

Interactions in both directions between changing objective circumstances and transformations in human consciousness are an inherent part of the historical process, and these connections become more obvious the longer the time span under study. One might have imagined, therefore, that a neo-classical view of long-term economic development would be impossible: what use are neo-classical axioms of choice in the context of the medieval mind? Indeed, orthodox economists have, partly for this reason, traditionally taken a diffident approach towards economic history. In recent years, however, neo-classical economics has extended its domain of applicability to long-term historical development.

A relatively serious and sober example of this approach is *The Rise of the Western World* by North and Thomas. For them 'Efficient economic organization is the key to growth; the development of an efficient economic organization in Western Europe accounts for the rise of the West. Efficient organization entails the establishment of institutional arrangements and property rights that create an incentive to channel individual economic effort into activities that bring the private rate of return close to the social rate of return'.[5] If the institutional arrangements give no material inducement to those individuals in the society who undertake activities which lead to economic growth, say North and Thomas, the result is a steady state. The existence of appropriate property rights would appear to be a necessary but not a sufficient condition for economic growth, but while 'individuals in the society may choose to ignore such positive incentives . . . casual empiricism suggests that most people prefer more goods to fewer goods and act accordingly'.[6]

Would North and Thomas's re-ordering of incentive schemes[7] have improved economic growth in Western Europe? Perhaps. In a period covering almost a millenium, from AD 900 to 1700, it is not difficult to pick out state activities which were so blatantly dysfunctional that alternative measures would have brought about 'Paretian improvements'. But, overall, is this a constructive approach to the problem of economic growth? Let the historian reply:

> What would a present day economist do . . . if some unkind providence transported him to the land of Philip the Fair in 1302, to Venice in 1600, or even introduced him to Law, the magician, in 1716, and then asked him to take stock, draw up the requisite balance sheets, and draft a plan to accelerate the growth of the economy concerned? He would, of course, only be allowed the bare means available in 1302, 1600 or 1716 respectively, and not those at his disposal today . . . [More] than anything else, his efforts would come up against insurmountable obstacles: the hazards of harvest, the slowness or lack of transport, incomprehensible and contra-dictory demographic movements, hostile attitudes, lack of reliable statistics, and the chronic deficiency of power resources.[8]

The development and expansion of markets in the early modern period is a function of the gradual easing of these objective constraints, coupled by, as North and Thomas correctly point out, a more 'rational' attitude to the protection of property rights by governments in some countries, most notably the Netherlands and Great Britain. But inseparable from these developments and an historically necessary prerequisite was the en-gendering and dispersion of broadly based 'rational' attitudes linked to capitalist habits of thought and mentality. This process of transformation is continuous, and on-going. Marx, Sombart and Schumpeter each believed they were living at a time in which the evolution of the capitalist mentality had approached or reached its epitome. But each of these thinkers was succeeded by a new generation – Marx by Sombart, Sombart by Schumpeter – to whom all earlier conduct of business affairs appeared old fashioned and tradition bound, and who could see in the previous generation enormous remnants of pre-capitalist formation. Just as it is a mistake to judge the efficiency of a technological process in some absolute sense and not relative to its time, it is similarly inappropriate to speak of the 'rationality' of the capitalist:

> Does this mean that we must attribute to our capitalists a . . . mentality made up of calculation, reason, cold logic, a lack of normal feelings, all subordinated to an unbridled appetite for gain? [On the contrary] our capitalist . . . stood at a certain level in social life and usually had before him the decisions, advice and wisdom of his

peers. He judged things through this screen. His effectiveness depended not only on his innate qualities but also on the position in which he found himself, whether at the intersection or on the margins of the vital currents of trade, near to or far from the centres of decision-making – which had very precise locations in every period.[9]

Though Braudel's discussion concerns the mentality of the early capitalist or the pre-capitalist merchant, it can be generalised. In each generation, capitalist 'rationality' and, equally important, the number of capitalists with this level of rationality are moulded and determined by the social formations of the day. It is constrained not only by the limitations imposed by the capitalist's own entrepreneurial imagination and technical facility at executing plans, but the availability and quality of the surrounding infrastructure, human and institutional, as well as the objective limitations imposed by the technologies associated with business organisation, transportation and communication. There is no obvious tendency for developments in these areas to cease. The continual unfolding of the capitalist system's internal logic seems to have no obvious limit even in our present age.

The Expansion of 'Markets'

The 'market', that image so beloved of all economists, was, in its substantive manifestation, most ubiquitous in the late Middle Ages. As Braudel comments:

> Markets in towns were generally held once or twice a week. In order to supply them, the surrounding countryside needed time to pro-duce goods and to collect them; and it had to be able to divert a section of the labour force (usually the women) to selling the produce. In big cities . . . markets tended to be held daily . . . whether intermittent or continuous, these elementary markets between town and countryside, by their number and infinite repetition represent the bulk of all known trade, as Adam Smith remarked.[10]

But by Adam Smith's time the dominance of this general market had already declined. With the increase in the volume of trade there emerged first, as in England in the sixteenth and seventeenth centuries, a gradual specialisation of markets and then, after 1720, the development of shops open for trade every day, backed up by the development of warehousing and wholesale trade in commodities. These latter forms of specialisation became a necessity as the volume of trade increased: 'trade circuits became established . . . the merchant built up his connections, and . . . such connections although completely by-passing many areas still untouched by trade, came to create coherent trading zones. Our imperfect vocabulary calls such zones "markets"'.[11] The expansion of the market in a figurative sense was thus coincident with its decline in a literal form: the persistence of this imagery in economic orthodoxy is symptomatic of the latter's failure to describe economic evolution in a satisfactory manner.

Market expansion was engendered by the activities of so-called merchant capitalists who had been making money, and sometimes building fortunes[12] throughout the late Middle Ages by 'taking advantage of price differences in space and time, due to the prevailing immobility of producers and their meagre resources – price differences which it sought to maintain, and even widen by its privileges of monopoly'.[13] Juridical changes, sometimes discontinuous, as in the case of the English and French revolutions curtailed such monopolistic privileges, as did the vast expansion of trade itself and increase in the number of competing merchants. Whether the expansion of trade that had taken place by the eighteenth century was by itself a cause of the subsequent industrial revolution is still an issue of great controversy.[14]

It is essential to note the unevenness and lumpiness of the dispersion of the new techniques of production. Even within Britain, the industrial transformation took place in a highly localised manner, the origin usually dictated by resource availability. Areas of intense specialisation then developed – the Midlands nail makers, with twenty districts each making a different nail, and the Sheffield cutlery industry – all islands of intense, and perhaps unprecedented competitiveness. These areas emerged due to the external economies generated by the creation of a physical infrastructure of canals and roads, as well as the existence of the relevant firms for supplying capital goods. Equally important was the generation of a human infrastructure of labour relevant to that industry: 'It is difficult to realise how scarce these specialised skills were in the late eighteenth century; how few the centres where precision metal-work in iron on a large scale could be conducted and learned; how limited the institutional means of acquiring such skills'.[15] The revolutionary nature of the new industrial system and the enormous infrastructural and human prerequisites of capitalist economic development dictated that diffusion to other European countries took place in an extremely uneven manner, often with the assistance of the 'visible hand' of government.

In the end, the revolution was accomplished. There was a ninefold increase in the value of world trade between 1820 and 1880, and a doubling between 1900 and 1910. For the period 1750 to 1913, the increase is supposedly fiftyfold.[16] Figures for increases in shipping tonnage seem to tell a more modest story – a doubling from 1850 to 1880, an increase of 77 per cent from 1900 to 1913, and an approximately twelvefold increase from 1800 to 1913.[17] On either set of figures[18] the increases indicate a remarkable expansion in the domain of the market in the nineteenth century.

But even these statistics tell only a fraction of the story of market expansion in this period. Until the 1850s and 1860s steamships were an uneconomical means of transport. Not until the 1870s and the 1880s did steam exert a downward pressure on rates, and the reduction in shipping costs was never as important as that achieved by railways.[19] The emergence of the railway was crucial to the development of the modern capitalist economy. We have already seen how railways engendered the managerial and financial transformations which became characteristic of other industries in the twentieth century. Of equal importance was the 'invisible' market expansion which railways brought about through increases in the volume of intranational shipments. Such lowering of costs of transport for both buyers and sellers promoted the breakdown of regional submarkets and of local monopolies, the intensification of specialisation, and the introduction of goods and business practices hitherto unknown. By the beginning of the twentieth century, the railway had effected an expansion of the market and an intensification of competition within national economies which were probably even more significant than the statistically visible increases in market extent brought about by the growth of international trade.

For both intra- and international competition, however, changes in the intensity of the competitive process or even the rate of expansion of markets cannot be properly measured by movements in the *ex post* value of shipments. For the nineteenth century, the dispersion of capitalist techniques and mentalities reinforced the regime of competitiveness brought on by market expansion, even though these developments were sometimes accompanied by the appearance of industrial and financial entities of unprecedented size. For this reason, the proposition that the nineteenth century was a period of increasing competitiveness is relatively uncontroversial.

In the twentieth century, markets have continued to expand, a development accompanied by the emergence of giant enterprises. The thesis developed here is that, as in the nineteenth century, the dispersion of capitalist techniques and mentalities in the twentieth century has continued to cause competitive pressure to increase. Why for the twentieth century has this proposition been so controversial? There seem to be two reasons. First, the growth of large firms and their exercise of economic (and political) power have been so conspicuous that for many observers declining competitiveness has been a self-evident proposition. Secondly, a widely held but implicit proposition in most discussions is that since, at the beginning of the twentieth century, countries like the United States and the United Kingdom *were already fully capitalist*, one does not have to consider the effect of the continued dispersion of capitalist techniques and mentalities on the competitive process, as would be necessary in the nineteenth century or in a contemporary developing country. Such an attitude is reinforced by the methodology of orthodox economics, where an unchanging rationality is assumed axiomatically.

The nature of the trend in competitiveness in the twentieth century will underlie the remainder of this chapter. A crucial role in the conceptualisation of this problem is played by technology and technological change.

Technological Diffusion

Technology may influence the conditions of competition in a number of ways:

1 Improvements in transport secularly increase the domain of the market: commodities such as steel and cars are now subject to high levels of trans-oceanic competition. This development is in part due to technical changes which have reduced transport costs.

2 Technical developments have helped generate an information revolution. How competitively participants act is in part a function of the quality and quantity of the information available to them. The competitive decision may demand a wide variety of different kinds of information, including that relevant to a competitor's, or potential competitor's behaviour and/or performance. All of these kinds of information are progressively more rapidly, cheaply and widely dispersed, a process facilitated by developments from the invention of printing to the transmission of data by computer.

3 A typical concomitant of technological change is the standardisation of product specifications, a process that is particularly strong in the inter-industry sector, especially the engineering and electrical fields.[20] Even where products are themselves differentiated, the tendency in natural science to reduce these differences to measureable parameters will make competing goods ever more commensurate. Even among consumer goods, long-term movements in the direction of uniformity (e.g. the pasteurisation of milk) may be of greater significance than the much vaunted development of product differentiation in the twentieth century.

4 Technological change can have an effect upon the size distribution of firms. In some sectors such as aircraft or mainframe computers in which competitive rivalry is inherently tied to a high level technological change in a relatively non-decomposable manner, the industries concerned often consist of a few large, integrated firms. It is in these very cases, however, that market concentration figures are of relatively little significance for an evaluation of the state of competition, as the heterogeneity of the products and the rapid transformations in the technological parameters often dictate that competition in sub-sectors is far more intense than would be indicated by market share figures.

5 The same technological transformations that facilitate the monitoring of the performance of rival firms and the pursuit of other information relevant to the competitive decision will also be applicable to the internal running of firms in a more 'rational' manner: this facilitation of co-ordination, control and information retrieval (e.g. with the advent of the telephone and later with the mainframe computer) is of great importance to large firms attempting to function efficiently. In some cases, such developments may be of no less benefit to smaller entities, who find that best-practice techniques become available to them at their own scale of

operation (e.g. desktop computers). Improvements in internal monitoring brought about by technical change may be as significant in engendering competitiveness as those which advance monitoring outside of the firm.

6   Changes in technology may facilitate alterations in the forms that competition may take: it has been suggested, for instance, that current developments encourage a 'flexible specialisation' as opposed to the tendency in much of the twentieth century towards uniform mass production of commodities.[21]

7   Lastly, and most importantly: technological innovation itself is a form of competition, both within industries and across industrial boundaries. Indeed, it is a commonplace of the literature of industrial innovation that crucial competitive breakthroughs derive almost invariably from outsiders to the industry.

Are advances in technology to be viewed as fully exogenous events? Nineteenth century advances would then be only fortuitously related to increases in competition, and further developments in the twentieth century might well have had the opposite effect. If, however, technological change is an integral part of the competitive process, it becomes more difficult (but not impossible) to conceive that rapid technological change in the twentieth century is associated with declining competitiveness.

While technological developments can never be wholly explained in economic terms, neither these developments nor their economic implementation can be treated as wholly exogenous to the economic system and the competitive process. Companies' decisions about technological change (including the passive decision not to indulge in it) are no less relevant than, for example, strategic price decisions. Other aspects of business decision making have intensified in the twentieth century, and this development has encompassed the choice of new technology.

The central perspective adopted on technology here puts an emphasis on the continuous process of change and refinement which is inherent in the competitive process, as opposed to the exogenous shocks and 'gales of creative destruction' which are part of both the neo-classical and Schumpeterian traditions. Our focus therefore is upon the diffusion of techniques rather than their initial conception, both because diffusion is inherently more amenable to economic analysis than is invention, and because its role *vis-à-vis* Schumpeterian innovation has been underestimated.

Bracketing the orthodox and Schumpeterian approaches to technology may seem surprising, but the two have much in common. It is a commonplace among modern historians that technological advance is overwhelmingly due to anonymous increments rather than to the discontinuous events known as inventions. This is true not only of a host of fundamental advances made in the early modern period and during the Industrial Revolution in such areas as machine tooling and metal working, but also of more recent changes.[22]

For Schumpeter, innovation, defined as 'the setting up of a new production function', implies 'by virtue of [its] nature, a "big" step and a "big" change'.[23] These innovations, thought Schumpeter, were in the long-term of far more consequence than the static forms of competition focused on in economic orthodoxy. Schumpeter has, therefore, been placed in the role of the most radical critic of the orthodox approach to competition: even for Hayek, the short run decisions of the firm on such questions as the price of the product were critical, but were seen from a different perspective. From Schumpeter's point of view, such short-term decisions were well-nigh irrelevant.

Nathan Rosenberg has pointed out that the analytical foundations – and indeed the implications – of Schumpeter's theory have close parallels in economic orthodoxy:

> Individual isoquants are usually presented for convenience as smooth and continuous curves, representing a wide range of alter-natives of varying factor intensities. They constitute a spectrum of what Schumpeter called 'eligible choices' . . . in what precise sense is it likely to be the case that a wide range of technological alternatives will ever be 'known'? Since . . . the production of knowledge is itself a costly activity, why should technological alternatives representing factor combinations far from those justified by present prices be known?

If we proceed in this way, suggests Rosenberg, 'we are really allowing factor substitution to swallow up much of technological change',[24] so that much technological change is not Schumpeter's setting up of a new production function, but a mere movement along the isoquant. One firm introduces change and then different firms through the process of diffusion explore and develop the ramifications of what from a neo-classical and Schumpeterian perspective should have been a complete blueprint of techniques. The Schumpeterian emphasis on the discontinu-ous jumps involved in an innovation is deceptive too in ignoring the enormous number of incremental improvements which are necessary prerequisites for its success, improvements both in the product itself (e.g. developments in car production and design at the turn of the century), and in complementary activities (e.g. the building of roads and the provision of fuel).

The very radicalism of Schumpeter's approach is, paradoxically, congruent with the traditional practice in orthodox economics of pushing the question of technological change to one side: if indeed technological change results from discontinuous 'gales of creative destruction' and if the source of these changes are the very large firms otherwise accused of monopolistic behaviour, then technological change has little to do with ordinary economic analysis of the competitive process. There is little then to do but to study this topic separately from the 'normal' processes of business behaviour and competition. If technological change is, however, largely incremental then much of it may be analysed as an aspect of business behaviour and competition. While there is a well-recognised literature on the existence of learning curves with established technology – so-called 'learning by doing', there has been little emphasis in economics on gradual improvements in new technologies and their diffusion. Such improvements make it extremely difficult to measure the interval between invention and innovation, since much of it is taken up by further inventive activity which improves the product.

Adoption of the new technique is thus critically affected by the rate of these improvements: Rosenberg suggests that 'If it is true that inventions in their early forms are often highly imperfect and constitute only slight improvements over earlier techniques', it follows that 'the pace at which subsequent improvements are made will be a major determinant of the rate of diffusion' and 'the state of development of the capital goods industries'[25] is the single most important factor governing these improvements.

Clearly the opposite proposition also holds: not only does the rate of subsequent improvements govern the rate of diffusion of new techniques, but the more rapid the rate of diffusion – the larger the number of firms attempting to improve the new techniques and adapting them to their special needs – the more quickly such improvements are likely to come about. The pace of diffusion of new techniques is, therefore, not only an important determinant of the level of an economy's competitiveness, but of technical change itself, broadly considered.

Exogenous shocks and gales of creative destruction can obviously have a critical effect on the competitive environment and on the size distribution of firms. If indeed there were to be a significant increase or decrease in the number of these shocks over time, such a change would of its own accord affect the trend in economy-wide competitiveness. A change in the incidence of such shocks could have an indirect effect on the competitive environment as well, if such shocks were to cause movements in the efficient scale of operations in certain sectors and therefore the size distribution of firms in these sectors. Economists, however, have very little to say about trends in society's overall level of inventiveness, and have reached agnostic conclusions on whether technical change is biased in favour of larger units. Therefore the focus here will be upon whether there is a tendency for the rate of diffusion to increase. The emphasis will be largely on a priori arguments, since there is only slight evidence on the subject, which seems to point in the direction of greater diffusion of innovation in the US over time.[26] But relevant here are the reservations raised by Rosenberg about the setting of a well-defined date for 'the' introduction of the innovation compared with its subsequent diffusion.

Of the existing literature on the general rate of diffusion, little of it is helpful to a discussion of the rate of change in this diffusion over long periods of time. Even Rosenberg's focus on the role of the capital goods sector may be of little assistance: for any technology, the 'state of development of the capital goods sector' can only be calculated relative to the 'newness' of that sector so that, for instance, the more revolutionary an innovation in electronics, the more backward may appear the existing capital goods industry. The state of development of the capital goods industry includes not only technical factors, but a whole set of entre- preneurial and infrastructural attitudes to new products which may facilitate or impede innovation. Since, however, discussion of such attitudes is part of the broader issue of trends in competitiveness, it would be inappropriate to introduce such arguments into a discussion of diffusion *per se*.

If we put aside more general considerations of 'animal spirits', are there any other reasons to believe that the rate of diffusion has increased? In recent times changes in governmental attitudes in many countries may have made it less easy for dominant companies to use the possession of patents as a means of maintaining market power.[27] But such a change is far from the long-term and more purely economic forces for which we are searching. The responsiveness of the capital market in making available funds both for research and for new investment is clearly crucial but is, like entrepreneurial attitudes, an issue apart from intrinsic changes in the underlying potential for the diffusion of new ideas.

What factors have been critical in affecting the speed and direction of diffusion of innovation? One element is the rapidity with which new ideas are dispersed. It would be wrong to underestimate the speed of dispersion of new ideas in earlier times. But science in the eighteenth century was still largely the province of enthusiastic amateurs. In England periodicals such as *Monthly Magazine* and *Gentleman's Magazine* popularised ideas and experiments from the professional literature of the Academies. On the continent, the *Britannique* (1796–1815) translated English publications on the arts and sciences.[28] In the nineteenth century a critical role was also played by exhibitions in the displaying of the fruits of innovation in concrete forms.[29]

Such diffusion of knowledge was but a trickle compared with the present day inundation. As the volume of scientific research increased in the nineteenth century, it became possible to argue that while diffusion itself was a competitive force, the large volume of information available and its wide dispersion favoured the growth of large industrial units. The economies of scale to large enterprises engaging in research and develop- ment were highlighted by Edison's creation of the Menlo Park research laboratory in 1876, followed by the General Electric and DuPont labs at the turn of the century, and only more slowly by European firms.[30]

The intrinsic economies of scale in research and development are easily confused with the benefits which accrued to these research laboratories in acting as monitoring stations for new ideas. Large companies could allocate specialised personnel to the difficult and expensive task of keeping track of new discoveries. This advantage seems to have evapor- ated during the present century. Despite an exponential increase in scientific knowledge, the difficulties of monitoring change have decreased enormously to the benefit of relatively smaller entities. When Menlo Park was created by Edison, literally no other profit-oriented entity in the world existed which was monitoring scientific invention. Since that time specialist firms in a wide variety of scientific areas now feel they can monitor world-wide developments almost as well as the subdivisions of multinationals which are studying the same problems. They simply subscribe to the same periodicals.

There is a related aspect to the problem of technological diffusion. The further back we go in the history of innovation, the more they are craft, and not science based. In earlier times, the critical blockage in the diffusion of technology was specialised expertise and engineering – not science. A central reason for the lumpiness of diffusion during the early Industrial Revolution was the need to create pools of individuals who could personally pass on arcane skills to each other. The diffusion of innovation from Britain meant the diffusion of engineers themselves – masters of the skills and 'tricks' necessary to make the machines work. In the words of Peter Mathias:

It is remarkable how quickly formal knowledge of 'dramatic' instances of new technology, in particular steam engines was diffused, and how quickly individual examples of 'best practice' technology in 'showpiece' innovations were exported. The blockage lay in the effective spread of technical change and more widely diffused average technology rather than single instances of best practice technology in 'dramatic' well-publicized machines.[31]

In absolute terms, these skills, this 'know-how' is still probably of overwhelming importance in commercial success. Relatively speaking, however, industrial innovation has become progressively more science-based, with predominance to science having taken hold in about the middle of the nineteenth century. The inherent nature of science is that it can be taught relatively abstractly and impersonally, and that new achievements can be written down relatively objectively in a verifiable form. The pool of individuals capable of monitoring, replicating and imitating new innovations and therefore competing with them is far larger than if we were in a world with an equal number of scientific minds, but where commercially relevant innovations possessed the same percentage of incommunicable 'craft-mystery' as they did in the eighteenth century. The movement to science-based innovation has clearly been a key aspect of the acceleration of the speed of diffusion of these innovations in the twentieth century. Initial inventive conceptions which are science-based rather than craft-based spread more rapidly, and the dispersion of the techniques for the reproduction of the resultant commodities in a science rather than a craft-based production system is also more rapid.

In summary, reductions in the cost of acquiring information about new innovations have accelerated the rate of diffusion of new ideas and reduced the relative size of enterprise necessary to receive this information. Furthermore, the assimilation of this information has been facilitated by the lowering of the component of incommunicable craft-based technique in innovation. The concomitant world-wide expansion in the number of individuals with scientific facility more closely corresponds than formerly to an increase in the numbers capable of assimilating new technology in a commercial context.

There are, on the other hand, important aspects of technological change in the twentieth century that have been of substantial benefit to large, integrated firms. First, there has been an 'inexorable rise in the development costs of new projects',[32] which implies an even greater weight than heretofore to the role of the capital market in the distribution of funds for research and development.

Even more significant is the relationship between innovation and the expansion of managerial perspective. In the contemporary world, the extension of the business planning horizon among very large firms has implied that innovation must be co-ordinated to take into consideration a progressively broader range of supply and demand based complementarities. In order to create the compact disc system, Philips had to co-ordinate research between its electronics and optical divisions (as well as with Sony). Within its electronics division, vertical co-ordination of research had to proceed so that integrated circuits appropriate to the system could be developed. On the demand side, the Philips record division (which is part of Polydor) not only had to develop new processes for the production of these discs, but had to devise a world-wide strategy for the marketing and repertoire of these discs, all of which had to be timed and co-ordinated with the production and sale of the players themselves.

Thus, the pattern of diffusion of technology in the twentieth century seems to be reinforcing the bi-polarisation tendencies outlined in chapters 6 and 8 – there is movement in the direction of a highly marketised environment as innovations become more rapidly diffused, while contrarily, large integrated entities, capable of embodying and co-ordinating a host of supply and demand complementarities in their research and development strategies are even more than ever before the vehicles through which many new innovations will invariably pass.

If, as Schumpeter thought, there are great dynamic advantages to large firms, they are not merely the indeterminate advantages of 'bigness', or even less, the advantageous aspects of 'monopoly', as certain of his interpreters have suggested.[33] The benefits would seem to be first, the economies of integrated research, so that a company such as Philips can avoid the high transactions costs that would have been involved had individual companies attempted to plan and co-ordinate the development and marketing of the compact disc system. But this highly integrated approach is likely to be limited to ventures capable of generating extremely high levels of output, and in a competitive atmosphere specialised producers may be able to compete successfully when and if the technology stabilises or becomes segmentable upon maturity.

A second potential advantage of bigness in technological change relates to the nature of the capital market. In Schumpeter's words:

within big units . . . [conscious] policy towards demand and taking a long-time view towards investment becomes possible. Although credit creation still plays a role, both the power to accumulate reserves and the direct access to the money market tend to reduce the importance of this element in the life of a trust . . .[34]

The issue of the time horizon of firms has been discussed extensively earlier: whether correct or not, its contemporary relevance is undeniable, though the role of the capital market in discussions of the Schumpeterian hypothesis has been ignored. Having pushed aside the one element which could have given coherence to the doctrine as he expressed it, the on-going discussions have centred on two supposedly Schumpeterian propositions. First, his ideas have been interpreted to suggest that the presence of monopoly qua monopoly could promote innovation, which besides being incorrect in formal theoretical terms[35] is unsustainable as an historical generalisation; secondly, his ideas were linked to an association between 'bigness', only vaguely conceptualised and innovation, which in this form is vacuous. Without an explicit discussion of the nature of the capital market, Schumpeter's theory lacks any real substance. If capital market advantages to large firms have a secular tendency to decrease, the specifically Schumpeterian advantages to large firms in innovation may be declining.

II: THE TWENTIETH CENTURY: INCREASING MONOPOLISATION?

An Overview

The central empirical thesis here is that increasing competitiveness is an aspect of the development of the capitalist market economy. In recent years this view has been put forth most strikingly by James Clifton:

Capitalism is . . . a period distinguished by its own economic laws, of which competition is one. [It] is a mode of production, itself subject to development. . . . Does a mode of production . . . unfold over time, gradually developing its own tendencies and characteristics, or does it emerge from another epoch immediately in its purest, most highly developed form and become increasingly imperfect with its own development?[36]

Clifton's answer to his own rhetorical question is in the negative: a mode of production does not emerge full-blown and become increasingly imperfect, but gradually unfolds itself, so that contemporary capitalism is more competitive than in earlier times. From Clifton's perspective, the process seems inevitable, one that is inherent in the laws of capitalism. Here, however, increasing competitiveness in the capitalist market economy will be considered in the context of substantive historical developments.

The thesis of increasing competitiveness developed is centrally concerned with changes in the capabilities and attitudes of the principals involved in creating the competitive environment. In order to demonstrate that this is an empirical proposition and not one true by tautology, we suggest conditions in which developments in the capabilities and attitudes of principals (which indubitably *have* taken place) would not necessarily be associated with increasing competitiveness:

1 'Capitalist' attitudes and mentalities may have always existed, either among the general population or, at very least, among sufficient numbers of individuals 'at the margin' who could push the economy in a competitive direction. Such a position is made explicit in the writings of economic historians such as North and Thomas. But by emphasizing rationality merely sufficient to achieve a static equilibrium, the whole evolution of the dynamics of the competitive process – of the *speed* of convergence to any such equilibrium – is by-passed. Little can be said in this context about whether convergence is more or less rapid than it used to be.

2 The evolution of skills and tools of managerial decision-making may have always been adequate for the facilitation of tasks in the existing economic environment. Clearly, this notion presupposes an exogenously specified environment, one not substantially determined by the activities of the participants themselves.

3 Expanding managerial capabilities may act to facilitate greater co-ordination and therefore less competition between enterprises than would have otherwise existed. In a given market, co-ordination may *ceteris paribus* be facilitated by the ability of each firm to calculate its average costs precisely, but, generally speaking, such expansion in the facility of firms has historically been accompanied by significant widening of the relevant domain of competitive activity both geographically and across product 'spaces'. Firms functioning in a given product area have seen the relevant markets shift from local submarkets to national markets, and then to transnational competition; movements across product domains have also become more fluid, as firms have become more aggressive in the pursuit of profitable opportunities.

4 The process of competition can be seen to be self destructive: random process effects (when entry is restricted), economies of scale and financial factors may all contribute to an environment which is progressively dominated by giant firms. These initial advantages have, with growing sophistication, been used to reinforce market control through advertising and other forms of market manipulation, including various predatory practices.[37] Underlying these developments are networks of financial control through which these large firms co-ordinate their behaviour and from which they derive a continuing ability to squeeze their (smaller) rivals.[38] High levels of competitiveness may be seen as an intermediate

stage, after which the economy (or sectors within it) settles down to a monopolistic equilibrium.

Clearly, objections 3 and 4 to the presumption of a relation between expanding capabilities and increasing competitiveness are the more powerful: ultimately, the proposition can be resolved neither in a priori terms, nor with a single decisive statistical test, but only through investigation of the historical events themselves.

The case being presented in favour of a secular tendency towards increased competitiveness is not to be confused with Austrian-style contentions that all private property relations are competitive, no matter how monopolistic they appear. There is no doubt, furthermore, that financial advantages have historically accrued to larger firms functioning in the 'higher' capital market layers. The crucial issue is whether the distance between these layers has tended to expand over time with the progressive development of webs of finance capital for the largest firms, or whether as suggested here these layers have a secular tendency to be squeezed in the direction of a more uniform treatment of capital units of all sizes.

Competitive developments in both the general economy and in individual sectors may be crucially affected by the policies of governments. Such policies may make the discernment of underlying tendencies in the economy extremely difficult. But the line between the structural tendencies in the economy (e.g. the progress of semiconductor technology) and 'volitional' governmental decisions (e.g. government procurement policies in the electronics industry) cannot be drawn in a simple way. However, it is still meaningful to suggest that, for instance, underlying competitiveness has increased in the steel industry due to lower costs of transport, etc., *despite* the neutralising effects of governmental impositions of quotas and other barriers to trade. Furthermore, a postulated delineation between economic and governmental factors makes possible the development of a potent political economy, as in Gabriel Kolko's famous thesis that the genesis of the legislation of the so-called Progressive Era in the US at the turn of the century was big business's attempt to restrain the increasing competitiveness of the capitalist economy.[39] An examination of the inherent tendencies in the private economy may, therefore, be crucial to the future development of a coherent conception of state action.

Contemporary writings often interpret indications of increasing competitiveness in recent times as if they resulted from a series of discontinuous and exogenous factors – rising imports and reductions in the minimum efficient scale of production, and of changes in government policies towards regulation and anti-trust.[40] Such interpretations suggest, among other things, that current manifestations of increasing competitiveness may well be temporary, and even reversible. We believe however that the long-term and fundamental nature of this tendency is present in the historical record.

Even for earlier periods, there is no longer unanimity among analysts who use market concentration as their fundamental index of competitiveness that the period before the emergence of giant firms was a golden age of competition. As Scherer says: 'Whether there was more or less monopoly power in 1904 than in 1830 no one can say with confidence, because the whole economic environment had been transformed so radically. (Note: Another broader developent [was] a long-run structural shift [towards manufacturing and] away from the more competitively structured economic activity [agriculture].)'[41] The source of this agnostic conclusion is clear: the effects of a rise in market concentration may have been reversed by the vast expansion of the internal markets in the US in this period, as well as the introduction of an enormous number of new products and, no less dramatically, new ways of doing business by firms.

It is the retention of agriculture in the above quotation as the standard of a 'competitively structured economic activity' which signals the difference between the market structure approach and that taken here. We would contest the idea that agriculture was a highly competitive sector in anything other than the tautological sense that it had low market concentration. Nineteenth century American agriculturalists are considered to have been both technically advanced and culturally more entrepreneurial – more 'capitalist' than their European counterparts. It is difficult, however, to escape the conclusion that from the perspective of capitalist economic development, agriculture in the US, as in other countries represented a substantial residual domain of uncompetitiveness – of ignorance and 'slothfulness', with a psychology substantially geared to habitual ways as opposed to 'rational' calculation compared with the emergent urban alternatives of commerce and manufacturing: transformations in farmers' ways of doing business in the nineteenth century almost invariably originated outside this sector (manufacturers' inventions of farm implements and government sponsored agricultural research) and had to be 'pushed' on them. From the perspective of a dynamic approach, there is little that could be called competitive about this sector.

In general, such behavioural criteria are essential for an understanding of the evolution of the competitive process. Thus, the British economy before the First World War appeared far more competitive than in subsequent periods if evaluated on the basis of trends in market (or aggregate) concentration, but 'only a close study of actual buying and selling practices will show the extent to which habit, personal ties and sheer inertia distorted the play of competition'.[42] It would be convenient for the market structure approach and indeed for all analysts of the competitive process if manifestations of X-inefficiency on the part of British manufacturers could be located exceptionally in areas of relatively high market concentration. Indeed, the absence of competition – generated first by Britain's overwhelming predominance in the nineteenth century, extending in many sectors through the inter-war period with Imperial and Commonwealth preference and even through the early days of the post-war boom until new competition emerged – is relevant as part of an explanation for the engendering of dilatory habits of behaviour in much of British industry.

But in individual sectors in Britain, the failure to respond competitively, either in the period before the First World War or in the inter-war period[43] seems in no way associated with sectors containing high levels of market concentration. On the contrary, the culprits were often in areas of low concentration such as the engineering industry where, for instance, British international competitiveness in ploughs collapsed due to an 'unbelievable lack of standardisation'[44] on the part of British manufacturers compared with their German and North American counterparts. Furthermore, far from there being any clear lines of causation from high market concentration to uncompetitive response, there are important instances in both the inter-war period (e.g. the formation of Imperial Chemical Industries in 1926)[45] and in the post-war world ('The growth of competition in the postwar world was . . . a significant cause of a major series of acquisitions in the late 1960s and led to considerable restructuring of the British electrical industry')[46] in which industrial amalgamation and high concentration have *resulted* from a competitive response to an increasingly competitive environment.

The phenomenon of the 'unbelievable lack of standardisation' in many areas of British engineering compared with their German and American rivals raises the issue of the overall significance of standardisation for trends in the competitive process. The importance of this question can be seen in the context of the role of trade associations, be they government sponsored or purely private. Such associations were widespread in each of these three countries from the nineteenth century onwards, but there were significant national differences. First, while all associations endeavoured to control the 'excesses' of competition, this desire was inhibited in the United States by the presence of the anti-trust laws, prosecuted in different periods with varying degrees of severity, but almost always (the NRA period from 1933 to 1935 excepted) looking askance at the overt cartel-like controls which were frequently exercised in Germany as well as Britain.[47]

Secondly, however, the trade association was used aggressively in Germany and the US for the imposition of scientific and industrial standardisation. In the US the development of standardisation took place for many years with, perhaps surprisingly, much of it promoted by government, most prominently during the First World War and during Herbert Hoover's tenure as Secretary of Commerce in the 1920s.[48] The effect of these co-ordinated and sometimes imposed standardisations was to create an environment which was more competitive[49] than in countries, like Britain, which made fewer efforts in that direction. The environment was more competitive in the sense that goods which emerged from this regime were more attractive – more 'competitive', as in the case of ploughs, but the environment was more competitive as well in the literal sense.

From the perspective of orthodox economics, little of interest emerges from the history of trade associations and similar organisations except for their anti-competitive, cartel-like features. In fact, the role of standardisation in the evolution of the competitive process is critical. In the 1890s in the US, there was still

> a confusion and a duplication of effort unknown to later generations of Americans ... the market was flooded with competing types of electrical apparatus and chemical products peddled by the new companies, in addition to the plethora of machined goods and machinery itself. Since each company was concerned above all with promoting its own products, and devised unique means of evaluating their quality and performance, *comparison between competing products was difficult*. And since each manufacturer used its own specially machined parts, *replacement by those of another was virtually impossible*.[50] (italics added)

Standardisation *per se* is of little interest in orthodox theory, except for the presumption that in oligopolies it might facilitate co-ordination on price. Economic orthodoxy *implicitly* assumes that the economic system inherently contains that minimum amount of standardisation which is necessary for goods to be commensurate, so that the price system can approximate the workings of the model. But such a state of affairs is in reality the result of a long historical process.

Orthodox economics presumes that for a given state of the art, the level of competitiveness will be limited solely by the success of participants at conspiring in restraint of trade. But this presumption proceeds as if this state of the art, including the level of standardisation were exogenous – outside the perimeter of the behaviour of participants. But an environment can be uncompetitive not because of any success participants have at conspiring together, but because the environment in which firms are functioning – which is to a great extent of their own creation – is dysfunctional for a direct comparability and interchangeability between products. The 'confusion and duplication of effort' found in earlier periods was as great an obstacle to competition as any monopolistic conspiracy.

While one may find examples even in the contemporary world (especially in cases of substantial market power, e.g. IBM) where a policy of avoiding standardisation and interchangeability is purposefully pursued in order to maintain a special niche for the product, the overwhelming long term tendency is in the direction of standardisation and comparability of products, a movement which is reaching new levels in this digital age. Note, for instance, GM's recent efforts to enforce compatibility among its suppliers of computer equipment. The standardised communications system to emerge – manufacturing automation protocol (MAP) – is meant to facilitate computer integrated manufacturing, in which every part of the production process will be interconnected through a central nervous system. Failures to take advantage of potentially available standardisation appear not so much as conscious attempts to maintain product differentiation as atavistic remnants, as it progressively becomes clear that others, as in the case of the British ploughs, will reap (*sic*) the potential benefits of any such failures.

The current perspective from Alfred Chandler and others[51] on the turn of the century emergence of giant firms in the US is clear: those entities which survived evidenced real advantages over their rivals – they had succeeded through their greater competitive prowess – and those combinations which demonstrated no such advantages were soon eliminated. A Golden Age of competition has never existed. Despite prominent examples of conspiracies in restraint of trade and of 'dirty tricks' which can be documented within the great oligopolistic industries which emerged, and despite the fact that the efficiencies which these firms sometimes manifested had little to do with most peoples' normative notions of socially beneficial efficiency (e.g. the marketing advantages of the great cigarette producers) the dominant movement has been towards a progressively more competitive environment. The forces which are contemporaneously making increasing competitiveness so manifest were already present earlier in the century, when the great oligopolies seemed at their most invulnerable.

The great firms which emerged at the turn of the century evidenced competitive advantages over their defeated rivals, but clearly, any such even implicit use of a survival of the fittest criterion must be viewed with caution.[52] One aspect we would like to focus on here is the role of government. The interpretation and evaluation we impose upon these developments is contingent on the range of tactics which were permissible to defeat and maintain dominance over rivals, and the constraints on such behaviour will depend partially on the rules of the game dictated by public policy. Stated in its most extreme form, a government which granted monopoly charters, or permitted gangsterism to constrain competition might well have engendered a 'survival of the fittest' regime which had little relation to the survival of the most economically competitive, in the conventional sense of the term.

The environment established by government can thus have an important effect on the evolution of the competitive process. Government policies may well have engendered for a sustained period a lessening of competitiveness in the US telephone industry;[53] on the other hand, the failure of the dissolutions early in the century of American Tobacco and Standard Oil to generate any dramatic change in their co-operative ways of doing business in their respective industries should restrain any tendency to overestimate the direct effect that government policy might have on the competitive environment.

The governmentally created environment may also affect the behaviour of firms indirectly. For instance, in the inter-war and early post-war period American multinationals had a reputation for being aggressive and unco-operative compared with their potential rivals in other countries. Such behaviour was often attributed to the habits engendered by US domestic anti-trust policies. Once again, conclusions must be cautiously drawn: the promotion of co-operation among firms in Japan by MITI seems to have had little effect either in limiting competition in the domestic environment or in dampening the international habits of competitiveness so manifestly displayed by Japanese firms.

In the post-war world, there has clearly been a movement away from the inter-war tendency to view cartel-like integration as desirable. Exceptions such as present co-ordination of output in the West European steel industry have been justified on the basis of special circumstances which, it is promised, will be self-liquidating. Of greater significance has been the state's changed role in the international sector in the post-war world with the long-term reductions in tariffs and other barriers to trade emerging from the General Agreement on Tariffs and Trade, and the accompanying inhibition of the kind of explicit international cartel agreements which were prevalent before the war.

Viewing the pre-war cartels,[54] it is easy to take an overly sanguine attitude retrospectively, since most of the cartels were unsuccessful in constraining competitive behaviour. Those which seemed most sinister – those for the control of raw materials – increasingly have their commodities traded in highly competitive markets in the post-war world. But the explicit carving up of the world by the electrical giants and the great (including American) chemical firms[55] had an important inhibiting effect on price competition (a serious temptation in high fixed cost industries, especially in periods of excess capacity) and more importantly on the forms of international competition involving new investment and research and development which we have observed in these industries since the war.

American post-war designs for a world relatively free of the impediments to free trade which existed in the inter-war period were successfully consummated.[56] If, as has been claimed[57] we have only in the last two decades entered into a situation of industrial competition which is truly international, the future trajectory of developments in the competitive process may be importantly affected by public policy decisions made in the international arena. The proliferation of more 'exceptional' international agreements such as that for the steel industry could signal a return to the pre-war environment for international cartels, thereby creating an important force countervailing against the underlying tendency for competitiveness to increase in the world economy.

Two general observations before we proceed with the sectoral studies. The first is about the mode of analysis. The categories which we shall be using – explicitly and implicitly to evaluate the changes in sectoral competitiveness are those conventionally to be found in industrial economics, such as firm turnover, the speed of technical diffusion and even changes in leading firms' market shares. Why have we not used these concepts in a more formal statistical way here? The answer is that the purpose of the exposition will be as much to explore the prerequisites of an appropriate mode of analysis for the competitive process as to verify the empirical hypothesis of increased competitiveness. Each of the factors mentioned above may be symptoms of competitiveness, but *do not measure competitiveness itself*. A sector may have relatively stable market shares over time, but maintain that stability only by an aggressively competitive (but among its members symmetrical) response to threatened imports. Furthermore, if we are interested in the underlying *dynamic* of competitiveness and not merely evidence in the naive sense, the search for a plausible story may demand greater use of qualitative, non-quantifiable variables than is possible in a statistical analysis.

The second observation is that there are bound to be severe limitations in an analysis of overall trends in the competitive process which is limited to two countries, the UK and the US, and to a few sectors. A perspective on the historical evolution of the steel industry is likely to be viewed very differently from the UK or the US on the one hand, and Brazil or South Korea on the other: changes which have impinged themselves relatively slowly on old and established industrial powers may appear in the newer countries as complete transformations in their industrial life and ways of doing business. Furthermore, the restriction to specific sectors, most of which are old and established, raises obvious difficulties for viewing overall trends. The problem develops a particular piquancy if the invisible hand is not in operation, so that there is great difficulty in choosing a few representative sectors. If 'inventory control among UK book publishers [and] furniture manufacturers ... is pretty awful ... but food and drink producers and capital and electronic equipment makers handle it better',[58] we may be able to form only hesitant global generalisations from particular sectors on trends in the competitive process and the evolution of ways of doing business. In an economy regulated not so much by an invisible hand as a whole set of invisible hands, the destinies of individual sectors may easily diverge and hesitant generalisation may be the best we can hope for.

Sectoral Surveys

Steel

We consider first two traditional sectors, steel and cars. For most of the century, both have represented common denominators of industrial development, at the same time prerequisites and indicators of maturity for newly developing economies. Both sectors emerged, especially in the US, as paradigms of the New Industrial State: US Steel and GM were taken to be classic examples of firms in the new age, in which scale economies and planning techniques (including those which would facilitate 'illegitimate' forms of competition) were sweeping away the remnant of a competitive environment. Such a perspective has become unrecognisable, as we are faced with the beleaguered, sick nature of these sectors in recent years. But the root cause of present developments is not to be found in a miscalculation – a crisis of overcapacity in the steel industry, or, in both sectors, the wizardry of the Japanese: the evolution of both the steel and car sectors illustrates fundamental aspects of industrial development in the twentieth century.

In the early 1960s it still could be written that 'The capacity of a modern industrialized society is best measured by its steel production. Steel in one form or another, from tinplate to girders and rails, from turbine rotors to the most delicate parts of precision instruments, is the matrix of modern life.'[59] Note that a nation's steel production is here identified with high volume steel usage as a prerequisite of industrial development – the use of steel in large amounts by a nation necessitates that it produce the stuff. And so it has been throughout much of the nineteenth and twentieth centuries.

Large scale steel making was initiated, as would be expected, in those countries which already possessed highly developed iron industries. Steel production, however, was largely introduced by newcomers, and it was often seen as a threat by existing iron producers rather than as an alternative activity. Starting in the late 1850s there burst forth a series of innovations, first the Bessemer process and the Siemans-Martin open hearth process, which together created the modern industry, followed by the Thomas-Gilchrist basic technique for removing the phosphorus found in much iron ore, which made the general dispersion of the new industry possible. Before this time, steel had been a rather expensive, somewhat esoteric material used for cutlery, surgical and precision instruments – as in, for instance, the famous Sheffield product, refined from Swedish bar iron in small furnaces. But by the mid-point of the century, military uses for steel and its potential role on the railways motivated the activity which resulted in these inventive successes.

Britain's early predominance and inventive success in steel was soon challenged. While by the turn of the century Britain had acceded first place in Europe to Germany, steel production was still largely restricted to the traditional centres of iron production, with Britain, Germany, the US (whose output by this time was greater than the latter two countries together) and Belgium producing 80 per cent of world production. But developments in other areas such as Russia were already indicating the much wider dispersion of production that would take place over the new century.

By the turn of the century, the world predominance of the American steel industry was unquestioned, not only for its unparalleled scale of operation, but for its creative adaptations of the relevant scientific and technical innovations, both indigenous and European. The erection of enormous integrated steel works in the latter part of the century had itself necessitated major innovations in the designing, equipping and arranging of the new establishments. From our present perspective of the steel industry as a tired sector producing a relatively homogeneous product, it is difficult to grasp the imaginative and innovatory nature of the vast act of co-ordination which was associated with running the giant integrated firm

– the orchestration of the sub-units within the works, such as the coke ovens, blast furnaces and open hearths with the mills for producing the finished goods, such as rails, wires and beams. The introduction of the sale of a wide variety of commodities of the latter kind by integrated producers such as Carnegie Steel represented major acts of diversification. These changes necessitated the introduction of new systems of cost control – a voucher system which attempted to keep track of expenditure within the organisation – but which still remained primitive, with little explicit attention to overheads and depreciation.

The American industry after the turn of the century fell into a kind of paralysis after its brilliant beginnings. The creation of US Steel in 1901 was not, as may first appear, the consummation of nineteenth century developments in the direction of integration. It was motivated more by a desire to realise monopolistic and (as a result) speculative gains than by any potential gains in real efficiency: the vast size of the American market had already permitted the emergence of an industry which had, simultaneously, firms with unprecedented levels of scale and efficiency and an unconcentrated, highly competitive environment. The company which emerged, far from setting any new standards for the level and sophistication of the integration of its processes, functioned as a rather lethargic and benign (from the point of view of competitors) holding company.

The market share of Big Steel (as it was known) in steel ingot production declined constantly in subsequent decades from its initial two-thirds level, and the effect of the 'pools, associations, trade meetings, and social dinners' and the *sub rosa* basing point system by which it ran the industry in the early years was lasting. The 'sprawling, inert giant' which was observed in a famous report of 1938 did not succeed in stifling the activities of rivals, who by this time had over 60 per cent of the market and continued to be more innovative than the dominant firm. But the lead set by US Steel was not conducive to the creation of competitive modes of behaviour, especially among the large integrated steel producers.

Despite this state of affairs, the American industry remained the world standard during the inter-war period, with its consumption of finished steel products per capita remaining twice that of Britain and at least 50 per cent greater than Germany, and its output per blast furnace two-and-a-half times that of the British and 70 per cent greater than Germany: there was no question of any competition from abroad.

In Britain, the situation was quite different. The common complaint there continued to be the overly large number of firms, each functioning at a level of efficiency far below the world standards being set in the US and Germany. The relatively low levels of concentration (it took 20 firms to produce three-quarters of national output, as opposed to only 8 in the US) did not, however, create an environment more competitive than that of the US: the general crisis in British industry had created a state of 'chronic depression and wild uncertainty'[60] in the steel industry of the 1920s, resulting in political pressure which led to the tariff of 1932, and to (successful) attempts by the British Iron and Steel Federation to restrict new investment by steel producers. Producers did little which broke the mould of traditional behaviour and ways of doing business. It will remain an open question here whether this lack of dynamism or aggression was characteristic of the whole industry, or whether there existed smaller producers or outsiders who, if they had not been constrained by the social structure of the industry and the limitations of the capital market would have pursued a different, more competitive strategy. Whatever the case, it is evident that the relatively low concentration in the British industry was not by itself sufficient to engender competitive behaviour.

The events of the post-war steel industry must surely rank as some of the most fantastic in the history of capitalism. In the inter-war period the British and US steel industries faced the difficulties of deficient demand but were secure in their relative status on a world-wide basis. These industries found themselves in the immediate post-war world not only with buoyant demand for their output, but, furthermore, with renewed leadership in the world market-place. In the UK, the re-found post-war status was shortlived. For the countries which were to comprise the EEC, however, there was a recovery in their share of the world market in raw steel between 1950 to 1960 from one-quarter to almost 30 per cent, before falling below one-quarter for the first time in 1970 and below 20 per cent in 1980. The UK's relative decline within this group was even more severe, so that by the mid 1980s it had only about 13 per cent of EEC rolled steel capacity, less than half of that of Germany, and only 60 per cent of the capacity which existed in Italy, a country without a comparable tradition for steel making and, furthermore, with no reserves of either coal or iron ore.

The American decline was even more remarkable. After the Second World War, the US was able to recapture the position it held at the end of the First World War of producing over half the raw steel in the capitalist market economy. By 1960, this share was under 30 per cent, and by 1970 a little over 20 per cent; by 1980, the share had fallen under 15 per cent, a lower percentage than in 1870. By the mid-1980s, US Steel's Tom Graham was speculating on whether the US industry might become mainly a finisher of imported steel. Indeed, with oil and gas accounting for more than one-half of US Steel's revenues by the mid 1980s, it was not surprising, but still somehow disconcerting, to see the word 'steel' exorcised from the name of Graham's once mighty company – as of 1986 it will be known as USX Corporation. Thus, within a few decades of a secure position in the post-war world, the extinction of the steel industries in the US and the UK as major forces in the world steel market seemed a serious possibility. How did such a strange turn of events come about?

Some of the developments which have taken place in recent years in the steel industries of the US and the EEC can be accounted for by the general effect of the macroeconomic crisis on this capital intensive sector. The malaise is so deep, however, that (unlike the 1930s) even the boom of the 1980s failed to stem the mounting losses and rising debt of the integrated steel sector in the US. Some of the failure is accounted for by the decline in the use of steel in advanced economies – the 'income elasticity' of demand for steel appears to be less than unity in those countries with growing shares of national income devoted to services and to high technology industries. Furthermore, there has been a tendency in recent decades for substitutes to be found for steel in a wide variety of uses. This circumstance too may give the impression of being wholly exogenous to the process of competition. But here it is relevant to note that, according to a 1966 National Science Foundation study in the US, all of the industries producing steel substitutes – aluminium, cement, plastics and glass – spent a far greater percentage of their sales revenues on research and development than did the steel industry: their competitive pursuit of new uses and adaptations for their products may well have exacerbated any 'natural' decline in the use of the more traditional material. Much of this natural decline, furthermore, has come about because steel users themselves such as car makers have in recent years been taking a more aggressive attitude to the use of new materials as the competitive temperature in their own sectors has risen.

Growth of competition has also taken place within the US steel market. Until the mid-1960s, for instance, the price discipline among the integrated producers was legendary, or notorious: for decades no deviations were observed between transactions (actual) and quoted (nominal list) prices, even for large buyers. This pattern was broken in the late 1960s with the first substantial import penetration, and by the mid-1980s one could speak of 'rampant discounting'[61] in a period of relatively moderate prosperity – acts of unconscionable bad behaviour to whose temptation these firms had not succumbed even during the 1930s.

Some of the reasons for the new competition seem to have a technological basis. Within the US, the rise of the mini-mills since the 1950s has acted as a spoiler in the steel market, especially in the West and the South which have been poorly served by the integrated firms, and as of the early 1980s they had about a 13 per cent share of national steel tonnage, a share that seemed to be rising rapidly. These firms emerged with the development of the electric furnace, which could be used to by-pass the pig iron stage by processing scrap. Using this technique, a narrow range of steels can be efficiently produced by small fabricators producing as little as 100–500 thousand tons a year. This development may appear to have emerged for purely technological reasons, but observers of the industry point to the new competitive spirit manifested by these manufacturers, indicated by their more rapid assimilation of the innovatory technique of continuous casting (a technique, admittedly, which is well-suited to mini-mill production) than either American or even Japanese integrated producers. A similiar innovatory spirit has been found among the group of small producers of specialty steels.

But competition has also manifested itself, and more profoundly, on a world-wide basis. Steel has now become an international commodity. Between 1950 and 1977, internationally traded steel as a percentage of total production has risen from 10 to 25 per cent in capitalist market economies, and from 9 to 18 per cent, if intra-EEC trade is eliminated (intra-EEC trade had risen from 7 to 27 per cent of production within the Community). If import penetration in the US was still under 5 per cent of national raw steel production as late as 1960 (two-thirds of which came from the EEC), by the late 1970s it was ranging consistently over 15 per cent and would have gone much higher in the absence of government imposed restraints on imports. The composition of these imports now changed, with the EEC accounting for only a quarter to a third, Japan for 30 per cent, Canada 10–15 per cent, and significantly, the rest of the world accounting in some years for a proportion as high as 35 per cent. For the EEC as a whole in this period imports as a percentage of production rose from 6 to 12 per cent from 1960 to the late 1970s. For individual countries, import shares including EEC trade rose from 7 to 21 per cent of production in the UK, 16 to 30 per cent in West Germany, and from one-quarter to almost one-half in France.

An insight into the progressive internationalisation of the steel industry can be gained from a reflection on the reasons for the early predominance of US Steel, and on why these advantages have become progressively less relevant. One reason for the early dominance of US Steel was connected with its success at tying up with a few other firms the key sources of raw material, especially iron ore. Control of these rich sources of supply was of great benefit to the major integrated firms in keeping discipline within the industry, and gave a substantial cost advantage to the American industry as a whole *vis-à-vis* foreign producers.

But this advantage has been dissipated in the post-war world. In 1950, 15 per cent of the iron ore used in the world was involved in international trade, but this figure was 50 per cent in 1980. As a result of this increased activity, the differential advantages accruing to the US have been dissipated. In 1960, the price paid for coking coal was 63 per cent higher for Japan and 61 per cent higher for the EEC than for the US, while in 1980 Japan paid 5 per cent more and the EEC 23 per cent more. For iron ore, the changes have been even more striking – in 1960, Japan paid 20 per cent more, and the EEC 10 per cent more than the US, while by 1980 the US was paying 31 per cent *more* than Japan and 33 per cent *more* than the EEC. It has thus progressively become true that 'The ability of foreign [i.e. non-US] producers to shop around the globe for the cheapest and highest grade ore seems to be a greater advantage than the ownership of captive mines.'[62]

A second aspect of the early predominance of the large integrated American steel producers was their success at managing the industry at an unrivalled level of sophistication and complexity. From our present perspective, the task of management in the industry would seem to have been relatively straightforward, even in large firms producing and selling a relatively homogeneous product with seemingly few problems concerned with the advertising and the selling of the output. The largest firms in the industry were able to run their operations for long into the twentieth century with relatively straightforward functional (U-form) lines of control, compared with the sophisticated modes of management which were emerging in other industries. But at the turn of the century Carnegie's decision to move his fully integrated plants into the production of a broad line of finished steel products such as tubes and wires was an unprecedented act of diversification for the industry. It signalled the substantial lead which the US had over other countries in the techniques of managerial co-ordination, both for the production and for the marketing of such a wide range of commodities. These managerial advantages have long ago not only been dissipated, but to a great extent reversed: 'Compared to the largest Japanese companies, the world's most efficient steel producers, the integrated US producers suffer from significant outmoded capacity, poor location and layout, mismatched products and markets, and significant technological backwardness in energy productivity, resource utilization, and finishing capacity.'[63]

The Japanese industry – the battering ram of the new competition – is a phenomenon worthy of study all on its own. Without denying its unique characteristics, its post-war emergence can be viewed in the context of broader developments. Not many years ago, before the Japanese phenomenon had imposed itself upon the consciousness of economists, it was common among students of comparative economic systems to point to the self-evident irrationality of the decision of the pre-1956 regime in Hungary to ape the Soviet Union and build a steel industry, despite the absence of coal and iron ore reserves in the country. And yet this is precisely what the Japanese have done, with great success, but not uniquely: the difficulties currently being undergone by the Italian industry, in common with other countries in the EEC should not blind us to the immensity of their achievement – they are now after West Germany the largest producer of steel in Western Europe.

But it is the Japanese industry which has become by far the greatest producer in the capitalist world, and the general standard of excellence. For American economists looking for easy lessons to learn, the Japanese experience poses difficulties: while the high concentration in the US industry seemed to encourage the X-inefficiency which led to its downfall, the even higher concentration in the Japanese industry – overseen furthermore by a MITI whose views on co-ordinated behaviour have been a good deal more benign than those of the US Justice Department has been consistent with a tremendous dynamism. In two of the major innovations of recent decades, the basic oxygen process and continuous casting, the figures for the early 1980s are 80 per cent of the relevant capacity in Japan versus 65 per cent in the US for the first, and 58 versus 17 per cent for the second innovation, and this is after substantial reductions of total (and presumably the most obsolescent) capacity in the US industry.

What is even more instructive for the theory of competition is that many of the supposedly exogenous changes which seem to have facilitated the development of the Japanese industry *were to a great extent brought about by actions consciously taken by the Japanese themselves*. Falling world raw materials prices were aided by important new discoveries for which the

Japanese had provided finance and technical assistance; falling bulk transportation costs were partially engendered by the Japanese industry's pioneering innovation of the giant bulk carrier for raw materials. They also constructed their plants in modern, deep water port locations to facilitate the necessary imports of raw materials as well as the export of steel products. All of these activities had to be planned and co-ordinated together, and the range and success of this planning was as always a major determinant of the extent of the world market for steel.

Furthermore, at a time when the slothfulness of the large integrated companies in the US and the dynamism of the mini-mills seemed to be pointing in the direction of a decline in minimum efficient scale in the steel industry, the Japanese made their great success first with blast furnaces and then with plants functioning at hitherto unprecedented scales of output and levels of integration – beyond any magnitudes that could have been predicted on the basis of changes in the technical parameters of production. Their adaptation of already existing, but latest technology (e.g. the use of basic oxygen steelmaking furnaces) to their own needs was a prominent example of managerial, rather than technological innovation.

If such kinds of innovation have a Hayekian role in pushing out the boundaries of what had previously been perceived to be the objective, technical constraints on the scale of operation, and if such problems manifest themselves in an industry as straightforward as steel, they point to the gravest limitations to the possibility of using *ex post* data for the purposes of estimating the *ex ante* envelope of economies and dis-economies in an industry: earlier estimates of minimum efficient scale in the steel industry seem to have only an historical interest in light of what the Japanese have demonstrated to be possible. If indeed at any moment the constraints upon the firms in an industry are unknowable and unobservable, so that for extended periods *all* firms within an industry may be operating inside the frontier of the production function, it points to the possibility that the implementation of the whole Samuelsonian paradigm of constrained maximisation may not be operational in the context of industrial economics.

A focus on Japan in the context of steel, however, could be deceptive for an understanding of long run developments in this sector, because even nations far behind Japan in managerial sophistication have had demonstrable success in recent decades. The integrated steel mill was once emblematic of the highest levels of managerial co-ordination; relative to many other industries, however, such co-ordination is now a straight-forward proposition. Countries possessing the requisite managerial skills and a sufficient infrastructure of skilled labour have been able to launch their own steel industries, since an indigenous supply of raw materials is no longer a prerequisite.

Thus steel is a basic industry where some newly industralising countries have made substantial advances *vis-à-vis* the developed countries, so that, between 1965 and 1980, crude steel production grew by 48 per cent in the advanced market economies (by 25 per cent excluding Japan), while it grew by 410 per cent in Brazil, 184 per cent in Mexico and 4200 per cent in South Korea. The orders of magnitude of this production are not trivial, since Brazil is now the sixth largest producer in the capitalist world, about equal to the UK, while South Korea is the tenth and Mexico the fourteenth largest. It is important not to exaggerate the significance of these developments: in individual cases, these national industries may not have arisen and grown with such rapidity for purely economic reasons and, for the Third World as a whole there is still a substantial net deficit on the steel trade, with South Korea the only substantial net exporter. But there is no gainsaying that the development of the steel industries in these countries has widened the scope of the steel market internationally and exacerbated the problems of surplus capacity in developed countries.

More importantly, these developments have signalled future tendencies: in 1960, Japanese labour costs were 45 per cent of those in the US per ton of steel, and 30 per cent at their lowest (relative) point in 1970. By the 1980s, South Korea's labour costs in steel were estimated at between 6 and 14 per cent of those in the US, and only 15 to 17 per cent of those in Japan.[64] Labour costs make up only a small part of total costs in this industry, but for many of the new competitors, the managerial obstacles to operating new, purpose built factories on greenfield sites have not seemed insurmountable. Even in this relatively capital intensive industry the wage differential advantage to poorer countries may prove to be crucial as long as the production of steel continues to demand an important component of backbreaking labour.

As of the 1980s, only about 20 per cent of world steel production – double the share of 1970–takes place in less developed countries. But even the possibility that steel, this former symbol of western economic dominance, may move the way of textiles – where high value specialty items are produced in the rich countries, while much of the mass produced item is shipped in from the poor countries is an astounding turn of events. Even if in the future factory automation should remove the poor country advantage in steel production, it is inconceivable that the industry should ever return to the situation of a few decades ago, in which only a few firms, in a few countries could maintain within themselves the world standard of production on the basis of their exclusive possession of sources of cheap raw materials and their monopoly of the technical and managerial facility necessary to function efficiently in this sector.

Cars

Contemporary events in the car industry are even more remarkable. If steel was for a long time the province of a few great producers with the US playing a central role, in the car industry the role of the US was even more pre-eminent, and if anything, even more secure. With hindsight, it might have been possible to predict that the dissipation of the raw materials advantage possessed by the leading countries in steel production was likely to lead to a dispersal of the industry world-wide, since integrated steel manufacture for the last few decades had possessed the reputation of being an old-fashioned, straightforward managerial operation. The production and distribution of cars, on the other hand, seemed to be much more solidly based on the enormous economies of scale in their manufacture and – equally important – on the demands upon managerial coordination made by an operation of this scale and complexity: GM, after all, was simultaneously the epitome of the giant multi-faceted organisation, and a progenitor of the new managerial forms which had been developed to deal with business at this scale and complexity of operation.

The vagaries of government policies and exchange rates may yet dictate that the spectacle of the magisterial trio of US manufacturers GM, Ford and Chrysler losing one-fifth to one-third of their home market to imports in the 1980s will reverse itself. But these events are merely a symptom of the changes which have been transforming the world industry. A major problem with relating this story is the need to put into proper perspective the distinctive role of the Japanese industry as the – shall we say? – sparkplug of this explosion of competition. The issue is two-fold: first, the role of the Japanese has been so dramatic and unforeseen as to disguise the deeper processes which have made the transformation in the industry possible; secondly, Japanese firms have been so successful, all the while violating what had been the accepted canons of this well-established and supposedly well-understood industry that many accepted ideas about industrial structure and competition need re-examination in light of these events.

The overwhelming dominance of the US industry was established even before the First World War, with North American production making up 73 per cent of the world total in 1910, 88 per cent in 1929 and 79 per cent in 1937. The Big Three (GM, Ford and Chrysler) alone reached an all-time peak (including overseas production) of 75 per cent of world production in 1935. In addition to overseas production, the North American industry had an important presence in international trade, having 80 per cent of world exports in 1929 and 61 per cent in 1937.

The early ascendancy of the US car industry was partially a function of the unprecedented level of sophistication of the operation. The famous assembly line at the Ford plant, for instance, was made possible by an already existing system of interchangeable parts in the US engineering industry, a system which did not exist in Britain. The car industry above all others depended on a rich undergrowth of associated industries and technologies, where in many cases the US was already setting a world standard. Even in the present day, developing countries sometimes propose creating a car industry merely for the sake of its supposedly beneficial effects on the development of infrastructure: "'I'm not stupid,'" says Chao Yao-Tung, 67, Taiwan's minister of economic affairs and an MIT-trained engineer. "The real reason for promoting a big auto plant is to develop our machinery industries, which will make parts'".[65]

The response by European firms to this American challenge was surprisingly robust, especially in Britain. In the 1920s, Morris and Austin proceeded to adapt both the steel body building technology and the flow production techniques of the American companies. By the 1930s the British industry (including Ford UK) had emerged as the second greatest in the world (in one year – 1937 – achieving as much as 18 per cent of US production). Domestic firms were holding their own against Ford – the giant from America who had set up shop in Britain: Ford, after having become the largest seller in Britain in 1923 had been pushed decisively to third place by the late 1930s.

But the overwhelming advantages of American production in world-wide terms were the economies of scale which could be exploited in the American market and nowhere else. Thus, before the Second World War the Ford plant at Dagenham – with the most modern facilities – had substantially higher costs than Detroit due to lack of volume. The development of economies of scale in the car industry in this period appears almost inexorable. According to one estimate, minimum efficient scale in the industry was at a volume of 20,000 cars a year before the 1920s, and had then risen to about 100,000 a year due to the co-ordination advantages of integrating the stamping, casting and machinery processes.[66]

The problem of the inherently low volumes in European domestic markets was exacerbated by the European tendency to offer up a greater variety of models than on the American market. Thus, in 1937 in the UK, the six largest producers made 350,000 private cars with 40 different engine types, and even more chassis and body models – more designs than the top three American producers with a production of 3.5 million cars per annum. Furthermore, the top three British models made up only 27 per cent of sales compared with 54 per cent for the top three models in the American market. The presence in Britain in the late 1930s of a one-third share by firms apart from the three largest seemed merely a reflection of the lesser dynamism of the British industry, rather than a sign of a highly competitive market. There appeared to exist in the car industry a substantial volume effect – a major non-convexity coupled with a steep trade-off between product differentiation and cost minimisation.

The share of firms outside the Big Three was under 13 per cent in the US by the 1930s compared with almost 50 per cent in 1913. This long-term movement is generally taken to be a reflection of a 'survival of the fittest' development coupled with substantial and growing advantages of size. But questions remain about the nature of economies of scale in the inter-war period. The fall in market shares by the smaller firms in the US may be divided into two stages, first, a decline from 48 per cent in 1913 to 32 per cent in 1923, much of which must have embodied the impact of the new techniques of mass production, and then a precipitous drop from 28 per cent in 1929 to 13 per cent in 1933, from which the fringe sector never significantly recovered. This share of almost 30 per cent of the market sustained throughout the 1920s by the fringe firms is larger than the share taken by imports in the US market in most of the post-war world. Unquestionably, there is a good deal more to the analysis of a competitive process than the calculation of market shares, and, furthermore, the post-war challenge posed by importers in the US market has been far greater, and of a qualitatively different kind from that offered by fringe firms in the US in the 1920s. And yet the size of the share of these firms was substantial, and undoubtedly limited the ability of the Big Three to exercise their hegemony on the US market.

Whether the sudden collapse of the fringe sector during the great depression was purely a result of their weakness in real terms is a matter of doubt. The wash out of small firms between 1929 and 1933 may be interpreted in orthodox, or, more definitively in Hayekian terms[67] as an expression of the correct workings of the market-place. In this interpretation, the process of restructuring which takes place in a depression is seen as a form of economic purgation – it eliminates the excesses of overcapitalisation, and redistributes capacity into more productive hands. A contrary interpretation is that it is precisely in such periods of crisis that the financial advantages which accrue to large firms in a less than perfect capital market may be most strongly manifest: it is these financial advantages, as much as any real advantages accruing to the largest firms that determine which firms succeed in weathering a crisis.

Whatever interpretation is imposed upon these events, the changes which took place in the US car industry during the great depression illustrate the critical role of macroeconomic conditions to the general state of the competitive environment. Even for the central core of established firms, the deficiency of demand for their goods during a depression is disconcerting, as is the commonplace breakdown of industry discipline, as manifested by the (often secretive) outbreaks of price cutting among firms desperate to cover their costs. The consoling nature of such an environment is that it is highly unsalubrious for an overexpansion of capacity by existing core firms, for the entry of new firms and for the survival of fringe firms. All of these factors dictate that a depression leads to the development of an environment which in the long-term is less competitive than it otherwise would be.

But the period after the Second World War witnessed the greatest and most sustained period of economic growth in the history of capitalism, and the consequent explosion of competition which took place would have been inconceivable in any other context. This increase in world competition took place, furthermore, in a period when technological developments – an increase in minimum efficient scale to a half million cars a year – would seem to have improved the relative position of established producers in the car industry. It is not surprising, therefore, to read as late as 1959 of the hopelessness of matching American standards: 'Even the largest British motor manufacturers are too small for it to be profitable for them to adopt methods as highly automatic as those now being introduced into the American industry.'[68] And yet within a few years, a country whose industry and market was in 1959 tiny compared with that of the British would be setting new standards for the efficiency of the industry worldwide.

Long before the Japanese industry made its presence felt in the international arena, events had taken place which set the stage for the dramatic changes to come. The 1950s and 1960s were notable for a long-term erosion of the American dominance, as well as a gradual but significant increase in the international trade in cars. In the immediate post-war world, North America was able to recover its previous position, in 1950 accounting for about[69] 80 per cent of world production, as opposed to 15 per cent for Western Europe; by 1960, the North American share was just over 50 per cent, its lowest since the beginning of the century, and by 1970, Western Europe was producing over 40 per cent of the world total (one-quarter of this production from American owned firms), while the North American share was just over 30 per cent. Japanese production was now significant on a world scale, being half that of North America, where it had been less than one-tenth of either North America or Western Europe as recently as 1965.

But this introduction of some geographical symmetry in the world production of cars would not have been of such significance for the competitive environment if it had not been accompanied by a vast increase in the share of car production devoted to world trade. This share in 1950 was about 9 per cent, less than the shares achieved during the inter-war years, but by 1960 the share was unprecedented at almost 20 per cent, reaching almost 30 per cent in 1970 and almost 40 per cent in 1980.

Major national markets were transformed. After a brief foray in 1959 in which Europeans managed to take an unprecedented 10 per cent of the US market with small, fuel-efficient cars, they retreated to half that share of the market for most subsequent years. As late as 1975, however, they were able to divide a 20 per cent share of the US market evenly with the Japanese, and while European exports to the US in 1980 were only 30 per cent of Japan's when measured by volume, their high priced offerings were worth 54 per cent of Japan's sales.

It was the Japanese, however, who permanently transformed the American market. European entry to the US market has attempted to fill various niches, first that for small fuel-efficient cars and later for luxury cars. Japanese entry was also predicated on the sale of small cars, but where they differed from the Europeans was their success in taking maximum advantage of the cost saving possibilities of mass production. Thus, if in the 1960s the share of imports in the US market never exceeded 10 per cent, once the Japanese entered in force in the 1970s the shares were reaching 20 per cent, and by the 1980s were up to 30 per cent of the US market, even with 'voluntary' quotas in force.

The other great market which has been transformed by international influences has been that of Western Europe. Post-war multinational investment in the car industry had a direct influence in disseminating American practices, and indirectly by engendering competitive responses from domestic firms. The other great influence has been that of international trade. Imports of Japanese cars, with 10 per cent of the West European market by 1980, have been of less significance than the increase in trade among West European countries. Trade within Western Europe increased from 19 per cent of total production in 1960 to 36 per cent in 1980. Within the key producer nations – France, Italy, the UK, West Germany, Spain and Sweden – nations which in earlier times had taken care of their needs almost solely with domestic production – the share of intra-European trade had increased from 7 per cent in 1960 to 22 per cent of production in 1980. By the latter date, the shares of the domestic market in cars taken by international trade in these producing countries was between one-quarter and one-half.

Part of the general increase in the world trade in cars was due to technological developments – in the post-war world the international trans-shipment of cars became a more viable procedure than previously, the pre-war problems having been a major motivation for the construction of the large number of assembly plants in different countries by Ford and GM. The general lowering of tariffs and other obstacles to trade has also had an important expansionary effect on trade, especially for countries within the EEC. But these factors have combined with a general extension of the horizon of car manufacturers, most especially in the direction of a renewed determination to realise the potential gains from volume production.

The question of the limits and the extent of economies of scale in the car industry is a complex one. It has been suggested[70] that the advantages of high volume production are significant enough to dictate that even in 1970, the cost of similar cars was 30 to 60 per cent higher in Western Europe than in the US. Europe was still paying a high price for its great variety of product models and national industries, which prevented the cost savings of high volume production from being realised.

This imperative to realise volume effects has been central to the development of car manufacture outside of North America. In Western Europe, exports (including intra-regional sales) have taken one-half of post-war production throughout the whole period. In Japan, exports made up only 22 per cent of total production in 1970, and only accounted for half of production as late as 1980. But it is the Japanese car industry, with the conjuncture of the two oil shocks and the maturation of the Japanese industry in the 1970s which has been responsible for setting off an irreversible set of changes in the industry world-wide. The new situation resulted in an unprecedented opportunity to sell large amounts of small, fuel-efficient cars on the American market.

What has been the secret of Japanese success? According to one authority it has been due to 'low labour costs, harmonious labour relations, a well-educated workforce, a high level of process automation, advanced quality control, and a flexible relationship between car firms and component suppliers (helping, for instance, to reduce stocks to a minimum). Japanese firms have now established a new standard of best practice in the organisation of automobile production'.[71] But how had this system been brought about? For several years, many foreigners believed that Japanese success could be explained purely by the first factor – it was a result of the low wages paid in Japan. It seems clear that deeper forces have been at work.

The Japanese experience in the car industry offers up encouragement and disappointment both to the advocates of planning and to defenders of the efficacy of market competition. The principles for the industry were established by MITI in 1952: 'unnecessary' introductions of foreign capital and technology (including multinational entry) were restricted, while 'desirable' forms were encouraged, so that in 1952 Nissan made a seven year agreement with Austin (UK) to assemble completely-knocked-down kits of 2000 cars a year under royalty, with domestic production of the components to be achieved within three years. In the Law for the Development of the Machinery Industry of 1956 and in subsequent extensions, MITI pushed for the rationalisation of the industry, encouraging mergers and setting target dates for the achievement of US quality and productivity standards.

But Japanese producers were not docile and compliant in the manner of the foreign stereotype of Japan, Inc. Smaller producers often rebelled against being 'rationalised', and adherence to MITI's directives was often far from complete by the larger companies. The forces behind the great international success of the Japanese car firms include both the protection from overseas competition and takeover in the early years and the framework of long-term planning afforded by the government, as well as the aggressive attitude engendered in these firms by a domestic market which is by reputation a ferociously competitive one.

Whatever the underlying impetus to the Japanese industry, its distinctive aspect in world terms has been its great success in managerial innovation. While using the same underlying technology as other developed countries, it has managed to demonstrate that even such exalted institutions as GM were operating well within the interior of the industry's 'production function'. One aspect of these innovations has been the substantial savings in inventories through the *kanban* system discussed in chapter 8. Superficially, it may seem odd that the Japanese have been so successful at the integration and co-ordination necessary for such a system, since the levels of vertical integration (ratios of value added to sales) by the major car assemblers in Japan appear to be much lower than in the US – in fact, the levels are much closer to those existing in a nation whose car industry has not been notable for excellence in co-ordination and control – Britain. But such close collaboration seems to have been maintained between Toyota and the most crucial of its 44,000 suppliers, not only for its present needs but in forward planning for new products and other future developments, that inventory holdings in the assembly plant are measured in hours, while the norm in North America was traditionally measured in months.

We have noted in chapter 8 that in this skilfully co-ordinated relationship with suppliers Japanese firms have made a substantial alteration in the pattern of managerial decision-making on the factory floor of the main assembly plant. In the 'classic' US pattern, it was the job of 'the line' – part of the administrative staff – to see to it that the assembly line ran smoothly. It was the job of workers to work. In the Japanese system, workers, co-operating in teams are apparently given a good deal more autonomy and responsibility for the smooth operation of the assembly line and they actively participate both in the genesis and in the installation of new techniques and processes of production. These changes on the factory floor of the assembly plant are probably a necessary concomitant of the *kanban* innovations, since the active participation of the workforce is undoubtedly necessary if manufacture is to proceed smoothly with such narrow margins for error in inventories.

As in the steel industry, the major Japanese innovations have been almost wholly managerial: 'Our assessment at MIT ... is that the Japanese operate with only 60 per cent of the labour force employed by a US company using identical machinery.'[72] Japanese firms have not altered the fundamental aspects of the technology of the assembly line. It is somewhat unclear whether the techniques employed by Japanese management are *in extenso* transferable abroad: on the one hand, GM executives were said to have been 'stunned' by the efficiency of the Toyota run plant in California in their joint venture, and the Nissan plant in the UK appears to be the most efficient in the country. On the other hand, Japanese executives have claimed that overseas plants can never be as efficient as those in Japan.

Normative interpretations of this system are not easy to make. Is the relationship between the great assemblers and the suppliers in the Japanese car industry to be interpreted as a successful balance between the co-ordination advantages of vertical integration and the flexibility of a market form, or is it merely a device for exploiting workers in the supplying industries, who receive far lower wages and who do not receive the benefits of the famous lifetime employment contract of workers in the assembly plants? Does the greater responsibility of workers in the Japanese assembly plant signal a liberation from the older Taylorist view of the narrow role of workers in the process of manufacture, or is it an extension of traditional modes of authoritarianism and paternalism – the giving of responsibility without power? Sadly, such questions are beyond our scope here.

What is clear is that with the Japanese intervention on the world scene, the world car industry will never be the same. In the mid 1980s, it was claimed that, in the absence of quotas and other inhibitions, Japanese, European and Third World imports could have captured over 40 per cent of the US market. While this particular circumstance may be at least in part a function of such temporary factors as the value of the dollar internationally, the flood of new competitors is now taken to be a permanent aspect of the scene, so that the traditionally captive car dealers in the US are starting to operate 'supermarkets', offering a dozen different brands to their customers. There are fears in Western Europe that changes in US government policy and in exchange rates could re-direct international competition in their direction, either in the form of a combination of Japanese and Third World imports, or through US–Japanese co-operation, forged through their recent joint ventures. In Europe, as in America the pressures of this competition have engendered new pressures on the workforces of the major car firms.

The main economic factors determining the nature of the future competitive environment are first, the response of rivals to the methods introduced by the Japanese; secondly, the role of the Third World, both as a supply source and as the initiators of new competition; thirdly, the 'new flexibility', with its implications for the building of a 'world car' and for minimum efficient scale in the industry, and lastly, the role of the rapidly emerging series of joint ventures between firms. What is the likely effect of these ventures upon competition, and what effect will they have upon minimum efficient scale in the industry, and upon established firms' perspectives of their vested interests?

The response of US firms to the new wave of competitiveness and to the challenge of the Japanese methods is of especial interest. As late as 1984, GM and Ford executives in Europe could complain of a failure of their companies to adapt products to the European market due to a 'not-invented-here' syndrome – a disbelief in anything not generated in Detroit. But in the most advanced thinking coming out of America 'The old ideas that financial integration [i.e. vertical integration], top-down decision making with tight control of product information, multiple sourcing and geographic dispersion [i.e. the traditional American system] are the keys to production efficiency have given way to operational coordination combined with financial disaggregation, increased single sourcing, and geographic concentration [i.e. the Japanese conceptions].'[73]

The manifestations of this new approach in the great American car firms are as yet rather oblique. In an immediate sense, the influence of the Japanese system has slowed the development of what had until then been taken to be one of the grandest conceptions of modern American management – the development of the 'world car'. One aspect of this conception – of a uniform, internationally acceptable product, sourced from the cheapest producers world-wide – has run against the new-found orthodoxy that suppliers should be close to final assembly to maximise co-ordination and to minimise the holding of inventories.

More profoundly, contemporary events have generated a palace revolution among the great American car companies, most strikingly at GM. GM, it is claimed, is proceeding with a total revamping of the system of control inherited from Alfred Sloan. In the self-proclaimed stream-lining of 1984, two super groups were created to replace the old structure of seven divisions and a major subsidiary. The real jewel in the new crown, however, is the Saturn project, supposedly a self-contained entity intended simultaneously to be the focus for the design and production of a car under new, and unprecededly automated conditions, and to be a laboratory for experimenting with new techniques of all kinds. All of these reforms take place under the fashionable precept of engendering autonomy for the subgroups involved, but this seems unlikely: the formation of these massive supergroups comes across as nothing less than a re-centralisation – a movement away from the M-form structure.

The purpose of this re-centralisation seems to be to gain maximum advantage from the massive expenditures that GM has made in recent years on 'hi-tech' companies such as Electronic Data Systems. It is unsurprising that GM should be trying to take full advantage of its size with a high level of integration and tight co-ordination of its affairs. For all their fashionability, contemporary managerial doctrines of the autonomy of 'self-contained decision units' within the larger organisation seem to have little to do with the practice within the great Japanese giants, which exhibit great flexibility, but within the context of highly centralised organisations which are able to reap the benefits of integrated planning and co-ordination.

The competitive response by the giant American firm has not at present proved very successful, but the effort being made is symptomatic of the tremendous pressures coming forth from this new environment. Whatever the long-term outcome of these grand projects, it appears that the new situation has already had its effect on ways of doing business in the US car industry: 'A recent Commerce Dept. study concludes that better management, automation, changed work rules, and other efficiencies have slashed the breakeven point of domestic producers by an impressive 30% since 1980.'[74]

The Third World enters into the picture of the state of competition in the contemporary car industry at two levels – as a cheap labour source for components and as an originator of new competition. Certainly many car firms must find the statistics tempting – hourly wages in manufacturing industries in Brazil, South Korea and Mexico were respectively 9, 10 and 13 per cent those of the United States.[75] But these possibilities have been analysed for the US[76] and there appears less likelihood of these kinds of developments than is first apparent. Major mechanicals (engines, transmissions) are highly capital intensive, and under the best possible conditions could yield savings, but as of the mid 1980s would still leave the American firm with higher costs than its Japanese rivals. 'Finish' parts (exterior body stampings, seats, etc.) are bulky to ship and must meet precise specifications. Moreover, wide geographical dispersal of these parts militates against the contemporary desire to centralise the sourcing of inputs, especially those which might interfere with the flow of production. Only minor mechanicals (starters, radiators, etc.) which involve much simpler techniques might be amenable to Third World sourcing, but the very simplicity of the techniques involved may make them suitable for automated manufacture in the future.

In the 1980s, much sourcing in Third World countries is done not for the sake of cost savings but to gain access to their markets by meeting domestic contents requirements. Among Third World nations, South Korea would seem to be the only producer with the possibility of emerging as a significant exporter in the near future, as it tries to fill the low price segment of the US market partially abandoned by Japan. The latter nation's offerings have become more 'up market' in the face of the constraints on the volume of their imports into the US. But by the early 1980s other Third World nations, including Brazil, Mexico and Taiwan were producing cars with high levels of local content (60 per cent in the case of Mexico and Taiwan, and 98 per cent in the case of Brazil), and they may yet demonstrate that car manufacture is not the exclusive province of developed countries.

A further factor entering into the contemporary equation has been the development of the 'new flexibility': 'Because of the changes in the technological outlook of the industry, the view has been put forward that it is going through a process of "dematurity" where the technology is diverging rather than converging. This results in a less vertically integrated industry where medium sized producers stand a much greater chance of survival through skilful exploitation of particular technologies and market niches'.[77] Thus contemporary technological developments seem to be nullifying the traditional trade-off between highly automated manufacture of a standardised model and the more labour intensive demands of manufacture which contain fundamental alterations in design. With the use of robotics and computer-aided design, it should become easier for medium sized producers to bring out variants on their basic model: minimum efficient scale should fall to a fraction of its present level. A given production run of, say, one-quarter to one-half million cars a year is now capable of yielding only one model on a cost-efficient basis, but with the new techniques, it is suggested, a medium-sized firm could offer up a full line of products without any loss in efficiency. The development of these new modes of manufacture, along with tariffs, quotas, local content requirements and government support for medium-sized firms make it unlikely that a homogeneous world or even European car is likely to dominate markets in the future.

But the events leading to an increase in competitiveness and a lowering of minimum efficient scale in the contemporary car industry have not been purely of a technical nature. Despite their superficially anti-competitive appearance, the development of joint ventures between firms internationally has also tended to generate a reduction in minimum efficient scale and to increase competition in the world car market. Thus, new entry to the US market is facilitated for Hyundai of South Korea when Mitsubishi agrees to market cars for them; Daihatsu (part of the Toyota group) announces that entry into the European market could be profitable with sales of as few as 50 to 100 thousand cars and other vehicles a year if its entry could be part of a joint venture with a European firm. As of the early 1970s, GM, Ford and Chrysler have had substantial minority stakes in the Japanese car firms Isuzu, Toyo Kogyo and Mitsubishi respectively and have distributed these cars under their own name in the US. Medium-sized producers are able to use these joint ventures to fill out their range (e.g. the sale of small Renaults by Volvo through its Scandinavian dealer network), for the cross-purchase of major components with other suppliers and for the joint development of products and technologies.

The long-term effects of the development of close relations between the great international car companies may yet engender patterns of oligopolistic familiarity like the ones seen in earlier times in many domestic markets. As of the mid-1980s, however, help received by the great American firms from their Japanese rivals in developing, manufacturing or importing cars to the US market – in order to stem the tide of Japanese imports – is either facilitating the sale of cars manufactured abroad for smaller producers who lack developed marketing facilities in the US, or, in the case of Toyota's plant in the US established in co-operation with GM, it gives Toyota useful experience in the problems of producing cars in the US.

These close relations between firms could be a transitional phase, prior to the eventual dominance of the world industry by one, or a handful of firms. Such outcomes seem unlikely on the basis of past experience. For the foreseeable future, the car industry will continue to exhibit the symptoms of being increasingly competitive, and the deeper causes which brought about this condition are unlikely to abate.

Semiconductors
Some readers may have derived a special satisfaction from the use of the terms 'market' and 'industry' and the use of market share data in the context of the above discussion of these traditional sectors, steel and cars, and some indeed may have convinced themselves that the events taking place in these industries can be reformulated and satisfactorily understood in the context of the structure → behaviour paradigm. Such temptations will be less present in the discussion to follow of the semiconductor and electronics industries.

But these problems are not qualitatively different from those found in our more traditional sectors. It is simply that, because events are moving so quickly in electronics, the essential nature of the competitive process is revealed, undisguised by atavism and tradition. In other sectors, such as steel and cars, the *failure* of firms for long periods to compete technologically when such opportunities were available could give the illusion that there existed structural, technological constraints inherent in these sectors which then determined firm behaviour. In the electronics industry, the existence of such objective, well-defined constraints and exogenously determined boundaries are self-evidently illusory.

In reviewing the competitive history of the semiconductor industry, the relevant questions are not about the possibility of describing the electronics industry through the categories of the structure → behaviour model, because it clearly cannot, but what kind of dynamic approaches – Schumpeterian, Hayekian, or otherwise – can be used to help explain the behaviour of firms, behaviour *which shaped the environment* in this fast moving sector. The transformations still emerging in this area have little to do with the effects of exogenous technical change, nor can they be explained in Schumpeterian terms as the result of a great, discontinuous innovation put forth by a giant firm. These changes are more closely associated with the ways in which institutional factors and the *economic* response of firms re-formed the structure of the environment in which these firms function, which then reflexively caused changes in the behaviour of firms inside and outside of this market.

The second issue is the nature and the significance of the changes which the semiconductor industry has generated beyond its own borders. In an immediate sense, the sector has been intimately shaped by its relationships with its users, most especially with the military but more profoundly with the computer industry. But the progress of semiconductors has in its wake created new and unforeseen products – industries such as microcomputers and various new forms of household electronics, and is continuing to transform older ones such as telecommunications. Through these changes the distinctions between all these sectors has proceeded to blur, including those which in former times seemed to separate semiconductor technology and semiconductor firms from other branches of electronics.

The competitive history of the semiconductor industry focuses on two periods, the transistor phase, which lasted from the inception of the industry in the late 1940s to the early 1960s and the integrated circuit phase from the early 1960s to the early 1970s. The industry was born in the US with the invention of the transistor at Bell Labs (the research constituent of AT&T) in the late 1940s. A distinguishing aspect of this technology is that, like nuclear power but unlike most previous developments of economic significance, it was brought forth by a scientific, abstract conception. The crucial, and central role of science in this sector should not obscure the fact that semiconductors are only of economic significance if they can be produced in large numbers, and cheaply. The exceptional characteristic of the American industry, and the factor that permitted it to develop – and remain so dynamic – was the almost ecological symbiosis which was established in the 1950s and the 1960s in the industry between different classes of firms.

There were, first, a few large manufacturers, epitomised by AT&T (which like IBM later on, produced only for its own needs), but including as well such vertically integrated giants as RCA and General Electric and six others – the traditional manufacturers of vacuum tubes (valves) – most of whom eventually left the industry (though some re-entered later through merger). These firms managed to simulate almost perfectly the model of the Schumpeterian large firm which plans in the long-term and produces fundamental innovations. In the mid-1950s, for instance, these tube manufacturers, with a one-third (and declining) share of the semiconductor market were receiving half the patents in the industry, while one-quarter were going to Bell. In the case of Bell Labs, not only was fundamental research undertaken (in 1959, a majority of major innovations in the industry were attributable to Bell, and even in the 1970s 80 per cent of the basic research in the industry emerged from AT&T and IBM), but great efforts were made to see that the new technology was widely dispersed, the symposia held under their auspices in 1952 and 1956 being critical to the development of the industry.

But while the semiconductor industry was born in science, the rapidity with which problems of economic viability were solved cannot simply be attributed to a fortuitous malleability of Nature in this field of endeavour. It was not the great tube manufacturers with their fundamental research who accomplished in half a generation the feat of transforming the semi-conductor from a scientific curiosity with limited commercial application to the dominant phenomenon of modern technology. The key agents of this change were a set of interlopers – the merchant manufacturers – firms whose only commitment to and experience in the electronics industry was connected to the production of semiconductors.

With the demonstration of the scientific reality of the semiconductor effect, the main problems to be solved were not theoretical ones, but were related to the techniques – the arts of manufacture in this field. In this most scientific of fields, it was knowledge of almost an empirical, craft-based kind which was the bottleneck to development. In their eagerness to make money in the short-term, rather than to confront fundamental theoretical issues, it was largely the new (and at the time small) merchant firms who solved crucial problems – Texas Instruments was the first company to come out with a silicon transistor in 1954, long before it had been perfected in every respect. Silicon, moreover, was not the best semiconductor material from a theoretical point of view, and in a different economic environment more elegant, but less practical solutions to the problems of semiconductor material might have been pursued.

A second landmark in the practical application of the semiconductor was the development at Fairchild in the late 1950s of the planar technique, which greatly facilitated batch processes for the large scale reproduction of semiconductors, making the integrated circuit possible (which then emerged from Texas Instruments and Fairchild in the early 1960s). Lastly, the introduction of the MOS semiconductor in the mid-1960s by General Microelectronics and General Instrument made possible the introduction by Intel in 1971 of the microprocessor – a computer's central processing unit on a single chip.

It was thus a complex interaction of institutions with differing time horizons which appears to have been crucial to the development of the industry in its critical phases. Bell and the other established vertically integrated manufacturers were the greatest source of fundamental break-throughs. An intermediate term perspective was provided by the more ambitious of the merchants such as Fairchild and Texas Instruments. Even these firms were constrained in their actions by a growing host of smaller merchants with even shorter time horizons, happy either to fill market niches left open by the larger firms, or to copy the designs of their superiors and to undercut them on price if given the opportunity. Since customers often demand that a second source be available for their purchases of a particular item, the activities of these firms as imitators have not always been as unwelcome to the great merchants as might first appear.

How and why were the merchants so successful at defeating the established vertically integrated tube manufacturers? Note that the competitive dynamism displayed by the great merchant producers in the US overwhelmed not only the established electronics producers in their own country, but overseas as well: European firms, also predominantly vertically integrated and with a long-term history of involvement in the electronics industry, seemed well equipped to compete technically with the US industry in the 1950s, and managed to keep the European industry relatively self sufficient in this period. But the Europeans were left behind by the innovations made by the US merchants in the 1960s and 1970s. Japan as well failed to begin to match technological developments within the US industry until the mid-1970s, and the industry probably survived because of government protection. The semiconductor divisions of Japan's vertically integrated firms, like many of the defeated US firms and most European firms (but unlike the two most successsful vertically integrated firms – IBM and AT&T) were largely dedicated to the production of electronics for consumers goods, a sector whose demands were far from the frontiers of technology.

It would be easy to attribute the success of the American merchants to the freedom of action and the added incentives of being 'their own bosses'. But such an explanation fails to suggest why this merchant phenomenon should have been so much more prevalent in the US than in Europe. The aggressive nature of the American merchant firms in forms of technological competition was at least partially engendered by their key end users, the military and the computer industry who were primarily interested in products that advanced the state of the art. The military, with its enormous funds, was willing to invest in long-term and often somewhat speculative projects – purchasing, for example, all of the early production of integrated circuits and well over half the production through the mid 1960s. The sustained influence of users in the relatively large US computer and (to a lesser extent) telecommunications industries was probably of even greater importance in the development of a long-term bias in the American semiconductor industry in favour of forms of competition which advanced the technology of semiconductors. But even here, the substantial military support which went to the computer and telecommunications industries was clearly of enormous indirect benefit to the development of the semiconductor sector, since US government contracts covered all computer production in the mid-1950s and half of production as late as the early 1960s.

But where did these merchant firms come from, and why did they arise primarily in the US, and not in Europe? By the end of the Second World War, the US not only had a vast scientific and engineering establishment, but was turning out graduates whose central commitment was to the *commercial* application of their knowledge,[78] an attitude which appears to be significantly different from that which existed in Europe at the time. It might be suggested that such a phenomenon is uniquely American, but even in the US no earlier period of history can point to such commercial aggressiveness from such a large body of scientists and technicians.

The striking characteristic of the scientists and technicians in the American industry was the alacrity with which they left secure positions at the great establishments such as Bell Labs to form their own firms, only to spin off into new ones. Fairchild Semiconductor was formed in 1957 by eight individuals who had previously worked for Shockley Semiconductor Laboratories, Shockley himself having been one of the inventors of the transistor at Bell Labs. Fairchild itself later engendered other firms. At a conference in California in 1969, of 400 semiconductor people present, less than two dozen had never worked for Fairchild: as of the late 1970s, at least 41 companies have been formed by former Fairchild employees. This rapid job mobility engendered rapid dispersion of ideas and techniques, reinforced by a culture which, while extremely commercially minded, had as well a scientific conviviality which generated relatively free exchanges of ideas and techniques in the industry.

Thus the indubitable *potential* for technological developments in this area was reinforced in America by the emergence of firms which were capable of realising these possibilities in a remarkably short period of time, making for an environment which was highly competitive at the level of technological innovation. Reinforcing this competitive atmosphere were the significant learning curve and volume effects present in the production of semiconductors: in the mid-1960s Texas Instruments estimated that, as a general rule, its costs fell to 73 per cent of the previous level every time the volume of production doubled. The existence of these effects generated a highly competitive pricing policy among producers based on forward projections of costs at high volumes (though some companies like Intel have tried on occasion to take advantage of temporary monopoly positions with high initial prices). The problem of industry 'discipline' is further exacerbated by the fact that much of the new demand is not to replace existing electronics, but is for new applications, so that co-ordinated price and product forecasts between firms are especially difficult. The following reminiscences from US semiconductor executives gives some flavour of the atmosphere which emerged in the industry in the 1950s and 1960s:

> most managers in semiconductors really believe they can make something at any given day for half the cost that their accountants tell them to make it for and the net result is to fire the accountant and get a new one. . . . I grew up on it. I grew up in situations where I figured out I could make something for $8 and my boss said you gotta make it for 6 and I said I can't make it for 6 and I saw behind his eyes that if you can't make it for 6 I'll go hire someone else who will make it for 6. Then I realized the other guy was just a better liar. So I said all right and I'll figure out how to make it for 6. I made it for 6. By then some other company was offering it for 5 because they had a

bigger liar. . . . If the semiconductor managers weren't such idiots, we might not have integrated circuits where they are today, because somebody would have said, 'Look, I can't manufacture them at the cost I've got to sell them.' It was the wrong decision, but it has benefited us all.[79]

The coming of the integrated circuit in the early 1960s witnessed the victory of the merchants over the vertically integrated tube manufacturers in the US and the absolute domination of the world industry by US producers. Between 1960 and 1969 imports from the US as a percentage of the markets for semiconductors in France, Great Britain, West Germany and Japan rose from 11 to 37 per cent, to which should be added the additional output derived from the construction of additional assembly and fabrication plants abroad by US firms, the total of which rose in this period from 8 to 39. (Subsequent falls in the percentage of direct US exports to these countries, with the exception of Japan, can be accounted for by increases in output from these plants.)

The reasons for an increase in the gap between the US industry and the rest of the world in the 1960s are a continuation of tendencies which had been present in the 1950s. These are, namely, the lower share of the US industry devoted to consumer goods (under 20 per cent in the US compared with over 30 per cent in Western Europe), the exceptionally high level of government (especially military) support, with the US government still accounting for one-half of all expenditure on electronics in the country in the mid-1960s and one additional factor: the introduction of the integrated circuit signalled a rapid acceleration in the rate of innovation in the US industry, with the developments taking place in a highly cumulative fashion. The lag in the introduction of the integrated circuit technology in Europe, which was of the same length as the earlier lag in transistor technology now led to a bigger shortfall than previously in the state of the art.

As late as the mid-1980s, the US had just under 50 per cent of the world's merchant semiconductor production (i.e. excluding production for firms' internal consumption), with the Japanese at 40 per cent, Western Europe at about 10 per cent and with only a small fraction for the rest of the world (including a rapidly emerging South Korean presence). Japan has now emerged as the world's leading producer, with Japanese firms holding the top three places in dollar sales. The most remarkable development has been the rise of the Japanese industry, which had as little as one-quarter of the world market as recently as 1980, at which time the US share had been about 60 per cent. Even this change underestimates the transformation in the Japanese industry, which with 5 per cent of the US market in Dynamic Random Access Memories – D-RAMs (which temporarily store the data being processed in a computer) in 1980, had control of 90 per cent of that market by the mid 1980s.

The rise of the Japanese industry as a major threat to the US predominance has come about in Japan in the usual manner – a co-ordinated effort by the large integrated firms starting in the mid-1970s directed towards the production of high volume standardised commodity components, most especially RAMs. In the 1980s Europe has responded to its generally dependent position in semiconductors and to the dual threat of Japan and the US production with the purchase of several American semiconductor producers by large European firms (for instance, the purchase of Signetics by Philips), but also by attempts to match the centralised research funding of MITI and the US military with the EEC's co-operative research programme Esprit, which includes work on advanced chip technology, and the Joint European Facilities, a joint research project between the largest semiconductor manufacturers in Europe, Philips of the Netherlands, Siemens of West Germany and Thomson of France.

The response of American firms to the Japanese challenge (they attribute the precipitous fall in 256K RAM prices [from $84 in January 1984 to $3 by the Autumn of 1985] to Japanese 'dumping') has been five fold. They have asked for import controls, accelerated the process of moving assembly plants to cheap labour areas, promoted Sematech, a government funded co-operative research project among these traditionally fiercely independent semiconductor manufacturers and increased joint ventures with, among other groups, the Japanese. There has also been a substantial retreat of the major American producers (except Texas Instruments) from standardised commodity production in favour of customised, or semicustomised chips. Once again, the Japanese seem unrivalled in arm's length forms of mass production, where significant volume effects can be exploited.

What is the likely shape of the industry in the future? In chapter 8, we noted two countervailing tendencies in firm integration at present. A first tendency – the expansion of modern management's horizon to all aspects of the business operation – implies a further movement in the direction of vertical integration. In electronics, the most prominently successful firms at present – IBM and the great Japanese companies – are all highly integrated operations, and it is natural to think these firms represent the future shape of the industry. The second tendency, however, implies that increasing competitiveness in many sectors (e.g., those producing raw materials) makes possible a greater use of the market in a vertically disintegrated way. Either of these tendencies, or some combination of them, could emerge as dominant in the relation between semiconductors and the electronics industry.

In the first case high volume production of standardised semiconductors could continue to lower the cost per function of these elements so rapidly and to such an extent that customisation of semiconductor devices ceases to be cost effective: if the chips are cheap enough relative to their desired uses, it may prove economical to use standardised versions of these components in a 'wasteful' manner rather than customised versions. Semiconductors could indeed become a commodity (like iron ore!) and no motivation for integration between semiconductor manufacturers and others would be likely to emerge. In the 1970s, for instance, firms like Texas Instruments integrated forward into calculator manufacture and electronic games, thinking that their production of the semiconductors at the heart of these devices would give them a commercial advantage; the commodification of the kinds of semiconductors used in calculators – the fact that they could be purchased easily and cheaply on the open market by any (non vertically integrated) manufacturer dictated that no great advantage has accrued to the great semiconductor producers in these fields, and in many cases they have withdrawn from this kind of production.

In the second case, which at the moment seems the stronger possibility, there will be further integration within the industry, either following the successful example of the great Japanese firms and IBM, or in the form of joint ventures and partnerships of various kinds between suppliers and purchasers. The motivation for integration is of two kinds. There is a strong feeling in the industry that cross-subsidisation of the integrated firms' semiconductor divisions has promoted long-term growth both in semiconductors and for these firms as a whole by avoiding interruptions in semiconductor development brought about by (temporary) periods of low profitability. Furthermore, there is a desire to minimise transactions costs between suppliers and purchasers. This development is linked to the growing importance of semi-custom chips (application specific integrated circuits – ASICs), which came about with the growing automation of chip design and the desire of computer manufacturers to minimise the number of semiconductors used. The use of semi-customised devices makes closer links between suppliers and purchasers imperative if the new product is not to be delayed. As Pat Brockett, managing director of National Semiconductor's European Semiconductor Division has said 'If we are going to develop a piece of technology of the complexity we are now dealing with, we have to understand exactly what our customers want.'[80] Thus, many of IBM's rivals in the computer industry integrated backward in the late 1970s to the production of semiconductors, while others have started to make *kanban*-like demands upon their suppliers for customisation of product and 'just-in-time' delivery.

The second issue to be discussed here concerns the influence that the transformations in the semiconductor industry have had on other sectors. This question may be conveniently addressed in the context of the third phase in semiconductor history, the Large Scale Integration or LSI phase (merged for our purposes with a fourth phase, the Very Large Scale Integration – VLSI phase, beginning in the 1980s). The LSI era was initiated in 1971 with the introduction by Intel of the microprocessor, a computer's central processing unit on a chip and in 1972 with the introduction by Texas Instruments of the microcomputer, which adds memory and input–output devices to the microprocessor, so that a complete system or subsystem was now available on a single chip.

The introduction of the microprocessor signalled a new role for the semiconductor in electronics, and for electronics in the whole economy, even though changes have been continuing apace both before and after the year 1971. Silicon transistors fell in price from $18 in 1951 to under $1 in 1965, and integrated circuits went from $50 in 1962 to $8 in 1965 to $1 in 1972. The fall in the cost per electronic function (per gate) has been even more astounding, a decline of 500 fold in the period 1960 to 1980 having been estimated.[81] But it is not the decline in price *in isolation* which has made such a difference in the status of the semiconductor industry in the whole economy since the early 1970s: it is more how these changes in the cost per function and in the size of semiconductors have permitted other areas of the economy to initiate qualitatively new uses for these components.

The issue of quality, and of qualitative change, leads us to question once again the fundamental presuppositions of orthodox economics in this domain. There are two approaches in this tradition – the general equilibrium approach, in which any changes in quality would cause a new commodity to be defined, and the various attempts which have been made to measure the 'price equivalent' of a quality change. But as Peter Swann has pointed out, these latter approaches 'seem to suggest that the difference between quality innovation and price reductions is not necessarily of great economic significance ... Indeed, the very expression "quality-adjusted" seems to suggest that quality is a nuisance, which obscures the conventional price and quantity analysis ... from the point of view of competitive strategy, quality innovation – indeed product innovation in general – is seen as a means of avoiding price competition; [but] the product innovation and the cost reducing process innovation are rather different. A framework within which they are indistinguishable is to some extent missing the point'. Miniaturisation is an example of a change which cannot be given a simple equivalent in price terms: 'When miniaturisation is important – in many control systems, instruments, microcomputers, watches, calculators etc. – a new miniature component is not merely equivalent to a collection of old bulky components.'[82]

There are two forms of this qualitative change which are of special interest to us here. There are those changes emanating from the semiconductor industry which blur the lines of demarcation within the electronics industry itself, and then there are changes which are helping to transform the modes of behaviour – the competitive practices – of firms outside of this domain. The effects of these changes are complex and reflexive: the peculiar dynamism of the semiconductor industry, which has always been associated with the telecommunications and computer industries, has now caused all of these areas to interact in unforeseen ways. Firms outside the electronics industry are also under the pressure of forces in the direction of greater competitiveness, and both influence and are influenced by the electronics industry. Indeed, in the absence of a business world desirous of and intent on making use of these new tools, the electronics industry, as a servant exclusively of military and scientific needs would have taken a very different form than it has today.

In Britain, the state of the electronics industry has been summarised as folllows:

> 'The problems that all the British electronics companies face have nothing to do with a general economic downturn', says Mr. Mike Sperring of stockbrokers Scrimgeour Vickers. 'They have to do with oversupply in the market, be it of microchips, mainframe computers, microcomputers or telecommunications equipment.' In all these sectors, international competition has been sharpened by fierce price cutting and massive capital investments by the dominant US and Japanese suppliers. Moreover, barriers, which have been long separated parts of the industry have been crashing down under the impact of technological convergence.[83]

While few would deny that this picture of a cumulatively more competitive environment accurately describes the state of the British electronics industry in relation to the rest of the world, one might think this notion has less relevance in other contexts. In the mainframe computer industry in the US, for instance, the magisterial IBM actually increased its share by ten percentage points to about 70 per cent of the market between the mid-1970s and the mid-1980s. An application of the orthodox methodology of competition might well suggest that such a high and increasing level of market concentration signals the existence of an environment which is uncompetitive, and which is in the process of becoming even less competitive over time.

But such an approach is static, and fails to recognize the underlying *behaviour* which generates these market shares – the mainframe computer industry in this decade was manifestly competitive relative to other industries in this period if the competitive *actions* of participants, such as the innovation of new products and processes are taken into consideration. The 'evidence' of a substantial increase in IBM's market share in this period would appear to be deceptive. It was precisely in this period that IBM was subjected to new and unprecedented challenges to its pre-eminence in the data processing industry, and it was only through a series of highly competitive responses that it managed to maintain that pre-eminence. Developments in microprocessor technology had made possible a series of new products – middle range computer systems from firms such as Digital Equipment and Data General, which for a fraction of the cost could handle computing tasks that once required mainframes, and the personal computer, a product which is helping to transform the conception of the role of the computer in the workplace and further blurs the lines with fully fledged mainframes.

By the mid-1980s, the IBM personal computer was confronting serious competition, with plunging prices for memory chips and other parts, combined with highly successful replication of the design by others, especially South Korean and Taiwanese producers, bringing about commodity pricing for this product within five years of its introduction.

The launching in 1987 of the IBM Personal System/2 personal computer based on a 32 bit microchip was designed to defeat the 'clones', but few believe the advantage will remain for long. If indeed IBM in the future should maintain a significant market share in the personal computer market, it will be because it succeeds in *competing* against its rivals through either price or quality competition (if we exclude the possibility of any forms of 'unfair' or extortionate behaviour): it would not be an indication of an absence of competition in this market.

But neither the introduction of the middle range computer, nor (by itself) the personal computer represent decisive examples of the kinds of qualitative change discussed above. It is rather in the convergence of the computer and telecommunications technologies that we can begin to see an example of the refashioning of existing industries generated by the innovations in microprocessor technology. Convergence between these industries has been taking place from both directions, as microprocessor technology has demonstrated the superiority of digital methods (i.e. the form in which information is carried in a computer) for both data and voice transmission.

From the telecommunications side, the pressures of increased competition have manifested themselves quite independently of movements in the direction of so-called deregulation and the breakup of AT&T in 1982. The pressures for these developments have come not from the consumer market but from business, where demands for the transfer of the ever increasing amounts of voice, data and paper documentation seem limitless. Within the office, business demand has engendered the development of PBXs (private branch exchanges) in which desktop devices combine the roles of the personal computer and telephone, connected to both voice and data networks, and LANs (local area networks), linking the personal computers in the office for the transmission of data and communications of all sorts. Clearly, the entry of IBM into the LAN market, with its imposition of a standard of uniformity for such systems, poses the possibility of a conflict between the computer and telecommunications industries for the control of office communications.

Beyond the office, satellite and optical fibre technology have permitted the development of long distance communication networks in competition with established phone lines both from new telecommunications firms and from private networks set up by the larger firms. Once again IBM and other data processing companies have shown an interest in challenging the established telecommunications companies in their own domains, both for the sale of the requisite equipment and even in the setting up of competing systems (IBM has purchased a minority share in AT&T's leading rival in satellite communications).

From the contrary direction, questions which were formerly the domain of communications technology have been imposing themselves upon the computer industry. The notion of the computer as a 'number cruncher' is fast giving way to its role as part of an information system for the firm, in which communication within the whole firm (and not just within a given office) and between firms, suppliers and customers takes full advantage of electronics technology. Indeed, much of DEC's success against IBM in the mid-1980s resulted from the ability of their computers to communicate easily with one another and to use common software programs. IBM's incompatible family of computers could not, a fact which has been linked to the divisionalised nature of the IBM organisation.[84]

The question of systems compatibility has thus become a major issue within the data processing industry. The current discussions emerging over the appropriate systems protocol – the underlying systems architecture which will permit different mainframes and personal computers, etc. to talk to each other – are of such consequence because they will play a crucial role in the development of the industry: will the new protocol be oriented towards users, especially manufacturing users as in GM's MAP system, towards the needs of (at least one) computer manufacturer with, for instance IBM's SNA (Systems Network Architecture), or will it be oriented towards the telecommunications industry, as in the Unix operating system of AT&T? If a more general system is adopted, such as that developed by the International Standards Organization, will it prove to be so loose that true compatibility between machines remains unattainable?

This issue is important because of the convergence of two forces. The development of microprocessor and related technologies has simultaneously made possible the stationing of vast numbers of personal computers within the firm and the potential for them to communicate with each other. But the *potential* for such development is not sufficient to explain the direction and the rapidity of present movements for unified co-ordination of the firm by electronic means. Just as Charles Babbage envisaged the computer long before the technical prerequisites for such an invention existed, so movements in the direction of the total co-ordination of all aspects of firm activity have long preceded the development of the electronically integrated firm. The new technical tools available have enlivened and focused the imagination of management in much the same way that the invention of the clock stimulated Sombart's entrepreneur, but developments like the Japanese *kanban* system, it must be remembered, have long preceded the development of any electronic systems protocol.

There is now a demand by business for a level of integration of electronic facilities – and of the whole operation of business – which is unprecedented. Within the factory, the vision has gone beyond Computer Aided Design (CAD) and Computer Aided Manufacturing (CAM) to Computer Integrated Manufacturing (CIM) where a common database permits information to flow from design drafting to modelling, analysis and manufacturing in one smooth continuum. If a system with such co-ordination and such manifest flexibility, in which new designs are instantaneously linked to the manufacturing process is at present only visionary, the demand for 'on-line' services on the part of retail stores, banks, airlines and others for instantaneous checking of reservations, credit, etc. is not, nor is the move by the Automobile Industry Action

Group (AIAG) to link electronically 300 suppliers and the car assemblers in the US. In the latter case, the obvious question arises:

> If electronic interchange makes so much sense, why didn't the [automotive] industry convert to it years ago? For one thing, microcomputers have only recently become cheap enough to allow data interchange to extend to the bottom of the supplier chain. But a much more telling reason may be the one offered by James R. Oravec, an AIAG member and a systems manager for EDS [the electronics subsidiary of GM]: 'Everyone was pretty fat and sassy at one point', he says. 'Now the Japanese have forced us to look at other ways to make our industry more profitable.'[85]

But what of the Japanese? In some areas, the electronics revolution seems to have passed them by, with their offices surprisingly 'low tech' by the latest Western standards. (While this phenomenon has often been attributed to tradition, or problems with the adaptation of the Japanese language to mechanised office work, it may simply be due to a certain perspicacity: a recent study can find no gains in productivity from office automation in the US!)[86] However, one of the key manifestations of the new approach to information technology in the firm is in the development of Value Added Networks (VANs), which are in active implementation in several countries, but especially in Japan. In such systems a central computer is to be linked by satellite, wire or fibre optic cable to all aspects of the business process, so that for example a customer's order of a new car would automatically cause the relevant parts to be ordered from suppliers or added to inventories, as well as passing on the (customised) order to the assembly line.

All such developments may still seem visionary, on the one hand, or manifestations of the 'wonders of technology' on the other: in truth, they are a continuation of tendencies long present in the capitalist market economy. These tendencies are now aided by a technology which in great measure has been moulded to serve the needs of this economic system. It would be unsurprising if the Japanese were the first economy to make successful use of these networks of electronic co-ordination on a large scale, given their previous and present successes at co-ordination even with minimal use of advanced electronics. The present profound changes being observed in ways of doing business in much of the world economy have at least as much to do with the imperatives and tendencies embedded in the economic system as in the limits and logic of the technology.

Food Retailing
Let us leave the heady sphere of high technology for a brief examination of a seemingly more mundane aspect of world economic development, the food retailing business in Great Britain (we restrict most of our discussion here to the grocery trade, though such distinctions are less important now than in former times). The sector is still in the midst of profound change,

much of which seems to be a repetition of events already experienced in other countries, most notably in the US. A central aspect of these developments has been the growing long-term competitiveness which has been evidenced in the food retailing sector, in spite of, and perhaps even because of increases in nominal market concentration. Unlike our other sectors, this increasing competitiveness owes as yet little to developments in high technology (though the relevance of the aforementioned discussion of changes emerging from the electronics industry should be obvious), and nothing to the influence of the Japanese.

In the UK and the US, the role of retailers has been crucial to overall economic development. In the absence of counter-examples like the Japanese (whose system of retail distribution has remained backward by Anglo-Saxon standards), it would have been tempting to build a theory of economic development for capitalist market economies in which retailers played a central role. Galbraith in his writings on countervailing power[87] called for a re-evaluation of the role of distribution in the competitive process, and its link to other economic developments should be self-evident: the traditional general store, with the shopkeeper blending and preparing his or her own commodities fitted in uncomfortably with the emergent world of mass-produced pre-packaged commodities like Kellogg's Corn Flakes and other such delectations.

In the contemporary world, the supermarket unites two developments which in fact took place separately, both from a logical point of view and in historical time, the first being the development of the multiple (known as the chain store in America) and the second being the innovation of self-service. The multiple appears superficially as a form of geographical diversification, but in fact has its origins in the desire of ambitious retailers like Thomas Lipton to integrate backward into wholesaling, using the multiple shops as outlets for his superior purchasing power. Underlying the development of multiples in Britain starting in the 1870s were the vast possibilities opened up by improved transport, both by rail and for goods from overseas. Certain contrary tendencies existed for the role of the independent wholesaler in this period. On the one hand the higher rate of urbanisation, with the consequent decline of local markets and producer/retailers accentuated the role of intermediaries, while improvements in transportation and communications made possible in principle the development of a system with progressively fewer links and even the by-passing of wholesalers.

The new multiples, in contrast to the traditional grocery, focused their sales on a handful of items in which they concentrated their buying power, staples of the working-class diet such as ham, cheese and tea. For the sake of substantially lower prices, the consumer was expected to forgo the privilege of buying from a retailer knowledgeable enough to undertake many of the tasks which were now becoming the province of the wholesaler or even the manufacturer such as the blending of tea, the mixing of spices and the curing of bacon. More significantly, the customer had to do without the extension of credit which was part of the traditional retailer's service to known customers. There were additional attractions to the new shops: for many working-class patrons, the relative cleanliness, the ordered displays, the clear marking of prices, the absence of haggling and the unadulterated and consistent quality of the goods to be found in the multiples and the emerging co-ops marked an improvement in living standards.

From our present perspective, the restriction by the multiple to only a handful of goods makes it in this sense less recognisable than the old-fashioned grocery. This policy was maintained for two reasons. First was the necessity of retaining bulk buying power, including the possibility of purchasing large consignments from distant localities by concentrating on a small number of items. Secondly, the restriction of the number of goods handled permitted efficient organisation of storage, processing, distribution and sales – in other words, constraints upon managerial efficiency restricted the number of goods that could be dealt with by a multiple.

The coming of the multiple was coincident with a continuing shift in consumer habits away from bulk purchases of semi-processed goods to the frequent buying of pre-packaged commodities from the shop around the corner. The multiples and the co-ops (which followed similiar policies) together, with these self-imposed limitations (as well as, in later periods the limitations imposed by resale price maintenance) managed to capture only about one quarter of the groceries and provisions market by the turn of the century, somewhat over a third in the inter-war period, and still less than half by 1950. (These figures are roughly similiar with those to be found for chain stores in the US at this time.)

Part of the reason for the survival of the independent grocery was the fact that there was a competitive response from this sector, especially from the wholesalers, who improved their delivery and credit services to retailers. The pre-packaging of goods by manufacturers and the offering of window displays to advertisers also eased the ability of small grocers to survive both the challenge of their larger rivals and the inundation of new commodities on the market which they were expected to carry. Furthermore, the development of grading and marking and the use of standards, particularly for imported foodstuffs, also reduced some of the advantages the multiples had with their specialist buyers.

In the period since 1950, the most significant phenomenon has been the progressive dominance of the supermarket. Smaller operators by the mid 1980s were maintaining less than 20 per cent of the grocery trade (three-quarters of these connected to voluntary groups linked to wholesalers), while the five largest multiples alone (Tesco, J. Sainsbury, Dee, Asda and Argyll) had over one-half of grocery market sales,[88] including over 400 superstore outlets. What interpretation are we to impose on these events? In the context of the traditional methodology of industrial economics, it might well be suggested that the substantial rise in concentration in the retail sector has had anti-competitive implications.[89] Indeed, it is undoubtedly true that the high levels of concentration which have emerged, with their attendant strong levels of mutual awareness may well inhibit price competition in the future. In the words of the chairman of Tesco, 'nobody needs to rock the boat and start a new price war',[90] and indeed there are indications that, as of the mid-1980s, overt price wars on branded products may be a thing of the past. Why is it contended here, therefore, that the period since the war is characterised by a continuing tendency for competitiveness to increase?

In order to consider this proposition we must examine in detail the reasons for the emergence of the supermarket – first, the advantages of bulk buying and/or the integration of wholesaler and retailer, and secondly, the logic and dynamics of self-service, which are tied to the issues surrounding economies of scale. The most obvious advantage of bulk buying for retailers would appear to be their ability to share with manufacturers any cost reductions accruing due to volume effects and reductions in near term uncertainty about orders. As noted above, the great majority of small retailers are now connected to voluntary groups, so that their wholesalers should be in a position to receive appropriate volume discounts from manufacturers.

If volume discounts were the only kind of advantage accruing in a backwards direction, a fair part of these gains would seem to be capable of capture by the small retailer through the use of wholesalers. However, other advantages exist which can only be gained through the integration of wholesaler and retailer, such as, for instance, the saving of the wholesaler's advertising and selling expenses in dealing with retailers. Other aspects of integration are less intrinsically beneficial: whether links between whole-sale and retail functions in the same organisation actually can be used to improve the flow of information between consumers and manufacturers depends on the ability of the 'hierarchy' within the integrated company to function better than the 'market' of separate wholesalers and retailers; cost savings may accrue to integrated retailers if they can make relatively long-term commitments to manufacturers which facilitate plant expansion and development, but such commitments can prove to be costly mistakes for retailers if they have guessed incorrectly about demand in their own market.

A last advantage to wholesaler–retailer integration is the one discussed in chapter 8: if indeed a retailer with superior managerial technique such as Marks and Spencer is in a position to guide a manufacturer in the direction of successfully marketable products, improve the manufacturer's production techniques and even his or her bookkeeping practices, then such a retailer may be better able to take advantage of such skills by direct control of manufacturing (which of course presupposes a wholesaling role) than by maintainimg an arm's length distance from their manufacturers.[91] Any such advantages of integration, however, are balanced by potential disadvantages, since they further complicate managerial control of the company. Present moves in this direction are a function of the expansion of the managerial capacity and horizons of actors in this sector.

The other aspect of the supermarket is its large size and its self-service aspect. The self-service store – the Piggly Wiggly – saw the light of day for the first time in Memphis, Tennessee in 1916, but its logical consequence, the supermarket chain, did not really emerge in a big way until the early 1930s, especially with the expansion of the A & P chain. In Britain, supermarket development in any substantial magnitude only came in the 1950s, with the emergence of the Tesco multiple.

Given that very wide ranges of pre-packed foods had been produced by food manufacturers since the latter part of the nineteeth century it appears remarkable that the logical consequence of this development – the supermarket – took so long to develop. After all, in neither country can a French or Italian fastidiousness about food quality be claimed as an excuse. Partial explanations for this slow development include the need for the possession of complementary commodities by consumers, especially cars, refrigerators and freezers to permit the closing of the many small branches of multiples and chain stores and the opening of fewer, larger ones to facilitate less frequent, bulk shopping, and the inhibition of resale price maintenance agreements on the development of low price, low service stores (these agreements having some potency in the US through the early 1950s and in Britain to the early 1960s).

But such explanations seem insufficient. Many of the advantages of big retailers discussed above may well be inconceivable without the capital market advantages to large firms discussed in chapter 7, but such advantages, like the ones discussed above, have potentially been around for a long time. Why has it taken so long for these giant entities to emerge? In Britain, supermarket development proceeded even more slowly than in the US, partially because the prerequisites of its emergence such as the pre-packaging of food and related products had not gone as far as in the US, with, for instance, biscuits not pre-packed in the UK until the mid-1950s.

But if supermarket development was relatively retarded in the UK compared with the US because of the lesser sophistication of many sectors of the economy, including its food producers (these words are meant to be understood purely in economic, and not in normative terms), in both countries the standards of managerial efficiency in retailing were feeble compared with those to be found in their respective manufacturing sectors. For decades in both countries, the selling of groceries was a sector whose crucial characteristic was its relative ease of entry both in terms of the requisite capital needed and of the low level of specialised knowledge required. The central aspect of the development in the grocery industry in Britain over the last three decades has not been any increase in monopoly power due to the rise in market concentration, but the elimination of the industry's managerial deficit *vis-à-vis* other sectors. The new modes of behaviour have created an environment that apppears highly competitive in comparison with that in former times.

The development of the supermarket posed unprecedented managerial problems for food retailers in Britain. Tesco, for instance, has had to undergo a continual series of reorganisations from the late 1960s to the present in order to impose central direction and co-ordination on its operation and J. Sainsbury proceeded with extreme caution, its trade being dominated by counter service until the late 1950s, with large numbers of supermarkets not emerging until the late 1960s.

A substantive example of the problems of large-scale co-ordination may be seen in the dramatic change which has taken place in the last few years in wholesale distribution. In the past, separate vehicles delivered to retail outlets from each source of supply. In the 1980s, J. Sainsbury has been a leader among the large food retailers in investing in enormous central warehouses to which deliveries are made. These new arrangements impose an unprecedented burden on the internal organisation of distribution for these companies, but at the same time they give far greater control over the levels of stocks and the timing of deliveries to outlets. Other food retailers have been rapidly pursuing J. Sainsbury in this minor manifestation of the 'just in time' approach to distribution. Such developments are only a foretaste of the possibilities for stock control and co-ordination emerging from the improvements in management information with the introduction of laser scanning and computer co-ordination.

This growth of centralisation and integration on the part of retailers is complemented by an increasing tendency for manufacturers – partially in response to these pressures to pursue a policy of disintegration – to contract out their distribution operations to a growing number of third party specialists. A subsidiary effect of this development of a rich 'market' in distribution services is that in the future relatively unintegrated entities, such as independent wholesalers and retailers, may well find it easier than previously to purchase distribution services at attractive rates, so that one of their existing disadvantages *vis-à-vis* large retailers may be lessened in the future.

But managerial changes have not been purely of a technical kind. Improvements in the facility of management have also been co-extensive with an expansion of the horizon of these firms, with rapid movement in recent years beyond the traditional grocery lines and into competition with other kinds of retail outlets in a wide range of food and non-food items. Furthermore, these large retailers have for many years been manifesting increased aggressiveness *vis-à-vis* both rivals and suppliers. Indeed, it has been suggested that the emergence of the supermarket in the UK in the 1950s was at least in part a 'countervailing power' response to the growing power and aggressive marketing of the large food manufacturers, especially American multinationals such as Heinz, Nabisco and Kellogg; the largest retailers have consistently been able to extract special discounts from manufacturers, which have been reflected in the lower prices charged to customers.[92] According to the Office of Fair Trading, these lower wholesale prices which the large retailers extract from manufacturers seem to be accounted for by cost savings on high volume.

There remains, however, another possibility, and it is connected with a small mystery: according to the same Office of Fair Trading report, there does not seem to be any difference between the gross margins to retailers on own brand goods compared with national brands. Now, if we exclude the unlikely possibility that significant price elasticity effects on the demand for the low-priced own brand products generate a higher rate of return on capital for the own brand products than on national brands, and if we consider the substantial capital and managerial commitment involved in the creation and maintenance of an own brand, there is a strong implication that the rate of return on investment on such own brands might well be lower than on the sale of national brands.

Why then have other firms been rushing to follow J. Sainsbury (well over half of whose sales are in own brands) as a producer of own brand products? Our conclusion is that if the OFT estimates are correct, the main utility of the own brands to the large retailer is not because they are intrinsically more profitable, but that they serve as a lever on manu-facturers for the extraction of large discounts on the name brand goods. In either case, whether own brand products are produced for their own sake or as a lever on manufacturers, the rapid expansion of this practice in recent years on a vast range of goods represents a significant escalation in the tasks of management, especially when retailers get seriously involved in the character and quality control of the products. Thomas Lipton in the nineteenth century also sold a high percentage of his own brands, but only from among the small range of products to which he restricted himself. The present developments are taking place in the context of a sector whose range of offerings to the public is still expanding rapidly and which has only emerged into the supermarket age in the last quarter century.

What will the future yield? Certain aspects of present developments could lead to a mitigation of the increasing competitiveness that this sector has manifested in recent decades. Perhaps even more significant than the rise in market concentration is the likelihood that all available superstore sites will be tied up by the major retailers in the next few years. But such an approach may be an overly static one for dealing with this sector. At the moment, the sector is unprecedently competitive, with laggards being punished severely for their failure to respond adequately to the changed environment.

Firms facing the onslaught of the big firms have also changed their behaviour, and this too is part of the new environment. Wholesalers confronted with the possible loss of their custom have been trying to match the big retailers by manufacturing their own brands and by expanding lower priced cash and carry facilities for retailers. Small retailers and voluntary groups have revived the nineteenth century practice of keeping their stores open long hours, and have attempted to extend their range of offerings beyond the ever wider selection sold by the big retailers. The net effect on society of all these changes may be far less unambiguously beneficial than industry publicists would suggest, but there is no doubt that, from the point of economic analysis the present atmosphere is far more competitive than anything seen in the past:

there has been a virtual revolution in the techniques of retailing from sleepy, passive local shops servicing immobile, tradition-bound customers to aggressive high turn-over, cost-conscious institutions dealing with a car equipped and knowledgeable constituency. We have phrased our case in a deliberately provocative way – but is it really so far from the truth?[93]

Notes

1. Mathias, P. The *Transformation of England* Methuen 1979, pp. 64–6.
2. See, for instance Weber, M. *The Theory of Social and Economic Organization* Free Press of Glencoe n.d.; English translation 1947.
3. Sombart, W. *The Quintessence of Capitalism* T. Fisher Unwin n.d.; English translation 1915, p. 125.
4. Ibid., ch. 25.
5. North, D. and R. Thomas *The Rise of the Western World* Cambridge University 1973; all citations and paraphrases are from ch. 1.
6. Anthropological evidence makes it highly questionable whether any such easy generalisations about 'human nature' can be drawn: see Sahlins, M. *Stone Age Economics* Tavistock 1974, chs 1 and 2.
7. North and Thomas on occasion become overly enthusiastic about their incentive schemes to encourage growth, such as their 'law assigning exclusive rights to intellectual property including new ideas, inventions and innovations'. The idea that these forms of legal protection would invariably have led to greater effort is an attractive notion a priori, but is not always borne out historically: compare the quantity of music produced by Handel and Haydn with their nineteenth century equivalents when copyright protection was available. Would Mozart have written almost two dozen piano concertos if copyright royalties had been available, or would he have played more billiards?
8. Braudel, F. (vol. I of *Civilization and Capitalism 15th – 18th Century*) *Capitalism and Material Life 1400–1800* Fontana 1967; English translation 1973, p. xiv.
9. Braudel, F. (vol. II of *Civilization and Capitalism 15th – 18th Century*) *The Wheels of Commerce* Collins 1979; English translation 1982, pp. 401–2.
10. Ibid., p. 29.
11. Ibid., p. 138.
12. Ibid., pp. 142–4–see the story of the merchant Simon Ruiz.
13. Dobb, M. *Studies in the Development of Capitalism* Routledge and Kegan Paul 1963, p. 20; and see Pirenne, H. *Economic and Social History of Medieval Europe* Harcourt, Brace and World 1933; English translation n.d., pp. 44–9.
14. The debate is contained in Hilton, R. *The Transition from Feudalism to Capitalism* New Left Books 1976, and see Polanyi, K. *The Great Transformation* Beacon 1957, and Dobb (note 13). An excellent recent summary is to be found in Holton, R. *The Transition from Feudalism to Capitalism* Macmillan 1985.
15. Mathias (note 1), p. 35.
16. Woodruff, W. 'The Emergence of the International Economy 1700–1914' in

Cipolla, C. (ed.) *The Fontana Economic History of Europe* vol. 4 part 2 Fontana 1973, pp. 656–716.

17. Woodruff, W. *Impact of Western Man* Macmillan, St Martin's Press 1966, p. 255, Table VI/3.

18. These data must be treated with caution, as can be seen by the greater increase in goods by value rather than by weight in the two series. This seems an anomalous result: the lowering of shipping costs should have encouraged relatively more lower-valued goods later in the period.

19. Woodruff (note 17), p. 240.

20. See Hannah, L. *The Rise of the Corporate Economy* Methuen 1976, pp. 186–91. This discussion is to be found in the first edition only; see as well Lamoreaux, N. *The Great Merger Movement in American Business 1895–1904* Cambridge University 1985, ch. 2.

21. This case is put forcefully in Piore, M. and C. Sabel *The New Industrial Divide* Basic Books 1984.

22. Kellenbenz, H. 'Technology in the Age of the Scientific Revolution – 1500–1700' in Cipolla, C. (ed.) *The Fontana History of Europe* vol. 2 Fontana 1974, pp. 177–272 and Landes, D. *Unbound Prometheus* Cambridge University 1969, ch. 2. Rosenberg, N. *Inside the Black Box* Cambridge University 1982, ch. 2 suggests that this was also the view of Marx.

23. Schumpeter, J. *Business Cycles* vol. I McGraw Hill 1939, pp. 87, 101.

24. Rosenberg, N. *Perspectives on Technology* Cambridge University 1976, pp. 63–5.

25. Ibid., pp. 196, 200.

26. Mansfield, E. *The Economics of Technological Change* Longman 1968, ch. 4.

27. For an example of the use of patents as a device for restricting entry, see Brock, G. *The Telecommunications Industry* Harvard University 1981, ch. 6, where the decline of competition in the period 1907–1935 is charted. Patents on the whole are not often thought a good way of protecting knowledge: see Rogers, E. 'Information Exchange and Technological Innovation' in Sahal, D. (ed.) *The Transfer and Utilization of Technical Knowledge* Lexington Books 1982, pp. 105–23, where the question is discussed for the solar and micro-processor industries. For a contrary view, see 'The Surprising New Power of Patents' *Fortune* 23 June 1986.

28. Mathias (note 1), p. 128.

29. Landes (note 22), p. 151.

30. See Birr, K. 'Science in American Industry' in Van Tassel, D. and M. Hall *Science and Society in the United States* Dorsey Press 1966, pp. 35–80. On the spread of research laboratories to Europe, see Layton, P. 'Education in Industrialized Societies' in Williams, T. (ed.) *A History of Technology* vol. 6 part 1 Clarendon 1978, pp. 138–71. The Menlo Park research laboratory was by modern standards a cosy affair and should not be pictured in late twentieth century terms: see Clark, R. *Edison* Macdonald and Janes's 1977.

31. Mathias (note 1), p. 29.

32. Rosenberg, N. (note 22), p. 284.

33. A review of the evidence on the 'Schumpeterian hypothesis' (hypotheses?) so interpreted may be found in Kamien, M. and N. Schwartz *Market Structure and Innovation* Cambridge 1982, chs 2 and 3.

34. Schumpeter, J. 'The Instability of Capitalism' *Economic Journal* 38 (September 1928): 361–86.

35. Arrow, K. 'Economic Welfare and the Allocation of Resources for Invention'

in Nelson, R.R. (ed.) *The Rate and Direction of Inventive Activity* Princeton University 1962, pp. 609–25.

36. Clifton, J. 'Competition and the Evolution of the Capitalist Mode of Production' *Cambridge Journal of Economics* 1(2) (June 1977): 137–51.
37. See Blair, J. *Economic Concentration* Harcourt Brace Jovanovich 1972, part 3.
38. For a contemporary description of the 'webs' of financial control, see Grou, P. *The Financial Structure of Multinational Capitalism* Berg 1985. For references on the doctrine of monopoly capital see ch. 2.
39. Kolko, G. *The Triumph of Conservatism* Quadrangle Books 1967.
40. See Shepherd, W. 'Causes of Increased Competition in the US Economy, 1939–1980' *Review of Economics and Statistics* 64(4) (November 1982): 613–26.
41. Scherer, F. M. *Industrial Market Structure and Economic Performance* Rand McNally second edn 1980, pp. 68–9.
42. Landes (note 22), p. 338.
43. Aldcroft, D. (ed.) *The Development of British Industry and Foreign Competition 1875–1914* George Allen and Unwin 1968; Aldcroft, D. *The Inter-War Economy: Britain 1919–1939* B. T. Batsford 1970.
44. Saul, S.B. 'The Engineering Industry' in Aldcroft *Development of British Industry* (note 43), pp. 186–237.
45. See Reader, W. J. *Imperial Chemical Industries, A History* Oxford University 1970, especially ch. 15.
46. See Channon, D. *The Strategy and Structure of British Enterprise* Macmillan 1973, p. 141.
47. On the interwar cartel-like behaviour of British trade associations, see Aldcroft *Interwar Economy* (note 43), pp. 141–5.
48. See Noble, D. *America by Design* Oxford University 1979, ch. 5 and Sobel, R. *The Age of Giant Corporations* Greenwood 1972, ch. 1.
49. The role of trade associations in lowering minimum efficient scale through the dispersal of information in the US for the period 1912–1933 is (surprisingly) noted in Burns, A. R. *The Decline of Competition* McGraw-Hill 1936, ch. 2.
50. Noble (note 48), pp. 69–70.
51. See Atak, J. 'Industrial Structure and the Emergence of the Modern Industrial Corporation' *Explorations in Economic History* 22 (1985): 29–52. Atak uses data on plant survivorship to suggest that the great corporations had emerged to a significant extent by making use of the new, large-scale production processes.
52. On the limitations of the survivor technique, see Scherer (note 41), pp. 92–4.
53. See Brock (note 27).
54. See Stocking, G. and M. Watkins *Cartels or Competition ?* Twentieth Century Fund 1948, appendix B, and Burns (note 49), ch. 1 for a summary of the effect of cartels and monopolies on the American economy in the inter-war period.
55. See Stocking and Watkins (note 54), chs 2–5; on the chemical cartel, see Reader (note 45) and Reader, W. J. *Imperial Chemical Industries, A History* vol. 2 Oxford University 1975, especially part II on the inter-war cartel.
56. On the American policy, the path-breaking study is Kolko, G. *The Politics of War* Vintage Books 1968; see especially ch. 19.
57. Stopford, J. and J. Turner *Britain and the Multinationals* John Wiley 1985, ch. 2.
58. 'The High Cost of Poor Control' *Financial Times* 28 February 1986.

59. Crankshaw, E. *Khrushchev's Russia* Penguin revised edn 1962, p. 28.
60. Warren, K. 'Iron and Steel' in Aldcroft, D. and Buxton, N. (eds) *British Industry between the Wars* George Allen 1979, pp. 103–128.
61. 'Is Bethlehem Investing in a Future it Doesn't Have?' *Business Week* 8 July 1985.
62. Adams, W. and H. Mueller 'The Steel Industry' in Adams, W. (ed.) *The Structure of American Industry* Macmillan sixth edn 1982, pp. 73–135.
63. Borrus, M. 'The Politics of Competitive Erosion in the U.S. Steel Industry' in Zysman, J. and L. Tyson (eds) *American Industry in International Competition* Cornell University 1983, pp. 60–105.
64. 'How Roles Have Been Reversed' *Financial Times* 16 October 1985 and 'Korea's Big Push Has Just Begun' *Fortune* 16 March 1987.
65. Quoted in 'The Third World's Bid to Export Cars' *Fortune* 5 September 1983.
66. White, L. 'The Automobile Industry' in Adams (note 62), pp. 136–190.
67. See Hayek, F. A. *Prices and Production* Augustus M. Kelley 1967; originally published in 1931.
68. Maxcy, G. and A. Silberston *The Motor Industry* George Allen 1959, p. 61.
69. 'With the worldwide growth of component making, the former clear divisions between integrated manufacture and completely-knocked-down assembly have almost disappeared. The point at which national "assembly" becomes "manufacture" tends to vary according to the source used.' Bloomfield, G. *The World Automotive Industry* David and Charles 1978, p. 143.
70. Jones, D. 'Motor Cars: a Maturing Industry?' in Shepherd, P., F. Duchêne and C. Saunders (eds) *Europe's Industries* Frances Pinter 1983, pp. 110–38.
71. Ibid.
72. Quoted in 'GM Learns from Japan: the Empire Strikes Back' *Financial Times* 24 January 1985.
73. Altshuler, A., M. Anderson, D. Jones, D. Roos and J. Womack *The Future of the Automobile* George Allen 1984, pp. 146–7.
74. 'Can Detroit Cope This Time?' *Business Week* 22 April 1985; see as well 'Detroit's Cars Are Really Getting Better' *Fortune* 2 February 1987.
75. These data are taken from 'Brazil: Big Upturn as Price Controls Continue' *Financial Times* survey *The Motor Industry* 11 September 1985.
76. This discussion is summarised from Altshuler *et al.* (note 73), pp. 175–9.
77. Jones (note 70).
78. This issue is originally and exhaustively discussed in Noble (note 48).
79. Braun, E. and S. MacDonald *Revolution in Miniature* Cambridge University 1978, pp. 94 and 144.
80. Quoted in 'Why the Speed of Technology is Chipping Away at the Independents' *Financial Times* 27 May 1987.
81. Swann, P. *Quality Innovation: An Economic Analysis of Rapid Improvements in Microelectronic Components* Frances Pinter 1986, pp. 75–6.
82. Ibid., pp. 7–8.
83. 'In the Shadow of IBM: the Desperate Struggle to Stay in the Race' *Financial Times* 22 April 1986.
84. 'How IBM Is Tackling its Tower of Babel' *Financial Times* 2 April 1987.
85. 'Detroit Tries to Level a Mountain of Paperwork' *Business Week* 26 August 1985.
86. 'The Puny Payoff From Office Computers' *Fortune* 26 May 1986.
87. Galbraith, J. K. *American Capitalism The Concept of Countervailing Power* Houghton Mifflin Co. revised edn 1956.

88. *Retail Business* No.333 November 1985, p. 6 and 'Major Fight for Sheer Bulk' *Financial Times* survey *Retailing* 10 June 1987.
89. This is the strong implication contained in Aaronovitch, S. and M. Sawyer *Big Business* Macmillan 1975, ch. 5.
90. 'Food Retailing – Catering for Changing Tastes' *Financial Times* 25 July 1985.
91. For more on this red hot issue, see 'The Chilling Story of the M & S Chicken' *Financial Times* 2 February 1984.
92. Office of Fair Trading *Competition and Retailing* June 1985 and the survey of grocery prices in *Which?* October 1982 and the corrections in December 1982.
93. Auerbach, P. and P. Skott 'Concentration, Competition and Distribution – A Critique of Theories of Monopoly Capital' *International Review of Applied Economics* 2(1) (January 1988): 42–61.

10

Perspectives and Prospects

The review undertaken in the previous chapter of some representative sectors in the economy casts serious doubt on the utility of orthodox approaches to industrial analysis. Some of the failures of orthodoxy seem straightforward. For example, in industry after industry we have observed that a central concern of participants is to achieve volume effects in production. Such a perspective is far different from that which would be gained from a study of orthodox microeconomics, which in all its manifestations, from standard textbooks to high theory, almost exclusively presumes the existence of cost curve convexities, in spite of a growing literature on learning-by-doing and comparable effects. The main reasons for the continued popularity of the convexity assumption seem to relate more to its analytical convenience – especially for yielding standard free trade, free market type conclusions – than because of any deep-seated belief in its empirical validity.[1]

But it is not our purpose here to suggest the universal presence of scale economies or to criticise orthodoxy simply for a specific empirical fault, its failure to recognise the existence of non-convexities, when the difficulties are of a more fundamental nature. These volume effects are only tangentially related to simple static propositions about, for instance, the level of minimum efficient scale in an industry. What one invariably observes is a complex relation between the processes of internal planning and co-ordination pursued by participants within a sector, their (implicit or explicit) time horizon and their methods of finance. The techniques which end up being best practice and the relevant minimum efficient scale in this sector emerge out of a process of historical change, contingent on sets of decisions made at each historical moment: there are no simple technical parameters which set exogenous constraints on behaviour.

'Laws of nature' and the broad-based 'blueprint' of available knowledge undoubtedly impose boundaries on participants at any given time. But, contrary to the dictates of orthodoxy, it is not these constraints which are observed by the economic analyst, but merely an inner set of constraints contingent on the cumulative effect of past *social and economic* decisions. And just as the existing levels of minimum efficient scale which we observe in a sector are the product of past decisions and not simply exogenous parameters imposed upon actors, they can be transformed by present decisions of economic actors, even when no change in the underlying blueprint of techniques has taken place. Thus, the provision of finance to a sector at a given moment can determine the levels of real scale economies in the future: what at one moment started out as a financial advantage for some participants may be subsequently transformed into a real one, in which historically existing constraints, including the optimum scale of operation, have been transformed. Many of the standard perspectives offered up by orthodoxy – the separation of the 'real' and the 'financial', the exogeneity of technology and so on – come across not so much as wrong but irrelevant to the analysis of substantive issues.

This complex and interactive relation between volition and objective constraints manifests itself as well in relation to our old nemesis, the market concentration ratio. Even when such a ratio can be meaningfully defined in specific instances, it certainly does not function as an exogenous constraint on behaviour. Rises in concentration, far from being invariably a cause of reduced competition, are often responses to an increasingly competitive environment, and sometimes these rises result in more, rather than less competition. Joint ventures and other forms of co-operation between firms may indeed signal reduced competition in specific instances, but have often appeared as competitive responses to a changing environment; certain forms of co-operation, for instance co-operation on the setting of uniform standards, can themselves be instrumental in changing the parameters of the existing environment in a more competitive direction.

In a similar way, substantive cases demonstrate the nebulous nature of the dichotomy between planning and the market. Markets are not in fact things to be used by economic actors, but relationships chosen by these actors, so that the extent and richness of a market will be contingent on the behaviour of participants in that market. Just as the market environment indubitably has its effect on the behaviour of participants, so too will the actions of participants affect the nature of the market. For any individual participant, a choice may exist between planning and using the market, but the nature of the planning decisions made by participants will collectively influence the environment in which these decisions are made. Thus at present we may be observing an acceleration in the development of markets and disintegration, while at the same time there is movement by many firms in the direction of more extensive and sophisticated planning and integration than ever before.

If we accept the notion of a world growing increasingly competitive, what implications might this have for the future? To our knowledge, only the monopoly capital school has tried to make explicit statements about the effects of changes in the economy's overall level of competitiveness. To oversimplify greatly, in the classic formulations of this doctrine by Michal Kalecki and his successors growing monopolisation of the economy – a decrease in competitiveness – generates a redistribution of national income from wages to profits. These developments tend to engender a long-term macroeconomic stagnation in the economy as income is redistributed from a class with a high propensity to consume (workers) to a class with a low propensity to consume (capitalists).

If the purpose of our discussion here were purely polemical, it would be possible to stand such notions on their head: in a world becoming increasingly competitive, then given the premises of the theory of monopoly capital it could be argued that the economic system generates the possibility of continuous growth and development. In fact, any such conclusion – in either direction – would be inappropriate. The notion of competition found in the theory of monopoly capital is an adaptation of the approach of orthodox theory, and thus has a rigid, unidirectional line of causation from the levels of competition to the levels of profitability within an industry. It does not picture competition as part of a behavioural process in which the actions of participants in the economy generate tendencies in the direction of the elimination of excess profits.

Within a sector, contrary to the presumptions of orthodox and monopoly capital theory, no simple generalisations are possible on the relationship between the level of competitiveness and the level of profitability: an initial impetus to greater competitiveness may generate for individual participants either higher or lower profits, contingent on the myriad of considerations which have been discussed throughout this book. For instance, contrary to the presumptions of orthodoxy and the theory of monopoly capital competitive entry into a sector might well generate increased profits for a substantial period, as participants in the sector are stimulated to reduce X-inefficiency, to look beyond the sector's conventional boundaries to compete in rival areas, or even to create products for heretofore non-existent sectors.

The theory of monopoly capital further assumes that relationships between competitiveness and profitability within industries can be generalised at an economy-wide level. The possibility of spillover effects between one industry and another is just one reason why the monopoly capital procedure of extrapolating from each individual sector to the economy as a whole is fraught with danger. Factors initially generating increased competitiveness in the semiconductor industry, for instance, might induce lower profits in that industry, but the overall effects of this increased competitiveness on sectors using semiconductors as inputs (such as watchmakers) are ambiguous. At first the effects might be favourable as watchmakers' costs are lowered. However, as increased aggressiveness causes semiconductor manufacturers to move in the direction of watch production, profits might eventually be dampened in this sector as well. The unstable nature of industry boundaries in the real world means that such outcomes are real possibilities, and not just academic exercises. For this and many other reasons, the net effects on the economy as a whole of increased competitiveness are unclear, even if increased competitiveness should be observed in every sector individually.

At any moment, countervailing forces to the underlying tendency towards increased competitiveness might prevail, such as the inhibiting effects of macroeconomic stagnation on the creation of new capital, government actions of various kinds and any advantages to large entities of the existence of layers in the capital market. But, despite the optical illusion created by the return to hegemony of the Anglo-Saxon powers in the years immediately following World War II, increasing competitiveness is the underlying tendency in the world economy. The post-war buoyancy, which reinforced this illusion of dominance by a few producers in key industries in the US and the UK was precisely the atmosphere which made possible the rise of new competitors both within these countries and world-wide. Periods of subsequent stagnation in the post-war world superficially appear to be more competitive than the periods of expansion because of phenomena such as price cuts in the steel industry. They are in fact likely to result in a slowing down in many sectors in the rate at which competition will increase.

It has been convenient for our purposes to isolate the role of government from these underlying economic tendencies, but at a deeper level this is clearly impossible. Governmental action has always had a crucial impact on the nature of the environment in which business operates, from the establishment of property rights and the relationship between labour and capital to the nature of the macroeconomic and capital market conditions which it helps to engender. In all of these areas, it is pointless to talk about a non-interventionist policy, since governmental decisions – explicit or implicit – on each of these questions are unavoidable. Especially in recent decades governments have intervened more directly in industry through nationalisation as well as industrial and competition policy. Government not only responds to the existing competitive environment with such acts as the setting of tariffs, but in a deeper sense is instrumental in the creation of that environment.

The present world-wide fascination with the efficacy of market processes, with fashions having clearly shifted from various forms of *dirigisme* to deregulation sits uncomfortably with simultaneous attempts by nations to protect themselves from international competition. At present the strongest advocates of free trade come, as usual, from among those nations and those groups which appear to be accruing the greatest benefit from it. But overall there is little doubt that the founding of the EEC has promoted an increase in competition within Western Europe in the post-war years, and its creation was partially due to a changed perception compared with the inter-war period – it has come to be believed that competition is a Good Thing. Any such change in attitude can have a crucial effect on the environment in which firms function.

The role of finance in the evolution of the competitive process is one of the most difficult issues in economics. Once we leave the comfortable assertion of the existence of a wall separating the real and the financial, explicit consideration of financial institutions and the behaviour of financial markets is seen to be central to an understanding of competition in non-financial sectors. While all business decisions ultimately take place through the nexus of money, the complexity of such interactions is so great that, even in our sectoral discussion above, we largely proceeded as if the destinies of these sectors could be discussed in real terms. In fact, the disentangling of the real from the financial advantages of size which accrue to, for instance, a giant supermarket can barely be done conceptually, much less in practice, and how much financial factors 'by themselves' have contributed to a gratuitous centralisation of the economy cannot be calculated precisely.

What can be stated with more certainty is that the financial sector is subject to many of the same forces as other areas, and its increasing competitiveness may in the future tend to mitigate biases in favour of larger entities emanating from the capital market. However, the present changes in financial arrangements world-wide are so dramatic, and the financial sector has so many elements peculiar to itself, that any such predictions may prove of limited use: if the present growth in entre-preneurial spirit in the financial sector continues apace, its most important influence on non-financial sectors may not be the direct effects of its increasing competitiveness but, conceivably, the indirect effects of an increasingly unstable financial environment.

What conclusions can be drawn about the effects to be observed of a world economy and its constituents growing increasingly competitive? Almost by definition, it appears to be true that laggards within the world economy are likely to be punished more quickly and more severely than in earlier times, and not just in Great Britain. Such an observation is straightforward, though its political and social consequences are pro-found. It is perhaps not too extreme to suggest that increasing competitive-ness, along with macroeconomic fluctuation are the most important factors defining the politics of our day.

Can any less obvious effects of increasing competitiveness be deduced? One fairly unambiguous effect of contemporary events is that the pressure on many workers within developed economies is intensifying significantly. The historic substitution of machines for people in many industrial processes is continuing, and with new technologies it will reach into areas heretofore thought safe from mechanisation. The new forms of mechan-isation are motivated not only by the traditional desire to substitute capital for labour in the context of the increasingly competitive environment, but in order to use automation in conjunction with contemporary ideas about integrated production and distribution. But the substitution of robots for people has as yet taken place on a small scale, and there have been few instances of such dramatically increased productivity from the new forms of mechanisation as to lead one to believe that a discontinuous change in the role of machinery in the workplace is imminent.

A second factor putting pressure on workers also relates to the new forms of technology, but unlike mechanisation *per se* it is relatively unprecedented in its effects. The new electronics technologies lend themselves far more than any earlier developments to a precise monitoring of the comings and goings of individual workers, and a precise measurement of their performance on the job.[2] The imposition of such controls does not necessarily have to take place as part of a conscious attempt by the employer to impose Taylorist methods. On the contrary, many of these new mechanisms of control appear as 'natural' forms of modernisation in the context of an increasingly competitive environment: precise stockroom measurement and control are not necessarily implemented primarily to monitor the productivity of workers in the stockroom, but they yield this information none the less. Such innovations have as yet had only limited impact, but the increasingly competitive environment may cause them to reach maturity much more quickly than equivalent developments in earlier times.

Thirdly, it is clear that the intensified conditions of the contemporary environment, as well as the expanded horizons of management, have caused businesses to look much further afield for labour than heretofore. Many parts of the working class in developed countries find their labour competing with that from workers in developing countries, both in the form of goods originating from enterprises in these countries and in goods produced abroad by multinationals using Third World labour. The labour force in advanced countries is faced with a severe decline in its potential bargaining power, as it competes with workers whose conditions and pay resemble those existing during the Industrial Revolution.[3] For workers in the Third World, benefits received from these developments may often prove to be temporary, since many of the industries involved lend themselves to high levels of mechanisation and producers in the future may find it convenient to locate production close to their markets in advanced countries, especially in areas where high technology permits flexible adaptation of the product to changing market conditions.[4]

A last effect of the new environment is the growing irrelevance of national boundaries as traditionally conceived for an analysis of the competitive environment. Let us return to the quotation from Dr. Playfair cited in chapter 8. In mid-nineteenth century Britain, he was already suggesting that 'Raw material ... is being made available to all ... and Industry must in future be supported, not by a competition of local advantages, but by a competition of intellects.' Like many visionaries, Dr. Playfair was somewhat premature, but contemporary developments are beginning to make his notions look commonplace. However, even specific intellectual skills may be purchased across national boundaries in today's highly fluid conditions.[5] It is thus not the possession of raw materials nor of any specific technology which seems to hold the keys to success or even survival in the contemporary world, but the adaptation of social organisations, be they firms or nations to the environment, in the context of their specific histories and institutional development. The forms which these adaptations take is then a crucial determinant of the environment itself.

Orthodox theory, even when it is elaborately modified, is still generated from individual preference functions subject to exogenously specified technological constraints – all suspended in a setting in which substantive historical and institutional developments have only a tangential role. Such a theory is of very little use in analysing those processes of historical change and institutional development which are the essence of the competitive process.

Notes

1. Of course a strong belief in the existence of pervasive cost convexities is often empirically based: see Prais, S. *The Evolution of Giant Firms in Britain* Cambridge University second edn 1981 and Geroski, P. and A. Jacquemin 'Industrial Change, Barriers to Mobility and European Industrial Policy' *Economic Policy* 1 (November 1985): 170–218.
2. See 'Time Clocks Catch Up With the Computer Age' *Business Week* 26 November 1984 and 'How the Satellite "Helps Them Earn More"' *Financial Times* 29 October 1984.
3. For an overview of the expansion of manufacturing exports from developing countries, see 'A New Wave of Industrial Exporters' and 'Change and Continuity in OECD Trade in Manufactures with Developing Countries' *OECD Observer* No. 119 November 1982, pp. 26–30 and No. 139 March 1986, pp. 3–9 respectively.
4. See Kaplinsky, R. 'The International Context for Industrialisation for the Coming Decade' *Journal of Development Studies* 21(1)(October 1984): 75–96.
5. 'Japan is Buying its Way into US University Labs' *Business Week* 24 September 1984. Xenophobes in the US should be reminded that America has always been happy to drain brains from other countries.

Index